Hugh Thomas was an English historian, writer and life peer in The House of Lords. Best known for *The Spanish Civil War* (1961), for which he won the Somerset Maugham Award, Thomas wrote a number of political works and histories. By the end of his life, Thomas had been appointed Commander of the Order of Arts and Letters by the French government, and received the Grand Cross of the Royal Order of Isabella the Catholic from Spain as well as the Mexican Order of the Aztec Eagle.

T0113046

Other titles in the series

Madrid,
A Traveller's Reader

Introduced and edited by
Hugh Thomas

ROBINSON

ROBINSON

First published in Great Britain as *Madrid: A Traveller's Companion* by Constable and Co. Ltd, 1988
Revised edition published by Robinson, an imprint of Constable & Robinson Ltd., 2002
This edition published in 2018 by Robinson

10 9 8 7 6 5

A CIP catalogue record for this book
is available from the British Library.

Every effor t has been made to trace and contact copyright holders. If there
are any inadvertent omissions we apologise to those concerned, and ask that
you contact us so that we can correct any oversight as soon as possible.

ISBN: 978-1-4087-1032-6

Typeset by Hewer Text UK Ltd, Edinburgh
Printed and bound in Great Britain by Clays Ltd, Elcograf S.p.A.

Papers used by Robinson are from well-managed forests and other responsible sources.

MIX
Paper | Supporting
responsible forestry
FSC® C104740

Robinson
An imprint of
Little, Brown Book Group
Carmelite House
50 Victoria Embankment
London EC4Y 0DZ

An Hachette UK Company
www.hachette.co.uk

www.littlebrown.co.uk

This book is dedicated to all my friends in Madrid,
particularly the hall-porters of
the Victoria, Palace and Ritz Hotels

Contents

MADRID

THE STREETS

Illustrations

Acknowledgements

I wish to express my gratitude to María and Gregorio Marañón y Beltrán de Lís, for much hospitality; to Ramón Tamames, for lending me books; to Fernando Chueca for several good ideas; to Carlos Zayas, with whom I first walked the magic streets of old Madrid thirty years ago; to Hermann and Gerda Miessner, whose bookshop was for years a university in miniature; to Dolores and Tom Burns y Marañón, 'Paco' Cuadras, Pedro J. Ramírez, Juan Tomás de Salas, Pedro Schwartz, and many *madrileños* of vision, wit and intelligence. Roger Lockyer helped me in relation to the visit of the Prince of Wales to Madrid (1623) and Ian Gibson reminded me of Dalí's cocktail.

I am also grateful to the patient and efficient staff of the London Library; and the dedicated assistants in the most beautiful library in Europe, the round reading room of the British Museum. I am also grateful for the help of Carmen Herrera Valverde of the Museo Municipal in Madrid. Finally, I thank Prudence Fay of Constable for her patience, industry and skill, and Vanessa and Isambard Thomas for their work on translations from the French. The translations from the Spanish were done by the Editor, but he was much assisted by Ana Schwartz. She did the poems.

I should like to make acknowledgement to the following for permission to quote from their writings, editions or translations, where copyright permission was needed:

The Centro de Estudios Constitucionales for Fernando Díaz Plaja's *La Historia de España en sus documentos*; A.M. Heath and the Estate of Arthur Machen for *Memoirs of Casanova*; A.D. Peters & Co and V.S. Pritchett for *The Spanish Temper*; Editorial Prensa Española for Julián Cortés Cavanilla's *Alfonso XIII* and Agustín de Foxá's *Madrid de corte a checa*; to Sir Harold Acton and Hamish Hamilton for *Memoirs of an Aesthete*; to Yale University Press for Jonathan Brown and J.H. Elliott's *A Palace for a King: the Buen Retiro and the Court of Philip IV*; Longman for Cynthia Cox's *The Real Figaro*; Plaza y Janés for Luis Buñuel's *Mi último suspiro*; Ediciones Pegaso for Melchor Fernández Almagro's *Historia Política de la España Contemporánea*; Espasa Calpe for Pío Baroja's *Aurora Roja*, *Desde la última vuelta del camino* and *Las noches del Buen Retiro*, for José García Mercadal's *Viajes de extranjeros por España y Portugal*, and for Gregorio Marañón's *Antonio Pérez*; the Estate of Manuel Azaña for his *Obras Completas*; Michael Joseph for General Sir John Aitchison's *An ensign in the Peninsular War*, edited by W.F.K. Thompson; Jonathan Cape, Scribner and the Estate of Ernest Hemingway for *Death in the Afternoon*; James Lees Milne and Chatto & Windus for *Harold Nicolson, a biography*; Le Divan for Prosper Mérimée's *Correspondence Générale*; Jonathan Cape for John Nada's *Carlos the Bewitched*; Weidenfeld & Nicolson for Pérez Galdos's *Torment*, translated by J.M. Cohen; Penguin for Francisco de Quevedo's *The Swindler*, translated by Michael Alpert; Allied Publishers, Bombay for M.N. Roy's *Memoirs*; Darton, Longman Todd for M.H. Vicaire's *Saint Dominic and his Times*, translated by Kathleen Pond; Harvard University Press for Rubens' *Letters*, translated by Ruth Saunders; Ediciones Turner for *Cartas de Francisco Goya a Martín Zapater* by Mercedes Águeda and Xavier de Salas; the Estate of Miguel Maura for *Así Cayó Alfonso XIII*; the Estate of Ramón Sender, and Sir Peter Chalmers Mitchell, for *Seven Red Sundays*; Vision Press for Salvador Dalí's *My Secret Life*; Macmillan Publishing Co. and Dodd, Mead for Nina Epton's *Madrid*; the Estate of

Gamel Woolsey for *The Spendthrifts*; Alianza Editorial for S. Ramón y Cajal's *historia de mi labor científica*; and the Estate of Arturo Barea for *The Forging of a Rebel*, translated by Ilse Barea.

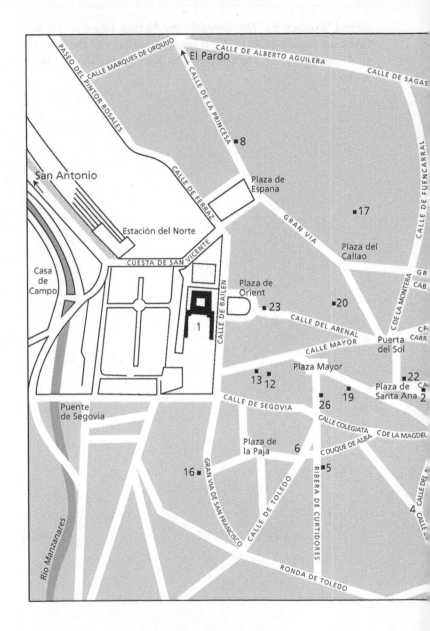

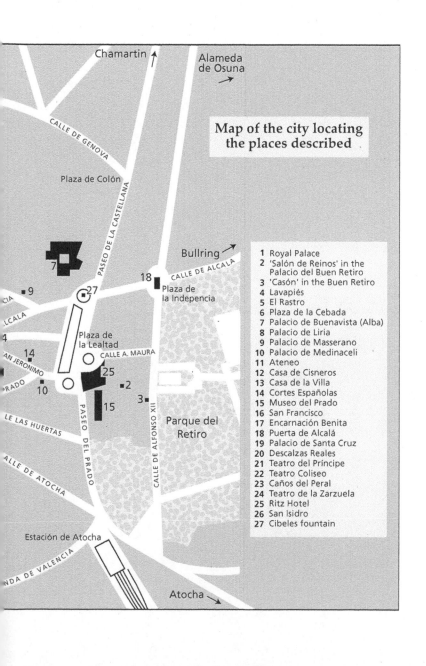

Map of the city locating
the places described

Chamartin

Alameda
de Osuna

CALLE DE GENOVA

Plaza de Colón

PASEO DE LA CASTELLANA

Bullring

CALLE DE ALCALA

18

Plaza de
la Indepencia

27

9

Plaza de
la Lealtad

CALLE A. MAURA

14

AN JERONIMO

25

PASEO DEL PRADO

10

2

3

15

CALLE DE ALFONSO XII

Parque del
Retiro

LE LAS HUERTAS

ALLE DE ATOCHA

Estación de Atocha

NDA DE VALENCIA

Atocha

1 Royal Palace
2 'Salón de Reinos' in the
   Palacio del Buen Retiro
3 'Casón' in the Buen Retiro
4 Lavapiés
5 El Rastro
6 Plaza de la Cebada
7 Palacio de Buenavista (Alba)
8 Palacio de Liria
9 Palacio de Masserano
10 Palacio de Medinaceli
11 Ateneo
12 Casa de Cisneros
13 Casa de la Villa
14 Cortes Españolas
15 Museo del Prado
16 San Francisco
17 Encarnación Benita
18 Puerta de Alcalá
19 Palacio de Santa Cruz
20 Descalzas Reales
21 Teatro del Príncipe
22 Teatro Coliseo
23 Caños del Peral
24 Teatro de la Zarzuela
25 Ritz Hotel
26 San Isidro
27 Cibeles fountain

Introduction

(In this introductory essay I have anglicized the names of kings (Charles III, not Carlos III) but not others (Juan de Villanueva, not John). I have rendered 'La Virgen de' as 'Our Lady of'. Spanish words frequently used are: calle *(street);* Conde *(Count);* convento *(nunnery or monastery);* Duque, Duquesa *(Duke, Duchess);* Marqués, Marquesa *(Marquis, Marchioness);* palacio *(palace);* paseo *(walk or promenade);* plaza *(square); and* puerta *(gate). The numbers in square brackets dotted about the Introduction indicate the extract which illustrates the point made, e.g. [No. 22].)*

1

In the summer of 1561, King Philip II travelled from Toledo, the ancient Visigothic capital of Spain, and established his court in Madrid. His father, the Emperor, Charles V, who had died three years before, at the Jeronomite monastery of Yuste in the Gredos mountains, nearly 150 miles west of Madrid, had advised Philip to make a stationary court, not the nomadic one which he had himself had, in common with the Spanish kings of the Reconquista. The Spanish Empire, the most ambitious political enterprise which the world had seen since the fall of Rome, needed sound administration: a capital to which despatches could be sent regularly, and where they would be at hand. King Philip had won his French wars, had married the French princess Elizabeth (not Elizabeth of England, as he had proposed), and needed to settle down. When a few years later one of his admirals offered to conquer China for him, if only he could receive another 20,000 men, Philip was unenthusiastic. Not for nothing was he called the prudent king.

King Philip had good reasons for choosing Madrid. Although some of its best known citizens had sided with the Comuneros in their revolt against his father in 1520, Madrid had not toyed with heresy, as Valladolid, the city most favoured by his great-grandparents, Ferdinand and Isabella, had done. Madrid had an immense royal fortress or Alcázar ('Al-Cassar') built by the Moors, rebuilt after a fire in the fifteenth century by King Henry IV of Castille and embellished by Charles V [Nos 104–118]. That edifice had been much used as a court by kings of Castille in the fifteenth century. It had served as a prison for King Francis I of France after his defeat at the battle of Pavia in 1525. Though still unappealing to Renaissance eyes, the Alcázar could be made into a centre of administration. Philip also thought it right that 'so great a monarchy should have a city fulfilling the function of a heart located in the middle of the body'*; and Madrid, though certainly central, was not, as Toledo was, under the day-to-day control of the city's Archbishop, the Cardinal Primate of the country: an advantage, since even prelates carefully appointed by painstaking monarchs (such as Philip) often developed habits of independence: Archbishop Guillermo de Croÿ had begun a long battle in 1518 against the building of a cathedral in Madrid – a struggle successfully maintained till the nineteenth century. Toledo, too, though clearly a great city, was marked by a mass of small steep alleys through which monarchs and noblemen could pass only slowly: in Madrid there were some fine straight streets, the central artery being

---

* Luis Cabrera de Córdoba, *Felipe Segundo, Rey de España*, Madrid, 1876, 3 vols., Vol. I, 298.

the line of an old *cañada*, or walk for transhumant sheep. The Emperor Charles, whose heroic life of struggle for the unity of Christian Europe meant so much to his son, had always liked Madrid, since he had there been cured of a special variety of malaria: an achievement which he attributed to the 'agreeable and healthy site' and the 'fertile soil and abundant water'*. Madrid, being 696 metres high, was drier than Toledo (529 metres). It was also green, more so than now, with many *huertas* or orchards and vegetable gardens outside the walls. There was good hunting – boar, bear and wolf – in the nearby oakwoods of El Pardo [No. 225], the 'dun-coloured' estate to the north, which the Emperor Charles had also used in the 1540s. He had built a small palace there, on the site of a much older hunting-lodge turned by Henry IV into a castle during the fifteenth century. These pleasures made the capital's modern coat of arms appropriate at the time: a bear climbing an oak tree. Henry IV had used Madrid a good deal. Bad king though he had been, it had been he who had first called Madrid by its famous style, '*muy noble y muy leal*: very noble and loyal'.

The plan to take the court to Madrid was one of the few decisions taken by a King who was always, in the words of Dr Gregorio Marañón, 'permanently in a state of hesitation and had no optimistic or expansive moments'. It was a fateful choice, which has for ever after affected, and surely weakened, Spain and perhaps, through example, the entire Spanish world. For Madrid, unlike other capitals of Renaissance Europe, such as London and Paris, or Vienna and Amsterdam, had no navigable river. All goods, therefore, had to be carried to it by land, mostly by mule, at great expense. The two-line report of a young English diplomatist in 1697 to London may, therefore, be the most significant of all in this book, even if it concerned only precious metals [No. 8]. It was only when railways were laid in the 1830s, motor-roads in the early 1900s, and with aviation in the 1950s, that the benefits of a centrally placed capital could be seen. Until then, Madrid was merely an administrative capital. Heart of the country though it was geographically, heart too of an empire which stretched

* quoted in Ramón Guerra de la Vega, *Historia de la Arquitectura en el Madrid de los Asturias*, Madrid (no date), 74.

from Peru to the Philippines, Madrid bred a population ignorant of business. The bureaucrat Pez, in the nineteenth century
in the novel *La de Bringas* by Benito Pérez Galdós, the greatest
of Madrid's novelists, is only a slight caricature: 'He was
always saying "we must have more administration" but it
was preaching in the desert. All the public services had gone
to the dogs. He himself had an ideal which he always kept in
front of him – but how could it be realized? His ideal was the
perfect administrative system, with eighty or ninety ministries.'
There should be 'no manifestation of the national life which
escaped the wise tutelage of the State'*. Pez was an authentic
heir of Philip II, not only a typical *madrileño*, but a characteristic man of the Spanish Empire. In the sixteenth century, the
only people to know anything of commerce in Madrid were the
Genoese banker friends of the soon-to-be ruined royal favourite, Antonio Pérez.

    Alongside such civil servants as Pérez and Pez, there soon
followed the churchmen, the servants, the noblemen, the
place-hunters, the providers of food and wine, and the thieves:
particularly, at first sight, at any time between the sixteenth
and the early nineteenth century, the first: Ramón de la Cruz,
the inspired memorialist of eighteenth-century Madrid, has a
character in one of his charming playlets known as *sainetes*
[e.g. No. 176], say, 'The capital has more churches than
homes, more priests than laymen, and more altars than
kitchens; even in the entrances of the filthy houses, even in
the vile taverns, small paper altar pieces can be seen, along
with a medley of wax articles, small basins of holy water and
religious lamps. One can hardly take a step without meeting
some brotherhood in procession, or an assemblage of people
reciting the rosary as they march, or hear the brayings of the
subchanters and the sacred jargon of the musicians entertaining devout souls with *villancicos*, couplets in praise of Our
Lady . . . Even the most recondite and venerable mysteries of
religion are chanted by blind men at doors of taverns to the
pleasant and majestic accompaniment of the guitar. Every
corner is covered with announcements of novenaries, and, at

---

* tr. as *The Spendthrifts* by Gamel Woolsey, Weidenfeld and Nicolson,
London, 1951.

every corner, accounts of miracles are sold as credible as Ovid's *Metamorphoses*'*.

An exaggeration? A French traveller, Jean-François de Bour-going, wrote that these *sainetes*, performed in the intervals of more pretentious plays, were not pictures of life but 'the thing itself'.

The liveliness of Madrid's low life was equally persistent. The picaresque novels of the sixteenth, and early seventeenth, centuries show both the energy and ingenuity of the innumerable rogues (*pícaros*) [see No. 41] who came hopefully to the court from all over Spain in those days, and whose descendants have contributed such vigour to the more southern quarters (*barrios bajos*) of the capital ever since. 'The first thing you've got to know is that in Madrid you can find all types, half-wits and very sharp minds, the very rich and the very poor,' the hero of Quevedo's *El Buscón* is assured.

We gain a vivid glimpse of this creative low life in the late eighteenth century from the paintings of Goya of the *manolos* or *majos* and *manolas* or *majas* of the district of Lavapiés. *Majo* and *maja* simply mean 'dashing' or 'sharp' or 'smart', when used as adjectives; while *manolo* and *manola* perhaps derive from a *sainete* of de la Cruz, called *Manolo*, subtitled *A Tragedy for Laughing or a Comedy for Crying* [No. 77]. They indicate young men and girls of poor origin who challenged convention by stylish if extravagant dress and behaviour. Lavapiés was the centre of popular hostility to foreign (particularly French) influence. By use of private language and customs, those who lived there set up a private domain, almost impossible for outsiders to penetrate. This world of 'manolería' was not only self-sufficient. It influenced the conduct and dress of aristocrats, such as the brilliant, charming, restless Duquesa de Alba [Nos 99 and 100]. The inter-relation between masters (and mistresses) and servants was always specially free in Madrid, as another French traveller Beaumarchais discovered in 1764 and drew from his experience there the basis for his famous plays *The Marriage of Figaro* and *The Barber of Seville*, for so long considered politically subversive. It will

* Ramón de la Cruz, *Pan y Toros*, quoted in Charles Kany, *Life and Manners in Madrid* 1750–1800, University of California, Berkeley, 1932, 396.

be recalled that it was in the Prado of Madrid that Count Almaviva first caught sight of Rosina, according to the last of these two plays.

2

In 1561, Madrid was a hill town with a population of between 20,000 and 30,000. It was not a city (*ciudad*) but a mere town (*villa*): if not as lowly as a mere *pueblo*. In comparison, cities such as Toledo and Seville had 80,000 each and Valladolid 50,000. Madrid was easily defended from the west and south but not from the north as would become evident in both the War of the Spanish Succession and the Napoleonic Wars. To the west, a slope from the Alcázar ran sharply down, across what has since the eighteenth century been known as the Campo del Moro (after the Arab king Tejufin who camped there while he besieged Madrid in 1109) to the River Manzanares: a waterway at that time less impressive than it is today [Nos 220–223]. To the east, a lesser slope led to a brook which meandered along what is now the Avenida de Castellana and the Paseo del Prado. These waterways met in the south a third one (which also for a time ran north-south, further to the east, beyond what is now the Retiro Park) at Vallecas. Within the town, there were – are – several hills; once, even ravines, in one of which, in the Calle Arenal (a word which means 'sandpit'), near the present church of San Ginés, a Christian community had lived, in caves, outside the walls of Muslim Madrid. (From the Manzanares to the Royal Palace, there is a rise of 200 feet, and to the site of the royal tapestry factory outside the gate of Santa Bárbara another rise, of 170 feet.)

Madrid (despite Moorish attacks in 1109 and 1197) had in the 1560s been a Christian city for nearly five centuries. Several hundred 'Saracens', however, lived there in the sixteenth century, not far from the Alcázar, in the quarter still known as the 'Morería'. In addition to the Alcázar, several buildings dating from Muslim days probably survived in 1561: for example, the undistinguished main parish church, Santa María de la Almudena (built near the Almudín or Alhondiga, the Moorish corn exchange), at the west end of what is now the

Calle Mayor, may have been reconstituted from a mosque to house Our Lady of la Almudena, an effigy said to have been hidden in the ancient walls throughout the Muslim occupation. This last story seems to be a myth. Madrid was almost certainly founded as 'Magerite' (which meant 'running waters' in Arabic) by the Arabs. Stories which give this capital a Visigothic or Roman past owe more to piety than to history. There is no evidence that there was once, on the site, a settlement known to Rome as 'Mantua' – or 'Mantua Carpentanorum', to distinguish it from the Italian city. The first historical record of Madrid apparently dates from the ninth century, when it was ruled by the Emir Muhammad I of Córdoba. The remains of Arab walls in what is now the Cuesta de la Vega have recently been dug up. The line along which those walls ran is easily identifiable [see De Wit's map of Madrid, illustration section]. It suggests that the city doubled in size, as probably in population also, between its capture by King Alfonso VI of Castille in 1083 and 1561.

Most inhabitants of Madrid in 1561 lived in single-storey, whitewashed houses made of brick and adobe similar to those still to be seen in many Castillian small towns [No. 85]. Although modern Toledanos would laugh at the idea, the view of Madrid from a distance would have looked in 1561, as the picture by the Flemish painter Anton van Wyngaerde suggests [see illustration section], rather as the historic centre of Toledo now does. Among the houses within the walls, a dozen parish churches and as many *conventos* stood out as the only buildings of any height apart from the Alcázar. These edifices had, as a rule, square brick towers, being mostly built by *mudéjar* architects (that is, by Arabs who had stayed on into Christian Madrid rather than fled, as many had done in 1083, through the Calle de la Cava Baja, a street whose old purpose as a ditch outside the town is still obvious to the naked eye). Two parish churches, San Salvador, opposite the present Plaza de la Villa, and Santa Cruz, near what is now the Foreign Ministry, had such high towers of this kind that they were known as the *atalayas* (watchtowers), 'of the city' and 'of the Court' respectively. An impression of what most churches of Madrid looked like in 1561 can be gained from visiting the surviving churches of San Pedro and San Nicolás de los Servitas. Both have fine, elegant, medieval towers, which some romantics (of a different generation to that which found a 'Mantua' in Madrid) believed once served as mosques. Both are probably *mudéjar*, and of the twelfth century. The finest Gothic tower was the most recent: the Renaissance chapel of the Bishop of Palencia, next to the old parish church of San Andrés, which was only finished in 1550.

The needle-like slate-tiled Flemish towers which became such a characteristic of Habsburg Madrid had not then appeared. Nor were there yet any domes in imitation of the Pantheon in Rome or the Duomo in Florence, such as the Jesuits would later favour. The Jesuits had, however, already founded a college in Madrid, and the new grand *convento* of *Descalzas Reales* ('Barefooted Royals') had just been begun by Philip II's aunt, ex-Queen Juana of Portugal, on the site of a house where her brother Charles V had used to stay and where she herself had been born, near the older Benedictine nunnery of San Martín [No. 194]. But they were old-fashioned buildings. There were four hospitals, all attached to *conventos*. Noblemen's houses were concentrated round the Plaza de la Paja (strawmarket), an old sloping square overshadowed by the church of San Andrés, which had been the main market in medieval Madrid [No. 83]. The finest of these houses was the Casa de Cisneros, in the Plaza de la Villa (still visible, as part of the expanded Town Hall [No. 138]). Next to it stood, and stands, the Torre de los Lujanes, belonging to an Aragonese family; in one of whose shabby upper rooms King François I of France is said to have been held prisoner for a few days in 1525. Some of these structures, including the hospital-monastery of La Latina built in 1504 on the orders of Beatriz Galindo, chief lady-in-waiting to Isabella the Catholic (in the Plaza de la Cebada [No. 81]), were by Moorish architects.

The walls of 1561 left much to be desired from a military point of view. They were probably complete, with 130 towers, but were mostly adobe, with about six stone gates. There was already much building outside them. This included the large establishments of several religious orders. Thus, since 1523, the Dominicans had had, in the south-east, their sanctuary dedicated to Our Lady of the Atocha (perhaps a corruption of 'Antioch', where its painting of the mother of Christ was said to have been found, after being completed by St Luke in her

lifetime [No. 187]. There was a Benedictine monastery of San
Martín founded by St Dominic of Silos, to the north. There
were the Jeronomites, to the east, with their church of San
Jerónimo el Real. St Dominic de Guzmán had in person
founded the nunnery of Santo Domingo el Real in 1218
[No. 182] while the Franciscans had been established to the
south-west by St Francis, though he seems to have been too ill
to visit Madrid personally during his stay in Spain in 1213–
1214 [No. 183]. These *conventos* were the focus for whole new
suburbs outside the walls, for they were able to communicate
with Madrid through small gates (*portillos*). Those who lived
from service to these foundations soon became citizens. Another suburb, with a different origin, had grown up near what
is now the Plaza de Lavapiés [Nos 76–78]: the ghetto, or
Judería, of Madrid, which several hundred inhabitants had
abandoned after 1492, optimistically taking with them the keys
of houses in the expectation of eventual return.

The centre of this Jewish population had been the street
rechristened, to exorcize it, the Calle de la Fe (Street of Faith),
(where the villain in Pérez Galdós's novel *Tormento* later had
his filthy flat). Their synagogue had been on the site of what is
now the undistinguished church of San Lorenzo in the Calle de
San Cosme y San Damián. In this quarter, too, perhaps because
there were empty sites, as a result of the Jewish emigration, the
Duque de Alba had built a large palace in the 1540s. St Teresa
of Ávila (whose own blood was far from 'pure') would sometimes stay there [No. 98]. Its site is still just identifiable in the
street called after the Duque.

The extension of the walls to embrace these suburbs was
King Philip II's first action in Madrid; the disused Puerta de
Guadalajara disappeared in 1570, and the 'Puerta' del Sol
(about whose name's origins there is controversy [No. 51]) was
also taken down, in 1580. Madrid's eastern entry was moved
to the present Plaza de Cibeles, where a new Puerta de Alcalá
was built. It became the main gate of the capital, where
customs duties were levied. These new walls were still only
of adobe. Further expansion soon made even them out of date.
Travellers from abroad continued to have the impression that,
in comparison with say, Rome or Vienna, or Toledo or Seville,
the capital of the 'most Catholic king' had no walls.

Madrid was still more medieval than Renaissance. Sheep and pigs, horses and cows, roamed in the streets. For two more centuries after 1561 pigs belonging to the monastery of San Antonio Abad were legally allowed to run wild in the streets, since that saint was the patron of animals. The monks and others abused this privilege. This added to the dirt for which Madrid's streets were, till a decree of Charles III in 1761, notorious. But some [No. 2] thought the air recovered automatically.

3

Philip II did not build much in Madrid. He may not have been quite certain that his capital would be always there. The drive of his strong narrow imagination was fixed on the Augustinian monastery of San Lorenzo, which he had ordered Juan Bautista de Toledo, trained in the other Spanish imperial capital of Naples, to build, thirty miles away, in 1562, at the village of El Escorial, in honour of his victory over the French at Saint Quentin on San Lorenzo's day in 1558. The monastery could be reached in three hours 'post-haste'. Still, what Philip did inspire in Madrid was important: there was the Puente de Segovia, the first stone bridge over the River Manzanares, built by Juan de Herrera (who in the end carried through the works at El Escorial) to take the place of a rickety, much repaired wooden crossing. Most of those who tried to depict Madrid either by painting or by the new technique of engraving in the next few generations did so to show the city from beyond this low, knobbly but stylish (and still in 1987 serviceable) crossing. (Engraving was little practised in Spain till the eighteenth century.) There was the reconstruction, also by Bautista de Toledo, of the 'Casa de Campo', on the west of the Manzanares, a summer house previously owned by the Vargas family, and the creation of a garden there [No. 224]. Thirdly, Philip began the transformation of the untidy Plaza del Arrabal, 'Suburb Square', so called since it was outside the Arab walls, popular with *converso* Jewish traders (Jews formally converted to Christianity instead of leaving the country), into the grand place of marketing and ceremony known thereafter as the Plaza

Mayor [Nos 64–70]. Fourthly, new works were begun on the Alcázar: both the royal stables and the Torre Dorada (golden tower) were given needle-like Flemish towers, covered by slate, which now became a feature of the city. A chapel was placed in the centre of the main patio. Apartments were given to the King to the west, the Queen to the east: an arrangement inspired by the Burgundian court etiquette introduced to Spain by the Emperor Charles V in 1548, whereby king and queen had separate households. Philip also continued what his father had begun at El Pardo, having told Gaspar de Vega in 1559 to cover its roof too with slate instead of old tiles, for safety reasons.

Philip's main impact on the population of Madrid, however, was to oblige the small 'Saracen' population to convert to Christianity, or to leave for Africa. This unjust echo of the treatment of Jews two generations before was the consequence of the continuing war with the Turks in the Eastern Mediterranean and the internal war against the Moriscos in the Alpujarra mountains south of Granada. Some Muslims who converted to Christianity nevertheless lived on in Madrid, in what was described by an Italian traveller, Francesco Vendramiano, as an 'incredible disgust', though that did not prevent them, he said, from increasing in numbers and in wealth, since, he said, 'all marry, never go to the wars and occupy themselves ceaselessly with money and commerce'*.

But if the King thought most of his monastery in the Sierra (and lived there a good deal), men dependent on the Court began to build extensively in Madrid. The population of the city soon doubled, mostly as a result of immigration from other cities of Castille. Industry, commerce and social life, continued to be centred upon Toledo and Sevilla. So did artistic life: Greco's residence in imperial Toledo was not an eccentricity. But clerks, lawyers, officials, priests, monks and nuns gathered in Madrid. New private palaces (for example, the Casa de Siete Chimeneas, still standing in the Plaza del Rey) began to be built, particularly along the Calle Alcalá which assumed the generous shape that it has today – being for 200 years looked

* Quoted in José García Mercadal, *Viajes de extranjeros por España y Portugal*, Madrid, 1952–62, 3 vols., Vol II., 279.

upon as the finest street in Europe [Nos 33–36]. Over a dozen new *conventos* were founded in, or outside, Madrid in Philip's time, including some, such as the Augustinian *convento* of Recoletos, well outside the King's attempt at new walls. Almost all were rough in architecture, with large orchards and gardens.

This was an important era in the history of Spain since it was then that Italian painters, such as Father de Urbino, the Carduchos, Zuccaro and Tibaldi, who were working on frescoes in the Escorial, began to transform Spanish art. They initiated an epoch when painters in Spain began to consider themselves, as they already did in Italy, as the companions of noblemen, not just as craftsmen producing visual propaganda for the Church. Travellers from northern Europe and Italy began to write about Madrid; these included Frenchmen such as the historian Brantôme, who wrote so admiringly of Spanish soldiers as they rode to the wars in Flanders in 'insolent grace'. There were ambassadors from the Valois Court, such as Fourquevaux and Longlée, and Venetian diplomatists, such as Antonio Tiepolo and Tomaso Contarini. From Belgium there was Jehan Lhermite, the Flamand Henri Cock, and the abbot of Saint Vaast, Jehan Sarrazan. There was the Roman priest, Giovanni Confalonieri, and a nuncio extraordinary, Camillo Borghese, who perhaps took back with him to Rome the idea which he made into a Bull when he became Pope Paul V, that *conventos* with fewer than five brothers should be abandoned.

Philip III, who succeeded his father in 1598, confirmed the establishment of the Court in Madrid, despite the efforts of his first minister, the Duque de Lerma, to return the capital to Valladolid. After five years of that vain endeavour, the King went back to Madrid in 1606. It was admitted then, that, as the saying was, '*Sólo Madrid es Corte*: only Madrid is the Court'. Thereafter, for sixty years, under Philip III and his son Philip IV whose faces are immortal because of Velázquez's inspired portraits of them, Madrid expanded even more. Builders and architects, carpenters and plasterers, tailors, hairdressers, domestic servants and men for hire, as well as place-hunters, playwrights, poets and painters crowded to the capital. Other Castillian cities such as Toledo, Alcalá, Segovia and Guadalajara diminished in both wealth and size. Noble families realized that they had to have a palace in Madrid if they were to have a chance of power; even of survival. Some of these palaces were immense: for example, that of Lerma, inherited in the next generation by the semi-royal Dukes of Medinaceli, on the edge of the Prado, described as resembling a small city of its own by Lady Holland, as it still seemed in the early nineteenth century [No. 103]. It can just be glimpsed in the illustration by Guesdon [see illustration section].

The largest new palace, however, was that built for Philip IV in the 1630s, the Palace of the Buen Retiro, opposite the Palacio de Medinaceli near the *convento* of San Jerónimo [Nos 129–135]. This was principally the work of the Court architect Juan Gómez de Mora (though the Italian Juan Bautista de Crescenzi played a big part). It was ordered by the King's new 'prime minister' – the expression was used then – the Conde-Duque de Olivares, who believed that his monarch should have a palace as graceful as those which he had seen in his youth in Italy. Hence the use which he made of Italians such as Crescenzi and Cosimo Lotti, who was the inspiration of elaborate gardens and water jokes. The palace was partly built to impress on the citizenship of Madrid the grandeur of their ruler, who now had two splendid residences, both where the sun rose and where it set. (Of this palace, nothing survives today save the Salón de Reinos, the Hall of Realms, disguised now as the Museum of the Army, where some of Velázquez's greatest paintings were panels; and the *Casón*, or ballroom, which, in the 1980s, housed the Prado's collection of nineteenth-century Spanish paintings and Picasso's *Guernica*.) But the gardens remain. Before the palace of Buen Retiro, the Paseos del Prado de San Jerónimo, de Recoletos and de Atocha also grew to look very like their modern shape: places for recreation, with trees and fountains to give shade in the hot summers [Nos 43–50].

Madrid's population reached 175,000 by the mid-seventeenth century. This figure made it the fifth largest European capital, after Constantinople, Naples, London and Paris. The physical expansion was to the north or the south, since the two royal palaces limited growth on the east and west. The climate worsened. The woods around the sixteenth-century city were cut. Though Madrid remained dry, the weather seemed to alternate between cold winters and hot summers. Travellers often returned from Madrid to London or Paris with two proverbs on their lips: 'three months of winter, nine of hell' (*tres meses de invierno, y nueve de infierno*); and 'the air of Madrid is so subtle that it kills a man but won't blow out a candle' (*el aire de Madrid es tan sutil que a mata un hombre pero no apaga un candil*). But others recalled the sharp, stimulating, clear air and the inexhaustible vitality of the underfed population which seemed to live in the streets.

The seventeenth century was a time of political stagnation for Spain. Philip IV himself dated the beginning of the national decline from the moment that his most successful general, Spínola (commemorated by Velázquez – for the Hall of Realms – as the generous victor in his *The Surrender of Breda*) returned from Flanders in 1630. This decline was scarcely evident in Madrid. Philip IV's reign continued to be a *belle époque* for painting, writing, theatre and architecture in the capital, as it also was for the Spanish Empire in the Americas, where, in addition to the building of churches, hundreds of monasteries and palaces, an administration was worked out for the continent, from California to Patagonia, which would give stability for 200 years. Plays flourished, particularly at the Palacio del Buen Retiro, intended not only as a worthy palace for a king but as a theatre for a monarch who looked on a theatrical production with ingenious sets as the greatest of human achievements. Cosimo Lotti inaugurated a great era of dramatic performances, whose climax was an aquatic masque, in which waves were caused artificially to break over the stage, while galleys were rowed majestically across it. Architecture was as ambitious. Thus under Philip III two famous still surviving *conventos* were built: that of the Encarnación [No. 185] and that of the Carboneras del Corpus Christi. The long reign of Philip IV inspired many substantial edifices. The Jesuits built their fine copy of the Gesú in Rome, the Colegio Imperial, with its great dome, the first in a city which became known for them. (This church became, after the expulsion of the Jesuits, the Cathedral of San Isidro [No. 192]). The Benedictines of Montserrat completed their equally splendid building in the Calle Ancha de San Bernardo. Smaller, but a baroque masterpiece all the same, San Antonio de los Portugueses was built in the heart of a then up-and-coming new quarter off the Calle de Fuencarral. Other religious buildings still to be seen which date from that epoch include the Chapel of San Isidro and the parish church of San Ginés, just off the Puerta del Sol. Surviving great palaces include those of the Duque de Uceda, now the Capitanía General, and the prison for noblemen, the Palacio de Santa Cruz (now – appropriately, it has been said – the Foreign Ministry [No. 146]). The town hall, the Casa de la Villa, was also built [No. 138]. The architects were mostly Spanish: Gómez de Mora being the favourite one in the early part of the century; while Fray Francisco Bautista, who designed both the Colegio Imperial and the Chapel of Cristo de los Dolores next to the *convento* of San Francisco, was probably the most imaginative.

A list of buildings does injustice to this 'golden age' since in the early seventeenth century artistic life flourished remarkably. Spain might be in 'decline' but this was the age of Velázquez, who commemorated it in painting not only the royal family [No. 169] but also the naturalistic figures in his *Bodegones*, of playwrights and poets such as Lope de Vega [No. 52], Calderón, Góngora and Tirso de Molina [No. 220], and novelists or satirists such as Quevedo [No. 46] and Cervantes. The residences of nearly all of these can at least approximately be still identified in the quarter of Madrid behind what is now the Palace Hotel (the successor to the Palacio de Medinaceli). It was then too that the low life of Madrid acquired that distinctive quality conveyed in the 'picaresque' novels. The life of Madrid became for the first time what it has remained, a mixture of the brilliant, the eccentric, the impoverished and the lively: 'Madrid is still as your lordship left it,' Lope de Vega wrote to a patron, the Duque de Sessa (Luis, the fifth Duque), 'Prado, coaches, women, dust, executions, comedies, a lot of fruit – and very little money.'*

The King, however, could still find money: gold and silver from the Americas brought up by trains of mules from Andalusian ports, such as Seville or Sanlúcar de Barrameda. The work of the North American historian Earl Hamilton (who described how the import of the American treasure brought

---

* Lope de Vega to the Duque de Sessa.

inflation) has made it hard for modern readers to realize just how beneficial these mule trains seemed at the time. They certainly produced enough to allow King Philip III to commission the then fashionable Giambologna in Florence to cast the fine equestrian sculpture of himself which, finished by that master's pupil Pietro Tacca, stood for a long time in the garden of the Casa de Campo and since 1848 has been in the Plaza Mayor [Nos 64–71]. Philip IV also invited Rubens to decorate a hunting lodge, the Torre Parada, in the Pardo [No. 114]. On a visit in 1603 that painter had spoken of the 'incredible incompetence and carelessness' of Spanish painters. But in 1628 he was able to talk to the immensely talented young Velázquez, who had received his first royal commission in 1623. Philip also invited Pietro Tacca to make an ambitious equestrian sculpture of himself, with the horse rearing – a construction never before achieved [No. 130]. The statue was a good example of collaboration between Spain and Tuscany, since Velázquez sent a small painting of Philip – probably the one now in the Palazzo Pitti – to guide the sculptor. Galileo is said to have advised on the mathematics of weights. Tacca's son and follower, Ferdinando, brought this work to Spain, for it to stand in the Palace of Buen Retiro before being moved in 1844 to its present site, facing the city, before the new Royal Palace in the Plaza de Oriente.

The seventeenth century was the time when the squares of the city, in which these and other statues and fountains stood, and stand, began to assume the character for which they are principally remembered: the Plaza Mayor was completed by Diego Sillera under Philip III, with its beautiful Panadería (bakery) on the north side [Nos 64–71]. It immediately began to be the stage for the trials of heretics (*autos de fe*); the burnings of those 'relaxed' by the Holy Office of the Inquisition were carried out by the 'civil power' outside the walls by the gate of Alcalá. The Puerta del Sol [Nos. 51–63] began to be the centre of Madrid life which it remained till the early twentieth century, with its popular fountain, the four-mouthed Mariblanca from which generations of *madrileños* drew water, and with the steps up to the now vanished church of San Felipe el Real converted into the gossip centre (*mentidero*) of the realm: Velázquez exhibited his first equestrian portrait of Philip IV there, to the general admiration. There was too the Plaza de la Cebada, for sales of grain and the start of the Madrid Feria [No. 81]; and the Plazas del Rastro (Cascorro) [No. 79] and de la Puerta Cerrada for general markets for everything else. Similarly, the two public theatres of Madrid, the Corral de la Cruz (on the site of the modern Calle Espoz y Mina) and the Corral del Príncipe (on the site of the still surviving Teatro Español) began their long careers (respectively in 1579 and 1583 [No. 209] in open courts or *corrales* (some of which can still be seen in summer), in competition with closed royal theatres in the Alcázar and the Buen Retiro. To these there was later added the Caños del Peral, or 'the font of the Pear Tree', since there was once such a conduit, close to the modern opera house. Finally, Philip IV, perhaps inspired by the visit of Charles, Prince of Wales in 1623, became a collector of paintings on an elaborate scale. He added over 2,000 pictures to the royal collection. If Prince Charles were indeed the inspiration of this passion, it was an unsung benefit of a most unsuccessful royal visit [Nos 7, 23, 45, 112, 224].

This new capital had, suitably, a new saint. There had previously been at Madrid's service Our Lady of the Atocha, in the *convento* of that name [No. 187], Our Lady of Solitude (*Soledad*) in the Church of Vitoria, just off the Puerta del Sol, and Our Lady of La Almudena, in Santa María. Henceforward, there was also San Isidro, a labourer on the property of the Vargas family and parishioner of San Andrés, in the thirteenth century, who was canonized with his wife, Santa María de la Cabeza, in 1622 (the only example of a married couple becoming saints [No. 200]). The fiesta of San Isidro in a field outside Madrid in May (commemorated by Goya) has been the most lively of Madrid's festivals from the seventeenth century onwards. The embalmed corpses of the two saints were sometimes brought from their place in San Andrés to try and revive dying royalties.

Northern Europeans have enjoyed themselves at the expense of the last Habsburg to reign in Madrid, Charles II. Macaulay's lurid pictures of this monarch and his court have entertained, as he would himself have put it, 'every schoolboy', and it has had a considerable effect on the attitude of Anglo-Saxons towards Spain. Much of his detail (for example his portrait of Cardinal Portocarrero) is, however, invention. The King on the other hand was indeed a freak, the descendant of incestuous intermarriages over generations and incapable of government, nearly illiterate, impotent and, therefore, childless. Worries over the succession dominated the time. Superstition was rife. Fears of witchcraft and of poisoners did preoccupy the Court. Even so, Madrid continued to see the construction of buildings of outstanding quality; for example, the elaborate, still-fashionable church of Las Calatravas in the Alcalá; the chapel of the Third Order next to the Convento de San Francisco; and the great church of the Comendadoras of Santiago, a masterpiece of the del Olmo brothers. In this last, banners mark victories of the order of Santiago during the Reconquista – Sanlúcar, 1266; Teba, 1328, where the Black Douglas threw forward the heart of Robert the Bruce and died in retrieving it – and give the modern visitor a sudden whiff of the Middle Ages. The Puente de Segovia, put up in the 1680s by Valenzuela, the favourite of the Queen Regent Mariana, was mocked. The wife of the French Ambassador, the witty Marquise de Villars, said that it would have done well over the Rhine; she advised Spain either to sell the bridge or buy a river [Nos 221–222]. All the same, it survives. Nor should the great fiestas of the Carnival [No. 196], the Burial of the Sardine (on Ash Wednesday), Holy Week [Nos. 197–198], Corpus Christi [No. 202], and the local parish *fiestas*, be dismissed, as they sometimes still are by Anglo-Saxons, as mumbo-jumbo. 'The Carnival', Baroja wrote later, 'has obviously a panicky and subversive basis and one understands that governments look on it with antipathy. The Carnival demands a certain grace and imagination . . . In contrast the public at a bull-fight or a football match does not have to display any imagination: it is a public mass of spectators.'* These ceremonies played an important part in offering the opportunity for participation to an impoverished population (*pace* Richard Ford [No. 200]). It

---

* 'El carnaval tiene evidemente un fondo pánico y subversivo, y se comprende que los gobiernos lo miren con antipatía. El carnaval exige cierta gracia e ingenio en el público . . . en cambio el público de una corrida de toros o de un partido de futból no exige ningún ingenio; es un público masa de espectadores.' Pío Baroja in Desde la última vuelta del camino, Madrid, 1948, 76.

would seem that Protestantism was the poorer without them. '*En vérité*', Mérimée wrote 150 years later, '*j'aime ces cérémonies catholiques et je voudrais croire.*'* The self-avowed atheist had his heart turned. Yet he allowed himself to forget that once among the most magnificent of the processions were those organized by the Inquisition [Nos 66 and 68].

4

Charles II did in the end die, leaving Europe to dispute his vast inheritance. The result was the War of the Spanish Succession whose consequence, in turn, was, ultimately, despite the first occupation of Madrid by foreign troops [Nos 9 and 10] and the efforts of Marlborough and of English historians to deceive themselves on the matter, a French triumph. Bourbons reigned in most of the old Spanish Habsburg dominions outside Italy and Belgium, except for Gibraltar and Minorca. Even Naples and Sicily returned to Bourbon rule after 1735.

The new King Philip V, Louis XIV's grandson, brought new ideas, architects and painters from both France and Italy (both Philip's wives, María Luisa of Savoy and Elizabeth Farnese, were powerful Italian influences). The new royal family busied themselves giving Madrid a modern classical carapace. Old churches received new façades. When, with the mute satisfaction of the monarch, the Alcázar burned down in 1734, a colossal classical edifice in Italian style was raised to replace it. A master plan was first conceived by the Sicilian-Piedmontese Filippo Juvarra, architect of the Palazzo Stupinigi outside Turin. After his death, a much modified version was carried through by his pupil, Giovanni Bautista Sacchetti [Nos 119–128]. Despite the loss of many famous paintings (for example Velázquez's first equestrian painting of Philip IV), and damage to many others, the Bourbons were glad of this opportunity to build anew. The old palace, with its memories of the imprisonment of François I and the mysterious deaths of two enchanting French Queens, Elizabeth [No. 110] and María

* Mérimée in *Lettres d'Espagne*, quoted in Trahard *La Jeunesse de Mérimée*, Vol. II, 204.

Luisa [No. 117], seemed a gloomy pile to anyone coming from France.

In the eighteenth century some new religious buildings were added to the skyline of Madrid: among those still to be seen are the large and impressive San Cayetano, half-destroyed, like so many in that quarter, during the Civil War of 1936–39; the Sacramento (now the well-kept church of the military chaplains); and, above all, the great dome of San Francisco. The latter appeared so elegant, as well as so grand, that it was proposed to make it the cathedral of Madrid: an idea dismissed because of its geographical position as well as the continued opposition of Toledo. But these clerical edifices were not typical of the age.

What a delightful world eighteenth-century Madrid was for those who, like Beaumarchais, in Spain for reasons as complicated as the plots of any of his plays, with his *'intarissable belle humeur'*, as he himself put it, could enjoy its *'soupers charmants'* or its gambling [No. 173]. Did he really pass on his exquisite lady, Madame de la Croix, to King Charles himself? Who can say?

Since, after all, as a *seguidilla*, which he quotes in a letter to his father, has it:

> The vows
> Of lovers
> Are light as the wind.
> Their enchanting air,
> Their sweetnesses
> Are deceiving traps
> Hidden under flowers.*

Such *'soupers'* might be held at one or other of the new noblemen's palaces, built for ostentation not protection, such as those of Miraflores or Grimaldi, Liria or Torrecilla, Perales or, the grandest of all, the Palacio de Buenavista, embarked upon in the 1790s by the Duques de Alba on property which they had recently bought on the corner of the Calles Alcalá and Barquillo [No. 99]. This still-extant edifice was later sold to Godoy and afterwards, till 1982, much enlarged, it was the seat of the Ministry of War or of Defence.

---

* Louis de Loménie, *Beaumarchais et son temps*, Paris 1846, Vol. I, 143.

The most characteristic eighteenth-century buildings were, however, institutions of enlightenment, particularly those built during the reign of Charles III in the second half of the century: the Observatory; Villanueva's Museum of Natural History (in which the Museum of the Prado was later housed [No. 142–145]); the Hospice of San Fernando, a foundling hospital (now the Museo Municipal); the Post Office, in the Puerta del Sol (now the seat of the Autonomous Government of Madrid); the barracks of the Conde-Duque, to house the King's bodyguards; the Academia de Bellas Artes in the Palacio Goyeneche, built by Churriguera; and the Custom House (Aduana), now the Treasury, designed by the Italian Francesco Sabatini, next door in the Alcalá. Thirty-two new schools were opened by Charles III in Madrid alone. The first modern bull-ring, specially designed for the increasingly popular spectacle of bull-fighting, was built outside the Puerta de Alcalá in 1749 [No. 206], though the *fiesta nacional*. continued too in the Plaza Mayor on special occasions [No. 71].

The inspiration of this modernization was King Charles III, 'Madrid's best mayor'. The Infanta Eulalia, returning with her brother King Alfonso XII, in the Restoration of 1875, remarked that everything in the capital '*seemed*' to have been built by Charles III [No. 127]. The exaggeration had an element of truth. Even the Royal Lottery was begun by some of Charles's Neapolitan friends – Charles had been an equally enlightened King of Naples before becoming King of Spain on succession to his brother in 1759. He was a patient, cold, hard-working monarch, who knew how to profit from the advice of able ministers, such as the Condes de Aranda or Floridablanca [No. 171]. He kept fit by hunting every day (shooting, as the English would call most of it) for, as he said, 'Rain breaks no bones.'

Sewerage was introduced in the 1760s. So was street lighting, having been previously non-existent save for a few lanterns behind sacred images at street corners. Houses began to be numbered, though only, most confusingly, by blocks (*manzanas*). Systematic paving of streets was introduced. So was cleaning of streets and the regular collection of rubbish [No. 25]. (Before this, rubbish could always be thrown out of the window at night provided the warning, '*Agua va*', 'water on the way', was given.) Excrement was not supposed to be thrown in places where there were crosses: an instruction of which Quevedo made fun by saying that crosses were being purposely placed at spots where he defecated. Flagellation in religious processions was banned in 1777. Nightwatchmen (*serenos*) were brought in from Valencia (the level of street crime fell sharply [No. 30]). A new line of walls, still mostly adobe, was laid out and several new stone gates built. The Jesuits were expelled in 1767 on the suspicion of wishing to build, like the Templars in the fourteenth century, a state within a State. The gardens of the Prado, used since the sixteenth century as a place to walk, were formally reconstituted as the 'Salón del Prado' by the architect Villanueva and the painter José de Hermosilla. The shape of the 'Salón' was supposed to reflect the hippodromic Piazza Navona in Rome. Part of the gardens of the Palace of Buen Retiro was opened to the public after the King moved from thence to the newly finished Royal Palace in the west of Madrid in 1767. This opening was subject to rules: men were not to wear capes, nor women mantillas. Similar regulations applied to the nearby Botanical Gardens, another inspiration of Charles III, which opened their gates in 1781.

These petty rules had a rational basis. The rate of crime in Madrid was high. The use of ground-length capes by men of all classes – itself justified by the dirt in Madrid – meant that it was easy to conceal one's identity during an act of robbery. Another side to the affair was a long-standing controversy over the merits of traditional Spanish dress (*traje de golilla*, or dress with cardboard neck-piece, breeches, and large hat, *chambergo*) or the new French styles brought by the Bourbons in 1713.

The arguments over the use of capes came to a head in some extraordinary events in 1766. King Charles had an unpopular Italian minister, the Marqués de Esquilache, who lived in the Casa de Siete Chimeneas. He decided that, since the streets were becoming cleaner, the long cape had no justification. He banned it, along with the *chambergo*. Tailors were appointed by the state to stand in doorways with orders to cut off the extra cloth from the capes of those who defied the decree. The aim was to cut crime rates further (see Zarba's lithograph, illustration section).

This aroused a patriotic and popular outcry against modernization of all sorts, but in particular against 'French ways'. There had before been much irritation over the alleged influence of French queens and shopkeepers. In the seventeenth century, dandified gentlemen who looked as if they were foreigners had sometimes been seized by *madrileños* and asked to pronounce *ajo* (garlic) and *cebolla* (onion): if they could not, they were beaten for the crime of being French. In the 1680s, at least one genuine *madrileño* was ill-treated by a crowd who found a French jacket among his clothes when he was bathing on the River Manazanares.

This so-called 'Motín de Esquilache', riot against Squillace, passed off harmlessly. The King abandoned the minister. The decree was rescinded. But there were ugly overtones. Popular hostility to modernization, if that could be identified with France, or '*Anti-España*' (Anti-Spain), played a large part in Spain's subsequent history. It was related to the popular support for anti-semitism in the fifteenth century and to the anti-modernist revolt of the Comuneros in the sixteenth. Thereafter the King and his ministers moved more cautiously. They did not, for example, carry through a plan to take cemeteries, in the interests of cleanliness, away from the precincts of churches to the suburbs. There was also a public outcry when a later minister proposed the introduction of shoe-cleaners in the streets. That idea was also held to come from the '*Gabachos*' (a nickname for the French pilgrims on the way to Santiago).

No such dramas affected one other typical manifestation of Madrid life of that time, the fan, which all women, even the poorest, used in innumerable ways, more elaborate than elsewhere in Europe, to indicate a vast variety of hopes, desires and hesitations, not just to keep themselves cool – a descendant of the courtly sign language developed in the seventeenth century. Queen Elizabeth Farnese had 1,600 fans (of which a selection is now shown in the Royal Palace). It was not a new fashion: there is a lady with a fan on an ivory casket made in the eleventh century, in the cathedral of Pamplona. Sennacherib had fans in Babylon. Nor was it specially Spanish: many of the fans sold as 'Spanish' were in fact made in France. But the fashion for the painted, folding fan (invented in Japan) had its heyday in Madrid in the late eighteenth century. Its use only declined in the twentieth century, when *madrileñas* began to smoke cigarettes heavily [No. 48].

If the King was the reformer of eighteenth-century Madrid, the best memorialist was Goya. This great painter, an immigrant, like so many others who have adorned Madrid, of Aragonese origin, could, due to his genius, move among every class: patronized by the King and Court, comfortable in the circles of the rival duchesses of Alba and Osuna (their rivalry was chiefly seen in their support for different actresses and bull-fighters [Nos 206, 226]), Goya also knew well the world of the *majos* and *majas*, and that of the bathers and picnickers along the River Manzanares. His letters show something of his personality, though less than a busybody from the twentieth century would like [No. 179].

5

The disadvantage of absolute monarchy is its reliance on the individual qualities of the kings. Charles III's son and successor, Charles IV, if less inadequate than Charles II, could not ride the whirlwind brought to Europe by the French Revolution. He, his Queen, and his prime minister Godoy, as well as the gay world of rival duchesses and their favourite bull-fighters, were swept away in the extraordinary events of 1808. The King was first persuaded to resign by Napoleon. A French army under Murat moved to occupy Madrid. There was a popular rising: it should have been no surprise to those who had observed the *Motín* of Squillace and a similar riot, six weeks before, at the royal country palace of Aranjuez, against Godoy. There was a famous clash between the French and the *madrileños* in the Puerta del Sol, immortalized by Goya in his *The Second of May, 1808* [Nos 55 and 56]. There was even fighting in the charming *paseo* of the Prado. The French later established their headquarters in, of all places, the porcelain factory in the Parque del Buen Retiro (approximately where there is now the *glorieta del Ángel caído*, the crossroads of the fallen angel). (French intelligence later successfully spread the *canard* that this factory was destroyed by the money-grubbing

English to prevent competition in chinaware!) Summary executions took place on the hill of Príncipe Pío, on the site of the modern Parque de la Montaña (in the early twentieth century a barracks famous during the Civil War). Goya's representation of those shootings, *The Third of May, 1808*, brilliantly captured the moment.

After some reverses and withdrawals, Napoleon led his army to Madrid [Nos 72–75] at the end of the year. Did he really say, when he reached the Royal Palace on his single day's drive round the capital, '*Enfin je l'ai, cette Espagne si désirée*'? And did he really tell his brother '*Vous êtes mieux logés que moi*' at the sight of the Palace? At all events, the reign of King Joseph Bonaparte was tumultuous [Nos 192, 225]. As a result of the victories of the Duke of Wellington, King Charles IV's son Ferdinand, known in what soon seemed golden days before 1808 as the Príncipe de Asturias (this title is the Spanish equivalent of the Prince of Wales), returned as King in 1814. On the suggestion of his second (Portuguese) Queen, Isabel de Braganza, he opened Madrid's most famous building, the Museo del Prado, to show to the public the paintings which his ancestors had collected.

All the same, nothing was the same as it had been before. The Empire collapsed; although a rich 'uncle in America' was a familiar figure in the life of Madrid for over another hundred years: for example, Agustín Caballero in Pérez Galdós's novel *Tormento*; or that elder brother in Antonio Machado's haunting early poem 'El Viajero', a figure 'familiar yet unknown', sitting, after years abroad, with his *sienes plateadas*, silvered temples, in the old kitchen. Even chocolate, the popular drink of Madrid in the eighteenth century, gave way to French coffee. The army of *la Gloire* left behind a regrettable taste for white bread, in Spain as elsewhere. Other traditional foods, such as the famous old stews (*ollas* and *pucheros*), began to be substituted for by French dishes. Some typical Spanish drinks such as *hipocrás* (red wine mulled with cinnamon) or *rosolí* (cane brandy, cinnamon and sugar) also lost their popularity. The behaviour of the French soldiery in Spain between 1808 and 1814 was as atrocious as their leaders were arrogant: '*la journée d'hier a donné l'Espagne à l'Empereur*', Murat is supposed to have said after the explosion and executions of

2 May 1808 (though the letter quoted here gives a less strident wording: [No. 56]). It seemed an absurd remark, indicating a general suffering from *folie de petit grandeur*. All the same, there is a sense in which, stylistically, it was true. For the tone of the nineteenth century in Madrid was given by Joseph Bonaparte. A reluctant monarch, '*el rey intruso*' imposed on Spain by his brother Napoleon, he started the clearance of small streets in front of the Royal Palace to begin the handsome Plaza de Oriente (he was given the nickname *el Rey de Plazuelas*, as well as *Pepe Botellas* – not because he drank but because he freed alcohol from crippling taxes). Really preferring a '*terre en Toscane*' to a throne in Spain, he brought a certain idea of liberty which Spain never forgot. At the same time, the brutal war which his brother fought led to the habit of undisciplined banditry, of smuggling and of taking to the hills ('*echarse al monte*') which had most destructive consequences. I have even heard Spanish people say that these wars led to national laziness, since so many people abandoned cultivation for robbery.

So far as legislation is concerned, the restored Bourbons continued what Bonaparte began. When, eventually, a constitutional Liberal government, inspired by French ideas, gained power in 1835, it embarked on the confiscation and sale of church lands. It was the most significant event of the century. In an apparent desire to remove from the city all trace of the Middle Ages, many landmarks vanished: even, at the end of the century, the old Santa María de la Almudena; even the three popular churches round the Puerta del Sol (San Felipe, loved for gossip; Soledad, known for lovers' trysts; and the hospital-*convento* of Buen Suceso, behind the life-giving Mariblanca fountain). The Palace of the Buen Retiro was, reasonably enough perhaps, also judged too ruined to be restored after the French occupation of its park. The site became a fashionable *barrio*. Many *conventos*, such as that of the Augustinians in the Recoletos, gave way to palaces, ministries, museums or apartment blocks. A new parliament, the Cortes Españolas [Nos 139 and 140], was in 1843 built by the fashionable architect of the day, Narciso Pascual y Colomer, on the site of the ruined Convento del Espíritu Santo (it was wrecked by fire in 1823 when the Duc d'Angoulême, the commander of the

French army of occupation, was at mass). The Inquisition was wound up in 1820: only one man, it is fair to say, was discovered in its prisons in the Calle Isabel La Católica at the time.

6

The nineteenth century saw another burst in the size of Madrid's population. In 1825 there were 200,000 *madrileños*; by 1875 over 300,000; by 1900 over 500,000*. Railways encouraged this growth after 1850. Vast new residential districts were created. Some of those, like the Salamanca district (called after its planner, the Marqués of that name, a man who resembled the Count of Monte Cristo in the turbulations of his career, and a statue of whom stands in the *glorieta* called after him) and the Argüelles district, became fashionable. Others, such as that in the north (Chamberí), became new centres of lively working-class life, based on new immigration. In 1911, the much discussed Gran Vía began to be crashed through the north of the old centre, in belated homage to Paris's Baron Haussmann, destroying a lively community around such streets as Calle Desengaño (where Goya had once lived) and the *quartier* described by Señora Pipaón de la Barca [No. 31] as well as some very slummy places. The new buildings along the Gran Vía (such as Ignacio de Cárdenas's Telefónica, taller than any church, of the late 1920s) gave a South American feel to the centre of the city, just as General Primo de Rivera gave a South American style to Spanish politics. The University was moved from the Calle Ancha de San Bernardino to the North American-style university city among the gardens and woods to the north-west of Madrid, where the mother of the Duquesa de Alba of Goya's day had

---

* David Ringrose gives the following estimates for Madrid's population: 1597 (65,000); 1630 (175,000); 1685 (125,000); 1723 (130,000); 1757 (142,500); 1769 (150,000); 1787 (175,000); 1799 (195,000); 1821 (160,000); 1842 (200,000); 1850 (220,000); 1860 (300,000) (David Ringrose, *Madrid and the Spanish Economy* 1560–1856, Berkeley, California, 1983.)

built a retreat, or '*palacete*', which was destroyed in the fighting during the most recent civil war. The move was much regretted by those who loved the old countryside [No. 80].

These extravagances left untouched Madrid's brilliant café life round the Puerta del Sol (*cafés portasoleños*) and the Calle Alcalá [No. 59]. The characteristic of this era in Madrid was the regularity with which people would in the evening repair to the same place, day after day, and hold court in a '*tertulia*': thus in the 1920s you could meet the playwright Benavente in the Café del Comercio, the politician Melquíades Álvarez (murdered in the Civil War) in El Oriental, the novelist Gómez de la Serna in the Café Pombo, and the biologist Ramón y Cajal in El Suizo [No. 95], while many writers would go after midnight to the Café Fornos [No. 94] in the Calle Alcalá, the café which the historian of Madrid's streets, Pedro de Répide, described as the most typical of all ('*madrileñísimo*'). During the summer, the gardens of the Buen Retiro were the site of *tertulias* of aristocrats, as well as of the literary world [No. 135]. The northern part of the site was, however, built upon between 1904 and 1918 for the overbearing new post office (Palacio de Comunicaciones) of Joaquín Palacios.

Throughout the nineteenth century, travellers from northern Europe had been wont to visit Spain in search of the exotic. Théophile Gautier's *Voyage en Espagne* in the 1840s began a new taste for Spanish painting. Prosper Mérimée ten years before had gathered impressions which he converted into the most famous of all Spanish stories, *Carmen*, published in Paris in 1847 and turned into an opera by Bizet (who never saw any need to visit Spain) in 1875. This was the heyday too of the English traveller: in Mérimée's *Carmen*, there is a note explaining that '*en Espagne, tout voyageur qui ne porte pas avec lui des enchantillons de calicot ou de soieries passe pour un Anglais*'. (The gastronomically minded will recall that in *Carmen* the gypsies of Andalusia nicknamed the English of Gibraltar '*écrevisses*', crayfish, because of the colour of their uniforms.) The best-known English traveller was Richard Ford, a gifted and learned man who wrote a very influential, if often misleading and mischievous, *Handbook to Spain* for the publisher John Murray. He hated the Catholic church and had no time for Madrid, being drawn to Andalusia. Like most people, I have enjoyed Ford's brilliant, mocking, learned, superior prose. That makes me even more pleased that I have lived into a time when his famous condescending injunction, 'Attend to the Provend', is a more appropriate one to a traveller in East Anglia than to one in Andalusia.

The political life of Spain after 1814 was turbulent. That partly accounted for Ford's disdain. Revolutions occurred often, usually coming to a head in the Puerta del Sol which, after the old post office had been made in 1854 into the Ministry of the Interior, was looked upon as the key to the kingdom. The great novelist of Madrid, Benito Pérez Galdós, remarked, in a well-known phrase, that the Spaniard 'left home' politically in 1808 and had 'not yet found his way home'. By the time that he wrote that in the 1910s, there had been two major civil wars (the first and the second Carlist wars, 1834–40 and 1870–75) and countless *coup d'états* (*pronunciamientos*). The monarchy had been overthrown in 1868, substituted for by Amadeo of Savoy, cousin of the King of Italy, who himself had given way to a Republic. The Bourbons had then been restored in 1875, in the person of the young Alfonso XII.

A generation of relative tranquillity followed. But there was also much frustration. Pérez Galdós's characters seem to be restless members of a parochial bourgeoisie. 'Where have my savings gone?' exclaims a character in his *Lo Prohibido*. 'If you could fly over this little Babel, its shops, its incredible and disproportionate luxuries, you would find a drop of my blood everywhere. You may say that I lacked will power . . . the *madrileño's* greatest defect is indolence, the disinclination to be disturbed by any serious subject; what matters is not to miss the show or the *tertulia*, to have a coach to drive about in, good clothes with which to impress people, the latest novelties which will enable our wives and daughters to be called elegant and distinguished . . . and here I must stop for there is no end to the list of futilities . . .'* Despite this criticism, Madrid in the Isabelline age – the days of Isabel II – had many charms. Some of them can be seen in, for example, Gautier's excited recollection of the Paseo del Prado [No. 48]. All the same, the

* Pérez Galdós, *Lo Prohibido*, 2 vols., Madrid, 1906.

combination of loss of empire, a stagnant economy and growth of population led many young men to dream of violent solutions. The aristocrats duelled over points of honour (there was a famous combat between the Duque de Alba and the son of the American minister in 1854). Young working men began to challenge the social order. In the long narrow Calle Fuencarral in 1868 the 'international' anarchist Giuseppe Fanelli preached the 'idea' of anarchism to a receptive audience of printers and lithographers [No. 39]. In a city where so much had been done by Italians in the past, from buildings to sculptures, it was suitable that an Italian should have inspired a new era in the history of Spanish workers.

Spanish socialism was founded in Madrid by Pablo Iglesias, a noble orator who was one of the few great Spanish public men who were indeed *madrileños*. His mother had been one of the washerwomen of the Manzanares. With the failure of 'Liberalism' and 'Conservatives' to evolve into national parties with deep roots, several efforts at regeneration were also launched from what was looked upon as the traditional clerical or national side of Spanish politics. Their task was made easier by the fact that the revolutionaries looked upon themselves as 'international' actors: the anarchists indeed so called themselves. Socialists and, later, communists were concerned to transform Spain into something closer to the northern European nations. An irony was that the last nationalist movement of regeneration on the right, the Falange Española, founded by José Antonio Primo de Rivera in the Teatro de la Comedia in Madrid in 1933, was always close to other European Fascist movements.

The result was the collapse of the monarchy in 1931 [No. 61], the failure of the Second Republic 1931–36, the disastrous Civil War of 1936–39 and the military dictatorship which followed. This is still a period of controversy. Contrary to what is sometimes believed north of the Pyrenees, these tragedies came less at the end of generations of decline than after a national revival. The first thirty-six years of this century in Spain were, after all, an epoch in the arts comparable to the golden age. Novelists such as Pío Baroja [No. 37], poets such as García Lorca, and the Machado brothers, painters such as Picasso and Juan Gris, film-makers such as Buñuel [No. 141], musicians such as Manuel de Falla, and countless other masters constitute the evidence. Most of these (including Picasso) had periods when they lived and studied in Madrid, even if they were born elsewhere. But this vitality could not be contained in the political systems available: neither a constitutional monarchical one, nor a republican democratic one, nor a well-intentioned *dictablanda* (mild military dictatorship), as offered by General Primo de Rivera. Anarchists and Fascists, Socialists and even Separatists (or Federalists) all offered uncompromising solutions to the nation's problems. The Cortes Españolas were the theatre of political drama, but the streets of Madrid were the stage for open clashes between the left and the right. It was an inspired period in the capital's life but it led to tragedy [Nos 37, 42, 62, 96]. After a war which was in many ways a foreign imposition, or at least could be so represented, the 'iron surgeon', General Franco, entered Madrid in 1939. Many frequenters of the great cafés of the Puerta del Sol fled to Buenos Aires or to Mexico. Many of the cafés themselves were transformed into banks. Later, many of even the nineteenth-century palaces in the Paseo de Recoletos and its newest extension, the Castellana, having been occupied by trade unions or hospitals during the civil war, also gave way to banks. A period of bastard Habsburg architecture – Franco believed in absolute monarchy – saw the completion of the 'new ministries' in the northern part of the latter avenue. For a time, famous streets exchanged their traditional names for those of General Franco's generals or allies. Even the Gran Vía was rechristened 'José Antonio', while the Recoletos became 'Calvo Sotelo'.

In the 1960s and 1970s, many new suburbs were formed of remarkable ugliness, hideous new roads were built along the banks of the Manzanares and much of what had kept Madrid so original for so long vanished during a hasty further modernization. Still, though much was taken, a good deal remains.

7

The charm of Madrid is elusive. It does not at first sight seem beautiful. Richard Ford was dismissive: 'the more Madrid is known, the less it will be liked.' 'I do not believe anyone likes it much when he first goes there,' Hemingway wrote in *Death in the Afternoon*. This disdain was shared by some who lived there: Unamuno described Madrid as 'an enormous owl getting ready to go to sleep', and 'a vast caravan of people with nomadic instincts – I shall resist going to it whenever I can'. Manuel Azaña and Ortega y Gasset were no less dismissive [No. 20]. All the same, young British officers in the Napoleonic Wars found Madrid the Queen of Cities [No. 13]. So did George Borrow [No. 16]. For those who know how to find it, Madrid has magic.

One can find that magic in the shadow cast over the present by the past. 'The past is not better than the present,' wrote Pío Baroja in his romantic novel, *Las noches del Buen Retiro*, a *Dame aux Camélias* for Madrid, 'but it is lit by a suggestive, crepuscular twilight both poetic and distinct from the crude and sour clarity of the present.' The best way to look for the real Madrid is to see what happened there in the days of our ancestors. Hence this collection. But, some will say, there is no discussion of the heroes of 2 May 1808, Daoíz and Velarde. There is nothing of García Lorca (I could not find anything of his about Madrid). There are too many murders. There is too much politics, too many Frenchmen, not enough *corridas*. I have forgotten the last Duque de Osuna, it will be said, the epitome of the romantic nineteenth-century aristocrat, last of his line and conscious of it, who ruined himself deliberately by his extraordinary extravagances, including his insistence that in every one of his many houses throughout Europe forty people would be able to lunch or dine any day that they liked: symbol of a spirit of generosity which has not altogether vanished in Spain. I have resisted that passage in Saint-Simon where the memorialist described in Madrid '*Jambons de co-chons nourris de vipères. Singulièrement excellents*'. Azorín is not here, nor, except in passing [No. 88], is the *cocido madrileño* or any variety of it. Some of the most beautiful women have been ungallantly omitted: where, it will be asked, are the Cuban-born Condesa de Jaruco, whom Lady Holland in 1803 described as 'extremely voluptuous and entirely devoted to the passion of love', and her daughter, the future Comtesse Merlin, 'the most magnificent glowing beauty I ever beheld'?* To dwell on dead beauties, I reply, is no business of mine. Yet the distinction between present and past is never absolute in Madrid. The miraculous liquefaction of the blood on the figure of San Pantaleón can still be seen, every 27 July, in the church of La Encarnación. That 'admirable purity' of the sky, of which Beaumarchais wrote in 1764 and which Salvador Dalí in his university days compared to the blue in the paintings of Patinir in the Prado†, can still often be seen, despite the pollution. There is still a 'Latina' in the Plaza de la Cebada but it is a cinema, not a hospital. A Bourbon king of Spain still receives visitors as his ancestors did, though he usually does so now in the small Palace of the Zarzuela, begun in 1635 in Palladian style by Gómez de Mora as a retreat for the brother of Philip IV, the Cardinal Infante Ferdinand, another of Velázquez's subjects, close to the Palace of El Pardo. There are still *tertulias* in the Café Gijón in the Paseo de Recoletos (which has resumed its old name), and I believe some in the Café Roma in the Calle Serrano, while Camilo José Cela, in *La colmena*, described *tertulias* of post-war Madrid as lively as any in the vanished Café Suizo. The *horchata*, a Valencian *refresco*, made from the roots of almonds and a root called *chufas*, is still for sale in the Puerta del Sol. The sellers of the successor to King Charles III's lottery still cry the lucky numbers '*para hoy*' (for today) in the streets, as if they were beginning a *cante jondo*. There are still gypsies in the Plaza de Santa Ana, between the Teatro Español and the bull-fighters' old favourite Hotel Victoria, next to the Palacio where the Condesa de Montijo held her enlightened *tertulias*, at the turn of the eighteenth and nineteenth centuries and where Prosper Mérimée visited her half-Scottish daughter-in-law [No. 84]. Our Lady of the Dove (*La Virgen de la Paloma*) is still carried in July along the Calle del Mediodía Chica and the Calle de Esperanza (white carnations are asked for: '*Como otro año más, saldrá la Santísima Virgen de la Paloma por las calles del Barrio. Y para que su carroza salga con flores, pedimos claveles – Blancos*'), while

* *The Spanish Journal of Elizabeth Lady Holland*, edited by the Earl of Ilchester, Longman Green and Co., London, 1910, 199.
† Salvador Dalí, *The Secret Life of Salvador Dalí*, Vision Press, New York, 191, 196.

two of the old gates of Madrid still stand – that of Alcalá, built by Sabatini for Charles III, an elegant adornment to a fashionable quarter; and that of Toledo, begun under Joseph Bonaparte but, ironically, finished as an 'arch of triumph' by Ferdinand VII, awful in its loneliness in what is for the moment a stretch of urban wasteland, almost resembling a gibbet. Many *madrileños* would regard that appearance as symbolically appropriate: for to leave Madrid for good is still for them akin to an execution. So thought Lope de Vega when, in 1587, the Velázquez brothers (no relations of the painter) launched a successful law-suit against him for libelling their families, with the consequence that the playwright was sentenced to 'four years' exile from this Court'. The Duke of Wellington was dismissive about the pleasures of Madrid. 'Yet', he told Stanhope*, 'the grandees seem to think no other place on earth worth living in. Yes, that is just their feeling. I remember the old Duchess of Osuna – you know her, María Pepa – spoke to me of the dreadful injustice and oppression which the Queen had practised on her husband. It was, she said, the cruellest thing in the world. On inquiry, I found it was nothing more than that the Duke had been appointed ambassador at Paris, and obliged to live there! Literally, that was the entire grievance!' Baroja recalls an old song:

¡*Álamos del Prado,*	Poplars of the Prado,
fuentes de Madrid!	fountains of Madrid!
¡*Como estoy ausente*	Since I am away
murmuráis de mí!	murmur of me!

Anyone who has come, as I (and other 'Anglo-Saxons' who suffer from the infirmity known as 'Byronia'†) have done, to find Madrid a most appealing city, hopes the same can be said of them.

In this collection, I leave Madrid as it was at the beginning of the 1930s. I have not sought to illustrate adequately the era of the Republic, the Civil War, nor the age of Franco. What happened in Madrid then can easily be found out. I include only one or two extracts which indicate the approach of the

* Philip Stanhope, *Notes of Conversations with the Duke of Wellington*, London, 1888, 123.
† An overwhelming desire to leave instantly for the Mediterranean.

catastrophe [No. 42]. I neglect the mid-twentieth century with
some relief. The blood-letting, after all, was beyond any that
could have been imagined in the Victorian (or, as the Spaniards
would say, the Isabelline) age. I do not forget the faces of
humble *madrileños*, whom the Mexican poet, Octavio Paz, in
The Labyrinth of Solitude, described as 'setting off for the
battle, expressing hope in a new way'*. All the same, what
tragic disillusion awaited them, whether they died or survived!
One benefit of the study of history is to realize that our own
times have no claim to superiority *per se* over what has gone
before, much less to perfection. Now that the latest of the
Bourbons, King Juan Carlos, has carried through his astonishing, brave, personal and successful transformation of General
Franco's dictatorship, and thereby shown himself the most
gifted king since Charles III, and Madrid, more alive than ever
before, has revived as a cultural and social centre, I can, I
believe, allow myself the luxury of concentration on the
remoter past.

I had at first hoped to include in this volume memories of the
numerous interesting places which surround Madrid: if not
Toledo, Madrid's predecessor as Spanish capital (which needs
a volume to itself), then the numerous *sitios reales*, royal
palaces, which are within a day's journey: leafy Aranjuez,
for example, 'an oasis of tall trees', according to Hemingway,
so famous for its strawberries in April, and the place where one
of the greatest plays begins:

> The happy days in fair Aranjuez
> Are past and gone.
>
> (Schiller, *Don Carlos*)

Or San Ildefonso (La Granja) with its wonderful fountains,
which so impressed Saint-Simon and where Lady Holland
repaired in the summer of 1803 because it was so cool when
'the baby was so ill'. Or the Escorial, where Richard Ford
allowed his pen to run riot in patriotic denunciation of Philip II,
and his 'bigot grey eyes cold as frozen drops of morning dew
. . . which even the pencil of Titian could not warm,' and where

---

* Octavio Paz, *El laberinto de la soledad*, tr. by Lysander Kemp, Allen
Lane, London, 1967.

strong feelings, either of awe or hatred (as in the case of Gautier) are usually aroused: rarely indifference. There are interesting small towns, such as Móstoles, whose mayor in 1808 declared war on Napoleon. There is decayed, if time-honoured, Alcalá de Henares, where Cardinal Ximénez de Cisneros founded the university which was later moved to Madrid; and arcaded Chinchón, where Goya's brother was once the priest; and there are several small royal pleasure places, such as ruined Balsaín, and royal stops on the way to Escorial (Aceca) or to Toledo (Illescas). In the event, I have left these delightful places for another work.

ARRIVAL IN MADRID

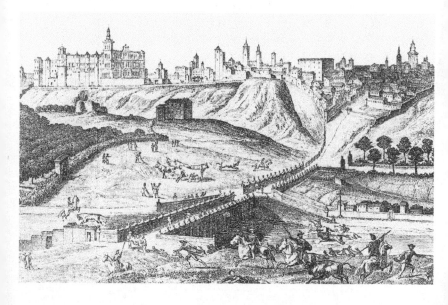

Differing Views
of the Approaches

[1] Saint-Simon (1721)
(The Duc de Saint-Simon (1675–1755) went to Madrid in
1721 to arrange the marriage (not destined to take place) of
King Louis XV and an infanta. He caught smallpox and
was made a grandee of Spain.)

We arrived at the edge of Madrid on Friday the 21st at eleven
o'clock in the evening. We found, at the entrance to the city,
which has neither walls, nor gates, nor barricades and no
suburbs, guards who asked us who we were and from where
we had come, and said that they had been put there expressly to
be warned of the moment of my arrival. As I felt so tired after
travelling all the way without rest from Burgos, and as it was so
late, I replied that we were the people of the ambassador of
France who would be arriving the next day.

Saint-Simon (1721), Vol. 38, 334.

[2] Casanova (1767)
(Casanova (1725–1798) went to Spain in order to escape an arrest (*lettre de cachet*) in Paris.)

At the gate of a town not far from Madrid I was asked for my passport. I handed it over, and got down to amuse myself. I found the chief of the customs' house engaged in an argument with a foreign priest who was on his way to Madrid, and had no passport for the capital. He shewed one he had had for Bilbao, but the official was not satisfied. The priest was a Sicilian, and I asked him why he had exposed himself to being placed in this disagreeable predicament. He said he thought it was unnecessary to have a passport in Spain when one had once journeyed in the country.

'I want to go to Madrid,' said he to me, 'and hope to obtain a chaplaincy in the house of a grandee. I have a letter for him.'

'Shew it; they will let you pass then.'

'You are right.'

The poor priest drew out the letter and shewed it to the official, who opened it, looked at the signature, and absolutely shrieked when he saw the name Squillace.*

'What, señor abbé! you are going to Madrid with a letter from Squillace, and you dare to shew it?'

The clerks, constables, and hangers-on, hearing that the hated Squillace, who would have been stoned to death if it had not been for the king's protection, was the poor abbé's only patron, began to beat him violently, much to the poor Sicilian's astonishment.

I interposed, however, and after some trouble I succeeded in rescuing the priest, who was then allowed to pass, as, I believe, a set-off against the blows he had received.

The door of my room had a lock on the outside but none on the inside. For the first and second night I let it pass, but on the third I told Señor Andrea that I must have it altered.

'Señor Don Jacob, you must bear with it in Spain, for the

* Leopoldo Gregorio, Marqués de Squillace (d. 1785), a Neapolitan minister who came over with Charles III in 1759, and was dismissed in 1767 following his orders about long cloaks – see No. 160.

Holy Inquisition must always be at liberty to inspect the rooms of foreigners.'

'But what in the devil's name does your cursed Inquisition want . . .?'

'For the love of God, Señor Jacob, speak not thus! if you were overheard we should both be undone.'

'Well, what can the Holy Inquisition want to know?'

'Everything. It wants to know whether you eat meat on fast days, whether persons of opposite sexes sleep together, if so, whether they are married and, if not married it, will cause both parties to be imprisoned; in fine, Señor Don Jacob, the Holy Inquisition is continually watching over our souls in this country.'

As I was entering the Gate of Alcalá, my luggage was searched, and the clerks paid the greatest attention to my books, and they were very disappointed only to find *The Iliad* in Greek, and a Latin Horace. They were taken away, but three days after, they were returned to me at my lodging in the Calle de la Cruz where I had gone in spite of Señor Andrea, who had wanted to take me elsewhere. A worthy man whom I had met in Bordeaux had given me the address. One of the ceremonies I had to undergo at the Gate of Alcalá displeased me in the highest degree. A clerk asked me for a pinch of snuff, so I took out my snuff-box and gave it him, but instead of taking a pinch he snatched it out of my hands and said, 'Señor, this snuff will not pass in Spain,' (it was French rappée); and after turning it out on the ground he gave me back the box.

The authorities are most rigorous on the matter of this innocent powder, and in consequence an immense contraband trade is carried on. The spies employed by the Spanish snuff-makers are always on the look-out after foreign snuff, and if they detect anyone carrying it they make him pay dearly for the luxury. The ambassadors of foreign powers are the only persons exempted from the prohibitions. The king, who stuffs into his enormous nose one enormous pinch as he rises in the morning, wills that all his subjects buy their snuff of the Spanish manufacturers. When Spanish snuff is pure it is very good, but at the time I was in Spain the genuine article could hardly be bought for its weight in gold. By reason of the natural inclination towards forbidden fruit, the Spaniards are extremely fond of

foreign snuff, and care little for their own; thus snuff is smuggled
to an enormous extent.   *Casanova, 71–75, (1767)*.

[3] M.J. Quin (1822)
(Michael J. Quin (1796–1843) was an Irish traveller whose
Visit to Spain enjoyed a vogue in the 1820s.)

When we arrived within about a league of Madrid, it suddenly
presented itself to our view with its numerous spires and
steeples, standing almost, like Palmyra, in the midst of a desert.
No shady groves, no avenues, no country seats, bespoke the
approach to a great capital. Not an object of any sort was to be
met worth describing, until we entered the barriers, which we
passed at half-past one o'clock in the afternoon.   *Quin, 46*

[4] The Marquis de Custine (1830)
(Astolphe Marquis de Custine (1793–1857) was a gifted
French writer best known for his *La Russie en 1839*
(1843).)

This plain has no beauty of any kind, not even of a bizarre
kind. It is cultivated, yet without variety; you scrape the fields
to scatter a bit of corn, which soon becomes dust-coloured, and
you reap it when it is yellow. These plains do not offer the eye
the richness of lands with good soil. They do not even have the
grandeur of complete solitude. The traveller arrives in the
capital of the kingdom feeling sad rather than annoyed. Since
morning he has not seen a tree and he has only passed through
dirty villages . . .
    This journey was made particularly disagreeable, for me, by
a rainstorm of the type that one finds only in hot climates. It
started raining at midday; and we entered Madrid under a
dense grey curtain, drawn across a hundred paces from us.
                                        Custine, 107, 133

[5] Edmondo de Amicis (1869)
(De Amicis (1846–1908), a popular Italian, wrote numerous successful travel books and novels between 1869 and 1908.)

Oh, *caballeros*, so pleasantly remembered, frequenters of all the cafés, guests at all the table d'hôtes, neighbors at the theatre, traveling companions on all the railways in Spain; you who so many times, moved by kind pity for an unknown stranger who glanced with a melancholy eye over the *Indicador del Ferrocarril* (railway guide) or the *Correspondencia Española*, thinking of his family, friends, and distant country, offered him, with amiable spontaneity, a *cigarrito*, and, taking part in a conversation which broke up the train of sad thoughts, left him calm and cheerful; I thank you. Oh, *caballeros*, so pleasantly remembered, whomsoever you may be, whether Carlists, Alphonsists, followers of Amadeus*, or liberals, I thank you from the depths of my heart, in the name of all the Italians who travel and all those who shall travel in your dear country. And I swear upon the everlasting volume of Michael Cervantes, that every time I hear you accused of ferocious souls and savage customs by your most civilized European brother, I will rise and defend you with the impetuosity of an Andalusian and the tenacity of a Catalan, as long as I have voice enough left to cry: 'Long live hospitality!'

. . . 'You have never seen Madrid?' my neighbour asked. I replied in the negative.

'It seems impossible,' exclaimed the good Spaniard, and he looked at me with an air of curiosity, as if he were saying to himself:

'Oh, let me see how a man is made who has not seen Madrid!'

Then he began enumerating the great things which I would see.

'What promenades! What cafés! What theatres! What women! For any one having three hundred thousand francs to spend, there is nothing better than Madrid; it is a great monster

---

* Followers respectively of Don Carlos, Alfonso XII and Amadeus of Aosta as King of Spain.

who lives upon fortunes; if I were you, I should like to pour mine down its throat.'

I squeezed my flabby pocket-book and murmured:

'Poor monster!'

'Here we are!' cried the Spaniard; 'look out!'

I put my head out of the window.

'That is the royal palace!'

I saw an immense pile on a hill, but instantly closed my eyes, because the sun was in my face. Every one rose, and the usual bustle of 'Coats, shawls, and other rags' began, which always impedes the first view of a city. The train stops, I get out, and find myself in a square full of carriages, in the midst of a noisy crowd; a thousand hands are stretched out toward my valise, a hundred mouths shriek in my ear. It is an indescribable confusion of porters, hackmen, guards, guides, boys, and commissioners of *casas de huespedes*. I make way for myself with my elbows, jump into an omnibus full of people, and away we go.

De Amicis, 109–11 (1869).

[6] Nina Epton (c. 1950)
(Nina Epton is known for her books on Galicia and Madrid and also for her work *Magic and Mystics of Java* (1974).)

Surely we would soon reach Madrid? The hours passed and the new Spanish train we had changed into was in no hurry to reach the capital. At first I did not mind because the mountains and starch-white villages of the Basque country were absorbing, but these were soon followed by endless barren plains. Where had the grass gone to? Who had burned it up? And where were the cattle?

The lonely earth stretched for miles, changing colour every so often as if weary of its own skin. Suddenly a fairy tale vision appeared on the naked horizon. This time nobody could tell it was the effect of the clouds. It was a real, solid town with a real solid wall all the way round it, and turrets. Everybody saw it this time – not just me and they exclaimed: 'Ávila!' A name like the beginning of a prayer. I was disappointed we could not leave the boring train to visit the city.

In the late, violet afternoon we reached the foothills of the

Sierra de Guadarrama and a tableland of rocks rising to a range of bare mountains upon which patches of snow glittered like fallen stars. Bluish-green bushes grew between giant boulders and aromatic plants threw out a sneezy perfume like chicken stuffing. Flocks of sheep and goats tinkled dreamily between stumpy trees that did not have any leaves, only immense birds' nests of dark green needles resting upon their branches. The birds that built them must be as large as the Roc in the story of Sinbad the Sailor. Mother laughed when I pointed at the nests and told me that the trees were umbrella pines.

'Ah, there is the Escorial,' somebody said. I rolled the word round and round my tongue. Escorial. It sounded hot and dry and twisted.

'Look at it,' my mother commanded in a crisp teacher-tone. 'It is the palace built by King Philip II, the king who made Madrid the capital of Spain.'

At the word 'palace' I leaped to the window and screwed up my eyes in the fading light. What I saw made me shiver. Had a king really lived in that large, dreary place? I could imagine soldiers or prisoners having to live there, but a king! Who could he show off his crown to? There was nobody there.

'We shall reach Madrid in an hour,' a man's voice said and Mother sighed.

'It is the longest hour of all.'

Now we could see nothing. The air of the Sierra poured in through the open windows, penetrating as incense. Soon lights began to appear, first singly and uncertainly, then in firm clusters and lastly in an intricate pattern of loops and curves and parallel lines – green, red and orange – like congealed fireworks; at the sight of them everybody in the compartment stood up and shouted: 'Madrid!'

'Madrid!' Mother echoed with tears in her eyes. People reacted as if there had been a free distribution of champagne. The sight of Madrid in the distance revived the drooping, unruffled the bad-tempered, bestowed the gift of tongues upon the inarticulate. Everybody waved, laughed, cried and shouted.

I have observed the same reaction, in greater or lesser degree, every time I have approached Madrid by train. (Aeroplanes are too rapid to allow for the pleasures of anticipation.) Why should Madrid have this effect? Is it perhaps the least beautiful capital of Europe and certainly one of the least beautiful cities of Spain – what, then, is the explanation?

'There is something in the air of Madrid,' people tell you vaguely, searching in vain for a concrete answer. 'It is because of the wind from the Sierra,' poets have assured me, 'which, married to the beautiful women of Madrid – most of whom come from Andalusia – creates a magic effervescence. It is a mystic marriage of sky and earth similar to those described in ancient mythologies.' Such chemistry defies analysis. All one can say is that the 'magic something' exists, but it is intangible.

The peculiar charm of Madrid cannot be defined in words and it has never been adequately painted by artists although Velázquez was obviously inspired by the city's skies. Madrid slips through one's fingers, shakes itself free of generalizations, laughs in the face of philosophers, mocks the solemn, shrugs at tragedy and befriends the light-hearted; Madrid loves pretty women and amusing men, luxury and pleasure. Madrid has no roots and only seeks to please. She does not expect anybody to be sentimental about her past, such as it is, and nobody is. The Madrileñas mislay the bodies of their most illustrious sons but they welcome the living with open arms. 'Nobody is a foreigner in Madrid,' says a refrain; so much so that the foreigner often wonders: 'Who and where is a genuine Madrileño?'

General Impressions

[7] Sir Richard Wynn (1623)
(Wynn (d. 1649), a Welsh baronet of ancient family,
accompanied Charles Prince of Wales, on his journey to
court the Infanta María, as groom of the bedchamber.)

The place resembles Newmarket, both for the country and for
the sharpness of the air. It is but a village, and lately grown to
this greatness by this King and his father's residing there. It
stands very round, thick with buildings, having neither back-
premises nor gardens in all the town. We were brought in at the
far end of the town, which lay near the place we were to alight
at. Coming through the streets, I observed most of their
buildings to be of brick, and some few of stone, all set forth
with balconies of iron, a number whereof were gilt. I found
likewise that some of their buildings were but of one story, and
the rest five and six stories high. Enquiring the reason, I was
told those low buildings were called in Spanish, *Casa de
Malitia* (i.e. *malicia*) – in English, House of Malice. For there
the King has the privilege, that no man can build above one

story without his leave, and for every upper story, the King is to receive half the rent, to save which charge, there be infinite numbers of houses but one story high.

We passed through a great part of the town, till we came to the Duke of Monteleone's Palace,* a house taken for us to lie in, where we continued that night; and the next morning, having one of the King's coaches sent for us, we went to the King's palace. By the way we found the streets wonderful full of people, and coaches in abundance, all covered with green cerecloth instead of leather. The buildings all along were like those I saw first. Their balconies, some of them, had richer trimming than the first I saw.   *D'Ewes II, 443–44.*

[8] Alexander Stanhope (1697): the mule-trains from the Americas
(Stanhope, son of the first Earl of Chesterfield, was in the English Embassy in Madrid in the 1690s.)

TO MR SECRETARY VERNON

Madrid, May 29, 1697
Yesterday came to town from Cádiz sixty mules laden with silver on the King's account.   *Stanhope, 36.*

[9] Entry of allied troops (1706)
(The historian Stanhope (1805–1875) describes the capture of Madrid by Austrian and Portuguese troops in the War of the Spanish Succession (1706). This was the first time the capital was captured by foreigners. Philip, fifth Earl Stanhope, wrote his history of the War of the Spanish Succession based on the papers of his ancestor, the first Earl, who was a son of the diplomatist quoted in No. 8.)

Madrid was now left open to the allied army, which had, without opposition, crossed the high mountains which line that city on the north, and divide the two Castilles. Their light

---

* The Palacio del Duque de Monteleone (a nobleman descended from Cortés through his Indian mistress) was in the Calle Alcalá.

troops were already hovering before it; and, on the 25th of June, the advanced guard of cavalry, under the Marquis of Villaverde, took possession of it. Galway* and Das Minas** made their triumphal entry two days afterwards; but their reception by the inhabitants was cold and sullen. To the Portuguese, especially, it was a glorious hour, – that they who but seventy years ago were the subjects and vassals of Spain, should now not only assert their independence, but enter, as conquerors, the very capital of their haughty tyrant! Unfortunately for them, their elation at this honour, together with the incapacity of Lord Galway, prevented them from pushing forward and securing their success. It was evidently their part to give Philip† no respite; to pursue, overtake, and crush his scanty forces and then, if they pleased, sit down and enjoy their laurels at leisure. Instead of this, the Generals took up their own quarters at ease in the palace of the Pardo, encamped their troops along the Manzanares, had King Charles the Third†† proclaimed in the streets, attempted to reorganize the public tribunals; and, in short, wasted a whole month in inaction; 'a halt,' says Lord Peterborough‡, in one of his letters, 'as fatal as Hannibal's at Capua.'[1] [*The Allies soon withdrew: see No.* 10.]   *Mahon, 192.*

1 Letter to General Stanhope, Aug. 1, 1706, MS. This is also Berwick's‡‡ opinion: – If, instead of amusing themselves at Madrid, . . . they had marched without delay after one they must infallibly have driven me to the other side of the Ebro . . .' (Mém. vol. i. 315)

* Henri de Massue de Ruvigny, Earl of Galway (1648–1720), Huguenot general in command of the English forces in Portugal.
** Antonio Luis de Sousa, 2nd Marqués de Minas (1644–1721), Portuguese commander.
† Philip V, King of Spain (1683–1746), the French candidate to the throne, grandson of Louis XIV.
†† i.e. Charles of Habsburg (1685–1740), the Austrian Pretender to the throne, brother of the Emperor Joseph I.
‡ Charles Mordaunt, Earl of Peterborough (1658–1735), was the English Commander in Spain: one of Macaulay's heroes.
‡‡ James fitz James (1670–1734), French marshal, first Duke of Berwick of the creation of King James II, of whom he was an illegitimate son by Arabella Churchill.

[10] Entry of Charles of Habsburg (1710)
(The Bourbon candidate Philip V reoccupied Madrid but
then had to withdraw again.)

Meanwhile Philip, from the battle-field of Zaragoza, had
hurried back to his capital. His reception was very different
from that usually given to a defeated and fugitive prince; and
the attachment of his subjects, like his own character, seemed
to be raised and strengthened by adversity. The people were
only incited to enthusiasm by what might have been expected
to dismay them – the royal decree removing the public offices
and tribunals to Valladolid; the permission given to the grandees to remain at Madrid, if they pleased; the preparations for
departure of the King and Queen and young prince of Asturias;
the terrified hurry and bustle of the courtiers; and the ill-
concealed exultation of the few Austrian partisans. The same
loyal flame seemed to burn in every breast. With very few
exceptions, all the nobles clung to what seemed the falling
cause, and escorted the King and Queen; the other classes
caught their spirit; crowded the road to Valladolid. Even ladies
of high rank were seen to follow on foot, rather than not follow
at all; and the people who remained attended the emigrants to
the gates with tears and prayers.

It was under such ill-omened circumstances that, on the 21st
of September, General Stanhope* and a thousand horse – the
vanguard of the allied army, – appeared in sight, and took
possession of Madrid. They found most of the shops, the
manufactories, and the private houses closed; the streets nearly
empty, and the few spectators silent. Charles himself made his
public entry a few days afterwards, with all military pomp;
some of his best cavalry before, and his household and guards
behind him. A pious or politic motive led him, in the first place,
to visit the church of Atocha†, much renowned throughout
Spain for its sanctity, and decked with all the standards lost by
the Allies at Almansa; he then entered the city, along with the
street of the same name: but neither curiosity to behold the

---

* James Stanhope, first Earl Stanhope (1673–1721), English comman-
der-in-chief, son of the author of No. 8, subsequently 1st Lord of the
Treasury.
† See No. 187.

prince who, during the last five years, had claimed the Crown and shared the dominions of Spain, – neither the love of show and splendour so common amongst the starers of a capital, – nor the proneness of all men to bow down before the rising sun, – could tempt the loyal inhabitants. Shut up at home, they left the deserted streets to silence and gloom. A few children who, when money was thrown amongst them, raised a faint and doubtful VIVA! were the only welcomers of Charles – their cry the only acclamations. Deeply mortified at a reception so contrary to his hopes, the Archduke soon stopped short, refused to continue his progress to the palace, and indignantly exclaiming, 'This city is a desert!' again left Madrid by the gate of Alcalá. For a time, he took up his quarters at a country house of the Conde de Aguilar, and attempted to gain the favour of the Castillians by various popular measures, – opening the public prisons; making promises (they cost nothing) of future gifts and largesses; filling up the vacant offices; and splendidly rewarding his ancient adherents, as the best means of attracting new. Nothing, however, could shake the stubborn loyalty of the people; and very few men of rank and influence espoused his cause. The Marquis of Mancera – that high-minded statesman, of whom the French, even when he was actively opposed to them, were obliged to own that he had no other guide than his duty*, and now oppressed in strength, but not in spirit, by the weight of a hundred years – had been kept at Madrid by his infirmities. Charles being naturally anxious to obtain the acknowledgement, which this venerable nobleman persisted in withholding, despatched Stanhope to press and persuade him. 'Sir,' replied Mancera, 'I have but one God, and but one King; and during my short remnant of life, I am determined to be faithful to both.' The few who pursued a different course soon began to undergo the slights and contempt of the very party they had joined; and Stahremberg† used sarcastically to call them 'the new Christians;' a term formerly applied, in Spain, to the converted Jews or Moriscos.   *Mahon, 318–19.*

* Antonio Sebastián de Toledo, Marqués de Mancera (1607–1715), exviceroy in Mexico (1664–73).
† Guido, Graf Stahremberg (1657–1737), Austrian field marshal.

[11] Napoleon 1 to his brother King Joseph
Bonaparte (1809)
(Napoleon in Madrid is discussed in the Chamartín section
[Nos 72, 74, 75]. This letter was written when he was
withdrawing towards France after his victory at the capital.)

Five-sixths of the population of Madrid are good; but respectable people must be encouraged, and that can only happen if
they are protected against the riff-raff.

You have done your best to obtain pardons for the riff-raff
arrested. I refused: I had them hanged, and have since learned
that at the bottom of their hearts people were glad that I did not
listen to them. I think it necessary for your Government to
show more firmness towards the mob, especially at first. The
mob love and value only those whom they fear; and nothing
but this fear on their part can bring you the love and esteem of
the whole nation.

Letter of January 16, 1809 (Valladolid), printed in 'Lettres
Inédites de Napoloéon I', 502. (This letter was shown at a
critical moment in the affairs of Mexico by the French officer
Pierron to the Emperor Maximilian to justify severity: see Egon
Caesar, Count Corti, *Maximilian and Charlotte of Mexico*,
New York, 1968, 575.)

[12] Joseph Bonaparte opposes force (1810)
(He was writing to his wife, Queen Julie.)

They do not know this nation, for it is like a lion; with rational
treatment it can be led by a silken thread, but not even a million
soldiers can crush it by military force . . . if they insist upon
setting up a military government, I am not the right man for it. I
cannot look on at the flogging of Frenchmen and Spaniards. I
shroud myself in my cloak and nothing is left for me but to
retire. Nobody will ever achieve anything by severity, and I less
than anybody . . .

*21 August, 1810, quoted in
'Lettres inédites de Napoléon I', 576-77.*

[13] A British military surgeon's enthusiasm (1812)

(Charles Bouffleur was a surgeon in the Second Somersets.)

On the 12th [August] we bivouacked about three Leagues from Madrid, and on the same day Lord W.* & Headquarters entered the Capital. Nearly the whole of the population came out to meet him, old & young, rich & poor; it was with difficulty we could get into the Town, so excessive was the joy of the People. On the 13th at daylight our Division marched towards Madrid, & bivouacked in a wood about a mile from the City, & close to the King's Country House†. I was in the town about eight o'Clock, & at this time the concourse of People was immense. The approach to Madrid within two miles of it was very fine, the Town itself is the most beautiful I ever saw; there are an immense number of Palaces, & other fine houses, and the Streets are wide and well built; it far exceeds the expectations of every one. – On the Evening of the 13th the Constitution as framed by the Cortes was proclaimed; the sight was truly affecting; the Houses of the Streets through which the procession passed were ornamented with silks of various colours; & the windows filled with remarkably fine women; everything bore the appearance of the most unsophisticated Joy. At length the Constitution was proclaimed amid the acclamations of thousands, who once more respired the air of liberty, after having for more than four years endured the galling Chains of the most odious Slavery. The rejoicings continued for three days, and for the same number of nights the town was most beautifully illuminated. In the midst of all this gaiety the preparations for carrying on the operations against the Retiro were carried on with vigour. On the night of the 13th the Outworks were stormed and taken, and on the following Morning at ten o'Clock a number of Troops deemed sufficient for the purpose were selected from the 3rd Division to storm the remainder of the work. Just as they were about to move off for the purpose, a flag of Truce issued from the Fort; the result of the conference, which lasted some time, was the surrendering up the Fort and all it contained to the Allied

---

* Arthur, Duke of Wellington (1769–1852), in 1812 merely an Earl.
† i.e. the Casa de Campo; see No. 224.

Army. The surprise excited by this most unlooked for event was so great, that it was with difficulty believed. At four o'Clock in the Afternoon the Garrison marched out with the honours of war, to the amount of two thousand; they were nearly all in a state of intoxication, and their gestures and language was very violent; they exclaimed that they were sold, and that their Officers ought every one to believe, that the Governor yielded to the '*Auri sacra fames*' tho' such an opinion is very assiduously scouted at Head Quarters; at all events it may very fairly be inferred that that Gentleman will never break his Parole. – In the Fort were found 190 pieces of Cannon, 20,000 Musquets, Ammunition in proportion, and immense Magazines of every description.

On the 18th our Division marched & bivouacked on the same ground we occupied on the 12th. On the 19th it reached the Escorial, where we still remain; I did not leave Madrid myself till the 19th and arrived here just at the same time with the Division. I will confess I never left a place with more sincere regret, having passed there a most delightful week. On the day of my arrival there I was particularly fortunate in being introduced to a Family of the first rank, and of the most amiable manners; from them I received attentions and kindnesses I can never forget; the father is an old General Officer, and in the time of Charles the 4th held the situation of Minister of war, and a Privy Counsellor of the Empire. The two great inconveniences we sustained at Madrid were the excessive heat (by far greater than I have ever before experienced it) and the hardness of the pavement, so much so that there was a general complaint of sore feet. – What most particularly strikes a stranger in Madrid is the elegance of the Women, the beauty of their dress, and their inimitable walk. *Bouffleur, 156–157.*

[14] Wellington's letters (1812)
(The Earl of Wellington (as he then was) captured Madrid on 12 August 1812, at the head of Anglo-Spanish forces.)

(a) to Earl Bathurst*　　　　　　　　Madrid, 13th Aug. 1812
It is impossible to describe the joy manifested by the inhabi-

* Henry, 3rd Earl Bathurst (1773–1847), secretary for War and Colonies.

tants of Madrid upon our arrival; and I hope that the prevalence of the same sentiments of detestation of the French yoke, and of a strong desire to secure the independence of their country, which first induced them to set the example of resistance to the usurper, will induce them again to make exertions in the cause of their country, which, being more wisely directed, will be more efficacious than those formerly made.

(b) to the Right Hon. Sir H. Wellesley, K.B.*

> Madrid, 23rd Aug. 1812

What can be done for this lost nation? As for raising men or supplies, or taking any one measure to enable them to carry on the war, that is out of the question. Indeed, there is nobody to excite them to exertion, or to take advantage of the enthusiasm of the people, or of their enmity against the French. Even the guerrillas are getting quietly into the large towns, and amusing themselves, or collecting plunder of a better and more valuable description; and nobody looks forward to the exertions to be made, whether to improve or to secure our advantage.

Wellington, 'Selections from the Dispatches', II, 86.

[15] Wellington's declarations to Stanhope (1836)

(Stanhope the historian later became fifth Earl Stanhope: see No. 9.)

Madrid was then a very good town, very loyal; but it is very curious that almost as soon as the Cortes came there they got it to be as factious and revolutionary as they could desire. Yet without a Court and without the grandees Madrid would be nothing at all. It would be a dismal village in the worst climate of the world. No place is both so hot and cold. The wind from the snow mountains is such that your true Spaniard is never without a leather waistcoat. It is a small town, hardly larger it looks than Canterbury, with which I have often compared it. Yet the amount of population is very different.

Stanhope's conversations with the Duke of Wellington (1836), 79.

* Sir Henry Wellesley (1773–1847), Wellington's brother, ambassador to Spain, later 1st Earl Cowley.

[16] George Borrow (1836)
(Borrow (1803–81) was agent in Spain to the Bible Society.
His *Bible in Spain* (1843) made him famous.)

I have visited most of the principal capitals of the world, but
upon the whole none has ever so interested me as this city of
Madrid, in which I now found myself. I will not dwell upon its
streets, its edifices, its public squares, its fountains, though
some of these are remarkable enough; but Petersburg has finer
streets, Paris and Edinburgh more stately edifices, London far
nobler squares, whilst Shiraz can boast of more costly fountains, though not cooler waters. But the population! Within a
mud wall scarcely one league and a half in circuit, are contained two hundred thousand human beings, certainly forming
the most extraordinary vital mass to be found in the entire
world; and be it always remembered that this mass is strictly
Spanish. The population of Constantinople is extraordinary
enough, but to form it twenty nations have contributed –
Greeks, Armenians, Persians, Poles, Jews, the latter, by-the-
by, of Spanish origin, and speaking amongst themselves the old
Spanish language; but the huge population of Madrid, with the
exception of a sprinkling of foreigners, chiefly French tailors,
glover-makers, and *perruquiers*, is strictly Spanish, though a
considerable portion are not natives of the place. Here are no
colonies of Germans, as at Saint Petersburg; no English factories, as at Lisbon; no multitudes of insolent Yankees lounging
through the streets, as at the Havannah, with an air which
seems to say, 'The land is our own whenever we choose to take
it;' but a population which, however strange and wild, and
composed of various elements, is Spanish, and will remain so as
long as the city itself shall exist. Hail, ye *aguadores* of Asturias!
who, in your dress of coarse duffel and leathern skull-caps, are
seen seated in hundreds by the fountain sides, upon your empty
water-casks, or staggering with them filled to the topmost
stories of lofty houses*. Hail, ye *caleseros* of Valencia! who,
lolling lazily against your vehicles, rasp tobacco for your paper
cigars whilst waiting for a fare. Hail to you, beggars of La
Mancha! men and women, who, wrapped in coarse blankets,

---

* Water-carriers in old Madrid came specially from Asturias.

demand charity indifferently at the gate of the palace or the prison. Hail to you, valets from the mountains, *mayordomos* and secretaries from Biscay and Guipúzcoa, *toreros* from Andalusia, *reposteros* from Galicia, shopkeepers from Catalonia! Hail to ye, Castilians, Extreménos, and Aragonese, of whatever calling! And lastly, genuine sons of the capital, rabble of Madrid, ye twenty thousand *manolos**, whose terrible knives, on the second morning of May† worked such grim havoc amongst the legions of Murat!

Borrow, 'The Bible in Spain', *(1843)*.

[17] Count Paul Vasili (1886)

('Count Vasili' was the pseudonym of Juliette Lamber (1836–1931), a well-known French writer of the late nineteenth century, director of the *Nouvelle Revue* and married to the politician Edmond Adam. Her salon was famous in the 1870s.)

This ugly capital, so dear to the heart of Philip II, will not remind you in any way of the Inquisitor King. Everything here is gay, even destitution; here you will find Don Quixotes, Sancho Panzas and Cesars de Bazán by the hundreds. Madrid society, unconsciously perhaps, is democratic; it is frank and sincere, and you do not find there any stiffness or affectation. The Castillian arrogance is only the covering for an optimistic self-sufficiency which does not wound, does not shock, which you will grow accustomed to, and in which you will drape yourself unknowingly on your return, since it clings to the bodies of the *madrileños*, like the folds of that elegant grey cloak, of that *capa* which you would like to wear and which you never know how to use properly, not being *gato*, that is to say, not being born in the very noble, very royal, very heroic city of the 2nd of May.

* *Manolo* is a difficult word to translate; it is applied to the flash or fancy man and his *manola* in Madrid only, a class fond of pleasure, of fine clothes, of bull-fights, and of sunshine, with a code of honour of their own; men and women rather picturesque than exemplary, and eminently racy, of the soil [Borrow's note]. See also No. 76.
† In 1808: see Nos 55 and 56.

Madrid is a very intelligent town, but influenced more than any other by religion. Wherever Catholicism darkens its spirit, it is a century behind. Careless of its political duties, and thereby a victim of the intrigues and ambitions of parties, its spirit is not free enough to be clear-sighted. You will very quickly see that the immorality of all large capital cities is doubled in Madrid by a strong dose of hypocrisy, a logical conclusion of its clerical education.

These are but little faults, when you think of all the vitality you meet with, all the warm responses to the least little call, the great-heartedness at the smallest emotion, the enthusiasm at the first onslaught of noble passion. The Spanish are a people whom you love for the sake of loving, where you fight for the sake of fighting, where the cult of Patriotism dominates all the joys of existence, where the supreme happiness is to give your life for an idea and for Spain.

What an admirable nation is the Spanish, and yet at the same time to be pitied! For she is constantly exploited both by the right and the left, in the name of liberty or monarchy, by priest or by general, by bulls or by *pronunciamientos*.   *Vasili, 2–3.*

[18] Ramón y Cajal (c. 1900)
(Santiago Ramón y Cajal (1852–1934) was Spain's greatest neurologist.)

Madrid is a most dangerous city for the hardworking provincial anxious to expand the horizons of his intelligence. The ease and charm of the social life, the abundance of the talent, the attractiveness of the learned societies, clubs and *tertulias** where grand personalities of politics, art and literature pontificate; the various theatrical spectacles and the other thousand distractions seduce and captivate the outsider who often finds himself without bearings and stupefied. In his life a radical metamorphosis is operating. The bee has turned into a butterfly, if not into a drone. Philosophy, art, literature, even politics and sport, draw out the soul with a thousand rigid and invisible

---

* A *terlulia* is a regular meeting of the same people, day in day out, for discussion. In the nineteenth and twentieth centuries these have usually been in cafés (see Nos 95 and 96); in the eighteenth in private houses.

threads. To the burdened worker there has succeeded the pleasant intellectual sybarite.

In addition the cerebral instrument forged during many years of solitude and abstraction is transmuted and whatever steel there is turned into one eaten up by rust. The special mentality carried from the provinces becomes little by little the same as everyone else's. The warts disappear and the hands become gloved. Time passes in admiring and imitating.

In vain we try to stop on the slippery slope, to abandon resolutely the road to Sybaris or Corinth, to return to the severe habits of yesteryear. Needled by a sense of punctiliousness, we get as far as to work out beautiful programmes of action. Unfortunately all miscarries. 'There is no time for that,' we say with bitterness.

Precisely, and to compensate for the excessive concentration of the life of the laboratory, I have always cultivated in Madrid two distractions; walks in the fresh air in the surroundings of the town, and *tertulias*.　　　　*Ramón y Cajal, 141–142 (c. 1900).*

[19] Arturo Barea (c. 1920)
(Arturo Barea (1897–1957) was a Spanish socialist born in Madrid, who, in his exile in England after the Civil War, wrote a fine autobiography, *The Forging of a Rebel*, published in London, 1941–4.)

Madrid smells better. It does not smell of mules, or of sweat, or of smoke, or of dirty farmyards with the warm reek of dung and of chickens. Madrid smells of sun. On the balcony of our flat, which is on the third floor, you can sun yourself in the mornings. The cat stays in a corner of the balcony on his square of rug, peers down into the street over the edge of the board placed against the foot of the railings, and sits down and sleeps. From time to time, he opens his golden eyes and looks at me. Then he shuts them again and goes on sleeping. In his sleep he twitches his nostrils and smells everything.

When they water the street below, the fresh scent of moist earth rises up to the balcony just as when it is raining. When the wind blows from the north you smell the trees in the Casa de Campo. When the air is still and the whole quarter lies quiet, the wood and plaster of the old houses smell, the clean linen spread out on the balconies, and the sweet basil in the flower-pots. The old walnut and mahogany furniture sweats beeswax; you smell it through the open balconies while the women are cleaning. In the basement of our house is a smart carriage yard, and in the mornings, when the lacquered carriages are taken out into the street, sluiced and brushed, you can smell them. The horses, white and cinnamon brown, come out for their walk covered with a blanket and they smell of warm hair.

Barea, 74–75.

[20] Manuel Azaña's scepticism (c. 1920)

(Manuel Azaña y Díaz (1880–1940) was a fine writer who subsequently became Minister of War, Prime Minister and President of the Second Spanish Republic.)

Enough to say that I am not *madrileñista*. *Madrileñismo* is a foppery imported from outside. Years ago a Catalan who sold paving stones to the Town Hall wished to become a Councillor and on his electoral posters he called himself a *madrileñista*. A typical entrepreneurial idea! Afterwards the idea was taken up by some gaming houses. Without being blinded by *madrileñismo*, I know that Madrid offers the idle traveller very tasty attractions. But, first, in Madrid there is nothing to do, nowhere to go, nothing to see. Second, Madrid is a town without history. An 'old city' of historic importance begins by infusing in me a provisional suspicion which turns into definite distancing when the history concerned is revealed as being plagued by stupidity. In Madrid nothing has happened because in two centuries almost nothing has happened in Spain, and the little that has occurred has done so elsewhere. The entire history of Madrid consists of handkissing and private or royal intrigues. . . . Between Madrid and a really historical city there is the same qualitative difference as there is between the Calle Ancha de San Bernardo* and Venice. I recognize that the fact that Madrid is not an old grand city is perhaps the most elegant charm that this town [*pueblo*] has for me.   *Azaña, I, 805–07.*

* A broad street running north-south in Madrid in which the University was established until its move to the University City following the reform of the 1920s.

[21] Ernest Hemingway (c. 1930)
(Hemingway (1899–1961) spent much of the late 1920s and early 1930s in Spain.)

The bad thing about going to Spain in the spring to see bull-fights is the rain. It may rain everywhere you go, especially in May and June, and that is why I prefer the summer months. It rains in July and August although it snowed in August of 1929 in some of the mountain summer resorts of Aragon and in Madrid it snowed one year on May 15th and was so cold they called off the bull-fights. I remember having gone down that year to Spain thinking spring would be well along, and all day on the train we rode through country as bare and cold as the badlands in November. I could hardly recognize the country as the same I knew in the summer and when I got off the train at night in Madrid snow was blowing outside the station. I had no overcoat and stayed in my room writing in bed or in the nearest café drinking coffee and Domecq brandy. It was too cold to go out for three days and then came lovely spring weather. Madrid is a mountain city with a mountain climate. It has the high cloudless Spanish sky that makes the Italian sky seem sentimental and it has air that is actively pleasurable to breathe. The heat and the cold come and go quickly there. I have watched, on a July night when I could not sleep, the beggars burning newspapers in the street and crouching around the fire to keep warm. Two nights later it was too hot to sleep until the coolness that comes just before morning.

Madrileños love the climate and are proud of these changes. Where can you get such a variation in any other large city? When they ask you at the café how you slept, and you say it was too bloody hot to sleep until just before morning, they tell you that is the time to sleep. There is always that coolness just before daylight at the hour a man should go to sleep. No matter how hot the night, you always get that. It really is a very good climate if you do not mind changes. On hot nights you can go to the Bombilla to sit and drink cider and dance, and it is always cool when you stop dancing there in the leafiness of the long plantings of trees where the mist rises from the small river. On cold nights you can drink sherry brandy and go to bed. To go to bed at night in Madrid marks you as a little queer. For a long time your friends will be a little uncomfortable about it. Nobody goes to bed in Madrid until they have killed the night. Appointments with a friend are habitually made for after midnight at the café. In no other town that I have ever lived in, except Constantinople during the period of the Allied occupation, is there less going to bed for sleeping purposes.

Hemingway, 'Death in the Afternoon', 50–51.

MADRID

MADRID

The Streets

[22] The complaints of Camillo Borghese (1594)
(Camillo Borghese (1550–1620) was papal Nuncio in
Madrid in the 1590s, and elected Pope in 1605 as Paul V.
He began the Villa Borghese.)

The city of Madrid was known in the Moorish language as
Magerite which means 'place of winds' . . . It is fairly big, full
of people, which suggests that there are 50,000 hearths. There
is a broad street [the Calle Alcalá] which would be beautiful if it
were not for the mud and filth which mars it. The houses are
bad and ugly and almost all made of mud and among other
imperfections have neither doorsteps nor closets; in consequence of which, all perform their necessities in chamber pots
which they afterwards throw into the street, a thing which
afterwards creates an insupportable odour; and Nature has
worked well so that sweet-smelling plants are in abundance,
without which one could not live; where if one did not use
diligence to clean the street frequently one could not move,
even if in spite of this cleaning it is impossible to walk.

Camillo Borghese, in García Mercadal, 'Viajes' I, 1472.

[23] Sir Richard Wynn (1623)

Thus did I pass our first day's being there, and at night did return to . . . our lodging, where, by the way, there were so many things emptied in the street that did almost poison us; for the usual custom there is, that at eleven at night every one empties those things in the street, and by ten the next day it is so dried up, as if there were no such thing. Being desirous to know why so beastly a custom is suffered, they say it's a thing prescribed by their physicians; for they hold the air to be so piercing and subtle, that this kind of corrupting it with these ill vapours keeps it in good temper. Notwithstanding all these ill smells, yet a plague is not a thing known in this town.

Sir Richard Wynn (1623) in D'Ewes, II, 446.

[24] Bertaut (1664)
(François Bertaut (1621–c. 1705) was in Spain as part of a French mission headed by Marshal Gramont [see No. 115].)

The streets are for the most part wide, but I do not think that anyone has ever removed a single cart-load of mud from them, so much of it is there everywhere, and so infected because of the dung thrown onto them, that I think it is for this reason that the Spaniards go to such pains to obtain scent. In winter the carriages have great difficulty in moving because of the mud, there are many places with mounds of drier mud, which have been there, it would seem, since the time of Charles V. In summer, this mud dries and produces a quantity of frightful dust, such that it never, whatever the season, seems as though the streets have been paved, though in fact they are.

Bertaut (1664), 45.

[25] Beaumarchais reports on the effects of Charles III's 'clean air' policy (1764)
(Pierre Augustin Caron de Beaumarchais (1732–1799) was in Spain for a year trying to persuade the writer José de Clavijo (1730–1806) to marry his sister Louise.)

The sky here is of an admirable purity, and it is an advantage that I sense a great deal more than natives of the country who have never seen the damp, grey winters that we have at home. Since the stubborn determination of the reigning Prince to clean the city of Madrid has beaten the obstinacy of the Spaniards to remain in filth*, this city has become one of the smartest that I have ever seen, very open, adorned with many squares and public fountains, which in truth are more useful to the people than agreeable to men of taste. A lively and appetizing air circulates everywhere easily, it is even sometimes of a vivacity that could kill a man where he stands at the entrance to a crossroads. But that only ever happens to a Spaniard exhausted by debauchery and *brûlé de vanille*†. These people combine superstitious devotion with a fairly large habitual corruption; and we have a very false opinion of the Spaniards when we think they are jealous: this frenzy perhaps survives in a few provincial towns, but no woman of the world enjoys such enormous liberty as those in this capital . . .

Letter to the Duc de la Vallière, 'Letters' I, 126.

[26] Henry Inglis (1830)
(Henry Inglis (1795–1835) was a Scottish journalist and writer who died of overwork.)

The streets of Madrid present a totally different aspect, at different hours of the day: before one o'clock, all is nearly as I have described it; bustling and busy, and thronged with people of all ranks, of whom the largest proportion are always females; for the women of Madrid spend much of their time in the streets, going and coming from mass, shopping (a never failing resource,) and going and coming from the Prado‡. But from one o'clock till four, the aspect of everything is changed: the shops are either shut, or a curtain is drawn before the door; the shutters of every window are closed; scarcely a respectable person is seen in the street; the stall-keepers spread cloths over their wares, and go to sleep; groups of the poor and idle are

* Charles III's decree on street cleaning was in 1761.
† Presumably brandy made from vanilla.
‡ The Prado; see Nos 43–50.

seen stretched in the shade; and the water-carriers, throwing their jackets over their faces, make pillows of their water casks. But the *siesta* over, all is again life and bustle; the curtains are withdrawn, the balconies are filled with ladies, the sleepers shake off their drowsiness, and the water-carriers resume their vocation, and deafen us with the cry of *agua fresca*. These water-carriers are a curious race, and are as necessary to the Spanish peasant as the vendor of beer is to the English labourer: with a basket and glass in the right-hand, and a water jar on the left shoulder, they make incessant appeals to the appetite for cold water, and during the summer, drive a lucrative trade; and so habituated is the Spaniard to the use of cold water, that I have observed little diminution in the demand for it, when the morning temperature of the air was such as would have made even an Englishman shrink from so comfortless a beverage.

Frequently, while in Madrid, I walked out early in the morning, that I might hear the delightful music that accompanies the morning service in the *Convento de las Salesas**: and then the streets wore a different appearance, – flocks of goats were bivouacked here and there to supply milk to those who cannot afford to buy cows' milk. Porters, water-carriers, stall-keepers, and market people, were making a breakfast of grapes and bread; and here and there a friar might be seen, with his sack slung over his back, begging supplies for his convent. One morning, I had the curiosity to follow a young friar of the Franciscan order the whole length of the *Calle de Montera†*; he asked upwards of forty persons for alms, and entered every sort of shop, and only two persons listened to his petition, – one of these was an old lame beggar, sitting at a door, who put half a quarto into his hand; the other was an old gentleman with a cocked hat, and certain other insignia of holding some government employment.

In my first perambulation of the streets of Madrid, I remarked, with astonishment, the extraordinary number of shops appropriated to the sale of combs. Throughout Spain,

---

* *Convento* of Salesian monks, on the site of the present Supreme Court.
† The Calle Montera runs north from the Puerta del Sol. Possibly so called because the beautiful wife of a huntsman (*montero*) of Philip II lived there.

but especially in Madrid, the comb is an indispensable and important part of every woman's dress, and a never failing accompaniment of the mantilla. A fashionable Spanish comb is not less than a foot long, and eight or nine inches broad; and no woman considers from nine to fifteen dollars too much to give for this appendage; accordingly, every tenth shop, at least, is a comb shop. Another very numerous class of shops appeared to belong to booksellers; and a third – shops filled with remnants and shreds of cloth of all kinds and colours, which partly accounts for the patched appearance of the garments of the lowest orders, who doubtless find in these repositories the means of repairing their worn-out clothes. I had one day the curiosity to walk leisurely through two of the principal commercial streets, and to take note of the different shops they contained. In the *Calle de Carretas** I found sixteen booksellers, ten vendors of combs, three jewellers, two hardware shops, two gold and silver embroiderers, two chocolate shops, two fan shops, six drapers and silk mercers, one woollen draper, one hatter, one perfumer, one fruiterer, one print shop, one wine shop, and one stocking shop . . .

Walking through the streets of Madrid, you are one moment arrested by a pleasant smell, and the next stunned by a bad one; among the former, is the fragrant perfume from the cinnamon to be mixed with the chocolate: at the door of every chocolate shop, a person is to be seen beating cinnamon in a large mortar. Another pleasant smell arises from the heaps of melons that lie on the streets. This custom, by-the-by, of heaping fruit on the street, requires that one unaccustomed to the streets of Madrid should look well to his feet, – melons, oranges, apples, and many other kinds of fruit, lie every where in the way of the passenger, who is in constant danger of being toppled over. Among the bad smells that assail one, the most common, and to me the most offensive, is the smell of oil in preparation for cooking . . .

. . . let me not omit one offensive sight, – I allude to the constant practice of combing and cleaning the hair in the street: in most of the less frequented streets, persons are seen at every

---

* The Calle de Carretas runs south from the Puerta del Sol: probably so called because the Comuneros in the revolt of 1520 (see No. 106) created a barricade of wagons (*carretas*) there.

second or third door intent upon this employment; and sometimes the occupation includes a scrutiny, at the nature of which the reader must be contented to guess; and even in the most frequented streets, if two women be seated at fruit-stalls near each other, one is generally engaged in combing, assorting, and occasionally scrutinizing the hair of the other . . .

I was prepared to find much more wretchedness and poverty among the lower orders in Madrid, than is apparent – I might perhaps say, than exists there. There is much misery in Madrid, but it lies among a different class, of whom I shall have occasion to speak afterwards: at present, I speak merely of the lowest class of the inhabitants, among whom, in every great city, there is always a certain proportion of miserably poor. I purposely walked several times into the lowest quarters of the city, but I never encountered any such pictures of poverty and wretchedness as are to be found abundantly in Paris, London, Dublin, Manchester, and other great towns of France and England. When the king* arrived in Madrid from *La Granja*†, there were at least 10,000 persons present at his *entrée*; and upon the occasion of the queen's accouchement‡, there were three times that number in the court of the palace; and yet I did not see a single person in rags – scarcely even a beggar. It is possible, however, that a cloak may conceal much wretchedness; and of this I had one day an example. Sauntering one morning in the retired part of the Prado, in front of the botanical garden, I sat down upon the low wall that supports the iron railing: a man, with a decent cloak wrapped around him, sat a few paces distant, seemingly in a reverie; he happened to have taken his seat upon some prohibited place, and one of the guards, unperceived by him, walked forward, and tapped him on the shoulder with his musket: whether the sudden start which this intrusion occasioned had unfastened the cloak, or whether he had accidentally let go his hold of it, is of no consequence; but the cloak dropped half off his body, and I discovered that it was his only garment, excepting his neckcloth: the man was no beggar; he hastily replaced the cloak, and walked away. He was probably one of that class

---

* King Ferdinand VII (1784–1833), King of Spain 1814–33.
† Country house of the monarchs at San Ildefonso near Segovia.
‡ Queen María Cristina of Naples, fourth wife of Ferdinand.

who, in Madrid, sacrifice all to the exterior; or, possibly, one of those very few Castilians, who yet inherit old Castilian pride, and who would die rather than ask an alms.

. . . Madrid has no manufacture, so that labour is not attracted to the capital, to be afterwards subject to the vicissitudes of trade; nor is there any spirit of enterprise, whose caprices demand a constant supply of superabundant labour. These may, or may not, be deemed sufficient reasons for the fact I have wished to account for, – the reader may probably be able to add others. The fact, however, is certain, that in no city of Europe ranking with Madrd, is there so little apparent wretchedness.

There is less appearance of business in the streets of Madrid, than in any city I have ever seen: the population seem to have turned out to enjoy themselves. Two things contribute mainly to give that air of ease and pleasure to the pursuits of the inhabitants of Madrid; the great proportion of women of whom the street population is composed, – and the extreme slowness of movement. The women of Madrid have nothing to detain them at home; the ladies have no home occupations as in London; nor have the majority of the bourgeoises any shop duties to perform as in Paris, – the street is, therefore, their only resource from *ennui*. And there is something in extreme slowness of motion, that is entirely opposed to business and duties, – a quick step, and a necessary one, are closely allied; but the street population of Madrid, with few exceptions, merely saunter; and wherever you reach an open space, especially the *Puerta del Sol** – a small square in the centre of the city, – hundreds of gentlemen are seen standing, with no other occupation than shaking the dust from their segars. The great numbers of military too, strolling arm in arm, and, above all, the innumerable priests and monks, with whom we at once connect idleness and ease, give to the street population of Madrid an appearance of pleasure seeking, which is peculiar to itself, and is perhaps little removed from truth.

Henry D. Inglis (1830), 70–80.

* See Nos 51–63.

[27] Marquis de Custine (1831)

The promenade by carriage risks yet another source of annoyance: it is the danger of encountering the holy sacrament. It is usual, when this happens, for even the king himself to get out, kneel in the road, and give up his seat to the priest, carrier of the Host. Whether from pride or from regard to etiquette, the priest never refuses.

This custom is the bane of the lives, and often the misery, of coachmen; they are trained to flee this meeting with the good Lord, whose passing they must anticipate far enough in advance in order that they can steer into a by-way, so as to avoid the necessity of their masters' ceding their places to him. If the unfortunate coachman has not heard the bell, if the holy sacrament accelerates towards him, if the road in which he is has no turnings, then he is sure to be hounded for letting himself be taken in by the holy trap.

Last winter the Duchess of . . . returned from a ball at 3 in the morning, and it was icy cold. There were 6 inches of snow on the streets of Madrid. Her coachman let himself be overtaken by the holy sacrament that was being taken to an invalid. The poor Duchess, forced to kneel in the middle of the road and yield her carriage to the priest, returned home on foot, in Court dress, and, during this perilous journey, contracted pneumonia, from which she thought she would die. You can easily understand why the coachman guilty of such a serious blunder was sacked the same day.

Custine, 224 (1831).

[28] Théophile Gautier (1840)

(Théophile Gautier (1811–1872) was a poet and a novelist whose *Voyage en Espagne* (1845) helped, with Mérimée's *Carmen* (1847), to create a great appetite for 'Romantic Spain' in Paris.)

Now let us roam the town at will, for chance is the best guide, especially since Madrid is not rich in architectural magnificence, and since one street is as interesting as the next. The first thing you notice, on raising your nose to the corner of a house or a street, is a clay plaque on which is written *Manzana, vicitac, gener**. These plaques used in the past to be the way of numbering houses forming islands or blocks. Today everything is numbered as it is in Paris. You will be surprised, also, at the quantity of fire insurances that bedeck the façades of the houses, especially in a place where there are no chimneys and where no one ever lights a fire. Everything is insured, even the public monuments, even the churches; the civil war, it is said, is the reason for this great eagerness to be insured: nobody being certain of not being more or less roasted alive by some *Balmaseda*† or other, everybody seeks at least to preserve his house . . .

One really surprising thing is the prevalence of the following inscription: *Juego de villar* which you see every twenty paces. Lest you imagine that there is something mysterious in these three words, I hasten to translate them: they merely mean 'Game of Billiards'. I cannot conceive what kind of devil could use so many billiard tables: everyone in the universe would be able to play a game. After the *juegos de villar*, the next most frequent inscription is that of *despacho de vino* (wine shop). There they sell *Valdepeñas* and other full-bodied wines. The displays are painted in striking colours, and are decorated with cloths and foliage. The *confiterías* and the *pastelerías* are also very numerous and fairly smartly decorated; the confitures of Spain deserve special mention; those known by the name of *cabello de ángel* (angel's hair) are exquisite. The pastry is as good as it can be in a country where there is no butter, or at least where it is so expensive and of such bad quality that one can hardly use it; it approaches what we call *petit four*. All these signs are written in small letters, which makes them at first difficult for the foreigner to understand, expert reader of signs though he may be.   *Gautier (1840), 48.*

[29] Alexandre Dumas, *père* (1846)
(Dumas (1802–1870) was in Spain to celebrate the wedding of the Duc de Montpensier, a patron of his, to the sister of the Queen of Spain. He was then at the height of his reputation.)

---

* *Manzana* is essentially a block, numbered in the 1760s for the first time.
† Presumably Juan Manuel Balmaseda (1800–46), a ferocious Carlist general.

In fact, everything was new to us. These grave and silent people who watched us pass with the stillness of a procession of shadows, these women, so beautiful in their rags, these men, so proud in their tatters, these children, already clothed in the shreds from the paternal cloak, all indicated to us not only a different people but a different century . . .

One day, I was nearly carried off in triumph. I was going along the Calle Santa Ana* in a gig. My gig was halted by an immense gathering of people. An elderly *marquesa* was walking along, followed by a pekingese and a servant, when all of a sudden a bull-dog, small but with jaws of steel, sprang on the unhappy pekingese, and got a firm grip on his fleshy hind-quarters. The pekingese howled, the *marquesa* cried, the servant swore and, it must be said, madam, to the shame of the inhabitants of the Calle Santa Ana, the public laughed.

A few more compassionate souls attempted to drag apart the two animals, but without success, which put the *marquesa* in despair.

I resolved to play the role of the antique god, my gig replacing the machine. I leant on the open apron of the carriage and, seizing hold of the situation:

'Bring me those two animals,' I said.

'Oh sir, save my dog!' cried the *marquesa*, with hands clasped together.

Someone gave me grappling-irons. As I had no knowledge whatsoever of bull-dogs, and as I was therefore hardly familiar with him, I tied my hand-kerchief round his tail and through it gave a hard bite.

The pekingese dropped like a ripe fruit, fell to the ground and ran to its mistress, while the bull-dog tried, writhing in pain, with blood-shot eyes and mouth agape, to seize hold of any part of my person.

But I knew my trade of bull-dog detacher. My lord had taught it me. I threw my animal ten feet away from me, and shouted:

'To the Institute!'

'Well, well!' said an old woman, 'it's no mistake that this gentleman is so clever, he is an academician.'

* This street runs off the Calle de Toledo. It is famous for a shrine to Saint Anne, once popular among gypsies.

Three days later, madam, the elderly *marquesa*, who had discovered my real profession and my true address, offered me her heart and her hand. If I had married her, I would have been a widower today, and I would have had 150 thousand francs of rent paid to me.

My advice to young people is to marry.

Dumas, 126–27 (1846).

[30] De Amicis on *serenos* (1869)

(*Serenos* were introduced in 1782 from Valencia. The crime rate fell. They disappeared in the early 1970s. The crime rate rose.)

. . . Finally you arrive at your house, but you have not got the door key.

'Do not give yourself any uneasiness,' says the first citizen whom you meet. 'Do you see that lantern at the end of the street? The man who is carrying it is a *sereno*, and the *serenos* have the keys of all the houses.'

Then you cry out: '*Sereno!*' The lantern approaches, and a man with an enormous bunch of keys in his hand, after giving you a scrutinizing glance, opens the door, lights you to the first-floor, and wishes you good night. In this way, by the payment of one lira a month, you are relieved from the annoyance of carrying the house keys in your pockets every evening. The *sereno* is an employé of the municipality: there is one for every street, and each carries a whistle. If the house takes fire, or thieves break in, you have only to rush to the window and cry: '*Sereno!* Help!' The *sereno* who is in the street whistles; the *serenos* in the neighboring streets blow their whistles, and in a few moments all the *serenos* in the quarter run to your assistance. At whatever hour of the night you wake, you hear the voice of the *sereno*, who announces it to you, adding that the weather is fine, that it rains, or that it is going to rain. How many things the nightwatchman knows, and how many he never reveals! How many subdued farewells he hears! How many little notes he sees drop from the window; how many keys fall on the pavement; how many hands, making mysterious motions in the air; how many muffled lovers stealing through little doorways; lighted windows suddenly

obscured, and dark figures gliding along the walls at the first
streak of dawn!   *De Amicis (1869), 140–41.*

[31] Pérez Galdós on the *quartier* near Santo Domingo el Real (1884)

(Benito Pérez Galdós (1845–1920), Spain's greatest and
most productive novelist, wrote many novels based on
Madrid life as he saw it. Señora Pepaón de la Barca in
Tormento (1884) assuredly had a real basis.)

Señora Pepaón de la Barca still not tired of praising her home and
congratulating herself upon it gave no rest to her tongue: 'As for
me, Candida darling, no one will drag me away from this district.
Nothing outside this little corner seems to me like Madrid. I was
born in the Plaza de Navalón and for a long time we lived in the
Calle de Silva. When two days go by without my seeing the Plaza
del Oriente, Santo Domingo el Real, the Incarnation and the
Senate, I don't seem to have been alive. I don't think I get any
benefit from the Mass unless I hear it in Santa Catalina de los
Donados or the Chapel Royal or the Buena Dicha. I admit this
part of the Costanilla de los Angeles *is* rather narrow but I like it
like that. We seem to have more company when we can see our
opposite neighbours so close that we could almost shake hands. I
like to have neighbours on all sides. I like to hear the tenant
running up his stairs at night; I like to hear people breathing
above me and below me. I find solitude quite terrifying and, when
I hear about families who have gone out to live in that suburb of
Sacramental that Salamanca* is laying out beyond the Plaza de
Torros, it gives me the shivers. Goodness how frightening. Now
this place is like a public balcony. Such a bustle! People talking at
all hours. Absolutely all night you can hear passers-by talking
and almost make out what they say . . . Then everything's so
close . . . The butcher's down below, the grocer's next door, and
a few yards away there's a fish stall. In the little square, there's a
chemist, a cake-shop, a chocolate-grinder's, a dairy, a haberda-
sher's and an oil shop . . .   *Benito Pérez Galdós, 'Tormento'.*

* The Marqués de Salamanca (1811–83) had a sensational career as
banker and politician. The *quartier* mentioned is now fashionable (1988).

[32] Arturo Barea's childhood games

Our *quartier* stretched farther on through a maze of old alleyways as far as the Calle Mayor*. They were narrow, twisting streets, as our forefathers had built them for some reason or other. They had wonderful names: the names of saints, like Saint Clara and Saint James; then heroic names of wars like Luzón, Lepanto, Independence; and lastly fancy names – Street of the Mirror, of the Clock, of the Stoop – which were the oldest and most winding alleys, those which were best for playing at 'Thieves and Robbers'. There were bits of waste ground with broken hoardings and ruins inside, old houses with empty doorways, stone courtyards with solitary trees, little squares narrower even than the streets. They twisted and intertwined so that it was easy to hide and to escape in them.

There we used to play at 'I spy'. The one who was left over waited until he heard the shouts of the gang which scattered into the alleys. 'I see you-oo-oo!'

He would start to run and behind his back the boys who had been crouching in the corners came out from the doorways, calling: 'Past and safe!'

He would run on, smelling out the holes like a dog until he caught one of the boys squatting on the ground or behind some worm-eaten door: 'I spy!'

Sometimes they both shouted at the same time, and then a quarrel would start and end in blows.

We had our *quartier* and our law. At times, the gang of a neighboring *quartier* invaded our territory, and then we defended our right with stones which ricocheted from the corners. The war usually lasted for days, and cost bumps and bruises. In the end, the attackers would get tired and leave us in peace. At other times, we ourselves attacked a neighboring *quartier* because the boys there were stinkers or because they had beaten up one of our gang who was passing through their territory.

Everything in our *quartier* was ours: the holes in the street where we played marbles: the railings of the square where we

* See Nos 41 and 42.

played hopscotch: the frogs and the toads in the fountain of the Plaza de Oriente*: the right to the planks of the hoardings which we could exchange for broken biscuits at the pastry-cook's in the Calle del Espejo†: the right to catch the hawk-moths round the street lights of the Calle del Arenal‡, to chuck stones at the gas lamps, to jump down the high steps leading up to the Church of Santiago, and to light bonfires in the Plaza de Ramales§.   *Barea, 76.*

* See No. 82.
† This street is said to have been so called because the Arabs fortified it against the Christians using a series of watchtowers which were known as 'speculas' and then 'espejos' (fourteenth century).
‡ This street running from the Puerta del Sol to the Plaza de Oriente is so called because the 'Arenal', a sandpit, was there in the time of the Arabs.
§ A square near the royal palace, once known as de San Juan, but changed to Ramales to commemorate a *pueblo* in Santander whose inhabitants fought Don Carlos there in 1840.

Alcalá

(This broad street runs from the Puerta del Sol towards the city of Alcalá de Henares. Until the twentieth century it ended at the Puerta (gate) de Alcalá, which was to begin with in what is now the Plaza de Cibeles and, since the eighteenth century, has been in the Plaza de Independencia.)

[33] The French army enters Madrid (1808) – General Bigarré
(General Auguste Bigarré (1775–1838) was aide-de-camp to the Emperor Napoleon.)

But when I heard the cannon thundering on all sides, when I saw the infantry making for Madrid, I forgot about defence, and I was not alone in so doing; I mounted my horse, as did Colonel Clermont-Tonnerre*, today Minister of War, and together we headed for the iron grille that stands at the entrance to the Prado at the highest place and, seizing the moment when the gunners led out a *pièce de quatre* beyond the walls, in order to drag it

---

* Clermont-Tonnerre, Aimé Marie Gaspard, Duc de (1779–1863), Minister of War under Charles X.

to the Alcalá gate, I stopped it on my own authority, and made them fire two cannon-balls which dismantled the lock of the grille, and opened up for us one of the gates of the town.

Clermont and I then quickly made for the fountain in Alcalá Street [presumably Cibeles] and, since there was there a battery of General Villatte's* division, newly arrived, I allowed myself to make it fire on the Puerta del Sol, where the Spaniards also had cannon and infantry.

On passing the houses in Alcalá Street, I managed, along with Major Daumesnil**, who was accompanied by a trumpeter of the light cavalry from his own regiment, to reach the trenches in the Puerta del Sol and pass myself off as a parliamentary. Then the Spanish general Morla† emerged from his redoubt, came towards me in an abashed manner, and said to me, before I had uttered the least word, that the people were furious, that they would in no way even hear of capitulation, and that perhaps, when he went back to the redoubt from which he had come in order to talk to me, he would be cut to pieces just as General Perales‡ had been. He beseeched me to tell the Emperor that the people were complete masters of the town and that civil and military authorities were no longer recognized.

Major Daumesnil and I returned by the same route which we had travelled on our way to this redoubt. Once returned to the fountain whence I had set out, I went immediately to the Emperor's tent to inform him of what I had just learnt. His Majesty was at this moment in an appalling temper with his aide-de-camp, general Lauriston§, who had spent an immense amount of time in bombarding the barracks of the bodyguards with a demi-battery of field cannon, without succeeding in making a break in the building; he treated him, in front of me,

---

* Eugène-Casimir Villatte (1770–1834), French divisional commander, later Comte d'Outremont.
** Pierre Daumesnil (1777–1832), French commander in the Puerta del Sol.
† Tomás de Morla, (1752–1820), Spanish patriotic commander.
‡ The Marqués de Perales was dragged from his house and murdered by the Madrid mob on the false accusation that he was hiding gunpowder. One of *The Disasters of War* (No. 29) by Goya shows the scene.
§ General Jacques Lauriston (1768–1828), grandson of the financier Law, died, a marshal of France and marquis, in the arms of a *danseuse* in the Opéra.

without care and without consideration. Then, turning towards me, he listened attentively to what I told him, then lost
his temper with General Morla, saying:

'Just look at this General Morla, he helped to put arms in the
hands of the people, yet now he has not the courage to take
them away; go and tell him from me, that if within two hours
he does not bring me the keys of the city, I shall set fire to all
four corners of it and put to the sword everybody found within
it at the moment we enter so in force.'

I returned, at the gallop, to execute the Emperor's orders, but
I learnt, when I arrived again at the redoubt at the *Puerta del
Sol*, that generals Morla and Don Bernardo Yriarte* had left
for Napoleon's quarters to give their surrender.

On the 4th, at 10 a.m., General Billiard† entered Madrid at
the head of a column of French army. He crossed the whole
length of this city to the sound of drums and music, and took
possession of all the positions and gates of the Spanish capital.

'Mémoires du general Bigarré', 232–233.

[34] Henry Inglis (1830)

As I have mentioned the Calle de Alcalá, let me speak of this
street as it deserves to be spoken of. I know of no finer entry
to any city; I might perhaps say, no one so fine, as that to
Madrid by the Calle de Alcalá. Standing at the foot of this
street, you have on the right and left the long, wide Prado,
with its quadruple row of trees stretching in fine perspective
to the gates that terminate it; behind is the magnificent gate
of Alcalá, a fine model of architectural beauty; and before
lies the Calle de Alcalá, reaching into the heart of the city, –
long, of superb width, and flanked by a splendid range of
unequal buildings, – among others the hotels of many of the
ambassadors; the two fine convents of Las Calatravas‡ and

---

* Bernardo de Yriarte (1734–1814), later adviser to Joseph Bonaparte,
died in exile in Bordeaux.
† General Augustin Billiard (1769–1832), later in the retreat from Moscow; there was '*aucun champ de bataille où il n'ail pas versé son sang*'.
‡ The domed church, built in the seventeenth century and refurbished in
the nineteenth, remains: the *convento* was demolished in 1868.

Las Ballecas* and the Customhouse.** But the Calle de Alcalá
is the only really fine street in Madrid; many of the other streets
are good, and very many respectable, of tolerable width, and
the houses lofty and well built; but there is no magnificent
street, excepting the Calle de Alcalá . . .

I happened to be walking one day in the Calle de Alcalá, when
the royal carriage drove up to the door of the Cabinet of Natural
History† and, being close by, I stopped to see the king and queen.
The king [Ferdinand VII] stepped from the carriage first; he then
lifted from the carriage, a very large poodle dog, and then the
queen followed, whom, contrary no doubt to royal etiquette, his
majesty did not hand, but lifted, and placed on the pavement;
and then turning to the crowd who surrounded the carriage, he
said to them, '*Pesa menos el matrimonio*,' which means, Ma-
trimony is a lighter burden than the dog, – a very tolerable jeu
d'esprit to have come from Ferdinand VII.   *Inglis, 82, 117.*

[35] George Borrow (1836)
(Borrow was in Spain during the revolution of La Granja
(1836), when General Vicente Quesada (1782–1836) staged
an unsuccessful *coup d'etat* in Madrid: see No. 57.)

There is a celebrated coffee-house in the Calle del Alcalá, at
Madrid, capable of holding several hundred individuals‡. On
the evening of the day in question, I was seated there, sipping a
cup of the brown beverage, when I heard a prodigious noise
and clamour in the street; it proceeded from the nationals§ who
were returning from their expedition. In a few minutes I saw a
body of them enter the coffee-house, marching arm in arm, two
by two, stamping on the ground with their feet in a kind of
measure, and repeating in loud chorus, as they walked round
the spacious apartment, the following grisly stanza:–

* Las Ballecas was destroyed in the early nineteenth century.
** The Customhouse, now the Treasury, was built by Francisco Sabatini
in 1769.
† Now the Academia de Bellas Artes, established in 1773 in the Palacio
de Goyeneche, built for a banker of that name by Churriguera.
‡ Probably the Café Fornos; perhaps the Café Suizo.
§ i.e. the anti-liberal side.

'¿Qué es lo que abaja
Por aquel cerro?
Ta ra ra ra ra.
Son los huesos de Quesada,
Que los trae un perro –
*Ta ra ra ra ra.'**

A huge bowl of coffee was then called for, which was placed upon a table, around which gathered the national soldiers. There was silence for a moment, which was interrupted by a voice roaring out, 'El pañuelo!' A blue kerchief was forthwith produced, which appeared to contain a substance of some kind; it was untied, and a gory hand and three or four dissevered fingers made their appearance, and with these the contents of the bowl were stirred up. 'Cups! cups!' cried the nationals . . .

'Ho, ho, *Don Jorge,*' cried Baltasarito†, coming up to me with a cup of coffee, 'pray do me the favour to drink upon this glorious occasion. This is a pleasant day for Spain, and for the gallant nationals of Madrid. I have seen many a bull *función*, but none which has given me so much pleasure as this. Yesterday the brute had it all his own way, but to-day the *toreros* have prevailed, as you see, *Don Jorge*. Pray drink; for I must now run home to fetch my *pajandi* to play my brethren a tune, and sing a *copla*. What shall it be? Something in *Gitano*? *'Una noche sinava en tucue'*.‡ You shake your head, *Don Jorge*. Ha, ha; I am young, and youth is the time for pleasure. Well, well, out of compliment to you, who are an Englishman and a *monró*, it shall not be that, but something liberal, something patriotic, the Hymn of Riego§. *Hasta después, Don Jorge!*'

Borrow, 205–207.

---

* Of these lines the following translation, in the style of the old English ballad, will, perhaps, not be unacceptable:-
    'What down the hill comes hurrying there? –
    With a hey, with a ho, a sword and a gun!
    Quesada's bones, which a hound doth bear.
    Hurrah, brave brothers! – the work is done.'
(note by Borrow).
† For this individual see No. 57.
‡ 'One night I was with thee.'
§ *Ei Himno de Riego*, the Spanish *Marseillaise*, was composed by Huerta in 1820, the words being written by Evariste San Miguel.

[36] 1898: the news of the catastrophe
(In this year the Spanish American War ended in disaster for Spain, leading to a defeat in Cuba and the Philippines and to a national self-analysis.)

A newspaper installed in Alcalá street in Madrid put up an exciting poster giving outstanding details of the hecatomb, stirring up the people and with the first lighting-up at night different groups of demonstrators appeared, all furious with the government . . . From time to time there were cries of angry '*mueras*'* and, inside the cafés, the clients were shouting, giving unmistakable signs of outrage. The picture took a bad turn. The often-foreshadowed torment of impetuosity was about to be unleashed. But after the momentary furore the cloud, from which we feared the fall of a thunderbolt, resolved itself in an unsubstantial tumult. There were people running about, agitated, a few blows exchanged in defence of order, demands for calm and tranquillity, and silence where anger burst out in a formidable and fearful manner; the atmosphere previously confused became serene; the multitude little by little was disappearing, and, on the stroke of twelve, everyone went home without the tragedy producing tremendous and fearful shocks. But the anguish was general, we felt near to the appalling conclusion of the war. The national disillusion was rendered more acute, for who did not consider that the position reflected on all those who had brought us the weaknesses, misapprehensions, and errors of an ever-temporizing political system? The gravest thing then began. Greater sadnesses lay in wait, more penetrating afflictions, even if the multitudes showed themselves indifferent . . .

'El año de la derrota', por J. Francos Rodríguez, 143.

* i.e. 'Death to' . . .

Arenal

[37] Pío Baroja (1906)
(See No. 32, footnote ‡ for origins of Arenal. Pío Baroja,
(1872–1966) was Spain's outstanding novelist after the death
of Pérez Galdós. This picture of Anarchist activity comes
from *Aurora Roja*, one of the best known of his novels.)

At this moment a battalion crossed the Puerta del Sol among
the people. The drums sounded excitingly, the bayonets and
sabres shone. On arrival facing the Calle del Arenal the band
began to strike up a *paso doble*.

Then they stopped.

'Here are the tommies (*mili*) as usual out to annoy us all,'
said Señor Canuto.

On passing the flag the soldiers formed a square. The
lieutenant ordered 'Attention' and he saluted with his sabre.

'The glorious rag,' said Señor Canuto out loud, 'symbol of
despotism and tyranny.'

A lieutenant heard the observation and stared at the old man
threateningly.

Canuto and the *madrileño* tried to cross through the middle of the soldiers.

'You can't pass,' said a sergeant.

'These bastards, because they have uniforms think they are superior to us,' said the *madrileño*.

A flag passed by and by chance stopped in front of us. The lieutenant approached Señor Canuto.

'Take off your hat,' he said.

'I?'

'Yes.'

'I don't want to.'

'Take off your hat.'

'I said I didn't want to.'

The lieutenant raised his sabre. 'Eh, guards,' he shouted, 'take him!'

A small man, a secret policeman, threw himself on Señor Canuto.

'Death to the Army! Long live the social revolution. Long live Anarchy!' cried the old man, trembling with emotion and raising his arm in the air.

Baroja, 'Aurora Roja', 344–45 (1906).

Caballero de Gracia

[38] The murder of Ascham (Clarendon, 1650)
(This old street, so called since there was once a well-known benefactor of that name, housed most of the few hotels which existed in Madrid during the seventeenth and eighteenth centuries. Clarendon, then Edward Hyde (1609–1674), was in Madrid as an ambassador of the English Royalist cause.)

The Parliament, in the infancy of their Commonwealth, had more inclination to make a friendship with Spain than with France, having at that time a very great prejudice to the cardinal; and therefore upon this encouragement from don Alonso they resolved to send an envoy to Madrid, and made choice of one Ascham, a scholar who had written a book* to determine in what time, and after how many years, the allegiance which is due from subjects to their sovereign comes to be determined after a conquest; and that from that term it ought

* Anthony Ascham's book was *Discourse of what is lawful during confusions and revolutions of government* (1648).

to be paid to those who had subdued them, or to the conqueror: a speculation they thought fit to cherish.

This man, unacquainted with business, and unskilled in language, attended by three others, the one a renegade Franciscan friar, who had been bred in Spain and was well versed in the language, another who was to serve in the condition of a secretary, and the third an inferior fellow for any service, arrived all at Seville or Cádiz in an English merchant's ship: of which don Alonso gave such timely notice, that he was received and entertained there by the chief magistrate, until they gave notice of it to the Court. The town was quickly full of the rumour that an ambassador was landed from England, and would be received there; which nobody seemed to be well pleased with. And the ambassadors [i.e. of the King, namely Lord Cottington and Mr Edward Hyde] expostulated with don Luis de Haro* with warmth, that his Catholic majesty should be the first Christian prince that would receive an ambassador from the odious and infamous murderers of a Christian king, his brother and ally; which no other prince had yet done, out of the detestation of that horrible parricide; and therefore they desired him that Spain would not give so horrid an example to the other parts of the world . . .

That the man might come securely to Madrid, an old officer of the army was sent from Sevilla to accompany this new agent to Madrid; who came with him in the coach, and gave notice every night to don Luis of their advance. There were at that time, over and above the English merchants, many officers and soldiers in Madrid who had served in the Spanish armies both in Catalonia and in Portugal; and these men had consulted amongst themselves how they might kill this fellow, who came as an ambassador or agent from the new republic of England; and half a dozen of them, having notice of the day he was to come into the town, which was generally discoursed of, rode out of the town to meet him; but missing him, they returned again to the town, and found that he had entered into it by another way; and having taken a view of his lodging, they met again the next morning, and finding accidentally one of the ambassadors' servants in the streets, they persuaded him to go

---

* Luis Méndez de Haro (1598–1661) was the nephew and in effect the successor of the Conde-Duque de Olivares as royal prime minister.

with them, and so went to the house where Ascham lodged*;
and without asking any questions walked directly up the stairs
into his chamber, leaving a couple of their number at the door
of the street, lest upon any noise in the house that door might
be shut upon them. They who went up drew their swords, and,
besides their intentions, in disorder, killed the friar as well as
the agent; and so returned to their companions with their
swords naked and bloody, and some foolish expressions of
triumph, as if they had performed a very gallant and justifiable
service. Notwithstanding all which, they might have dispersed
themselves, and been secure, the people were so little concerned
to inquire what they had done. But they being in confusion,
and retaining no composed thoughts about them, finding the
door of a little chapel open, went in thither for sanctuary; only
he who served the ambassadors separated himself from the
rest, and went into the house of the Venetian ambassador. By
this time the people of the house where the man lay had gone
up into the chamber; where they found two dead, and the other
two crept, in a terrible fright, under the bed; and talking with
and examining the persons who were there; and the rumour
was presently divulged about the town that one of the English
ambassadors was killed . . .

. . . [The two royal ambassadors] were both in extraordinary trouble and perplexity, dismissed their coach, and returned
to their lodging. Though they abhorred the action that was
committed, they foresaw the presence of one of their own
servants in it, and even some passionate words they had used in
their expostulation with don Luis against the reception of such
a messenger, as if the King their master had too many subjects
in that place for such a fellow to appear there with any security,
would make it be believed by many that the attempt had not
been made without their consent or privity. In this trouble of
mind they immediately writ a letter to don Luis de Haro, to
express the sense they had of this unfortunate rash action, of
which they hoped he did believe, if they had had any notice or
suspicion, they would have prevented it by the exposing their
own persons. Don Luis returned them a very dry answer; that

* The oratory of the Caballero de la Gracia was built (1654) on the site of
this house.

he could not imagine that they could have a hand in so foul an assassination in the Court (for all Madrid is called and looked upon as the Court,) of a person under the immediate protection of the King, that his majesty was resolved to have it examined to the bottom, and that exemplary justice should be done upon the offenders; that his own ambassador in England might be in great danger upon this murder, and that they would send an express presently thither, to satisfy the Parliament how much his Catholic majesty detested and was offended with it, and resolved to do justice upon it; and if his ambassador underwent any inconvenience there, they were not to wonder if his majesty was severe here; and so left it to them to imagine that their own persons might not be safe.

But they knew the temper of the Court too well to have the least apprehension of that: yet they were a little surprised when they first saw the multitude of people gathered together about their house, upon the first news of the action, insomuch as the street before their house, which was the broadest in Madrid, (the Calle de Alcalá), was so thronged that men could hardly pass. But they were quickly out of that apprehension, being assured that the jealousy that one of the English ambassadors had suffered violence had brought that multitude together; which they found to be true; for they no sooner shewed themselves in a balcony to the people, but they saluted them with great kindness, prayed for the King their master, cursed and reviled the murderers of his father, and so departed. They who had betaken themselves to the chapel were the next day, or the second, taken from thence by a principal officer after examination, and sent to the prison; the other was not inquired after, but, having concealed himself for ten or twelve days, he went out of the town in the night, and without any interruption or trouble went into France . . .

Clarendon, VIII, 136–43 (1650).

Calle de Fuencarral

[39] Foundation of Anarcho-Sindicalism: Anselmo
Lorenzo (1868)
(Anselmo Lorenzo (1842–1914) was an early Spanish
follower of Anarchist ideas.)

We came together then, in the house of Rubau Donadeu, with
Fanelli.*

 This man was about forty years old, tall with a face at the
same time serious and amiable, a black bushy beard, with black
expressive eyes which alternatively shone like sparks or assumed a look of affectionate compassion according to his
mood. His voice had a metallic quality and was capable of
every appropriate inflection, passing rapidly from tones of
anger and threats against the exploiters and tyrants to those
of suffering, pity and good advice when speaking of the
exploited; which things he understood without having suffered

---

* Giuseppe Fanelli (1827–1877) was a follower of Bakunin and at this
time a deputy in the Italian parliament.

them directly or in consequence of which by an altruistic sentiment he took pleasure in presenting as justifying an ultra-revolutionary ideal of peace and fraternity.

The curious thing is that he did not speak Spanish and his speaking French, which only some of those present half understood, or Italian, which we only understood a little by reason of its similarity to Spanish more or less, not only caused us to identify ourselves with his feelings but thanks to his expressive mimicry we all felt ourselves possessed of the same enthusiasm. One had to see and hear him describe the state of the worker deprived of the means of subsistence for lack of work as a result of excess production; after expressing in rich detail the desperation of misery, with an enthusiasm which reminded me of the tragic Rosi whom I had the pleasure of admiring a little time before, he said: '¡Cosa horrible! iterrible!' and we felt shudders and shocks of horror. He compared the so-tragic situation with that of the parasites of society who monopolize the riches and production to give themselves over to softness and idleness and, if they fly from this vice to show themselves intelligent and active, abuse the riches, carry to extremes the exploitation and usury and only think of accumulating wealth. This description shocked us to the highest degree. He showed us, in the end, the effects of the workers' international union conducted by resistance and study becoming a force capable of neutralizing capitalist pride and the foundation of a true economic science, which would correct the absurdities which prejudice, routine and ignorance have considered as social fundamentals, giving them legal sanction. We required them to be replaced by rational and worthy institutions which would protect the natural right of all individuals without anyone being humiliated or having to found their well-being on the misfortune of others or the ruin of their equals, and then a sweet hope animated us, elevating us to the sublime heights of the ideal . . . Fanelli gave us three or four sessions of propaganda, alternating with private conversations in *paseos* or in cafés in which I had the satisfaction, which I considered as an honour which caused me great happiness, of seeing myself specially favoured by his confidences . . . *Anselmo Lorenzo, 19–20.*

Calle Marqués de Cubas

[40] The murder of Prim (1870)
(This street was known as the Calle del Turco in 1870. Juan Prim (1814–70), one of the most remarkable of Spanish statesmen, was murdered when at the height of his powers by men whose identity was never discovered.)

. . . The Prime Minister [General Prim] left the Cortes last night at seven-thirty in a carriage which was directed towards the Ministry of War accompanied by his aides-de-camp Señores Nandín and Moya.

At the end of the Calle del Turco they met two coaches standing still at the point where it debouches into the Calle Alcalá.

The General's carriage had to stop before this obstruction, which appeared accidental and, in order to see what the delay consisted of, Señor Moya, who was travelling with his back to the coachman, went to the little door while General Prim and Señor Nandin remained in the front.

Señor Moya saw three men dressed in overalls pointing

carbines or shot-guns and he had not time to do more than say, 'Down, General, they are firing at us.'

Immediately three shots rang out from the left and some others from the right almost inside the coach, in such a way that General Prim had the grains of gunpowder marking his face.

The coachman, seeing what was happening, began to insult and give a verbal lashing to the assassins, whipped the horses and these started off brusquely, upsetting the two carriages. The distance from the Calle del Turco to the Ministry of War* is extremely short . . . Once they reached there they got out . . . and immediately went upstairs to the main reception rooms, and it was seen that the Prime Minister had a wound of considerable importance by virtue of which the first knuckle of the ring finger of the right hand had to be amputated, and a horrible wound in the left shoulder. General Prim went very steadily up the staircase of the Ministry, leaning on the banisters with the right hand wounded, and leaving on it various stains of blood†.

'El Imparcial', Madrid, 28 de diciembre de 1870

---

* The Palacio de Buenavista; see Nos 98–100.
† Prim died soon afterwards, on a couch in the Ministry which is still shown to the visitor.

Calle Mayor

[41] The murder of Escobedo in 1576 (Gregorio
Marañón)
(This murder took place in a side street, at the west end of
the Calle Mayor, approximately where there is now the
Calle Factor, against the walls of the church of Santa María
de la Almudena (now disappeared).

Juan de Escobedo, secretary to Don John of Austria, half-
brother of King Philip II, was killed with the king's connivance
since he feared an attempt by Don John to establish himself as
an independent monarch in Flanders. This account is taken
from Gregorio Marañón (1887–1960), Spain's best biographer
of the 1930s and 1940s, though always a doctor too.)

The day of the banquet there gathered to dine in the *Casilla* [in
the Calle Santa Isabel: on the site of what is now, and has been
since the sixteenth century, the *convento* of Santa Isabel]
Melchor de Herrera, the Conde de Chinchón, Nava de Puebla,
Escobedo and Pérez. The last, doing business with the Sover-

eign, made him believe that someone threatened him that night; and Don Felipe [i.e. the King] affectionately advised him that a friend should accompany him as far as La Casilla*. But the person who was threatened was not Antonio [Pérez].

The dining-room of La Casilla gave on to the countryside, and before it there was an empty room or anteroom and then a room with the serving side-tables. Every time that Escobedo asked for a drink, Enríquez† carried his glass and delayed to speak to Martínez‡ in the anteroom and poured into the wine a thimbleful of the poisoned water which the major-domo had hidden in a flask. He twice repeated the dose, as had been agreed. At the end of the banquet, Escobedo returned to his house as quiet as a farmyard chicken, and the others went to the gambling-room. Pérez with an excuse that he had to pass water – and perhaps that excuse was real, since he could not control his nerves – left the gambling-room and examined the quantity of poison used, which was sufficient to kill anyone other than the robust *montañés* [native of Santander].

Four days later, a Friday, he returned to the charge. It must have been the middle of February. Pérez again invited Escobedo to his house, this time to the one which he had in the Plaza del Cordón, with the same Nava de Puebla and others, and with Doña Juana de Coello. To each guest he gave a bowl of cream or of milk, and in that of Escobedo there was added 'some dust like wheat' which was certainly a kind of poison or arsenic. Antonio was very restless fearing that a mistake might be made and that the poisoned bowl might be given to one of his sons. In addition to the dust, Martínez poured into the glass of the unfortunate guest, once or twice, some of the same poisoned water. This time Escobedo felt ill. He had great pains and was sick, did not want to go on eating, and went back to his house where he had to keep to his bed several days, though neither he himself nor his doctors guessed the reason.

As he appeared to have also overcome the new attack on him, it was decided to double the dose of poison and, in order

* The friend was Jacobo Grimaldo.

† Antonio Enríquez, Catalan page to Pérez, aged twenty, later betrayed his master for money; see No. 137.

‡ Diego Martínez, an Aragonese, distant relation of Pérez, whose major-domo and secretary he became. Also later betrayed Pérez.

to do that, Martínez was put in touch with the cook of Escobedo, *el pícaro**, whose real name was Juan Rubio, a man very suitable for the task because of his intelligence and lack of scruples . . . They were making for the poisoned man a special soup for his illness; and Rubio managed to put in it more than once a thimbleful of poison powders which Martínez made available to him. Escobedo worsened, and this time realized an attempt was being made on him. A Moorish slave-girl was suspected. She was hanged a few days later in the public square. The unfortunate girl when she climbed the ominous stairway, cried: 'Hang me, but there are people alive who will avenge me.' Perhaps she was referring to her Moorish companions who then were plotting new rebellions . . .

Bustamante testified [later] in the prison of Saragossa that he once heard Pérez say that when telling His Majesty the modest effect of the poisons, 'the King had replied to him that he had heard it said that one had to give poison little by little, as if fattening someone up, since one could not give everything in one dose without the victim becoming aware of it' . . .

With the greatest naturalness in the world [Pérez] went to visit Escobedo in his house and asked after his health. He told the King of this visit and told him, with unconcealed joy, that he would not see the next day. But Escobedo did not provide him with any luck . . .

Antonio, with uncontrolled nervousness, called upon his old major-domo and confidant, Juan de Mesa, who lived retired in Bubierca, in Aragon. Juan . . . was already in Madrid, accompanied by another specialist called Insausti whose powers of decision and skill were not slow to be demonstrated. He, despite his name, was a Catalan, a nephew of one of those concerned in the works of El Escorial, and a man as daring as he was lacking in understanding. There joined together six 'brave men' – and during the following days they had various meetings . . . They discounted the crossbow and decided on the sword, in whose use Insausti was a master, and who was

---

* Rubio was an Aragonese, a page of Pérez, then a captain in the Spanish army in Naples. Everyone called him *el pícaro*, the scoundrel, one of the first occasions that that word, which later characterized a whole genre of 'picaresque' novels, was used, according to Dr Marañón. Rubio escaped after this to Naples, where he later died in prison (1589).

charged with the actual execution of the deed. Juan de Mesa brought a big weapon of this sort, with a corrugated blade, light, of Castillian style, . . . eating and drinking, without doubt at Antonio Pérez's cost, on the grassless soil of the suburbs of Madrid, they discussed the method of liquidating Escobedo with the same calm as if they had been playing cards . . .

That night, the last of his life, Escobedo spent a long time, until it was dark, in the palace of the Princess of Eboli*: for there he was seen. . . on his way to Doña Brianda [de Guzmán, presumed mistress of Escobedo], where he stayed a short time only, since towards nine he returned from there. That was the most populous quarter of Madrid, since it was close to the Palacio Real and since there was there an abundance of houses of grandees, *conventos* and parish churches, among them the aristocratic one of Santa María [now destroyed]. The Easter season and the wild night helped to make the streets animated and made difficult the task of the assassins shadowing their prey.

He was on horseback, thoughtful, accompanied by one of his household and preceded by torches. While crossing the alley called the Camarín de Nuestra Señora de la Almudena, which led from the Calle Mayor to the houses of La Eboli and of Escobedo, being close already to them, just beneath the walls of the church of Santa María, taking advantage no doubt of a moment when their prey was alone, the assassins attacked the group, and in the confusion Insausti like lightning pierced Escobedo with his sword clean through his body, knocking him off his mount.   *Marañón, Vol. I, 302–311.*

[42] An attempt on King Alfonso XIII (1906)
(The Anarchists attempted to kill King Alfonso XIII (1886–1941) and Queen Victoria Eugenia (1887–1969) on the occasion of their wedding.)

The royal procession was just about to turn from the Calle

---

* Ana González de Mendoza (1546–1592), widow of Antonio Pérez's predecessor as chief confidant of the King Philip II, Ruy Gómez, Príncipe de Eboli; possibly once a mistress to the King; intimate friend of Pérez, whose plans and disgrace she shared. The famous patch over her eye was probably to conceal a squint.

Mayor towards the Palacio Real when, in the middle of the acclamations, a dry detonation carried death to the pavement covered with flowers. There were some moments of horrible anguish. Don Alfonso, who was travelling with Victoria in the Carriage of the Crown, protected the Queen by making a shield of his body and with chilling serenity, when even the smoke of the explosion had not yet vanished, appeared at the windows crying, 'It is nothing! It is nothing!'

The delightful and triumphal marriage procession had, however, broken up in a terrifying noise, amid horses gone wild, shrieks of grief and the dismay of the people who uttered terrified screams. The King, recalling the scene, says that he noticed a strong acrid smell and during two minutes at least he was blinded by the thick smoke. 'When this cleared,' he went on, 'I saw that the lilies and roses on the wedding dress of the Queen were stained with blood. I came out of it unhurt, but several of our guards had been thrown from their mounts, blown to pieces. Men and horses bled profusely. The street was a terrible sight. Twenty-eight people were dead, forty wounded. Everyone was shouting frantically, "They have killed the King and Queen." Only thanks to the superhuman discipline of my regiment of Was-Ras who covered the road and did not break lines, an avalanche of panic was avoided. I took the Queen's arm and went on foot in search of the spare coach. Had it not been for my wish that the Queen should return the greetings of the staff of the official buildings [i.e. of the Municipality, on the left] we would not be alive; the bomb exploded on the right of the coach.'

On arrival with her sister Paz* at the Palace, the Infanta Eulalia† anxiously asked the King: 'What happened? What's been going on?'

'Bah,' replied Alfonso smiling, 'the well-known hazards of office. An anarchist – nothing. We shall soon see who has been wounded,' he said afterwards turning to one of his aides 'and ensure that they look after everyone.'

'Nothing was yet known,' the Infanta recalled, 'and the confusion was increased as more and more wedding guests arrived at the Palace. María Cristina, silent, serious, tried to

---

* The Infanta Paz; see No. 127, footnote 3.
† The Infanta Eulalia; see No. 127.

contain her emotion and sought in vain to counterpoise her spirit of queen to that of mother*. In the middle of the tumult, in the middle of the sea of bewildered courtiers, the King, only twenty years old, yet serene and smiling with his pulse still a little fast, lit a cigarette while he sought out, from among the sea of uniforms, General Lóriga†, his chief aide and tutor.

'How are you, Lóriga?' he asked. 'Are you wounded?'

'It is nothing! They killed my horse and gave me an unimportant knock,' replied the veteran of the Philippines. 'Your Majesty conducted himself like a hardened warrior.'

The blonde beauty of Victoria Eugenia thus dawned in the light of Spain on a vast pool of blood.

Cortés Cavanillas, 116.

---

* Maria Cristina (1858–1929), widow of King Alfonso XII, Regent of Spain 1885–1902.
† General Juan Lóriga (1853–1929), Conde del Grove.

Paseo del Prado

(The 'promenade of the meadow' in the shallow valley at the end of the main eastward-facing streets of old Madrid (Alcalá, Carrera de San Jerónimo and Atocha) was a fashionable place to walk or ride from the sixteenth century until the (lamentable) invention of the motor car.)

[43] View in 1543 (Pedro de Medina)

Towards the east of Madrid, in coming out of the houses, on a small hill there is a sumptuous monastery of Jeronomite brothers with apartments and rooms for the reception of, and hospitality to, kings and queens, with a large and beautiful orchard. Between the houses and this monastery there is, to the left on leaving the town (*pueblo*), a big and lovely walk (*alameda*) with poplars ranged in three lines making two very broad and long streets, with four beautiful fountains with delicious water at set distances, while there are many rose trees made to intertwine with the trunks of the poplars all along the way. Here there is a large tank of water which greatly assists the great beauty of, and recreation in, the *alameda*.

On the other, right hand of the same monastery, coming out of the houses there is another very peaceful *alameda* with two rows of trees which makes one very broad street as far as the road which is called Atocha. This *alameda* has its irrigation ditches and goes as far as some orchards. They call these *alamedas* the Prado of San Jerónimo, which in the winter gives sun and in the summer coolness, and it is a great thing and a great recreation to see the people who go there, some most splendid women, very well turned-out gentlemen, and many of the most important people in coaches and carriages. Here one can taste with great enjoyment the freshness of the wind every evening and every night of summer, and hear much good music, without damage, risks or robberies, as a result of the good care and attention of the court mayors.

> *Pedro de Medina, 'Grandezas y cosas memorables*
> *de España,' 1560 (describing events as they appeared*
> *in 1543), quoted Mesonero Romanos, 222.*

[44] Philip II received in the Prado (1569)

Coming to 26 November 1569, Sunday, the clarity and clemency of the sky continuing so that His Majesty's arrival could be the more easily solemnized and so that the great quantity of people, who had come from all over Spain to see it, could extend themselves over the fields, it was a thing to wonder at the great concourse and density of the crowd which, more than a league before His Majesty arrived at Madrid, had spread out on both sides of the road. There were more than 4,000 infantrymen, very smart-looking soldiery of singular uniforms, with over 1,500 arquebusiers. There were fifteen flags which beautified the entire countryside and which were most pleasurable to see. Don Francisco de Vargas Manrique . . . was captain-general . . . and organized and laid out his men with such meticulousness that it gave the impression of being a real battle. They went round the town more than a month before the King was due to enter, with fifes and drums collecting people together. On the days of fiesta a great parade and show was made in each company, and their captains made valiant gestures with free meals and private shops for their men.

A little before His Majesty arrived in sight of the town, the Conde de Feria, captain of the guard of His Majesty, organized all his people, both on foot and mounted, and from their houses with great music and fanfare set out to receive His Majesty . . . when the King drew near, entering by the Prado he was greeted by a beautiful figure representing Pales, goddess of the fields, [who] offered His Majesty a garland of flowers and begged him to receive and look with tolerance at a spectacle of such pleasure, and His Majesty then and there enthusiastically looked at the garland on which had been placed a notice reading:

> Receive this thing of flowers
> Since, because it has no equal,
> You will thus possess the world.

His Majesty also had much pleasure in seeing the gracious playing of the jets of water coming from the fountains . . . and also, at the end of the Prado, a large tank of water, about 500 feet long and 80 broad, of a good depth which had been put up with the greatest speed and diligence in the space of only ten days.

On one side of the Prado, on the left near the rise on which the monastery of San Jerónimo had been built, a very well-built castle had been put up with four towers at the corners. In the middle a tower had been raised which was called 'of homage', full of artillery. The base of this castle was on the edge of the tank, this making the water seem to beat against the wall. It seemed a very strong fortress, looking rather like Algiers with its artillery and site. Eight galleys had been fitted out, each with rowers and twenty fighting soldiers, gallantly dressed, four guns in each, with a great quantity of projectiles. The galleys had on their mastheads and sterns flags of crimson taffeta and on the bow the royal arms, as well as trumpeters and musicians, so that the whole appeared to be really well armed and on the point of going to war. Next to the tank of water there had been built a scaffold in the style of a throne of very great majesty, with fourteen steps going up on both sides so that by one way one could go up and kiss hands with His Majesty and by the other way go down. All the steps, and the summit as well, were covered by rich brocade . . . There was also a very

sumptuous canopy under which a seat of honour had been put
in which His Majesty sat in order to enjoy the dances and
inventions and follies which were represented there . . . His
Majesty got down from his coach with Prince Albert of
Austria* and, going up to the platform and being seated on
the throne, the official salutation was made and the Moors
fired from the castle with great energy, which in effect seemed
to be a naval battle such as the Roman emperors in their fiestas,
celebrations and triumphs used to represent. Although it would
not be too daring to say that he was more shaken by the
artillery and dust . . . the galleys by water and the infantry by
land made a most lively attack so that in a very little time they
placed their flags on the towers of the castle, even though it
defended itself with its artillery and though the number of
Turks and Moors inside was great . . . This was a most superb
battle which all the foreigners present said that they had never
seen the like of, and no one certainly had ever seen a better
organized body of troops.   *Mesonero Romanos, 355ff.*

[45] The Prince of Wales woos the Infanta María (1623): Endymion Porter gives an account to his wife

(Endymion Porter (1587–1649) was a gentleman-in-waiting
on Charles, Prince of Wales. His grandmother was 'a
relation of the Conde de Feria', Philip II's ambassador to
London, who had many illegitimate children.)

MY SWEETEST LOVE, . . . The Prince and my lord are well and
have been the braveliest received that ever men were. Yesterday
the King and Queen† came publicly abroad, and the Infanta‡
with them in the coach, where my master and my lord with the
Ambassador and myself in another coach (with the curtains
drawn in the street) stayed to see them go by, and the Prince

* Albert of Habsurg (1559–1621), subsequently Cardinal Archbishop of
Toledo.
† i.e. King Philip IV (1605–1665), King 1621–65, and Isabella of
Bourbon (1603–44).
‡ The Infanta María, later Queen of Hungary and wife of the Holy
Roman Emperor, Ferdinand III.

hath taken such a liking to his mistress that now he loves her as much for her beauty as he can for being sister to so great a king. She deserves it, for there was never seen a fairer creature. Although the Prince was private and the curtains of his coach drawn, yet the searching vulgar took notice of it, and did so press about the coach to see him, that we could not pass through the streets, insomuch that the King's guard was forced to beat them from it and make way through the multitude. They all cried 'God bless him,' and showed as much affection generally as ever was seen among people, only they took it ill he showed not himself to them in a more public manner. Last night the King of Spain had a great desire to see the Prince, and in a coach only with the Conde Olivares*, my lord Marquess† and myself, he came privately at eleven of the clock at night, and met the Prince in the fields without the town, who came with the two ambassadors only, and there they discoursed in the coach above an hour, and the King used him with so much love and respect, giving him the better hand still, that he is as well affected to his Majesty's nobleness and courtesy as to his sister's beauty.

Thy true loving husband,
ENDYMION PORTER

MADRID, *this* 10th day of March, 1623.

Dorothea Townsend, 48–49

[46] Quevedo's view (c. 1630)
(Francisco Quevedo (1580–1645) was one of the most brilliant Spanish satirists.)

So I went down to the Calle Mayor and stood in front of a saddler's, as if I were thinking of buying something. Up rode two gentlemen who asked me if I was thinking of buying the saddle I was holding, which was chased with silver. I put it down and engaged them for some time in flattering conversation. In the end they said they were thinking of having a little

* The 'prime minister', the Conde Duque de Olivares (1587–1645).
† i.e. George Villiers, then Marquess (later Duke) of Buckingham (1592–1628).

bit of fun in the Prado gardens and I said I'd go with them, that
is, of course, if they didn't mind. I left a message with the
shopkeeper that if my pages and a lackey appeared, would he
please send them to the Prado? I described their uniforms; then
I rode off between the two gentlemen. It occurred to me as I
rode along that nobody who saw us could tell whose were the
pages or footmen with us, nor which of us didn't have any. I
began to talk in a very self-assured manner about the jousting
at Talavera and a white horse I'd had; I boasted a lot about the
war-horse I was expecting from Córdoba. Every time we
passed a page, a horse or a servant I made them stop, asked
them who their master was, went over the horse's points and
asked if it was for sale. I made the horse trot up and down the
street twice, and even if it was perfect pointed out some fault in
the bridle and told the man how to put it right; as it happened, I
had plenty of opportunities of doing this. Now the other two
were wondering and, as I thought, asking themselves:

'Who on earth is this country bumpkin who's sticking to us
like a leech?'

You see, one of them had a noble insignia on his chest and
the other a diamond chain – that's insignia and estate lumped
together, or as good as – so I said I was looking for a couple of
good horses for myself and a cousin of mine as we'd put our
names down for some events in a competition. We reached the
Prado and, as we were going in, I took my foot out of the
stirrup and let my horse walk slowly with my feet hanging
loose. I wore my cape over one shoulder and carried my hat in
my hand. Everybody stared at me. Some said:

'I've seen that one walking,' and others:

'Pretty bugger, isn't he?'

I pretended not to hear any of it, and swaggered on.

Quevedo, 'El Buscón', 183–86 (c. 1630)

[47] Wellington in the Prado (1812)
(John Aitchison was a young officer in Wellington's army
occupying Madrid. He later became a general.)

It is the fashion to walk every evening until dark in the Prado – a
long broad space with six rows of trees each side enclosing a walk –

the middle space is for carriages and has some handsome fountains at certain distances which supply water for the trees, and it is conducted to their roots every morning and evening by channels cut and kept in order for the purpose. This space on one side is supplied with a great number of cane chairs where any person may sit down when tired. Lord Wellington regularly attends the Prado and it is very flattering to see the attention with which he is treated. The museum and other public institutions are open and every person in uniform is admitted without fee.   *Aitchison, 187*

[48] Gautier (1840)

The Prado, made up of many alleys and cross-alleys, with a carriageway in the middle for coaches, is shaded by trees, pollarded and thick-set, whose roots stand in little basins surrounded by bricks which funnel the water during watering hours; without this procedure they would very soon be devoured by dust and roasted by the sun. The walk begins at the Atocha convent, passes in front of the gate of that name, the gate of Alcalá, and ends at the gate of Recoletos. But society gathers in a restricted space by the Fountain of Cybeles and that of Neptune, between the Alcalá gate and the Carrera de San Jerónimo*. There you find a large space called the *salón*, lined with seats like the *grande allée* of the Tuileries; at the side of the *salón* there is a cross-alley called Paris; it is the Boulevard de Gand of the place, the rendezvous of fashion in Madrid; and since the fashionable people's imagination is not particularly struck by the picturesqueness, they have chosen the most dusty, the least shaded, and the least convenient area of the entire promenade. The crowd in this narrow space is so large, confined between the *salón* and the carriageway, that it is often difficult to put your hand in your pocket to get out a handkerchief: you have to shuffle and follow the line as in a theatre queue (when theatres had queues). The only reason that this place could possibly have been adopted, is that from it you can

* The magnificent fountains of Cybeles and Neptune still play in the Prado. They were made by Francisco Gutiérrez and Roberto Michael, and by Ventura Rodríguez, during the creation of the 'Salón' de Prado 1775–1782.

see and greet those who pass by in their barouches (it is always honourable for a pedestrian to salute a carriage). The turn-outs are not very brilliant; most of them are drawn by mules whose blackish coats, large stomachs and pointed ears give the most ungraceful effect; they look like the mourning coaches that follow the hearse: even the Queen's own carriage is extremely simple and merely bourgeois. A fairly rich Englishman would assuredly despise it; obviously there are some exceptions, but they are few. What are undoubtedly charming are the beautiful Andalusian riding horses, on which the fops of Madrid parade. It is impossible to see anything more elegant, more noble or more gracious than an Andalusian stallion with its beautiful plaited mane, its long thick tail which reaches right to the ground, its harness ornamented with red pompoms, its roman nose, its shining eyes, and its neck puffed out like a pigeon's chest. I saw one mounted by a woman, that was as pink (the horse, not the woman) as a Bengal rose glossed with silver, and of a marvellous beauty. What a difference between these noble beasts which have kept their beautiful primitive shape and those locomotive machines of muscle and bone called English runners, and which have no more horse in them than four legs and a dorsal spine to put a jockey on!

A glimpse of the Prado is in fact one of the most animated sights that can be seen, and it is one of the most beautiful promenades in the world, not because of the site, which is most ordinary (in spite of all the efforts of Charles III to correct its defects) but because of the astonishing assembly which gathers there every evening, from 7.30 until 10.00.

You see very few women in hats in the Prado; with the exception of some sulphur-yellow biscuits, which must once have adorned some learned donkeys, there are only mantillas. So the Spanish mantilla is a reality; I had thought they only existed in the romances of Monsieur Crevel de Charlemagne*: it is of white or black lace, but more usually the latter, and is worn at the back of the head on the comb; a few flowers placed on the temple complete this coiffure which is the most charming you can imagine. With a mantilla, a woman must be as ugly as the three theological virtues if she does not appear pretty;

---

* Louis Ernest Crevel, known as Napoléon Crevel de Charlemagne (born 1807), musician, poet, and writer of operettas.

unfortunately it is the only part of the Spanish costume which has been preserved, the rest is *à la française* . . .

The old costume is so perfectly adapted to the character of beauty, to the proportions and habits of the Spaniards, that it is really the only possible one. The fan corrects a little pretention towards *parisianisme*. A woman without a fan is something I have not yet seen in this happy country; I saw some wearing satin shoes but no stockings; but they had fans; the fan follows them everywhere, even to church, where you meet women of all ages, kneeling or squatting on their heels, who pray and fan themselves with fervour, intermingling all the many Spanish signs of the cross, which are much more complicated than ours, and which they execute with a precision and rapidity worthy of Prussian soldiers. To wield a fan is an art completely unknown in France. The Spanish excel at it; the fan opens, shuts, returns to their fingers, so quickly, so lightly, that a conjurer could not do it better. Some elegant people make collections of great value; we saw one which included more than 100 different types: there were fans from all countries and from all periods: ivory, tortoise-shell, sandalwood, spangles, gouaches from the era of Louis XIV and of Louis XV, rice paper from Japan and from China, nothing was lacking: several were studded with rubies, with diamonds and other precious stones: it is a luxury in good taste and a charming mania for a pretty woman. Fans which shut and open out again produce a little whistling sound which, repeated more than a thousand times a minute, throws its notes across the confused noise that floats over the promenade, and contains something strange to the French ear. As soon as a woman meets someone she knows, she makes him a little signal with the fan, and directs at him, while passing, the word *agur* which is pronounced *abouz* [i.e. *adieu*]. *Gautier, 101–105*

[49] Pérez Galdós's view through the eyes of Rosalía Bringas (late nineteenth century)
(La de Bringas (1884) is one of Pérez Galdós's most dazzling novels.)

The month of August slowly unrolled its tedious length. This is the month in which Madrid is not Madrid, but an empty frying pan. In those days the only theatre open in summer was Price's Circus, with its insufferable ponies and its clowns who played the same tricks every night. The Prado was the only pleasant place to be; and in the shadow of its trees the amorous couples and the *terlulias* passed the time in more or less boring conversations, trying meanwhile to defend themselves against the heat with waving fans and sips of fresh water. For the *madrileños* who are obliged to pass the summer in the city are the true exiles, and their only consolation is to declare that at least they are drinking the best water in the world . . .

As she [Rosalía] sat in the semi-obscurity of the Prado and watched the dizzying procession of passers-by, she saw among them various men whom she knew to be rich and who consequently drew her attention. The street lantern nearest the place where they were sitting lighted these passing forms sufficiently for her to recognize them as they went past, and then they were lost again in the dusty shadows. Thus she saw the Marqués de Fucar, recently returned, she knew, from Biarritz, plump, pompous and simply padded with bank-notes; and then Trujillo the banker, and then Mompous, the stock-exchange broker, and Don Buenaventura de Lantigua, and others of the same sort. Among these powerful personages there were some whom she knew personally and others whom she only knew by sight; some of them had given her what seemed to be amorous glances, while others were said to be of impeccable behaviour both at home and abroad.

Pérez Galdós, 'La de Bringas', 204

[50] Songs heard by Pío Baroja (c. 1900)

Now it seems the *chicas* [girls] scarcely sing in the streets and squares. Before, I remember having seen them singing and playing regularly ring-a-ring-a-roses in the Prado near the fountain of the Four Seasons and in the Plaza de Oriente.

Now I leave my house very little. But when I do I don't see the girls holding hands in a ring; as was frequent in another epoch.

In Madrid and in the provincial capitals in the squares and walks the girls used to sing regularly. In the streets of little traffic they used to come out at dusk to play and sing their *cantinelas* [refrains], most of them old:

A los siete colchones,	To the seven mattresses,
mi señora mía,	My dear lady,
que me ha dicho mi madre	My mother told me
que me dé usted la niña.	That you should give me your girl.

Also there was the tale of the sparrowhawk:

Al milano que le dan	To the sparrowhawk let them give
la corteza con el pan	Crust with bread;
si no le dan otra cosa	If they don't give it anything else,
las mujeres más hermosas.	[He will take] the most beautiful ladies.

Also there was one classic song which went:

Me casó mi madre	My mother married me off
chiquita y bonita,	Pretty and petite,
ay, ay, ay	Ay, ay, ay,
con un muchachito	To a boy
que yo no quería;	I did not love;
a la media noche,	
a la media noche,	At midnight, at midnight
el pícaro se iba,	The scoundrel used to flee,
la capa terciada	His cloak slung across the shoulder,
y espada tendida.	His sword at his side.

Most of these songs were graphic.

I suppose that they are collected up in books of folklore. But I don't think of speaking any more than of what I have heard and seen.

The Prado was a classic promenade of Madrid with its two baroque fountains very decorated – those of the Four Seasons and of Neptune. Years ago the Prado had no trees, only an iron bar on one side which showed where it ended, on which the boys would do gymnastic exercises. The girls used to sing a song which referred to the Prado, with Basque music, of the first civil war: the *¡Ay Ay Mutillá!* It went like this:

En el Salón del Prado	In the Salon of the Prado
no se puede jugar,	One can't play,

porque hay niños que gozan	Because there are children who enjoy
en venir a estorbar;	Coming to obstruct;
con el cigarro puro	With the Havana cigar
vienen a presumir,	They come to show off,
más vale que les dieran	Better give them
un huevo, y a dormir . . .	An egg and to bed . . .

Baroja, 'Desde', 84–85

Puerta del Sol

(This square was once the site of Madrid's east gate, removed by Philip II to the Plaza de Cibeles. The name may derive from the fact that the sunrise came into the city from this direction or because the Comuneros in their revolt (1520). – see No. 106 – had a placard of the sun there; or both.)

[51] Royal decree, 28 July 1541

'. . . that the houses of the public brothel which are near the Puerta del Sol (in the same site which once was filled by the alley and place of the Palace of Oñate) be transferred to another point further away and away from the road which leads to the monasteries of San Jerónimo and of Atocha; to whose care this transfer is ordered to avoid the scandals which have been presented to the faithful who go to those monasteries.'*

Qu. Mesonero Romanos, 'El Antiguo Madrid', 112

* The site of the new brothels was in the Cava de la Puerta del Sol where later the *convento* of Carmen Calzado was built.

[52] The murder of the Conde de Villamediana (Lope de Vega, 1622)

(On the western side of the square, on the site of the café Mallorquín there was once the Palacio de Oñate. In front of it, on the night of 21 August 1622, the Conde de Villamediana, poet, courtier and perhaps homosexual, was killed by means of a crossbow.)

Lope de Vega (1562–1635), the great playwright, wrote:

Mentidero* de Madrid	Gossips of Madrid
Decidme ¿quién mató al conde?	Tell, who killed the Count?
Ni se dice, ni se esconde	It is neither said nor hid;
sin discurso discurrid,	Without discourse, think.
Unos dicen que fué el Cid,	Some say it was the Cid,
por ser el conde Lozano;	Because the Count was Lozano;
¡ disparate chavacano!	Stuff and nonsense!
pues lo cierto de ello ha sido	For the fact is that
Que el matador fué Bellido†	the killer was Bellido†
y el impulso, soberano.	And the impulse, sovereign.

Qu. in Mesonero Romanos, 'El Antiguo Madrid', 113–114

[53] The Habsburg candidate's portrait burnt (1706)

(During the War of the Spanish Succession (see Nos 9 and 10), the capital was reoccupied by the Allies. But they soon left it (1706).)

No sooner had the Allies left Madrid, than Berwick despatched a squadron of horse, under Don Antonio del Valle, to take possession of that capital. Arriving before its gates on the 4th of August, the very day which had been fixed for the triumphal entry of the Archduke, they found themselves encountered by no opposition; but, on the contrary, received with most enthusiastic joy. The people could not be withheld from pillaging

---

* This alludes to the steps (*grada*) of San Felipe el Real, the gossip shop (*mentidero*) of Madrid.

† This killer was a prototype of the medieval traitor, the murderer of Sancho IV.

the houses of the chief Austrian partisans; but all the furniture
and other property seized there was publicly burnt by themselves in the streets, to show that their object was to punish
traitors, and not to profit by their spoils. The standards, and
the portrait of the Archduke, were likewise burnt in triumph at
the Puerta del Sol; and a few hundred Portuguese, who had
taken post at the royal palace, were compelled, by want of
provisions, to surrender in two days.   *Mahon, 206*

[54] Gil Blas in the Puerta del Sol (c. 1715)
(*The Adventures of Gil Blas* (first published 1715), the
engaging novel by Le Sage (1668–1747), was for at least a
hundred years the most popular novel.)

I was punctual in calling on Señor Mateo Meléndez. He was
a woollen-draper, living at the Puerta del Sol, at the corner
of Trunkmaker street.* No sooner had he broken the cover
and read the contents, than he said with an air of compla-
cency – 'Señor Gil Blas, my correspondent, Pedro Palacio,
has written to me so pressingly in your favour, that I cannot
do otherwise than offer you a bed at my house; moreover,
he desires me to find you a good master, and I undertake
the commission with pleasure. I have no doubt of suiting
you to a hair.'

I embraced the offer of Meléndez the more gratefully because
my funds were getting much below par; but I was not long a
burden on his hospitality. At the week's end, he told me that he
had mentioned my name to a gentleman of his acquaintance,
who wanted a valet-de-chambre, and, according to present
appearances, the place would not be long vacant. In fact, this
gentleman happened to make his appearance in the nick of time
– 'Sir' said Meléndez, pushing me forward, 'you see before you
the young man as by former advice. He is a pupil of honour
and integrity. I can answer for him as if he were one of my own
family.' The gentleman looked at me with attention, said that
my face was in my favour, and hired me at once. 'He has

* That is the Calle de los Cofreros. The house was thus on the site of the
present Café Mallorquin.

nothing to do but to follow me,' added he, 'I will put him into the routine of his employment.' At these words he wished the tradesman good morning, and took me into the Calle Mayor, directly over against the church of San Felipe. We went into a very handsome house, of which he occupied one wing; then going up five or six steps, he took me into a room secured by strong double doors, with an iron grate between. From this room we went into another, with a bed and other furniture, neat rather than gaudy.

If my new master had examined me closely, I had all my wits about me as well as he. He was a man on the wrong side of fifty, with a saturnine and serious air. His temper seemed to be even, and I thought no harm of him. He asked me several questions about my family; and liking my answers – 'Gil Blas,' said he, 'I take you to be a very sensible lad, and am well pleased to have you in my service. On your part, you shall have no reason to complain. I will give you six *reales* a day board wages, besides meals. Then I require no great attendance, for I keep no table, but always dine out. You will only have to brush my clothes, and be your own master for the rest of the day. Only take care to be at home early in the evening, and to be in waiting at the door, that is your chief duty.' After this lecture, he took six *reales* out of his purse, and gave them to me as earnest. We then went out, he locked the doors after him, and taking care of the keys – 'My friend,' said he, 'you need not go with me, follow the devices of your own heart; but on my return this evening, let me find you on that staircase.' With this injunction he left me to dispose of myself as seemed best in my own eyes.   *'Gil Blas', I, 130.*

[55] The battle of 2 May 1808: Pérez Galdós's description
(The French, under General Murat (1767–1815), occupied Madrid as part of the arrangements made by Napoleon, Charles IV, and Godoy at Bayonne (1808). Pérez Galdós's impressions come from the third novel of his famous series, *Episodios Nacionales*.)

The struggle, or, one should say, the bloodbath, was appalling in the Puerta del Sol. When the firing ceased, and the cavalry began to take action, the Polish guard and the famous Mamelukes* fell with sabres on the people, those of us who were in the Calle Mayor getting the worst of the onslaught because the ferocious horses fell upon us from two sides. The danger did not prevent me observing who was around me and so I can say that they sustained my wavering valour. There were, in addition to La Primorosa [a *maja* of the hero's acquaintance], a grave and well-dressed gentleman who appeared an aristocrat and two most honourable shopkeepers of the same street whom I had once known.

We had on our left hand the passage de la Duda as a strategic position which served us as a headquarters and the road to flight, and thence the noble gentleman and I directed our fire at the first Mamelukes who appeared in the street. I must point out that we riflemen formed a kind of rearguard or reserve, because the truest and most resourceful warriors were those who fought with knives against the horses. From the balconies also there came many pistol shots and a great number of projectiles were flying down, bricks, flowerpots, stewpots, clock weights and so on.

'Come here, Judas Iscariot' – screamed La Primorosa, directing her fists towards a Mameluke who was wreaking havoc on the door of the house of Oñate. 'And isn't there anyone who can put a pound of gunpowder in his body? What a sight you are! Why are you behaving in this contemptible way? You worthless lump, put fire in your gun or I'll scratch out your eyes.'

The imprecations of our general obliged us to fire shot after shot. But that badly directed fire was not worth much because the Mamelukes had managed to clear a great part of the street with their sabre slashes and were getting further along every minute.

'At them boys (*muchachos*)!' cried the *maja*, rushing forward to meet a pair of horsemen whose mounts were carrying them towards us.

* Polish troops took part under Napoleon's orders. The Mamelukes were a small unit of cavalry brought to Europe from Egypt.

Nobody can imagine what these partisan battles were like. While firing was beginning from the windows and the street alike, the *manolas* attacked, knives in hand, and the women clawed their fingers in the heads of the horses or leapt, seating themselves on the arms of the riders. This received support and, in the next few moments, there were two, three, ten, twenty, who were attacked in the same way and confusion took hold, a horrible and bloody hotpotch impossible to describe. The cavalry won in the end and went away at a gallop, and when the multitude, finding themselves free, rushed towards the Puerta del Sol, they were met by a hail of fire.

I lost sight of La Primorosa in one of these frightful clashes. But in a second she reappeared, furious at having lost her knife and she seized my rifle with such energy that I could not prevent her taking it. I found myself unarmed at the same moment that a strong charge of Frenchmen made us fall back to the pavement of San Felipe el Real. The old nobleman was wounded next to me. I tried to help him. But he slipped from my hands and fell shouting, 'Death to Napoleon! Long live Spain!'

That instant was terrible since they cut us to bits without pity. But my lucky star so managed it that, being among those closest to the wall, I had in front of me a human wall which defended me from the lead and the steel. But in exchange I was so tightly pressed against the wall that I almost thought that I would die by being crushed. The majority of the people fell back on the Calle Mayor and, as the violence of the withdrawal forced us to invade a house, which is today numbered 21 to 25 of that street, we entered it and decided to continue the struggle from the balconies. Do not complain of my vanity in using the first person 'we', since though I found myself to begin with among the fighters by chance, and without any initiative on my part, the heat of the combat, and the hatred of the French which communicated itself from heart to heart in a breathtaking manner, afterwards induced me to work energetically in favour of my own people . . .

Invading the house, we occupied it from the ground floor to the garret. We fired from every window, throwing out at the same time everything which the hard-working valour of the residents found at hand. In the second floor an old father, sustaining his two daughters who, half-fainting, clung to his knees, cried to us, 'Fire! Fire! Take what you want. Here are two pistols. Here you have my shot-gun. Throw my furniture over the balcony, let us all die, and destroy my house if that's the way to bury these *canaille* under it! Long live Ferdinand!* Viva España! Death of Napoleon!' . . .

These words revived the two girls, and the younger of them led us to a next-door house from which we could better direct our fire. But we had a shortage of gunpowder, we ran out of it at the end, and a quarter of an hour after our entry the Mamelukes were giving violent knocks on the door . . .

Pérez Galdós, 'El 19 de marzo y el 2 de mayo', 273–275.

[56] Murat to Napoleon I, 2 May 1808
(Murat's report to Napoleon gives a different impression from that in No. 55.)

Sire, Public tranquillity has been disturbed this morning. For the last few days, country people have been gathering in the town; pamphlets have been circulated to encourage them to revolt; a price has been put on the heads of the French generals and of the officers stationed in the town: in short, everything pointed to a crisis. This morning at 8 o'clock, the rabble of Madrid and its outskirts blocked all the roads to the palace and filled up the courtyard. One of my aides-de-camp, whom I had sent to convey my compliments to the Queen of Etruria† who was about to go out in her carriage, was stopped at the gate to the palace, and was assassinated by the wild populace, in spite of the 10 or 12 of your Majesty's grenadier guards whom I had sent to assist him. An instant later, a second aide-de-camp whom I had sent to carry orders to General Grouchy‡ was attacked with stones and wounded. In the field the call to battle was given; Your Majesty's guards took to arms, all the camps began moving and received the order to march on Madrid and occupy the positions which had been shown them in case of emergency.

* Ferdinand VII, recognized by patriots as King in 1808.
† María Luisa (1782–1824) married her cousin Luis of Parma (1773–1803), 'King of Etruria'.
‡ Emmanuel Grouchy (1766–1847), Marquis, Marshal of France.

Meanwhile a battalion of the Guard which is posted in my palace marched, supported by two cannon and a squadron of Polish light-cavalry, towards the Palace and on the crowd which had gathered, and dispersed it with gunshots. General Grouchy, for his part, massed his troops in the Prado, and received the order to go via the Calle Alcalá to the Puerta del Sol and to the Plaza Mayor and to that of the Fontana de Oro, where more than 20,000 rebels had assembled. Already, all the isolated soldiers who attempted to return to their posts had been killed in the streets; even those who found themselves at the quarter-master's stores were not spared. General Lefranc, who occupies the convent of San Bernardino with a regiment, took a brigade to the Fuencarral gate where three cannon had been put. The battalion of sailors have taken up their reserve position in front of my palace. Colonel Fréderic, with his two battalions of fusiliers, occupied the square in front of the Palace and the entrance to the streets Almudena and Platería; the Basque company went to the Plaza del San Dominic; Your Majesty's mounted Guard was engaged in battle in front of the barracks, in the El Prado Nuevo street, right to the gate of San Vicente. The *cuirassiers* marched from Carabanchel on Toledo bridge; the pickets were sent to the hospital, others marched to the arsenal. Such were my arrangements, when I ordered General Grouchy to go to the Puerta del Sol, and Colonel Fréderic to march to the same point via the Calle Platería and to break up the violent mob with cannon fire. These two columns set off and managed to clean up these streets, not without great difficulty since the scoundrels, when chased out of the street, took refuge in houses and formed a cross-fire against our troops, while the greater number went to the arsenal in order to make off with the cannon and guns. But General Lefranc, who found himself at the gate of Fuencarral, went through it with bayonets in front, and managed to take control of it and to recapture the cannon which these people had seized.

Consequently the columns went on to the Puerta del Sol, the Puerta del Toledo, and also the gates of Segovia and of Fuencarral. General Grouchy had the houses entered whence the cross-fire came, and put to the sword all those who were found therein. All the streets were swept clean. The country peasants, who had begun to try and escape from the town, met the cavalry and were cut down.

The cannon and gunfire were no longer heard and, receiving reports that nobody was left in the streets, I went to the Palace to see the Infante Don Antonio* to tell him to immediately disarm the whole town.

The proclamation was made at that moment; it was sent out to the provinces. The major-generals, the *Corregidors*, the *Alcaldes*, the heads of the clergy were made responsible for its execution and for the peace of the realm.

Sire, there were many killed. The riflemen of the Guard lost some men. Colonel Daumesnil was as brave as ever; twice he made his way through the mob with his infantry and his Mamelukes. He had 20 men out of action, 2 horses killed under him, he was wounded in the knee; his wound is slight. Tonight I will describe this event more exactly to Your Majesty, as soon as I myself have all the detailed reports from the differing commanding officers. In the twinkling of an eye, everyone was at his post. I owe the greatest praise to all Your Majesty's troops, but I owe it especially to General Grouchy.

Thirty of these knaves who took up arms were shot; another thirty whom we hold in prison, will be tomorrow. Lampoons and provocations against the army of Your Majesty were found on them.

During the shooting, I received Your Majesty's letter of the 29th; it was no longer possible for me to start an engagement. Your Majesty's other dispositions have been carried out. This event, though unfortunate, assures us the peace of the capital, and I hope of the kingdom, for ever.

I offered guards to the ambassadors of Russia, Holland, Denmark and to all the members of the diplomatic corps. Calm having been restored, these gentlemen thanked me kindly, and showed themselves to be sensitive to my offer.

P.S. *Le peuple des croisées* and all good citizens applauded as soon as the proclamation was published on the streets.

Murat, 319–321.

---

* The Infante Antonio (1755–1817), youngest son of King Charles III.

[57] George Borrow sees the 'Revolution of La Granja' (1836)

(This revolution soon failed.)

. . . I entered the Puerta del Sol at about noon. There is always a crowd there about this hour, but it is generally a very quiet motionless crowd, consisting of listless idlers calmly smoking their cigars, or listening to or retailing the – in general – very dull news of the capital; but on the day of which I am speaking, the mass was no longer inert. There was much gesticulation and vociferation, and several people were running about shouting, '¡Viva la constitución!' – a cry which, a few days previously, would have been visited on the utterer with death, the city having for some weeks past been subjected to the rigour of martial law. I occasionally heard the words '¡La Granja! ¡La Granja!' which words were sure to be succeeded by the shout of '¡Viva la constitución!' Opposite the Casa de Postas* were drawn up in a line about a dozen mounted dragoons, some of whom were continually waving their caps in the air and joining the common cry, in which they were encouraged by their commander, a handsome young officer, who flourished his sword, and more than once cried out with great glee, 'Long live the constitutional queen!† Long live the constitution!'

The crowd was rapidly increasing, and several nationals [anti-soldiers] made their appearance in their uniforms, but without their arms, of which they had been deprived, as I have already stated. 'What has become of the moderado government?' said I to Baltasar, whom I suddenly observed amongst the crowd, dressed as when I had first seen him, in his old regimental great coat and foraging cap; 'have the ministers been deposed and others put in their place?'

'Not yet, Don Jorge', said the little soldier-tailor; 'not yet; the scoundrels still hold out, relying on the brute bull Quesada and a few infantry, who still continue true to them. But there is no

---

* The Post Office was on the site of the present Dirección General de Seguridad, from 1768 to 1848. It was built by Jacques Marquet. The clock, which had been on the old church of Buen Suceso across the square, was placed there in 1854. The building served as Ministry of the Interior between 1848 and 1939.

† Queen Isabella II.

fear, *Don Jorge*, the queen is ours, thanks to the courage of my friend García, and if the brute bull should make his appearance – ho! ho! *Don Jorge*, you shall see something – I am prepared for him, ho! ho!' and thereupon he half opened his great coat, and showed me a small gun which he bore beneath it in a sling, and then moving away with a wink and a nod, disappeared amongst the crowd.

Presently I perceived a small body of soldiers advancing up the Calle Mayor, or principal street which runs from the Puerta del Sol in the direction of the palace; they might be about twenty in number, and an officer marched at their head with a drawn sword. The men appeared to have been collected in a hurry, many of them being in fatigue dress, with foraging caps on their heads. On they came, slowly marching; neither their officer nor themselves paying the slightest attention to the cries of the crowd which thronged about them, shouting, 'Long live the constitution!' save and except by an occasional surly side glance: on they marched with contracted brows and set teeth, till they came in front of the cavalry, where they halted and drew up in rank.

'Those men mean mischief,' said I to my friend D –, of the *Morning Chronicle*, who at this moment joined me; 'and depend upon it, that if they are ordered they will commence firing, caring nothing whom they hit. But what can those cavalry fellows behind them mean, who are evidently of the other opinion by their shouting? Why don't they charge at once this handful of foot people and overturn them? Once down, the crowd would wrest from them their muskets in a moment. You are a liberal, which I am not; why do you not go to that silly young man who commands the horse and give him a word of counsel in time?'

D – turned upon me his broad red good-humoured English countenance, with a peculiarly arch look, as much as to say, . . . (whatever you think most applicable, gentle reader), then taking me by the arm, 'Let us get,' said he, 'out of this crowd and mount to some window, where I can write down what is about to take place, for I agree with you that mischief is meant.' Just opposite the post-office was a large house, in the topmost story of which we beheld a paper displayed, importing that apartments were to let; whereupon we instantly ascended the common stair, and having agreed with the mistress of the *élage* for the use of the front room for the day, we bolted the door, and the reporter, producing his pocket-book and pencil, prepared to take notes of the coming events, which were already casting their shadows before . . .

We had scarcely been five minutes at the window, when we suddenly heard the clattering of horses' feet hastening down the street called the Calle de Carretas. The house in which we had stationed ourselves was, as I have already observed, just opposite to the post-office at the left of which this street debouches from the north into the Puerta del Sol: as the sounds became louder and louder, the cries of the crowd below diminished, and a species of panic seemed to have fallen upon all: once or twice, however, I could distinguish the words, 'Quesada! Quesada!' The foot soldiers stood calm and motionless, but I observed that the cavalry, with the young officer who commanded them, displayed both confusion and fear, exchanging with each other some hurried words. All of a sudden that part of the crowd which stood near the mouth of the Calle de Carretas fell back in great disorder, leaving a considerable space unoccupied, and the next moment Quesada, in complete general's uniform, and mounted on a bright bay thoroughbred English horse, with a drawn sword in his hand, dashed at full gallop into the area, in much the same manner as I have seen a Manchegan bull rush into the amphitheatre when the gates of his pen are suddenly flung open.

He was closely followed by two mounted officers, and at a short distance by as many dragoons. In almost less time than is sufficient to relate it, several individuals in the crowd were knocked down and lay sprawling upon the ground beneath the horses of Quesada and his two friends, for as to the dragoons, they halted as soon as they had entered the Puerta del Sol. It was a fine sight to see three men, by dint of valour and good horsemanship, strike terror into at least as many thousands: I saw Quesada spur his horse repeatedly into the dense masses of the crowd, and then extricate himself in the most masterly manner. The rabble were completely awed, and gave way, retiring by the Calle del Comercio and the Calle de Alcalá. All at once, Quesada singled out two nationals, who were attempting to escape, and setting spurs to his horse, turned them in a moment, and drove them in another direction, striking them in a contemptuous manner with the flat of his sabre. He was crying out, 'Long live the absolute queen!' when, just beneath me, amidst a portion of the crowd which had still maintained its ground, perhaps from not having the means of escaping, I saw a small gun glitter for a moment; then there was a sharp report, and a bullet had nearly sent Quesada to his long account, passing so near to the countenance of the general as to graze his hat. I had an indistinct view for a moment of a well-known foraging cap just about the spot from whence the gun had been discharged, then there was a rush of the crowd, and the shooter, whoever he was, escaped discovery amidst the confusion which arose.

As for Quesada, he seemed to treat the danger from which he had escaped with the utmost contempt. He glared about him fiercely for a moment, then leaving the two nationals, who sneaked away like whipped hounds, he went up to the young officer who commanded the cavalry, and who had been active in raising the cry of the constitution, and to him he addressed a few words with an air of stern menace; the youth evidently quailed before him, and, probably in obedience to his orders, resigned the command of the party, and rode away with a discomfited air; whereupon Quesada dismounted and walked slowly backwards and forwards before the *Casa de Postas* with a mien which seemed to bid defiance to mankind*.

Borrow (1907), 199–204.

[58] Pérez Galdós's memories (c. 1865)

In '63 or '64 – and here my memory is a little unclear – my parents sent me to Madrid to study law and I came to this 'Court' and entered the University where I distinguished myself by my frequent truancies. Escaping . . . from the lectures, I wandered about the streets, squares and culs-de-sac enjoying seeing the busy life in this large and motley capital. My literary vocation began with an itch to write plays and, if my days were passed in wandering in the streets, I invested a good part of my

---

* Quesada was executed at Hortaleza soon afterwards; see No. 35.

nights in scribbling dramas and comedies. I frequented the
Teatro Real and a café in the Puerta del Sol where there would
gather a good number of my contemporaries.

In that period, abundant in serious political events which
were precursors of the Revolution, I was present, mixed up
with the student mob, at the scandalous riot of Saint Daniel's
night – 10 April 1865* – and . . . the following year, on 22
June†, memorable for the Sergeants' revolt in the barracks of
San Gil, from the guest house in the Calle del Olivo I was able
to appreciate the tremendous events of that tragic day. The
cannon thundered; from nearby streets there came the groans
of victims, violent imprecations, streams of blood, voices of
hatred . . . Madrid was hell. At nightfall when we were able to
leave the house we saw plundering of the dead and the bloody
face of the beaten Revolution. As a most tragic spectacle, the
most tragic and sinister I have ever seen, I will mention the
procession of artillery sergeants carried in coaches to the
scaffold, two by two, down the Calle de Alcalá to be shot
against the walls of the old bullring.

I saw them pass by, carried away by grief. I did not have the
courage to follow the funeral *cortège* as far as the place of
torment, and ran home and there tried to find relief in my dear
books, and in imaginary dramas which enraptured me a good
deal more than real ones.

By recalling the thick revolutionary atmosphere of those
turbulent times I believed that my dramatic essays would bring
another profound revolution in literary achievement; a pre-
sumption very natural in juvenile brains of that generation.
Every lively boy (*muchacho*) born in Spanish territory is a
playwright before being anything more practical and realistic.

Pérez Galdós, 'Memorias', 35–37.

[59] De Amicis's impression (1870)

During the first few days I could not tear myself away from the
square of the Puerta del Sol. I stayed there by the hour, and

* This was perhaps the first specifically student riot in Spain.
† This famous rising in 1866 led to the shooting of their officers by the
artillery sergeants.

amused myself so much that I should like to have passed the day there. It is a square worthy of its fame; not so much on account of its size and beauty as for the people, life, and variety of spectacle which it presents at every hour of the day. It is not a square like the others; it is a mingling of salon, promenade, theatre, academy, garden, a square of arms, and a market. From daybreak until one o'clock at night, there is an immovable crowd, and a crowd that comes and goes through the ten streets leading into it, and a passing and mingling of carriages which makes one giddy. There gather the merchants, the disengaged demagogues, the unemployed clerks, the aged pensioners, and the elegant young men; there they traffic, talk politics, court girls, promenade, read the newspapers, hunt down their debtors, seek their friends, prepare demonstrations against the ministry, coin the false reports which circulate through Spain, and weave the scandalous gossip of the city. Upon the sidewalks, which are wide enough to allow four carriages to pass in a row, one has to force one's way with one's elbows. On a single paving stone you see a civil guard, a match vendor, a broker, a beggar, and a soldier, all in one group. Crowds of students, servants, generals, officials, peasants, *toreros*, and ladies pass; importunate beggars ask for alms in your ear so as not to be discovered; cocottes question you with their eyes; courtesans hit your elbow; on every side you see hats lifted, handshakings, smiles, pleasant greetings, cries of *Largo* from laden porters and merchants with their wares hung from the neck; you hear shouts of newspaper sellers, shrieks of water vendors, blasts of the diligence horns, cracking of whips, clanking of sabres, strumming of guitars, and songs of the blind. The regiments with their bands of music pass; the King goes by; the square is sprinkled with immense jets of water which cross in the air; the bearers of advertisements announcing the spectacles, troops of ragamuffins with armfuls of supplements, and a body of employés of the ministries, appear; the bands of music repass, the shops begin to be lighted, the crowd grows denser, the blows on the elbow become more frequent, the hum of voices, racket, and commotion increase. It is not the bustle of a busy people; it is the vivacity of gay persons, a carnival-like gaiety, a restless idleness, a feverish overflow of pleasure, which attacks you and forces you around like a reel without permitting you to leave the square; you are seized by a curiosity which never wearies, a desire to amuse yourself, to think of nothing, to listen to gossip, to saunter, and to laugh. Such is the famous square, the *Puerta del Sol.*

De Amicis, 118–119.

[60] A Communist's surprise: M.N. Roy (1921)

(Roy (1887–1954) was an Indian Communist despatched from Moscow to Madrid to persuade the Spanish Socialists to join the Comintern. He was unsuccessful.)

Madrid was the first European capital I visited. It was a gay city, all the more so because of the coming Carnival – the popular spring festival in the Catholic countries of Southern Europe. The merchants and industrialists had made money out of the war, and they flaunted their newly acquired riches with a reckless extravagance and graceful abandon. The numerous cafés and luxurious restaurants along the Puerta del Sol – the main thoroughfare of the city – were crowded practically for all the twenty-four hours. Milk actually flowed and honey was replaced by cubes of shining white sugar which were littered on the floor. When one ordered a cup of coffee, a waiter came carrying two big kettles and poured out simultaneously boiling milk and the steaming brown brew until as much splashed on the table as in the cup; another waiter threw on the table half-a-dozen sugar cubes neatly packed in paper. Each guest left several of them on the table to be swept on the floor. There was a similar surfeit and wastage of all other articles of food. Dandified young men lounged for hours in red plush sofas and easy chairs smoking, drinking and playing *dominó* for money. It was a spectacle fascinating as well as disgusting. But I could not watch it for any length of time, because of the noise and the smoke which filled the places. But the incongruity of an oriental bazaar in the heart of a European city, crowded with people of Western habits, was so very captivating that during my first short stay in Madrid I dropped in at one after another of the cafés, whenever I could spare the time.   *Roy, 230–31.*

[61] The fall of the monarchy: Miguel Maura (1931)
(Maura (1887–1971), son of the Conservative prime minister,
became Minister of the Interior in the new government of the
Republic.)

It was about six o'clock when, convinced of the uselessness of
my efforts to convince my comrades of the urgency of taking
power on our account that very evening, I left the library and
crossing the hall went up the first steps of the staircase. From
there, directing myself to the public which filled the ground
floor, I asked in the middle of an absolute silence: 'Are you
disposed to come with me to occupy the Ministry of the
Interior?'

The cry in reply was such that my friends precipitously left
the library and . . . they found that they could not return to it,
cut off by the vast human flood around me and around those
who with me went out into the street in search of cars.

I took the arm of Largo Caballero* who was the only one
who had agreed to my proposal during the discussion and went
to my car. My chauffeur drove; beside him there was an
individual totally unknown to me, and behind there were
Largo Caballero and myself. I did not occupy myself at all
with what happened to the others and as my car was in the
entry of the garden when we left the street my comrades were
still wandering about in search of the necessary vehicles. We
thus gained time because the danger of being blocked up, if we
remember the crowds which normally frequent the streets at
this time, was serious.

Without difficulty and thanks to this detail we soon arrived
at Cibeles. From there on we had to go very slowly because the
streets were full of people. Soon they recognized us and then
our calvary began. We took about two hours to travel up the
section of the Calle de Alcalá which goes from the Plaza de la
Cibeles to the Puerta del Sol, or little more than a kilometre.
The people opened up a path for us by shoves and pressures but
from time to time they jumped on to the running boards and
mudguards of my car in such a way that completely shut up the

---

* Francisco Largo Caballero (1869–1946) Socialist leader, Prime Minister
during the civil war, imprisoned by the Germans 1940–45, died in Paris.

windows and inside we almost asphyxiated. We had unfortunately to deal one or two blows in the stomachs to those who covered the windows in order to be able to breathe.

In the Puerta del Sol the agglomeration of people exceeded anything imaginable. The lamps, the trams stopped in the middle of the square, the balconies and rooftops were filled by innumerable products of humanity. The shrieking deafened me.

The cars which my companions were driving delayed in appearing at the entry to the Puerta del Sol which faces the Calle de Alcalá.

As we learned afterwards, Azaña*, who came with Casares Quiroga† in one of these last vehicles, was grumbling bad-humouredly, saying that we would be shot by the Civil Guard, saying that the whole thing was madness and calling me *Señorito chulo* ('young rascal').

In the end my car arrived before the main gate of the Ministry of the Interior. The door was shut.

On the principal balcony to my great astonishment there soon waved the Republican flag. It was Rafael Sánchez Guerra‡ and the man who was going to be my under-secretary, Manuel Ossorio Florit, who had gone in a little before by a door in the Calle de Pontejos and, seeing that we were arriving, hurried to raise the flag. Before the closed gate were only Largo Caballero and myself, surrounded naturally by a vociferous mass demanding the opening of the gates.

Soon these were gingerly opened and there appeared on the threshold a picket of the Civil Guard barring the way.

I pushed myself in front, declared who I was and said – 'Gentlemen, let pass the Government of the Republic!'

The soldiers, just as if they had been rehearsing the thing beforehand, in two files each on one side presented arms.

We passed, Largo Caballero and I returning the salute. On arriving at the great staircase, I went up the stairs in two or three jumps and went directly to the office of the Minister,

---

* Manuel Azaña; see No. 20.
† Santiago Casares Quiroga (1884–1950), lawyer and politician from La Coruña, prime minister 1936, died in exile.
‡ Rafael Sánchez Guerra (1897–1964), later Secretary-General of the Republic, prisoner 1940–1943, died in a Dominican monastery.

which I knew of old. There I met Mariano Marfil, a friend of many years, and, I repeat, a more than excellent person. He had not abandoned his post in the three days since the [municipal] elections, and day and night was in harness carrying out his duties. I said to him: 'Marfil my friend! Here you are not needed from now on.'

'I understand perfectly, and at this moment I shall leave,' and in effect he vanished.

He had to leave by the gate in front of the building because the others were full of people.

I repented then and I have repented since of the brutal discourtesy with which I treated on that occasion someone who, by his behaviour, deserved much and whom I so much admired. Months afterwards, in an extensive and warm conversation with him in my house, I asked for and obtained his pardon and we renewed our old, briefly interrupted, friendship.

This was, dear reader, the 'ceremonial' of the famous transfer of power . . .   *Maura, 169–71.*

[62] An Anarchist's plan: Ramón Sender (c. 1933)
(Sender (1902–1982) was a brilliant writer who sympathized with the Anarchists before 1936 and with the Communists afterwards.)

. . . I come to the Puerta del Sol. In the corner to the left, those out of work belonging to the building trade are airing themselves in the sun as usual. Very few of the bourgeoisie are to be seen in the streets. Workmen are much more numerous, and they proclaim themselves strikers by the mixture of amusement and suspicion with which they walk the streets. The streets belong to no one yet. We shall see who are going to conquer. The Civil Guard*, the Public Safety Agents, the Shock Police† lurk in the entrance-halls of public buildings and in the usual stations, the doors of which are half closed. In the Home Office there are black visors, chin-straps fastened, and eagle eyes looking in every direction. Telephone calls, telegraphic 'tickers',

* The para-military police force founded in 1844 to keep order in the countryside.
† La Guardia de Asalto, founded in 1931.

although there is still no reason for expecting anything outside Madrid. All the same the Regional organization has acted spontaneously. Although there are no newspapers, we have received word that the local Federations in the two Castilles are meeting to discuss the matter*. That means a lot. A pity that there is little to excite them. But the out-of-work people will soon put that right.

Voices, disturbances. This Puerta del Sol is like a bay of the sea, always in agitation. I have sometimes seen all the street openings occupied by troops which had cleared the open space completely, and suddenly men, coming as it were from the asphalt itself, began to gesticulate and shout. Suddenly, firing. The rebels appear on the great electric light standards and in the entrances of the metro. What happens in the Puerta del Sol happens all over Spain. The strength of our tactics is that the Government never knows where the enemy is. And these tactics are not our own, but come from the Spanish temperament. They say that the monarchy fell in that way. A moment comes when passion has infected the air, and no one can breathe, and the most extraordinary events happen independently of any of the preparations which have been made. We ourselves have determined on a general strike. No doubt we should be content with making the strike as complete as possible. But when we go into the street and see one of the Civil Guards, we feel that we have to kill him. The organization is always behind us ready to go forward to anything. Someone calls, 'So far,' and a thousand voices call, 'Onwards.' Amongst these voices workers and women, well-dressed people and beggars. We move on, and soon we see that the syndicalist plans are overruled. We halt a little, and resolve again, 'Thus far.' The air and the flagstones, the light and the buildings call to us, 'Further on.' We consult the Local Federation, and they say, 'Onwards,' signed and sealed. We go to the Regional and they say 'Onwards.' Next the National Committee and the Peninsular Central are consulted. All reply, almost without words, a single sign, the sign of today and tomorrow. The eternal sign. 'Always onwards.' Today the starting-point is in Madrid. Sometimes it is in

* The Anarchists were organized in the CNT (Confederación Nacional del Trabajo).

Barcelona or Sevilla. The whole organization, without conference or even telephonic communication, is behind us as we
are undermining, without discipline and without any real
organization, the defence system of the State. Whither we
don't know. Comrades Progreso, Espartaco and Germinal!
On the Sunday night they closed our syndicates, deployed
all their forces against us, but the general strike was agreed on.

Sender, 102–03 (c. 1933).

[63] Post-war impressions: V.S. Pritchett (c. 1950)
(Sir Victor Pritchett (1900–97), the English man of letters,
was much travelled in Spain.)

After midnight in Madrid, when one has just finished dinner,
one goes off into those packed, narrow streets lying off the
Puerta del Sol in the middle of the city. They are streets of small
bars crowded with men roaring away at each other, drinking
their small glasses of beer or wine, tearing shellfish to bits and
scattering their refuse and the sugar-papers of their coffee on
the floors. The walls are tiled and in gaudy colours. The head of
a bull will hang there, or some bloody painting of a scene at the
bullfight. Through the door at the back of the bar one makes
one's way into a room, tiled again, like a bathhouse, and
furnished only with a table and a dozen chairs. There one can
invite a guitarist and singers and listen to *cante flamenco*.

Less respectably, one can find some cellar in the same
quarter, some thieves' kitchen which will probably be closed
by the police in a week or two, and there one may hear *cante
flamenco* and, even better, the true *cante jondo*, or deep song,
brought up in the last thirty years from the south, and sung not
for the traveller's special entertainment but, as it were, privately, for the singer's own consolation. For, despite its howling, it is also an intimate music, perhaps for a singer and a
couple of friends only. It can be sung in a mere whisper. The
dirty room, lit by one weak and naked electric-light bulb, is full
of wretched, ill-looking men; the proprietor wanders round
with a bottle of wine in his hand filling up glasses. In one corner
four men are sitting, with their heads close together, and one
notices that one of them is strumming quietly on the table and

another is murmuring to himself, occasionally glancing up at his friends, who gravely nod. The finger strumming increases and at last the murmurer breaks into one low word, singing it under the breath in the falsetto voice of the gypsies. '*Ay*,' he sings. Or '*Leli, Leli*,' prolonging the note like a drawn-out sigh, and when he stops, the strumming of the fingers becomes more rapid, building up emotion and tension and obsession, until at last the low voice cries out a few words that are like an exclamation suddenly coming from some unknown person in the dark. What are the words? They are difficult to understand because the gypsies and, indeed, the Andalusians, drop so many consonants from their words that the speech sounds like a mouthful of small pebbles rubbed against one another:

> *Cada vez que considero*
> *Que me tengo que morí*

the voice declaims:
'Whenever I remember that I must die'
wavering on its words and then suddenly ending; and the strumming begins again until the rapid climax of the song,

> *Tiendo la capa en el suelo*
> *Y me jarto de dormí.*
> 'I spread my cloak on the ground
> And sleep and sleep.'

The manners of the thieves' kitchen are correct and unmarred by familiarity. A yellow-haired and drunken prostitute may be annoying a man by rumpling his hair, but otherwise the dejected customers at three in the morning are sober.

Pritchett, 107–09 (1950).

Plaza Mayor

(This great square was rebuilt by the architect Juan Gómez de Mora (1580–1648) in two years 1617–1619. Its first historic scene was the beatification of St Isidro (1621). The second was more tragic (see below). The Plaza Mayor was the place of public executions till 1790, if the deaths were by garrote (to the north side) or hanging (to the south). Burnings of prisoners 'relaxed' by the Inquisition to the civil powers were held outside the city walls, beyond the gate of Alcalá or the gate of St Bárbara.)

[64] The execution of D. Rodrigo Calderón (1621)
(Calderón was a friend of the late King Philip III's favourite, the Duque de Lerma. He suffered for this rather than for other crimes.)

At eleven-thirty the Mayor brought out from prison the afore-said Rodrigo Calderón, dressed in a great dress of baize, and a hood over the head, its collar flounced without starch, his beard and hair long, having grown in his time in prison, without his wanting to have it cut off. The Mayor said in a high voice, 'Let it be known that I hand over Don Rodrigo Calderón to the *alguaciles* of the Court by order of his Majesty in order that his sentence be executed on him.' And those who found themselves nearest Don Rodrigo asked him, with good reason, if he would pardon them and . . . he asked in a deep voice how he hoped, 'For the love of God, that they would pardon him if, at any time, he had said some disagreeable words.' And the executioner went up to him with a black mule*, saddled and bridled, with adornments of black handkerchiefs, and he mounted her with a good *brío* and liveliness, and great contrition; and Father Pedrosa of the order of San Jerónimo and his counsellor Father Gabriel del Sacramento, of the order of the Barefooted Carmelites gave him a Christ to carry in his hands. They began to leave the prison at half-past eleven, the bells of the church tolling and the two crucifixes accompanying them, with both *alguaciles* and the town criers crying: 'This is the justice for having killed treacherously and murderously a man, for being implicated in the death of another man, and the other crimes described; in the sentence he has been condemned to be beheaded; inasmuch as a man does so, he shall be responsible . . .' It was impossible to enumerate the people who filled the streets where he passed, and the windows and grids without number, filling all streets so that no coaches could go. Great lamentations of pity were heard. The Plaza Mayor was so full of people that it cost the *alguaciles* a great deal to get as far as the scaffold. The balconies, windows, roofs and ground before the houses were so full of people that it appeared a whole world. They arrived at the scaffold which was without drapery, next to which the aforesaid Don Rodrigo got down from the mule and, finding there Father Pedrosa and his confessor, said: 'Señor Pedrosa, now that we are going to lose the body we will win the soul,' and he went up the scaffold with his crucifix in his hand, while he said the Confession and heard the Absolution, kissed the planks three times, and then the monks who were there turned to speak of his salvation and he replied, with much devotion and signs of great Christianity and, with good heart, he rose

---

* A black mule symbolized humiliation but also the passage of the soul to the next world.

and sat in the chair and all the monks were by him and in a short time the executioner came and tied his legs and then his body and arms to the selfsame chair and the executioner begged his pardon and Don Rodrigo pardoned him and embraced him and gave him peace on both cheeks. The executioner turned and tied his hands and covered his eyes with a black *tafetán* and took away the collar that he had and beheaded him saying, 'Jesus,' giving his soul to the Lord at half-past twelve . . . At eight that night a lay sister who customarily shrouded executed persons and the executioner with her undressed the body on the scaffold and enshrouded it and put it in a coffin covered with black cloth and, on the shoulders of the Brothers of Antonio Martín, with the two crucifixes which had accompanied him to the scaffold, and the brotherhoods of Our Lady of Peace, of Charity and of the Holy Cross and clergy, bore the body back down on the street by which he had come and by the Calle Mayor below to the Calle de Alcalá went to deposit it in the monastery of the Barefoot Carmelites where it arrived at half-past eight, though there were so many people, coaches and populace in the streets to see it that it could scarcely pass. They put the body in the centre of the church on a tomb . . . God keep him in His glory. Amen.

Díaz Plaja, 'Documentos', II, 97–98

[65] A bull-fight (Clarendon, 1650)
(For background, see No. 37.)

The next day, and so for two or three days together, both the ambassadors [Lord Cottington, Mr Edward Hyde] had a box prepared for them to see the *toros*; which is a spectacle very wonderful. Here the place was very noble, being the market-place, a very large square, built with handsome brick houses, which had all balconies, which were adorned with tapestry and very beautiful ladies. Scaffolds were built round the first story, the lower rooms being shops, and for ordinary use; and in the division of those scaffolds all the magistrates and officers of the town knew their places. The pavement of the place was covered with gravel, which in summer time was upon those occasions watered by carts charged with hogsheads of water. As soon as the King comes, some officers clear the whole ground from the common people, so that there is no man seen upon the plain but two or three *alguaciles*, magistrates, with their small white wands. Then one of the four gates which lead into the streets is opened, at which the *toreadores* enter, all persons of quality richly clad, and upon the best horses in Spain, every one attended by eight or ten more lackeys, all clinkant with gold and silver lace, who carry the spears which their masters are to use against the bulls; and with this entry pay very dear. The persons on horseback have all cloaks folded up upon their left shoulder, the least disorder of which, much more the letting it fall, is a very great disgrace; and in that grave order they march to the place where the King sits, and after they have made the reverences, they place themselves at a good distance from one another, and expect the bull. The bulls are brought in the night before from the mountains by people used to that work, who drive them into the town when nobody is in the streets, into a pen made for them, which hath a door that opens into that large space; the key whereof is sent to the King, which the King, when he sees everything ready, throws to an *alguacil*, who carries it to the officer that keeps the door, and he causes it to be opened, when a single bull is ready to come out. When the bull enters, the common people, who sit over the door or near it, strike him, or throw short darts with sharp points of steel to provoke him to rage. He commonly runs with all his fury against the first man he sees on horseback, who watches him so carefully, and avoids him so dexterously, that when the spectators believe him to be even between the horns of the bull, he avoids by the quick turn of his horse, and with his lance strikes the bull upon a vein that runs through his poll, with which in a moment he falls down dead. But this fatal stroke can never be struck but when the bull comes so near upon the turn of the horse that his horn even touches the rider's leg, and so is at such a distance that he can shorten his lance, and use the full strength of his arm in the blow. And they who are the most skilful in the exercise do frequently kill the beast with such an exact stroke, insomuch as in a day two or three fall in that manner: but if they miss the vein, it only gives a wound that the more enrages him. Sometimes the bull runs with so much fierceness (for if he scapes the first man, he runs upon the rest as they are in his way) that he gores the horse with his horns that his guts come out, and he falls before the rider can get from his back. Sometimes by the strength of his neck he raises horse and man from the ground, and throws both down, and then the greatest danger is another gore upon the ground. In any of these disgraces, or any other by which the rider comes to be dismounted, he is obliged in honour to take his revenge upon the bull by his sword, and upon his head, towards which the standers by assist him by running after the bull and hocking him, by which he falls upon his hinder legs; but before that execution can be done, a good bull hath his revenge upon many poor fellows. Sometimes he is so unruly that nobody dares to attack him, and then the King calls for the mastives, whereof two are let out at a time, and if they cannot master him, but are themselves killed, as frequently they are, the King then, as the last refuge, calls for the English mastives; of which they seldom turn out above one at a time; and he rarely misses taking the bull and holding him by the nose till the men run in; and after they have hocked him, they quickly kill him. In one of those days there were no fewer than sixteen horses, as good as any in Spain, the worst of which would that very morning have yielded three hundred pistoles, killed, and four or five men, besides many more of both hurt: and some men remained perpetually maimed: for after the horsemen have done as much as they can, they withdraw themselves, and then some accustomed nimble fellows, to whom money is thrown when they perform their feats with skill, stand to receive the bull, whereof the worst are reserved till the last: and it is a wonderful thing to see with what steadiness those fellows will stand a full career of the bull, and by a little quick motion upon one foot avoid him, and lay a hand upon his horn, as if he guided him from him; but then the next standers by, who have not the same activity, commonly pay for it; and there is no day without much mischieve. It is a very barbarous exercise and triumph, in which so many men's lives are lost, and always ventured; but so rooted in the affections of the nation, that it is not in the King's power, they say, to suppress it, though, if he disliked it enough, he might forbear to be present at it. There are three festival days in the year, whereof midsummer is one, on which the people hold it to be their right to be treated with these spectacles, not only in great cities, where they are never disappointed, but in very ordinary towns, where there are places provided for it. Besides those ordinary annual days, upon any extraordinary accidents of joy, as at this time for the arrival of the Queen, upon the birth of the King's children, or any signal victory, these triumphs are repeated, which no ecclesiastical censures or authority can suppress or discountenance . . .

There was another accident upon one of these days, the mention whereof is not unfit, to shew the discipline and severity of that nation in the observation of order. It was remembered that at the last masquerade the almirante* and marquis of Leche† were sent to their chambers; and afterwards, the matter being examined, they were both commanded to leave the town, and to retire each to a house of his own, that was within three or four leagues of the town. The marquis of Leche was known to have gone the next day, and nobody doubted the same of the almirante, those orders being never disputed or disobeyed. The King going to the *toros* either himself discerned at another balcony, or somebody else advertised him of it, that the duchess, who was wife to the almirante, was there, and said, he knew that lady was a woman of more honour than to come out of her house and be present at that fiesta whilst her husband was under restraint and in the King's displeasure, and therefore concluded that her husband was likewise there; and thereupon sent an *alguacil* to that room, with command to examine carefully with his eye whether the almirante was there; for there appeared none but women. The almirante being a young rash man, much in the King's favour, and a gentleman of his bedchamber, thought he might undiscerned see the triumph of that day; and therefore caused himself to be dressed in the habit of a lady, which his age would well bear, and forced his wife to go with him; who exceedingly resisted his command, well knowing to what reproach she exposed her own honour, though she had

* The Almirante of Castille was an office hereditary in the family of Enríquez. The holder was Juan Gaspar Enríquez (1623–91).

† The Marqués de 'Leche', actually Heliche, was Gasper Méndez de Haro (1629–1687), son of the 'prime minister' Luis de Haro; later viceroy in Naples.

no fear of his being discovered. The *alguacil* brought the King word that he was very sure the almirante was there in the habit of a woman, and sat next his wife, amongst many other ladies. Whereupon the King sent the officer to apprehend him in the habit he was in, and to carry him to his, the officer's, own house. And as soon as the King returned to the palace, there was an order that the *alguacil* should the next morning carry the almirante to Valladolid, four days journey from Madrid, where he had a house of his own, where he was confined not to go out of the limits of that city; and under this restraint he remained for the space of full three years: so penal a thing it is amongst that people for any man, of how great a quality soever, (there was not in Spain a man of a greater than the almirante of Castile,) to disobey or elude the judgement of the King.   *Clarendon VIII, 80–84.*

[66] A French ambassador's wife's view of the *auto de fe* of 1680
(Marie Gigault de Bellefonds, Marquise de Villars (1624–1706) is the ambassador's wife. Her letters to Madame de Coulanges and Madame de Sévigné were turned into a book.)

On the last day of June we had here in Madrid something that has not been seen for 48 years: a general *auto* of the Inquisition, in which was conducted, with great ceremony, the public trial and condemnation of several people guilty of crimes against religion, who had been gathered from all the Inquisitions of Spain. For this function, a large stage in the Plaza Major of Madrid was erected, where, between 7 in the morning and 9 at night, people were looking at the criminals and listening to their sentences. Eighteen obstinate Jews, both men and women, two apostates and one Mohammedan, were condemned to be burned; fifty other Jews or Jewesses, arrested for the first time and repentant, were condemned to several years in prison and to wearing what is called a *sambenito*, which is a yellow cassock with the red cross of St Andrew before and behind; ten others guilty of bigamy, sorcery and other misdemeanours, appeared in large paper hats, ropes around their necks, candles in their hands: the punishment for these things is usually flogging, the galleys, or banishment.

The following night, those who had been condemned to the fire were burned outside the town, on a specially raised mound, where these wretched creatures, before being executed, had to suffer a thousand torments; even the monks who were present there burning them with small flames from torches in order to convert them. Several people, who had climbed on to the mound, struck them with swords and the populace showered them with stones.

Those who had never been brought up on this Spanish preoccupation, which causes people to treat this ceremony with veneration, found it strange that, during the performance (the Inquisitor was placed much higher up than the King and on what seemed a throne), the King, from morning till night, had before his eyes these criminals and all the tortures as an entertainment, and that in his presence, and right next to him, some of the criminals were maltreated by the monks who beat them several times at the foot of an altar to get them to kneel down by force.

One saw the Grandees of Spain acting as sergeants since, besides the servants of the Inquisition who led forth each guilty person, those who were condemned to the fire were led on to the pyre by two Grandees of Spain, who held them. One saw extremely ignorant monks impetuously haranguing these Jews, without giving them any sort of reason for destroying their religion, while some of the criminals replied with as much knowledge as coolness, and others were gagged for fear they should speak. They appeared at all these moments, right up to their death, with a bearing worthy of a better cause, and some even threw themselves on to the fire. These tortures do not greatly diminish the number of Jews to be met with in Spain and especially in Madrid where, while some of them were being punished so ferociously, others are employed in finance, well-considered and respected and nevertheless recognized as being from Jewish families.

Shortly after this execution, a certain Don Ventura Dionis obtained the title of Marquis, from the King, for 50,000 écus. His father had given even more for the order of St James and it was known that his uncle was one of the elders of the

Synagogue in Amsterdam*. There are quite a lot in the farms
and in the King's receiverships, where usually they are let alone
for a while until they are rich enough to be pursued. They are
made to pay considerable sums to avoid the final victimization,
which makes one think that this great apparatus for judgement
of a few wretches is more the result of ostentation on the part of
the inquisitors than a real religious zeal.

Marquise de Villars, 186–189.

[67] Saint-Simon's visit (1721)

As I was writing this reply, Don Gaspard Girón† invited me to
go and see the illuminations in the Plaza Mayor. I finished my
letter promptly; we got into a carriage, while the most important among the people I had brought with me got into
others of mine. We were taken by detours to avoid the glimmer
of the lights on approaching, and arrived at a beautiful house
which gave on to the centre of the Plaza, and which is the one
where the King and Queen go to see the fiestas. We saw no light
at all when we alighted, nor when we mounted the stairs;
everything had been very well shut; but on going into the room
which looked on the Plaza, we were completely dazzled, and
straight away, going on to the balcony, I was lost for words for
seven or eight minutes.

The surface area of this plaza is much vaster than any I have
seen in Paris or elsewhere, and longer than it is wide. The five
storeys of the houses which surround it are all the same level,
each with windows equal in size and distance apart, and each
with a balcony of which the length and breadth are exactly the
same, with iron balustrades also all similar in height and
workmanship, and all exactly the same on all five storeys.

* In a dispatch to the King, on 8 July 1680, the Marquis de Villars wrote:
'The Prince of Parma must leave immediately . . . the title of Marquis has
been sold to the son of a Jew for 15,000 pistoles.' On the other hand, an
Ambrosio Dionis is mentioned in the *Gazette* (news from Madrid of 23
February 1681) as one of the principal bankers of Madrid, besides
Domenico Grillo and Francisco de Montserrat. The latter obtained in
March 1681 the title of Marqués de Tamarit.
† Gaspard Girón (1652–1727), grand marshal of the household under
Philip V.

On each of all these balconies are placed two large flambeaux of white wax, one at each end, very simply leant against the curve of the balustrade, so as to appear leaning out without being attached to anything. It is incredible what light that gives out, the splendour is astonishing, and it has an indescribable grandeur which really grips one. You can read the smallest letters with no difficulty in the centre, and in all the parts, of the plaza without the ground floor being lit.

As soon as I appeared on the balcony, everybody in the square gathered under the windows and cried out to me 'Señor, *toro, toro!*' It was people asking me to obtain a bull-fight holiday, which is the one thing in the world which arouses their greatest passion, and which the King, for the last few years, has not wanted to allow because of principles of conscience.

Saint-Simon, Vol. 39, 2–3

[68] An *auto de fe* in the eighteenth century.

. . . *Relaxed* in effigy.* I. Francisco Jerónimo López de la Cruz, native of the city of Sigüenza, resident of this Court, married, a doctor by profession, the oldest in the General Hospital, aged 64 years, died in the prisons of this Holy Office; was condemned to take part in the *auto* in the form of a statue representing his person, with *sambenito*† and crown of flames, with his bones being exhumed and relaxed with his effigy for heresy, for being a Judaizer, a negative person and convicted.

2. Beatriz de León y Contreras, born and resident in this Court, widow, aged 58 years, dead in prison, condemned to be taken out in effigy representing her person, with *sambenito* and crown of thorns, her bones to be exhumed and relaxed in effigy, for Judaizing heresy, a negative person and convicted . . .

Relaxed in person. 7. Juan López, native of the city of Berganza, in the realm of Portugal, resident of this court, widower, by profession silk-weaver and retailer of tobacco, aged 80 years old, agreed that he practised Jewish rights by the

---

* 'Relaxed' meant, in those circumstances, handed over to the civil authority.

† *Sambenito* was a special garment of penitence; see No. 66.

Inquisition of Coimbra of that monarchy, in 1667, was condemned to leave the *auto* in *sambenito* and crown of flames, for heretical Jewry, fell back into criminal conduct and convicted; his person was relaxed to justice and the secular arm, and being penitent was garroted and his body burned . . .

9. Manuel Custodio de Sota y Herrera (alias) Manuel de Guzmán Castro y Herrera, native of the city of Granada, stepchild of Francisco de Robles and resident in this Court, bachelor; with no employment, aged 19 years, was condemned to leave the *auto* with *sambenito* and crown of flames for partaking of Judaizing heresy, denied the crime and was convicted as being impenitent and inconsiderately pertinancious in his error and his heretical blasphemy; and so maintaining himself, without having wished to reduce it, his body was tied to a stake and handed over live to the flames of fire.

10. Josefa de Vargas y Machuca (*alias*) la Josefina, native and resident in this Court; married, aged 39 years, left the Court in the dress of a penitent with *sambenito* with two crosses, a wax candle in her hands . . ., was reconciled according to the rules, with formal penitence, for her Judaizing heresy, with confiscation of goods, condemned to wear a cowl and remain in prison for one year . . .

12. Juan Pacheco, native of the city of Cuenca, resident of it but living in this Court, bachelor, unemployed, aged 40 years, left the *auto* as a penitent, with *sambenito* with two crosses, wax candle in hand, rope round the neck with two knots; was formally reconciled, with confiscation of goods, cowl and prison permanently, and the day after the *auto* was given 200 strokes of the whip in the streets of this Court . . .

Penitence with Abjuration of Levi. 21. Francisca Avendaño (*alias*) la Gitana, native of Aranda de Duero, resident in this Court, spinster, by profession saleswoman of clothes, aged 54 years, left the *auto* as a penitent, with a placard proclaiming her to be a cheat, crown, wax candle in the hands, rope with two knots round the neck for being a liar and for sorcery, confessed her Judaism, was absolved with a warning, and denounced and exiled from the Court and from the city of Aranda de Duero and twenty leagues around them for the space of ten years of which the first three would be passed shut up in the royal prison of La Galera in this Court and placed in charge of a

learned person who would instruct and fortify her with the
mysteries of our holy Catholic faith and dissuade her from her
superstitious frauds and the day after the *auto* she was to be
given 200 strokes of the whip in the public streets.

Díaz Plaja, III, 142–145 (1722).

[69] Description of the fiesta upon the occasion of
Charles III's public entry into the capital, 15 July
1760

We arrived at the balcony of the English Ambassador* in the
Plaça Mayor about half an hour after three in the afternoon,
and were at once struck with the chearfullest, gayest sight
imaginable. The *square*, which is large, was thronged with
people; the *balconies* all ornamented with different coloured
silks, and crouded from the top to the bottom of the houses; the
avenues to the square were built up into balconies, and a sort of
sloping scaffolding was placed round for the common people,
elevated above the ground or pit, if I may so call it, about eight
or nine feet, with openings in proper places, and wooden
doors.

First came in the coaches of the *cavaliers*, four in number, of
an antique and singular make, with glasses at the ends, and
quite open at the sides: The cavaliers were placed at the doors
of their coaches, from whence they bowed to the people, and
the balconies, as they passed round the square; and they were
accompanied by their sponsors, the Dukes of Osuna, of Baños,
of Arcos, and Medinaceli†. Before the royal family came a
company of *halberdiers*, after which the King's coaches in great
state, I believe about seven or eight in number, preceding his
Carosse de Respect, which was extremely rich, with red and
gold ornaments, and beautiful painted pannels: Then a coach
with some of the great officers, who go always immediately
before the King; next came the King and Queen in a very
sumptuous coach of blue, with all the ornaments of massive
silver, and the crown at the top; the trappings of the horses

---

* The English ambassador was George Hervey, 2nd Earl of Bristol
(1721–1775).
† These were the premier grandees of Spain then.

were likewise silver, with large white plumes. These were followed by the coaches of the Prince of Asturias*, the two infanta's, and Don Luis†, with their attendants.

Their Majesties were placed opposite to us, in a gilt balcony, with a canopy and curtains of scarlet and gold; the Queen on that occasion taking the right hand. On the right hand of the King's balcony were placed the rest of the royal family: and on the left were ranged the gentlemen of the bedchamber in a row; all dressed in a very fine uniform of blue and red, richly embroidered with gold. The *halberdiers* marched from the King's balcony, which was in the center on one side, and forming themselves into two lines, fronting different ways, instantly cleared the square of the croud, who retired into the scaffolding, erected for them round it. Next the halberdiers formed themselves in a line before the scaffold, under the King's balcony. Then appeared *two companies of boys*, dressed in an uniform with caps, and red taffeta jackets, ranged against the right and left hand side of the square, who carrying buckets of water in their hands, watered the stage as they crossed over to the side opposite to them. This being performed, the six chief *Alguazils* of the town, mounted upon fine horses, covered with trappings, and dressed in the old Spanish habits, black with slashed sleeves, great white flowing wigs, and hats with plumes of different-coloured feathers, advanced towards the King's balcony, under which they were obliged to stay the whole time to receive his orders; except when they were frightened away by the bulls, when they were obliged to ride for it, being absolutely unarmed and defenceless.

Having obtained the king's permission for the *bull-feast*, the troops belonging to the *knights* entered upon the stage in four large companies, dressed in liveries of *Moorish habits* of silk, richly and elegantly ornamented with lace and embroidery: These marched first to make their bow to the King's balcony, and then in procession round the square: and from the elegance, singularity, and variety of their uniforms, made one of the most delightful scenes that can be conceived. After them

* The future Charles IV. 'Prince of Asturias' is the title given to the heir to the throne in Spain.
† The Infante Don Luis (1727–85), ex-Cardinal Archbishop of Toledo, which post he abandoned in order to marry; an early patron of Goya.

came the *four knights*, habited in old Spanish dress, with plumes in their hats, and mounted upon the most beautiful horses: each carried in his hand a slender lance, and was attended by two men on foot, dressed in light silk, of the colour of his livery, with a sort of cloaks or mantles of the same; these never forsake his side, and are indeed his principal defence. After the *cavaliers* had done their homage to the King, their companies retired, and there remained with them only, besides those who walked by their side, a few dressed with mantles in the same manner, who disperst themselves over the stage. The cavaliers then disposed themselves for the encounter; the first placing himself opposite to the door of the place where the bulls are kept, the other at some distance behind him, and so on.

The King then making the *signal* for the doors to be opened, the bull appeared, to the sound of martial music, and the loud acclamations of the people: and seeing one of the attendants of the first cavalier spreading his cloak before him, aimed directly at him; but the man easily evaded him, and gave his master an opportunity of breaking his spear in the bull's neck. In the same manner the bull was tempted to engage the other cavaliers, and always with the same success: till having received the honourable wounds from their lances, he was encountered by the other men on foot: who, after playing with him, with an incredible agility, as long as they think proper, easily put an end to him, by thrusting a sword either into his neck or side, which brings him to the ground; and then they finish him at once, *by striking a dagger, or the point of a sword, behind his horns into the spine, which is always immediate death*. After this the bull is instantly hurried off by mules, finely adorned, and decked with trapping for the occasion.

My apprehensions were at first principally for the men *on foot*; but I soon perceived they were in no sort of danger: their cloaks are a certain security to them, as the bull always aims at it, and they can therefore easily evade the blow. Besides this, there are so many to assist each other, that they can always lead the bull which way they please, and even in the worst case they can preserve themselves by leaping into the scaffold, as they frequently did.

The *knights* are in much more danger; their horses being too full of fire to be exactly directed; they cannot therefore so well evade the aim, and are liable every moment to be overthrown with their horses, if the attendants by their side did not assist them. Two beautiful horses nevertheless we saw gored; one of which was overthrown with his rider, but fortunately the man escaped any mischief from his fall. The courage of these horses is so great, that they have been often known to advance towards the bull, when their bowels were trailing upon the ground.

After the knights had sufficiently tired themselves with these exploits, the King gave them leave to retire and repose. We had then bulls let out (one at a time always) from another door, of a more furious nature; these were encountered entirely by the men on foot, who were so far from fearing their rage, that the whole business was to irritate them more, by throwing upon their necks, and other parts, little barbed darts, ornamented with bunches of paper, like the *Bacchanalian Thyasus*, some of which were filled with gunpowder, and burst in the manner of a squib or serpent, as soon as they were fastened to the bull. Nothing can be imagined more tormenting than these darts, which stick about him, and never lose their hold. But the courage and amazing dexterity, with which they are thrown, takes off your attention from the cruelty of it. Another method they have of diverting themselves with the fury of the bull, is by dressing up *goat-skins*, blown up with wind, into figures, and placing them before him, which makes a very ridiculous part of the entertainment. Many of the bulls, however, would not attack them, and one of the most furious that did, shewed more fear than in encountering his most sturdy antagonists: so great is their apprehension from an object that stands firm, and seems not to be dismayed at their approach. There is likewise another kind of larger spear, which is held by a man obliquely, with the end in the ground, and the point towards the door, where the bull comes out, who never fails to run at it, with great danger to the man, as he is always thrown down; but greater to the bull, who commonly receives the point in his head or neck, and with such force, that we saw a spear broke short, that was much thicker than my arm. They also baited one bull with dogs, which shewed as much courage and obstinate perseverance as any of that breed in England. As to the laws of this spectacle, and other circumstances relative to the punctilios of the bull-feast, I cannot pretend to explain them, and imagine others, who have attempted it, have been obliged to take it mostly upon trust, nor do I think it very material . . .

Nothing can be imagined more crowded than the houses, even to the tops of their tiles; and dearly enough they paid for their pleasure, pent together in the hottest sun, and with the most suffocating heat that can be endured. Nor do I greatly wonder at them, when I consider how much my own country, that is certainly as humane as any nation, is bigotted to its customs of bull-baiting, cock-fighting, etc. – I do not deny, that this is a remnant of Moorish, or perhaps Roman barbarity; and that it will not bear the speculations of the closet, or the compassionate feelings of a tender heart. But, after all, we must not speculate too nicely, lest we should lose the hardness of manhood in the softer sentiments of philosophy. There is a certain degree of ferocity requisite in our natures; and which, as on the one hand it should be restrained within proper bounds, that it may not degenerate into cruelty; so, on the other, we must not refine to much upon it, for fear of sinking into effeminacy. This custom is far from having cruelty for its object; bravery and intrepidity, joined with ability and skill, are what obtain the loudest acclamations from the people: it has all the good effects of *chivalry*, in exciting the minds of the spectators to great actions, without the horror that prevailed in former times, of distinguishing bravery to the prejudice of our own species. It teaches to despise danger; and that the surest way to overcome it, is to look it calmly and stedfastly in the face; to afford a faithful and generous assistance to those engaged with us in enterprizes of difficulty: And in short, tho' it may not be strictly consonant to the laws of humanity and good nature, it may yet be productive of great and glorious effects; and is certainly the mark of qualities, that do honour to any nation.					*Clarke, 110–115.*

[70] The battle of July 1822
(These 'July days' were the culmination of two years of unsuccessful constitutional government, nominally under the King, Ferdinand VII. A French army soon returned to Spain, this time to put absolutism back.)

The attack on the Plaza [Mayor] was much more terrible. The principal aim of the enemies was to gain the square and particularly the Panadería whence one could dominate the square. The attacks were many and obstinate. But the fire directed by the company of grenadiers commanded by Don Juan Muguiro of the commerce of this court, the bravery and measureless audacity of the shooting men, and the skill with which the artillery was directed . . . frustrated the efforts of the enemy who had to retire defeated and with heavy losses.

Before the battle of the square began one of the enemy divisions had already captured the Puerta del Sol but were unable to penetrate the post office whose guard defended it shutting the great door, and as it had neither key nor keyhole it was attacked with an enormous stone which the robust grenadiers detached from the stairway.

A little later the enemy began to evacuate this point because they saw themselves attacked from the rear and had to retire fast. One of their columns began to mount in close order the Calle de Montera crying fiercely 'Viva el Rey,' and filling with consternation its inhabitants who believed themselves victors. But they then retreated and retired down the Calle del Arenal.

Put to flight, the assailants of the square directed themselves to the Palace to seek asylum.

The public was in expectation many hours waiting for the results of the next day's victory: when at three in the afternoon they received the happy news that the battalions of the Pardo had just given up their arms. But far from realizing such a favourable event, this obstinate unit left the city crossing the river. Immediately they were pursued and . . . the fugitives being caught near the inn of Alcorcón they were destroyed and completely dispersed.

Qu, Díaz Plaja, 'Documentos', IV, 162–63.

[71] Alexandre Dumas, 1846

(The Plaza Mayor was in 1846 the scene of celebrations commemorating the double marriages of Queen Isabella II (1830–1904) and her sister Luisa (1832–1897) to Prince Francisco de Asís de Borbón (1822–1902) and the Duke of Montpensier (1824–1890) respectively. For Dumas's role, see No. 29.)

The Plaza Major, as its name indicates, madam, is the biggest in Madrid, and as when Philip II built Madrid there was so much space, the Plaza Major is immense. After a month, preparations began; these preparations consisted of taking away the paving, spreading sand in place of the stones, erecting crash-barriers around the perimeter, establishing entrances for live horses and bulls, and exits for the dead ones, and of decorating the tiers.

These tiers only went up to the first floor of the houses. Starting from this level, the windows served as boxes. We found ourselves situated in the middle of one of the four façades of the Plaza, with the royal box on our left.

Under the royal box, which backed on to the street of San Jerónimo, a company of Halberdiers blocked an opening in the circle which could well have been thirty paces wide. These halberdiers had, under all circumstances, to stand as still as the wall they represented; if the bull were to charge them, they had to stop the beast by lowering their halberds; if, in the struggle they killed the bull, they kept it.

Opposite them, mounted on black horses, all clad in black themselves, were six *alguacils* in their ancient costumes; these six *alguacils*, who are only armed with a sword and a hand-whip, seemed to be placed there to amuse the people, alongside the tragedy. Indeed, the bull, who does not at all understand these six men with whips and dressed in black, took cunning pleasure in particularly attacking them; whence, the running, the jumping, which sent the people of Madrid into rapture.

The Plaza offers a unique spectacle, with its tiers, its balconies, its windows, its roofs full of spectators; one or two belfries surge skywards, overlooking the Plaza; on each protuberance of these belfries was suspended a man or child.

More than 100,000 people could see and be seen.

Dumas, 136–141, (1846).

Chamartín

(Chamartín in the eighteenth century was a village outside Madrid. It is now part of the city, known because the main northern railway station is there.)

[72] Napoleon's stay (1808)

Napoleon established himself in a place called Chamartín, one league from Madrid, in a country house built by the Duquesa del Infantado*, when the upheavals of the revolution forced this generous family to withdraw from Paris, where they spread so much kindness. Force of habit must be very great, since it is noticeable that this house, built in a modern style and with a very rigorous winter climate, by people accustomed to the studied elegance of the most beautiful dwellings in Paris, does not possess a single chimney.   *M. de Pradt, 200–201 (1808)*

---

* The dowager Duquesa, born Princess von Salm. Lady Holland describes this house as a 'most delicious residence' with 'extensive gardens, magnificent terrace, a tennis court' (in her *Journal*, 193).

[73] The French fail to impress the *madrileños* (1808)
(André François, Comte Miot de Mélito (1762–1841) was
Joseph Bonaparte's comptroller of his household, later a well-
known scholar.)

The strictest order and discipline were observed by the French
troops on entering Madrid after the capitulation, and the
inhabitants suffered only from the evils inseparable from the
presence of a foreign army. Entire tranquillity reigned in the
town from 4 December, and every one was free to return to his
ordinary occupations.

But this moderate conduct, which was rendered all the more
generous by the hostility of the inhabitants, obtained for the
French neither regard nor gratitude from those whom they
spared; and hatred, which the clemency of the Conqueror had
failed to abate, might be discerned in the gloomy and severe
countenances of the few inhabitants who showed themselves
outside their houses. None came to meet the French, none
sought to propitiate their new masters by attentions to the
generals and officers. Even curiosity seemed to have lost its
power. For several days no women appeared in the streets;
none even could be seen at the windows. The theatres were
reopened by order of the French Government, but no Spaniards attended the performances. At the houses in which the
soldiers were quartered, everything they required was either
given them, or they were suffered to take it, but nothing was
offered, and the masters of the house avoided as far as possible
all contact with their guests. Never did the inflexible Castillian
character display more obstinacy, and never was the greatest
misfortune that can happen to a capital city, that of falling into
the power of the enemy, borne with more dignity and pride.

Struck by the extraordinary deportment of the people,
Napoleon was obliged to recognize that he had been mistaken,
and that the seizure of Madrid had not produced the effect he
had intended . . .

In vain did the Emperor try to change the public mind by
using the means that had succeeded elsewhere. He had flattered
himself that his famous name, and the desire to behold so
extraordinary a man would have attracted the populace to him;
that the road from Madrid to Chamartín would be thronged

with a curious multitude; and that he would be watched and followed. Nothing of the kind occurred. He passed through the town to visit the palace of the Kings of Spain; no one followed nor even stayed to look at him on his way. He held a grand review of the army on the plain between Chamartín and Madrid. It had been announced two days beforehand in the hope that some of the inhabitants of the town would be attracted by curiosity, and that he should receive some kind of homage from them. In this also he was disappointed: the review took place, but there was not a single Spaniard present.

This determined enmity, and still more this disdainful indifference, were profoundly irritating to Napoleon, and were probably not without influence on his ulterior views for Spain. From the measures which he took after the capitulation of Madrid, and especially from his proclamation of 7 December to the Spaniards, it is clear that he already contemplated the annexation of at least a part of the Peninsula to his Empire. The proclamation ends with these remarkable words: 'If my efforts are in vain, if you do not respond to my confidence, it will only remain for me to treat you as conquered provinces and to place my brother on another throne. I shall then put the crown of Spain on my own head, and I shall know how to make evildoers respect it, for God has given me both the strength and the will to overcome every obstacle.'   *Miot, 293–297*

[74] Napoleon asks what possesses the Spanish people (1808)

In the midst of all this, some Spanish parliamentarians came to beg Napoleon's mercy in the name of all the inhabitants. His Imperial Majesty, who foresaw the irreparable misfortunes resultant from a capital taken by force, received them kindly and said to them, with the good-heartedness that characterizes great leaders: 'Who are the agents leading these infuriated people? Are they the monks, the wealthy, or the officers commanding the regular troops? If the latter want to fight, why don't they take up battle formations in the middle of a plain, instead of barricading themselves in a city, so that innocent people, women, children, and the old will be butchered? Only cowards and barbarians use such methods. Go at once,' he told them, 'and tell your commanding general that, if towards 3 p.m. I see no standards flying from the tops of the belltowers as a signal of your surrender, I will give the order to put everyone to the sword immediately.' This speech was delivered with so much energy and eloquence that the deputies, full of consternation and remorse, went directly to Madrid; and soon the firing ceased throughout.

> *From the report of General Dautaincourt on the capture of Madrid, published in Balagny, 486–487*

[75] Napoleon leaves (1808): letter to the Empress Josephine in Paris

Madrid, 22 December 1808

I am leaving directly to grapple with the English, who seem to have received their reinforcements, and to be making a show of courage. The weather is beautiful; my health is perfect; do not be anxious about anything.

NAPOLÉON

Napoléon, 'Correspondance', Vol. 18, 146

Lavapiés

[76] The square known as Lavapiés (also El Avapies) was the centre of a very special kind of *manolería* (Ramón Mesonero Romanos (1803–82) was the first modern historian of Madrid. *El Antiguo Madrid* (1843) is his best-known book.)

But returning to the special type of *manolo* of Madrid, according to what Goya has left us in his *caprichos* and in the delicious *sainetes* of Don Ramón de la Cruz* we must point out that they have suffered constant and successive modifications in their customs, manners and dress, their favourite professions continuing to be as in the past those of shoemaker, tavern keeper, butcher, or coachman, or salesmen in iron, clothes, tallow, and skins which constituted until recently the guilds of clothiers, kitchen utensil makers, horsedealers, and others. They have abandoned the cue and hairnet in their

---

* Ramón de la Cruz (1731–94), best known for his *sainetes* (from *saín*, a piquant sauce), one-act plays performed in intervals of theatres.

hair style, the stockings and the doublet, the short brightly coloured cloak with sleeves and the pointed hat with which they were wont to appear at the beginning of this century. Their present dress, modified with an imitation of those of Andalusia and of the more elevated classes, consists generally of a tight short jacket with a multitude of buttons, an open waistcoat and with equivalent buttoning but without fastening more than the top one; embroidered shirt folded round the neck and held by a handkerchief of striking colour, fastened with a ring on the chest; yellow or red skirt; trousers narrow at the ankle; white stocking, and short and fitted shoe. The round and high hat, glossy and shining, has been replaced by the little Andalusian hat with a low crown and broad brim turned up (*sombrero calañés*). No *manolo* has abandoned the stick in the hand and the terrible knife in the belt . . .

As for the *manola*, a precious classic type now vanishing from sight, and whose grace, elegance and ease of manner are proverbial in all Spain, who does not know the puffed up bell-shaped and well-adorned petticoat, the mother-of-pearl stocking, the tiny shoe, the generous *mantilla de tira*, and the skilful braided hair of Paca la Salada (the witty), of Geroma la Castañera (chestnut-seller), Manola la Ribeteadora (the seamstress), Pepa la Naranjera (orange-seller), and Maruja, Damiana and Ruperta, a flower-seller, radish-seller and cigarmaker? Who does not know from memory their graphic sayings, their impromptu epigrams, their proverbial ferocity and arrogance? Who does not see with feeling the confusion of this gracious specimen with the repugnant alter ego of the mondaine woman who in her desire to appear well has sought to parody the charm, the dress and the special ways of the *manola*?

Mesonero Romanos, 194–96.

[77] Gautier meets the last *manola* (c. 1840)

Once, walking through the *Rastro* quarter, the Temple of Madrid, having stepped over a large number of tramps sleeping stretched out on the ground covered with appalling rags, I found myself in a deserted alley, and there I saw, for the first and last time, the long-sought *manola*. She was a tall, strapping lass, about twenty-four years old, the oldest that a *manola* or a *grisette* can be. Her complexion was swarthy, her expression steady and sad, her mouth a little thick and something a trifle African about her features. An enormous tress of hair, so black it appeared blue, plaited like basket rushes, went all round her head, and was finally attached by a high, ornate comb; bunches of coral beads hung from her ears; her tawny neck was decorated with a necklace of the same substance; a mantilla of black velvet framed her head and shoulders; her dress, as short as those of the Swiss women from the canton of Berne, was embroidered cloth and showed her slim, wiry legs clad in tight black silk stockings; her shoes were satin, as in the ancient fashion; a red fan trembled like a vermillion butterfly in her fingers, which were covered in silver rings. The last of the *manolas* turned the corner of the street, and disappeared from my sight, as I marvelled at having seen a costume from Duponchel*, a disguise from the Opera, walking about the actual living world!

I also saw in the Prado a few *pasiegas* from Santander in their national dress; these *pasiegas* are reputed to be the best nurses in Spain, and their love of children is proverbial, as in France is the honesty of the people of the Auvergne; they wear a red cloth skirt with large pleats, edged with a wide braid, a corset of black velvet likewise braided with gold, and for headdress a handkerchief of gaudy colours, all accompanied by silver jewellery and other savage finery. These women are very beautiful, they have a very striking and grand nature. The habit of nursing children on the arm gives them an arched back posture which goes well with their well-developed chests. To have a *pasiega* in national dress is a kind of luxury similar to having a *Klephtle†* behind your carriage.   *Gautier, 84.*

[78] Barea (1920)

Old Madrid, the Madrid of my childhood, is a great surge of clouds or of waves, I do not know which. But beyond all those

* Charles Edward Duponchel (1795–1868), Director of the Academy of Music, opera director, jeweller, etc.
† A Greek people who fled to the northern mountains during the Turkish invasion.

whites and blues, beyond all the songs and sounds and vibrations, there is one predominant strain: El Avapies.

At that time it was the frontier of Madrid. It was the end of Madrid, and the end of the world. With that critical instinct for the right word, which two thousand years since earned the tag of *vox populi, vox dei*, the people had baptized the limits of El Avapies; there were the *Americas* and there was *El Mundo Nuevo*, the New World. It was another world indeed. So far civilization and the city reached, and there they ended.

There began a world of abstruse things and beings. There the city cast its ash and spume, and so did the nation. The seething waters of Madrid threw their scum from the centre to the periphery, and the scum of the seething waters of Spain was sucked from the periphery to the centre. The two waves met and formed a belt which spanned the town. Only the initiated, the Civil Guards, and we children penetrated into the live barrier.

Gullies and slopes bearded with rough ears of grass eternally yellow, dry and harsh. Fumes from factory chimneys and evil-smelling trickles from stables. Allotments with lumpy soil, black and putrid; foul streams and parched cracks in the earth. Epilatic trees, hostile thistles and thorns, gaunt dogs with angular ribs, dusty telegraph poles with their white china cups broken, goats browsing on waste paper, empty rusted tins, huts sunk to their knees in the ground. Gypsies with bold side-whiskers, gypsy women in motley, grease-stained petticoats, beggars with abundant beards and lice, children all bottom and belly, filth trickling down their legs, the navel button protruding from their dusky paunches. This was called the '*Quartier* of the Injuries'.

It was the lowest rung in the social ladder that began at the Plaza de Oriente* in the Royal Palace with its gates open to plumed helmets and diamond-spangled *décolletés*, and ended in El Avapies, which then spewed out the last dregs and deposited them in the other world, in the Americas and the *Mundo Nuevo*.

Thus El Avapiés was the pointer of the scales, the crucial point between existence and non-existence. One came to El Avapies from above or from below. Whoever came from above had stepped down the last step left to him before the final and

* See No. 82.

absolute fall. Whoever came from below had scaled the first step upwards, which might lead to anywhere and anything. Millionaires have passed through El Avapies before crossing the outer belt of the Rondas and turning into drunken beggars. Ragpickers, collectors of cigarette stubs and waste paper, filthy from spittle and trampling feet, have climbed the step of El Avapies and come to be millionaires. In El Avapies, all the prides exist side by side, the pride of having been everything and no longer wanting to be anything, and the pride of having been nothing and wanting to be everything.

If those tremendous and wantonly cruel forces were to clash, life would be impossible. But the two waves never break against each other. Between them lies a firm, calm beach which absorbs the impact of both and converts them into currents which ebb and flow: all Avapies works.

In its houses built with prison galleries running round their courtyards, passages open to the winds, a single lavatory for all the inmates, a door and a window per cell, live the plasterer, the smith, the carpenter, the newspaper vendor, the blind beggar from the corner, the bankrupt, the rag-and-bone man, and the poet. In those courtyards with their pavement of rounded pebbles, a dripping water-tap in the middle, all the tongues of one language meet: the refined accent of the gentleman, the shameless talk of the pimp, the slang of thieves and beggars, the high-flown rhetories of the budding writer. You hear horrifying blasphemies and exquisitely tender phrases.

Every day during many years of my childhood I walked from the gates of the Palace down to the gates of the New World, and scaled the slope on my way back. At times I went into the Palace and watched from the marble galleries guarded by halberdiers the pageant of the royalty, the princes and the grandees of Spain. At times I crossed the frontier into the no-man's-world beyond the New World and watched naked gypsies squatting in the sun and killing the lice which the swarthy fingers of their mother or sister plucked from their hair, one by one. I watched the ragpickers separating the mountain of refuse into heaps of food for themselves and their animals, and heaps of rubbish which they would be able to sell for a few coppers.   *Barea, 88–89*

Other Squares

[79] El Rastro: Baroja (1910)
(The Rastro is the antique and second-hand market of
Madrid, once much more lively than now.)

Some days we played truant from the Institute and went to the
Rastro.

At that time to get there, at the end of the Calle de Estudios in
what was then called the Cabecera of the Rastro, and now is a
statue of the 'hero of Cascorro'*, there was a block of old and
decrepit houses which intercepted the way to the Ribera de
Curtidores and which was called the *Tapón* (plug) of the Rastro.

To the right there opened the Callejón del Cuervo. This was
dark, full of shops selling black clothes, which had inside,
hanging up along the walls, second-hand trousers and jackets,
old and grimy hats, peasants' clothes, brown capes, lace,
tailors' dummies made of pasteboard, with painted faces and

* The 'hero of Cascorro' was Angel Gonzalo García (1876–97), a
Spanish soldier killed after a brave action in the Cuban war.

glass eyes, with long real hair, dummies who in their day had served in shop windows or in hairdressers'.

For a schoolboy, dressed as a spoiled upper-class child in bowler hat and new suit, to enter these culs-de-sac of the Rastro was something risky. I was liable to have a rotten tomato thrown at my head.

The Rastro was itself a curious place then, almost medieval. There was sold almost everything imaginable: used clothes, pictures, false teeth, books, medicines, chestnuts, coach wheels, trusses, shoes. There one met all types: Moors, Jews, blacks, travelling charlatans, rat-catchers and sellers of caged birds (*pajaritos sabios*).

There were also artful players of the three-card trick and small time swindlers and tricksters . . .

The Rastro did not then have this air of antique shops which it has acquired now, since the war, nor did elegant people go there, only second-hand dealers . . .

There were strange advertisements, such as one on a doorway in the Calle de las Velas written on a bit of cardboard which ran:

Here are sold	*Se venden*	
Tortoises	*galápagos*	
And other domestic	*y otros animales*	
Animals	*domésticos*	Baroja, 'Desde', 48–49

[80] La Moncloa: Azaña's regrets (c. 1928)
(The charming hills of the district known as Moncloa beyond Madrid to the north-west became the site of the University in the late 1920s: the University had already been moved from Alcalá de Henares to the Calle Ancha de San Bernardino in 1836–37.)

. . . At the end of the Calle de la Princesa I met the desolation of the ruined Moncloa. At that point there used to be a walk of old pines, twisted and rustic, towards the old engineering school.

All that part of the Moncloa, with the landscape as far as the river, was most beautiful, soft, elegant: the best of Madrid. Already nothing remains: 'a great avenue', new skyscrapers, the horror of urbanization.

I saw with pleasure that the University City was being built. But I could not imagine that in this upper part of the Moncloa they were going to wreak such havoc. Nor could I imagine how the destruction would cause me such sadness. Because really I have been sad all morning and even now the impression has not gone. How many evenings of autumn passed in that place! Its perfect time was autumn. Delicateness, tranquillity, admirable greys. And that serene light, so endearing, so melancholy! Had Madrid been an artistic city, they would not have been able to do away with the Moncloa. But here they pass weeks making pretentious and very 'madrileñista' lamentations for the destruction of the Apollo Theatre and nobody, that I know, has made any elegy of the Moncloa.

Today I have realized how much I used to like it. There I learned to be emotional about the landscape. In fifteen or twenty years the new place will be without doubt very beautiful: I don't doubt it – parks, groves, etc. But the luminous candour and elegant rusticity of the abandoned Moncloa, who will return them to us? And those who did not know them will never know what Madrid has lost.

Of the University City I have seen four or six enormous buildings under construction. Red and grey masses, resembling barracks or factories. I do not know what will become of it all.

Doctor Negrín* is already thinking of putting the school of engineering and I don't know what other establishment in the Casa de Campo. It is fatal. And afterwards or at the same time the Pardo. In half a century Madrid will have left to it none of the good which it has now. Fortunately I shall not see it.

Azaña IV, 221

[81] Plaza de la Cebada: the Marquis de Custine attends an execution (1831)
(This old market square was used as a place for executions from 1790 to 1834. It is still a large market place today.)

* Dr Juan Negrín (1889–1956) was Dean of the Medical School, and carried through the changes. He was Prime Minister of the Republic 1937–1939, and died in exile.

This morning a bookseller, a rich man, was hanged. He was well considered in Madrid. The reason for his death was stated in the *Diario de Madrid* roughly as follows: 'At 12.30, at the Plaza de la Cebada, the bookseller Myard will be executed. When he is dead a piece of paper will be stuck on his face with the inscription "For Political Crimes".'

Here is his crime as told me by trustworthy people. He used often to repeat that Spain lacked a constitution, and that now this country could hope to obtain one through the intervention of France!! . . . You will say that I am more of a traveller than a man, if I swear to you that I had an awful curiosity to see this wretch die, less to see him himself than to observe the passions of the people at such a solemn occasion. Half an hour before the designated time, I went to the market place at la Cebada, and I stopped very close to the scaffold. In Madrid, executions are a religious ceremony, since there the priest sanctions all the actions of the state: I was struck by the composure, the calm, the silence of the populace who, like myself, were walking towards the place of punishment.

An hour before the criminal was to be led to the scaffold, men ran through the streets, money boxes and little bells in their hands, asking for alms in the name of the condemned man. This money is destined to pay for masses for the repose of his soul. At the same time, priests went into all the churches where they awaited the signal of his death in order to fulfil this charitable office: thus the mystic sacrifice followed immediately upon the accomplishment of the legal sacrifice, and it diminished the horror. Compassion requires a glimmer of hope: evil without remedy drives a man into stupefied terror.

When I arrived near the scaffold, I found it surrounded by quite a large number of soldiers; this is an innovation, the display of military force not usually being deployed in Madrid on similar occasions. At 12.30 the noise of drums announced the arrival of the procession: officers and mounted dragoons kept back the crowd which seemed no more avid for blood than it was touched by pity; nobody around me was very moved.

I knew that the unhappy man's wife had yesterday been to Aranjuez to beg for his pardon; the King was the only injured party; I could not deny a secret hope. Many people say that, if pardon had been granted, there would have been fewer happy people than discontented ones. You would have to know public opinion well to appreciate this assertion; it is something not given to a traveller who has only been here eight days, in a country where mystery presides over life. You are assured that, if it had been a fine day yesterday, the condemned man would have been saved. The King would have gone out, he would have encountered the wife come to implore him, and he would have shown mercy. It rained; the King stayed at home; the rain decided the execution!

Looking at the side whence the procession approached, I first of all saw some mounted men appear, dressed a little like priests;

'What are these ecclesiastical cavaliers doing?' I asked my neighbour.

'They are not priests, they are *alguacils*.' So I asked why such myrmidons wore religious costume. No one could tell me. It is because of all this sort of intimacy with the police that the Catholic religion will become discredited in Spain.

The silence grew around me, the crowd was still; the cross appeared to be upheld by a group of men dressed in black and, following it, I saw emerge, at the bottom of a street made narrower by so many people, the wretch whose soul was about to ask for justice against vengeance.

He was dressed in white, about forty years old, mounted on a donkey, supported by his confessor, and assisted by another priest. His joined hands were black; I only learned the reason for this circumstance later, it was the effect of the cord binding them so violently together. The execution imposes this pain on the victim to spare him a greater one. Will not the thus swollen arms be numb to the axe's blow that cuts through the wrists? These murdered hands carried a piece of paper, on which was engraved the face of Christ.

At that moment, a man turned towards me and said in French: 'He is not afraid!' But I myself was not without fear: I had been warned to be extremely careful, above all necessary for a Frenchman exposed to the popular rage which could be suddenly aroused. Today in Spain, the authorities have so many prejudices against France, that they would not intervene to protect us, if a howling mob tore us to pieces in the streets

. . . I kept quiet; I would have broken my silence only to plead the cause of humanity against terror, and that would have been to anticipate a useless peril.

My eyes followed this victim of fear. Despotism is really only to be feared when it feels itself weak.

The unhappy man, although already very pale, grew paler still when he saw the scaffold: he turned his head away, he leant towards his confessor, and seemed to listen to the words of Christianity with a compassion that moved me to tears. A condemned man, one minute before his execution, is such an extraordinary being, so apart from other men, so close to God, that you can only contemplate with respectful astonishment this creature suspended between two worlds by creatures as wretched as himself, and who do not even understand all the impact of the sentence they have carried out. By means of the judicial execution, society presents Heaven with a victim in order to distance itself from the responsibility of the forfeit . . . But does this legal barbarity suffice to free the community of all responsibility? Will God accept the bleeding offering? Can the crime be redeemed by cruelty? Such were the thoughts that occupied me. And then I condemned myself, and reproached myself for having had the courage to come and watch a man perish for so little reason.

When he had come to within twenty paces of the scaffold, I suddenly moved away, asking myself under my breath if a government of monks was worth such sacrifices.

Also perhaps, in the century in which we live, it is no particular order of things which is defended by similar harsh acts, it is the possibility of maintaining anywhere any kind of government. I walked along absorbed by a train of contradictory reflections, when my heart was filled with an icy cold; the tolling of the bell told me that the punishment was over! This bell announces to the priests of the principal churches in Madrid that it is time to cease the prayers for the dying and begin the mass for the dead.

I do not know how to paint for you the mixture of indignation and pity which such an iniquitous sentence aroused in me, and the manner in which this truly Christian society executed it. There customs really do prevail over laws. Be present at the punishment of a condemned man with us: the populace has a brutality that seems to outdo the harshness of the institutions.

I went into the first church I found open: it was that of Our Lady of Victory*. There I found, right in the midst of day, the nave and the choir draped with black and, underneath a majestic hanging which served as dome to the high altar, I could see the Holy Sacrament sparkling with diamonds in the centre of an aureole, or rather of a sun of burning candles. I fell to my knees amongst the crowd prostrated, like myself, and profoundly meditative; I experienced feelings for which I cannot find the words. Seraphic music made my heart burst. Everything became confused in my mind . . . I wept and my tongue repeated involuntarily, like an echo, these words, the summing up of my day: 'What a marvellous religion, what a noble people, what a frightful government!'

Custine, 178–84 (1831).

[82] Plaza de Oriente: a *corrida* in 1455 (Mesonero Romanos's description)
(This square in its present shape was created in front of the new royal palace by Joseph Bonaparte. But there was always a square there of a sort.)

Henry†, endowed with an ardent temperament and given over to sensual pleasures, was an example of misconduct, and in proof people refer to the story of how despite having been only recently married to the beautiful Doña Juana of Portugal‡, he allowed himself to be carried away by a vehement passion for one of the ladies who accompanied the Queen called Guiomar de Castro§ who was also supposed to be very beautiful. Wishing one day to please her he arranged a *corrida* in the square in front of the Alcázar of Madrid. Once the Queen knew the object of that fiesta she forbade all her ladies to look out of

---

* This church, de la Vitoria, in the Puerta del Sol, has since vanished even though it was the home of the much-venerated Our Lady of Soledad (Solitude).
† Henry IV of Castille (1425–1474).
‡ Joanna of Portugal (1438–1475).
§ Guiomar de Castro, illegitimate daughter of the Conde de Monsanto.

the windows of the Alcázar. But this order was scandalously not carried out by the proud favourite, who appeared at one of them. The Queen, indignant, waited till she passed by a certain staircase and then, coming on her brusquely, whipped her with a clog. At the cries of Doña Guiomar the King came in hastily and put himself between the two women, and then launched violently at the Queen, protecting Doña Guiomar, with whom he thereafter continued his criminal relations, putting her in a magnificent *quinta* or country house which he had built near Valdemorillo*, a short distance from Madrid, where he went to visit her often.   *Mesonero Romanos, 15.*

[83] Plaza de la Paja: a speech of Cardinal Ximénez (1516)
(Francisco Ximénez de Cisneros (1436–1517) was a great Cardinal Archbishop of Toledo who was also a statesman. He was eighty when the conversation below occurred. Sandoval, the chronicler (1553–1620), was a Benedictine monk.)

The grandees of the realm felt angry that a friar**, whatever his quality, and a foreigner† of the same cloth should have been raised over the government of the Kingdom. They said that the Catholic King†† could not substitute for nor place someone else for the government, since he had not reigned but had only acted as Governor after the death of the Catholic Queen; nor had Doña Juana‡ reigned; so that the grant of powers had to be revised according to the law of the Kingdom.

   And they agreed that the Duque de Infantado‡‡ and the Constable§ and the Conde de Benavente¶ should ask the

---

* A small *pueblo* thirty kilometres to the north-west of Madrid.
** i.e. Cardinal Ximénez.
† The Dean of Louvain, 'ambassador of the Prince' – i.e. Charles V.
†† Ferdinand V.
‡ Doña Juana (1479–1555), daughter of Ferdinand and Isabella, married to the heir of the Habsburgs, Philip the Handsome, on whose early death in 1505 Juana went mad.
‡‡ Diego Hurtado de Mendoza, 3rd Duque de Infantado (d. 1531).
§ Iñigo Fernández de Velasco, 2nd Duque de Frias (d. 1528).
¶ Alonso de Pimentel, Conde de Benavente, general (died 1527).

Cardinal with what powers those realms should be governed. He replied that he was governing with the powers of the Catholic King. And with their replying that the Catholic King could not name others, he drew them to a window of the house* where they were and, pointing down into the square which he had had well provisioned with artillery, ordered his men to fire before them and said, 'With these powers that the King gave me I am governing and shall govern Spain until the Prince† our Lord comes to govern us.'

Fray Prudencio de Sandoval, 'Historia del Emperador Carlos V', 1,73–74.

[84] Plaza de Santa Ana: Mérimée takes leave of the Condesa de Montijo (1840)
(Mérimée, who did so much to promote the idea of 'Romantic Spain' with his *Carmen* (1847), writes to his friend and patroness.)

Dear Countess,

Before leaving your house‡ which I will perhaps not see again for a long time I want to say goodbye once again. We are separating at a very sad moment. You are remaining in the midst of the most abominable chaos and for my part I shall probably find an equivalent one at home, so that every time we say goodbye to each other it is at a moment of trouble and misfortune§. Will we never then see each other to chat and to laugh at the present without fear of the future? I will think much of you both on the journey and in Paris. Your dear children¶ engage my thoughts a great deal. For themselves and for yourself, for whom they are everything. May they have your courage and cleverness, since I greatly fear that they will have only too much need of them. I miss horribly those last two

* This was the house belonging to the Lasos de Castilla in which the Catholic Kings often lodged.
† Charles V.
‡ At the corner of the Plaza de Santa Ana.
§ Revolution threatened.
¶ The future Empress Eugenie and 'Paca', future Duquesa de Alba.

days passed in Madrid. It seemed to me as if I had to say farewell to every tree in Carabanchel*.

The news this evening is not reassuring. The ministers have appointed M. Ferrer Minister of Finance *ad interim* and have not officially told the junta of this nomination†. The latter is offended and it is said it has resolved not to lay down arms until everything it wished has been done. On another side, the Conde Belascoáin‡ arrives in Madrid tomorrow or later with many troops. It is said that Rodil has recognized him as captain-general. Espartero was received in Valencia with enthusiasm§.

He was called *el nuevo Pelayo*, laurel wreaths were thrown at him, even sweets. Apart from that it does not seem as if his programme, or his programmes since there are several, have as yet been approved by the regent. Purely and simply, she wishes to abdicate and these gentlemen do not want to hear of it. That is what I have learnt this evening. Nothing certain is known of Paris except that there is continual great uncertainty about the fate of the ministry.

Goodbye dear countess! . . . I wanted you to be the last person with whom I spoke here. May you and yours be happy.

P.S. – I fear I may have left at Carabanchel a little flowered satin 'housewife' with needles and thread. If you find it, keep it until you should come to Paris, it was made by V[alentine]. Is it not in one of the drawers of the dressing-table that was in my room?   *Mérimée, 448–49.*

* Delightful suburb (then) of Madrid to the south, where the Montijos had a country house, long since destroyed.
† Joaquín María de Ferrer (1777–1861), banker and politician, briefly prime minister.
‡ Conde Belascoáin was Diego León (1807–41), a general executed 1841.
§ General Bartolomeo Espartero (1793–1879), Prìncipe de Vergara, Duque de la Victoria, etc.

The Houses

[85] Seventeenth-century houses (according to
Angel Fernández de los Ríos)
(This writer (1821–80) was one of the first to write
seriously of Madrid's history, in a guide intended for the
Spanish, not the foreign, traveller. He died in exile.)

The blocks of houses were monstrous agglomerations of big
and small buildings, the big ones sometimes occupying
200,000 square feet, the small ones – the immense majority
– only having 400 or 1000 square feet; that is, without
counting those in the Plaza Mayor which varied from 300 to
600 square feet, nor those in the so-called Cinco Tejas (five
tiles) which really only meant the façade and only added up
to 30 feet on the surface. Rarely were the exterior walls
washed and almost never those properties known as Mos-
trencos (that is, in the hands of dead people or entailed,
which were infinite in number). Ridiculous façades crowned
with gutters which drenched water down on passers by, with
many balconies only of wood! Enormous grilles which ob-

liged one to go along the stream then in the centre of the streets! Little alleys which appeared to lead to dungeons by which one reached narrow steep stairways with no light which led to uncountable apartments, generally on top of one another, with small lightless alcoves, which almost always had their only ventilation through the dining-room, and with lavatories separated from the kitchen hearths by a simple partition: in that class of lodging, or in others even worse, there were gathered the local community, imprisoned . . . to such an extent that the Calle de Toledo in 174 houses had 400 inhabitants; that del Anguila, in 42, 4294; that of La Paloma, in 31, 1000; and that of the Comadre, in 95, 300, mostly day labourers and artisans; on the door of the hall which on one side had a drain and on the other a rubbish bin one could read the words 'Jesús, María and José', and on a tile 'general visit', house number so-and-so, but this numbering had been given to each block so that in a single street one might have five or six equal numbers . . .

One threw out rubbish from the windows and balconies. Later it was deposited in the hallways of the houses, where it was allowed to ferment from Sunday to Saturday when those who came to sell vegetables from nearby towns were obliged to take it away: in the end there came the cleaning wagons which received the name of the engineer Sabatini; sewers remained only a presentiment. The public way, thermometer of the civilization of a people, demonstrated the backwardness of the capital; the wells were full of rubbish; the walls sweated grease; greengrocers left on the ground the waste from their merchandise; donkeys of plasterers became white with their charges; coal-merchants scattered on the plaster the contents of their baskets; lamplighters dripped oil; drunks passed water on the sides of the streets; boys did more; the inhabitants interrupted passage by taking the air in the summer or making braziers to roast chestnuts, watering flowerpots, shaking out mats, throwing out of windows papers or old rags in every direction and at all hours; stonemasons converting the street into their workshop, masons saturating the atmosphere with chalk, and dogs, cats, goats, deer, oxen, peacocks, chickens stationed themselves in it as if their kennel, stable or piggery.

Madrileños . . . laugh when they see the effects of this abandon. Salas said:

Aun las personas más sanas	Even healthy people
si son en Madria nacidas	If born in Madrid
tienen que hacer sus comidas	Have to make their meals
con píldoras y tisanas	Of pills and tisanes

A. Fernández de los Ríos, *'Guía de Madrid'* (1876), 45–46.

[86] An English Embassy of the seventeenth century (Clarendon, 1650)

(The English Embassy in Madrid was in the Alcalá in the seventeenth and eighteenth centuries, on the site of the Bank of Spain.)

. . . They had a house provided for them in the Calle de Alcalá, belonging to the marquis of Villa Magna*, to whom the King paid four hundred pounds sterling by the year; a good house, wherein three grandees had lived; and yet, after it was put into their hands, they were compelled to defer their remove for at least a week, to devise a place where to make a kitchen, there being no chimney in the house but in the garrets, and of those not one big enough to roast a joint of meat; but rather hearths, upon which several pipkins might be set together, according to the custom and manner of living there in the greatest families. So that there being a stable adjoining to the house, they were compelled to build a chimney and ovens there, which accommodated them well. All the rooms of reception and entertainment were well furnished out of the King's wardrobe, with tapestry-hangings and chairs, which were changed upon the change of the season, with a cloth of state, and two very good beds for the ambassadors themselves; but they were put to hire all beds and other necessaries for the accommodation of their retinue and servants. The King's coach always waited upon them at their door.   *Clarendon, VIII, 91.*

---

* Alonso de Toledo y Mendoza, 1st Marqués de Villa Magna, a title created 1624.

[87] Calle Clavel (1802)

(The house of the French governor of Madrid, Junot (No. 11 nuevo) is still there. This account is by the great gossip of Napoleon's Empire, Laure Permon (1783–1834), Duchesse de Abrantés, the wife of Junot.)

After Junot* had embraced me and his daughter likewise, he told me that Alphonse Pignatelli† had not lied to us in warning us that his house was barely habitable.

'Imagine a sort of *posada* a little better arranged than the rest, but not having even one decent room.'

'Madame de Beurnonville‡ very much regrets,' said the General then to me, 'not to be able to offer you accommodation at the French Embassy, but we also are in a bad way, and ourselves have cause to complain.'

All this was spoken on the way to the Calle del Clavel, where Alphonse Pignatelli's house was situated. The two ambassadors got into my carriage and eventually we stopped in front of our temporary residence. I saw first of all a white house, looking exactly like an English house. A little door, such as one sees many of in Madrid as in London, many other differences though there be between the two towns, beautifully gleaming copper door-knocker, then a charming little hallway lit up by daylight, paved with marble and well-sanded as in a Flemish house. The staircase was small, just as the house was, but elegant and in good taste. We next reached an antechamber and a dining-room. It is all charming. The drawing-room, the bedroom, all were perfectly simple, something which, in this country where the least thing is as gilded as a chalice, would be bound to seem hardly suitable to a man like Don Alphonse. The bed in the bedroom was a gilt bronze basket, from which seemed to emerge a great quantity of admirably chiselled flowers. Above it, and passed through a golden ring, an

---

* Androche Junot (1771–1813), Marshal, made Duc de Abrantés after his victory there.

† Alfonso Pignatelli, later Conde de Fuentes. A great reputation for successful amours.

‡ Pierre Beurnonville (1752–1821), Marshal of France, was ambassador in Madrid at this time. He was married to a rich Creole from the Île Bourbon.

immense purple veil, embroidered with a strip of gold as wide as a finger, descended like a curtain, making what in hot countries is termed a mosquito net. The bed mattresses were made of white satin; the room hangings of Indian nankeen, with a broad band of embroidery in purple wool, forming arabesques. Large divans, the most comfortable pieces of furniture, completed the furnishings of this charming retreat, which costly tables, beautiful porcelain and French bronzes managed to make into certainly the most agreeable habitation in Madrid, after two houses belonging to the Osuna family* and to the Marquesa de Ariza†.

These two gentleman amused themselves at my astonishment. Junot told me he had organized this little conspiracy to give me the pleasure of a surprise and, in fact, it was total, since, after what Alphonse had told me in Paris, I had prepared myself to find a bachelor's house, untidy and uninhabitable.

Abrantés, 5, 220–21.

[88] Inglis (1830)

In Madrid, the whole of the middle classes, and, indeed, all excepting the very highest ranks, live in stories, or flats, as they are called in Scotland, – each story being a distinct house. The outer door of every house in Madrid is of an enormous strength, more like the door of a prison, or of a convent, than of a private dwelling-house; and in the centre, there is a small window, about six inches long by two broad, grated with iron, and with a sliding shutter. When one rings at the door of a Spanish house, the answer to the bell is a voice, which calls out '*¿Quién es?*' – who is it? or who comes? and the person wishing to be admitted, must answer '*Gente de paz*,' – literally, people of peace. But this assertion does not content the person within, who then shoves aside the shutter and peers through; and the usual colloquy is carried on through the grating, before the door be thrown open, unless the person without, be known to the servant within . . .

* The Osunas were among the most powerful, rich and interesting of Spanish families.
† Teresa de Silva, daughter of the Duque de Híjar, now Marquesa de Ariza.

The house which I select for a description of its interior, as a fair sample of the dwelling-houses of the middle classes in Madrid, belonged to a gentleman holding a government appointment of 50,000 reals (500l.) per annum: and, with very few variations, this house may be taken as an average specimen of the houses of professional men, *employées*, and independent persons, of from £500 to £1,000 per annum. The principal room, answering to the English drawing-room, is large, and well-lighted; a handsome straw matting, worked in a pattern of coloured flowers, and which looks quite as pretty as a carpet, entirely covers the floor, which is generally of brick. There is no fire-place in the room; the walls and roof are both what is called stained, and this is as well executed as I have ever seen it in England; and the furniture of the room consists of a large mahogany sofa, with hair cushion, covered with flowered black satin; mahogany chairs, with green and strawcoloured basket-seats; four small mahogany tables, of good material, and prettily carved, and a large round table in the centre of the room – just an English loo-table – upon which stands a handsome service of china; a mirror, and two marble slabs between the windows, and a few pictures – copies from Spanish masters, – complete the furniture: but let me not omit five or six low stools, scattered here and there; for every lady has her footstool.

At one end of this room, opening from the side, is a recess, twelve or thirteen feet square, and not concealed by any curtain. This is a bed-room, – a bed-room too in constant use. The bedstead is of steel or brass wire; the bed is covered with a counterpane, trimmed with broad lace; the furniture is all of mahogany, and the wash-hand basin and ewer are of brass.

A wide archway opening at the other end of the drawing-room, leads to an ante-room, covered with the same matting as the drawing-room, and furnished with a couch, chairs, and footstools, covered with blue satin. At the side of this ante-room is another recess, open like the other, containing two beds, between them a small marble slab, with a vessel of holy-water, and at the head of each a small image of Christ in ivory. This is the matrimonial chamber. The rest of the house consists of a long, tortuous, and rather dark passage, from which the other rooms enter: these are, a small parlour, or study, always poorly fitted up; a boudoir, with a low couch covered with black satin, a couple of footstools, a table, and very handsome looking-glass; this important room is either matted, or floored with Valencia tiles; and the walls are generally covered with a French paper, and adorned or disfigured as the case may happen, with a few pictures, religious, or of an opposite character, or both, according to the taste of the señora.

The worst room in almost every Spanish house, is the dining-room, or rather eating-room, for every meal is taken in the same room: the floor has generally no matting, – the walls are unadorned, – the furniture is of the commonest description, – and the room itself so small, that the table, which nearly fills the room, is rarely large enough for more than six persons. This at once lets a stranger into an important secret in the economy of Madrid society; that there is no probability of receiving an invitation to dinner . . .

I have omitted to mention the Spanish kitchen, which is provided with a stone table, in which there are six or eight circular holes for charcoal, and numerous earthen vessels to fit these holes. Generally speaking, respectable Spanish houses, whether in Madrid, Seville, or Valencia, are scrupulously clean. I have never in any country seen kitchens and bed-rooms so clean as they are in Spain . . .

In Madrid, and generally in Castile, there is somewhat more luxury in the table, though the Spaniards as a nation, may justly be characterized as abstemious, and little addicted to the plea-sures of the table. The *olla*, or *puchero*, is not the sole dish that graces the tables of the middle and upper classes in Madrid: there is generally a stew of some kind added, and dinner is always followed by cakes, sweetmeats, and fruit; but this is after all but an indifferent dinner for one with an income of 700l. or 800l. a-year. And there are still very many in Madrid, even in the upper ranks, who are contented with the *puchero* . . .　　　　*Inglis, 137–43.*

[89] Gautier's observations (1840)

The houses of Madrid are made of lath, of brick and clay, except for the supports, the piers and the beam braces which are sometimes of blue or grey granite, the whole carefully plastered and painted in fairly unusual colours, celadon green, or ash blue, fawn, canary yellow, pompadour pink, and other more or less convivial colours; the windows are framed by an ornamentation and an architecture simulated by vigorous scrolls and *enroulements*, little cupids and vases of flowers, and furnished with Venetian blinds, striped with wide blue and white bands, or with esparto hangings which are sprinkled with water to keep the wind which blows through them humid and fresh. The really modern houses are merely plastered with lime or distempered or whitewashed, like those in Paris. The corbels of the balconies and miradores break a little of the monotony of the straight lines and throw distinct shadows which vary the naturally flat aspect of the buildings of which all the reliefs are painted and treated like theatre decorations: brighten all that with a sparkling sun, plant at intervals, in these light-flooded streets, a few long-veiled señoras holding against their cheeks fans which they unfold like parasols: a few beggars, warped, wrinkled and draped in scraps of linen or threadbare rags, some half-veiled Valencians of Bedouin appearance; make loom between the roofs little hunch-backed cupolas, and curved bell-turrets topped with lead balls from a church or a convent, and you will obtain a fairly strange vista and one which will moreover prove to you that you are no longer in the rue Lafitte, and that you have definitely left the asphalt, when as yet the fact that your feet have been torn to shreds by the pointed pebbles of the Madrid paving has not convinced you.

Inside, the houses are vast and comfortable. The ceilings are high, and they do not economize anywhere with space; a whole house could be built in Paris in the space of a stairwell. You walk through long suites of rooms before you reach the part that is really inhabited; since all these rooms are only furnished with rough-rendering tinted either yellow or blue relieved with small coloured lines or panels of simulated *boiserie*. Dark and smoky pictures, representing some decapitation or disembowelling of a martyr, favourite subjects of Spanish painters, hang from the walls, for the most part without frames and all puckered in their stretchers. The parquet floor is unknown in Spain, or at least I have never seen one. All the rooms are laid with brick; but since these bricks are covered by rush mattings in winter and by rattan in summer, the inconvenience is greatly lessened; these mats of reed and rush are plaited with much taste; the savages of the Philippines or the Sandwich Isles could not do better. There are three things that are for me the exact indicator of the state of civilization of a people; pottery, the art of plaiting either rushes or straw, and the way in which the beasts are harnessed. If the pottery is beautiful, pure in shape, as accurate as the ancient pottery, with the natural tone of biscuit on red clay; if the baskets and the matting are finely done; if the harness is embroidered, quilted, adorned with little bells, woollen pom-poms and designs of the choicest, you can be sure that the people are primitive and still very near to their natural state; civilized people have no idea how to make either a pot, or a mat, or a harness . . . The few pieces of furniture that one finds in Spanish rooms are in frightful taste which recalls the *goût messidor* and the *goût pyramide*. The Empire shapes flourish in all their purity. There you will find tortoiseshell pilasters surmounted by sphinxes' heads in green bronze, copper beading and fes-tooned frames in the style of Pompei, which have long since disappeared from the face of the civilized world; not a single piece of carved wood, not a single table inlaid with mother-of-pearl, not a single lacquer cabinet, nothing; ancient Spain has completely disappeared: there only remain a few Spanish carpets and damask curtains. On the other hand there is an abundance of really extraordinary chairs and sofas stuffed with straw; the walls are daubed with false colours, false cornices, or white-washed. On the tables and the whatnots are spread little biscuit-china or porcelain figures of troubadours, Matilda and Malek Adel, and other ingenious subjects, but fallen into disrepair; poodles of spun glass, metal candlesticks filled with candles, and a hundred other magnificent things that would take too long to describe, but what I have described would seem suffi-cient; I have not the courage to speak of the atrocious illuminated engravings which have the misplaced aim of adorn-ing the walls.

Perhaps there are some exceptions, but few. Do not imagine that the rooms of the upper classes are furnished with better taste and richness. This description, of the most scrupulous exactitude, applies to people who possess a carriage and eight or ten servants. The blinds are always lowered, the shutters half closed, so that in the rooms there is a sort of half light to which you must become accustomed in order to discern the objects, especially when you come in from outside; those in the room see perfectly, but those who come in are blind for eight or ten minutes, especially when one of the previous rooms is light. It is said that clever mathematicians have made calculations on this optical combination which results in the perfect security for an intimate tête-à-tête in a room thus disposed.

Gautier, 115–119.

Hotels, Cafés, Tertulias

[90] A bottleshop of the eighteenth century: Gil Blas

Our first intention was to see what was to be seen upon the
Prado; but passing in front of a liquor-shop, it came into our
heads that we might as well go in.

The company was in general tolerably select at this house of
call. There were two distinct apartments; and the pastime in
each was of a very opposite nature. One was devoted to games
of chance or skill; the other to literary and scientific discussion:
and there were at that moment two clever men by profession
handling an argument most pertinaciously, before ten or twelve
auditors deeply interested in the discussion. There was no
occasion to join the circle, because the metaphysical thunder
of their logic made itself heard at a more respectful distance: the
heat and passion with which this abstract controversy was
managed made the two philosophers look little better than
madmen . . .

'Angels and ministers of grace defend us,' said I to my
companion: 'what contortions of gesture, what extravagance

of elocution! One might as well argue with the town crier. How little do we know our natural calling in society!' 'Very true indeed,' answered he: 'you have read of Novius, the Roman pawnbroker, whose lungs went as far beyond the rattle of chariot-wheels, as his conscience beyond the rate of legal interest; the Novii must certainly have been transplanted into Spain, and these fellows are lineal descendants. But the hopeless part of the case is, that though our organs of sense are deafened, our understandings are not invigorated at their expense.'

We thought it best to make our escape from these braying metaphysicians, and by the prudent motion to avoid a headache which was just beginning to annoy us. We went and seated ourselves in a corner of the other room, whence, as we sipped our refreshing beverage, all comers and goers were obnoxious to our criticism. Núñez was acquainted with almost the whole set. 'Heaven and earth!' exclaimed he, 'the clash of philosophy is as yet but in its beginning; fresh reinforcements are coming in on both sides. Those three men just on the threshold mean to let slip the dogs of war. But do you see those two queer fellows going out? That little swarthy, leather-complexioned Adonis, with long lank hair parted in the middle with mathematical exactness, is Don Julián de Villanuno. He is a young barrister, with more of the prig than the lawyer about him. A party of us went to dine with him the other day. The occupation we caught him in was singular enough. He was amusing himself in his office with making a tall grey-hound fetch and carry the briefs in the cases which were so unfortunate as to have him retained; and of course the canine *amicus curae* set his fangs indifferently into the flesh of plaintiff or defendant, tearing law, equity, precedent, and principle into shreds. That licentiate at his elbow, with jolly, pimple-spangled nose and cheeks, goes by the name of Don Qherubino Tonto. He is a canon of Toledo, and the greatest fool that was ever suffered to walk the earth without a keeper. And yet, he arrays his features in that sort of not quite unmeaning smile, that you would give him credit for good sense as well as good humour. His eye has the look of cunning if not of wisdom, and his laugh too much of sarcasm for an absolute idiot. One would conclude that he had a turn for mischief, but kept it down from principle and feeling. If you wish to take his opinion upon a work of genius, he will hear it read with so grave and rapt a silence, as nothing but deep thought and acute mental criticism could justify; but the truth is, that he comprehends not one word, and therefore can have nothing to say. He was of the barrister party. There were a thousand good things said, as there always must be in a professional company. Don Cherubino added nothing to the mass of merriment; but looked such perfect approbation at those who did, was so tractable and complimentary a listener, that every man at table placed him second in the comparative estimate of merit.'

'Do you know,' said I to Núñez, 'who those two fellows are with dirty clothes and matted hair, their elbows on that table in the corner, and their cheeks upon their hands, whiffing foul breath into each other's nostrils as they lay their heads together?' He told me that by their faces they were strangers to him; but that by physical and moral tokens they could only be coffee-house politicians, venting their spleen against the measures of government. 'But do look at that spruce spark, whistling as he paces up and down the other room, and balancing himself alternately on one toe and on the other. That is Don Agustín Morete, a young poet sufficiently of nature's mint and coinage to pass current, if flatterers and frauds had not debased him into a mere coxcomb by their misplaced admiration. The man to whom he is going up with that familiar shake by the hand, is one of the set who write verses and then call themselves poets; who claim a speaking acquaintance with the muses, but never were of their private parties.'

'Authors upon authors, nothing but authors!' exclaimed he, pointing out two dashing blades. 'One would think they had made an appointment on purpose to pass in review before you. Don Bernardo Deslenguado and Don Sebastián of Villa Viciosa! The first is a vinegar-flavoured vintage of Parnassus, a satirist by trade and company; he hates all the world, and is not liked the better for his taste. As for Don Sebastián, he is the milk and honey of criticism; he would not have the guilt of ill-nature on his conscience for the universe. He has just brought out a comedy without a single idea, which has succeeded with an audience of tantamount ideas; and he has just now published it to vindicate his innocence.'

Góngora's candid pupil was running on in his career of
benevolent explanation, when one of the Duque de Medina
Sidonia's household came up and said: 'Señor Don Fabricio,
my lord duke wishes to speak with you. You will find him at
home.' Núñez, who knew that the wishes of a great lord could
not be too soon gratified, left me without ceremony; but he left
me in the utmost consternation, to hear him called Don, and
thus ennobled, in spite of master Chrysostom the barber's
escutcheon, who had the honour to call him father.

'Gil Blas', 78–81.

[91] Alexandre Dumas *père*'s hotel, 1846

Arriving was not the only problem, I had to find lodgings; now
lodgings at such a period, and in such circumstances, were not
an easy thing to find.

But, your banker will say, you must anticipate the circumstances, write in advance, book a place at an hotel.

Firstly, Madam, you will have the goodness to reply to your
banker that we left at a moment's notice, so that as a result we
had no time to make preparations on this subject.

Secondly, you will add, and he will remember this fact since
because of this fact the funds were lowered by three francs; you
will add that the newspapers had announced that the whole of
Spain was in a state of revolution, the roads were infested with
guerrillas, and that there was fighting in the streets of Madrid
. . . Now that was our reasoning. If there is fighting in the
streets of Madrid, we will surely find room in the houses of the
people who are fighting, seeing that one cannot at one and the
same time fight in the streets and stay in one's house. Not a bit
of it, behold Spain enjoying the deepest peace, behold us having
travelled 150 leagues, from Bayonne to Madrid, without encountering the least guerrilla on the roads; behold us finally in
the streets of Madrid in their matutinal solitude, and full of
travelling theatres erected in advance for the festivals for which
we had come to take part; so the only thing left to us was to
lodge in a theatre.

It was so magnificent that it was heartbreaking.

We set off in quest, leaving our baggage at the desk; we flung ourselves at every hotel in Madrid, we visited every furnished house, every *casa de pupilos*: not a room, not an attic, not a cupboard that could house a page boy, a *cobolt*, a dwarf.

At each new disappointment we returned to the street, we looked questioningly at each other, and then, more and more crestfallen, continued our investigations. We had visited everything, we had almost lost final hope, when by chance I raised my head and I read above a door these words: 'Monnier, French bookseller.'

I gave a cry of joy, it was not possible for a compatriot to refuse us hospitality in his house, or at least not do all he could to find it elsewhere for us.

I looked for a door other than the shop door, I found a side door above which were written these three words: *Casa de baños*.

It was a miracle of fortune. What we needed most of all after a furnished house was a bath house.

I pushed open a little gate which rang a bell. I entered. I followed a long path, at the end of which I found a glass-covered courtyard. All round this courtyard there were entrances opening on to the bathrooms: above these rooms ran a little mezzanine.

Two women and five cats were warming themselves at a brazier.

I asked for Mr Monnier; but doubtless my displeased expression disturbed the house, for the women began to grumble and the cats to whine.

At this double noise, a window in the mezzanine opened; a head tied up with a scarf and a torso adorned with a shirt appeared at the window.

'Who is there?' asked the head.

I hasten to tell you, Madam, that this head, whose physiognomy it was at this junction so important for me to ascertain, I hasten to tell you that this head was endowed with the most pleasing aspect.

'My dear Mr Monnier,' I replied, 'it happens that I and my companions are in search of lodgings; that we have been looking since two o'clock in the morning, that if you do not put us up, we shall be obliged to buy a second-hand tent from some retired Carlist general, and to camp on the Plaza de Alcalá.'

Mr Monnier heard me, opening his eyes very wide.

'Excuse me,' he said to me, 'but you called me dear Mr Monnier. So do we know each other?'

'No doubt, since I called you by your name.'

'Oh, there is nothing very surprising about that, my name is on my door.'

'And so is mine.'

'What! your name is on my door?'

'Yes indeed! I read it there.'

'What is your name then?'

'Alexandre Dumas.'   *Dumas, 60–61.*

[92] Borrow in a café (1836)

Apropos of bull-fighters: Shortly after my arrival, I one day entered a low tavern in a neighbourhood notorious for robbery and murder, and in which for the last two hours I had been wandering on a voyage of discovery. I was fatigued, and required refreshment. I found the place thronged with people, who had all the appearance of ruffians. I saluted them, upon which they made way for me to the bar, taking off their *sombreros* with great ceremony. I emptied a glass of *val de peñas*, and was about to pay for it and depart, when a horrible-looking fellow, dressed in a buff jerkin, leather breeches, and jackboots, which came halfway up his thighs, and having on his head a white hat, the rims of which were at least a yard and a half in circumference, pushed through the crowd, and confronting me, roared:

'*¡Otra copita! ¡vamos Inglesito: Otra copita!*'*

'Thank you, my good sir, you are very kind. You appear to know me, but I have not the honour of knowing you.'

'Not know me!' replied the being. 'I am Sevilla, the *torero*. I know you well; you are the friend of Baltasarito, the national, who is a friend of mine, and a very good subject.'

Then turning to the company, he said in a sonorous tone, laying a strong emphasis on the last syllable of every word, according to the custom of the *gente rufianesca* throughout Spain –

'Cavaliers, and strong men, this cavalier is the friend of a friend

---

* 'Another glass; come on, little Englishman, another glass.'

of mine. *Es mucho hombre*. There is none like him in Spain. He speaks the crabbed *Gitano**, though he is an *Inglesito*.'

'We do not believe it,' replied several grave voices. 'It is not possible.'

'It is not possible, say you? I tell you it is. Come forward, Balseiro, you who have been in prison all your life, and are always boasting that you can speak the crabbed *Gitano*, though I say you know nothing of it – come forward and speak to his worship in the crabbed *Gitano*.'

A low, slight, but active figure stepped forward. He was in his shirt-sleeves, and wore a *montero* cap†; his features were handsome, but they were those of a demon.

He spoke a few words in the broken gypsy slang of the prison, inquiring of me whether I had ever been in the con-demned cell, and whether I knew what a *Gitana‡* was.

'*Vamos Inglesito*,' shouted Sevilla, in a voice of thunder; 'answer the *monró* in the crabbed *Gitano*.'

I answered the robber, for such he was, and one too whose name will live for many a year in the ruffian histories of Madrid; I answered him in a speech of some length, in the dialect of the Estremenian gypsies.

'I believe it is the crabbed *Gitano*,' muttered Balseiro. 'It is either that or English, for I understand not a word of it.'

'Did I not say to you,' cried the bull-fighter, 'that you knew nothing of the crabbed *Gitano*? But this *Inglesito* does. I understood all he said. *Vaya*, there is none like him for the crabbed *Gitano*. He is a good *jinete*, too; next to myself, there is none like him, only he rides with stirrup leathers too short. *Inglesito*, if you have need of money, I will lend you my purse. All I have is at your service, and that is not a little; I have just gained four thousand *chulés* by the lottery. Courage, English-man! Another cup. I will pay all – I, Sevilla!'

And he clapped his hand repeatedly on his breast, reiterating, 'I, Sevilla! I –'   *Borrow, 176–78 (c. 1835)*.

---

* i.e. gypsy language.
† *Montero* in Spanish means 'a hunter' and a *montero* cap, which every reader of Sterne is familiar with at least by name, is a cap, generally of leather, such as was used by hunters in the Peninsula.
‡ Twelve ounces of bread, small pound, as given in the prison [note by Borrow].

[93] Gautier's visit to the cafés (1840)

The cafés of Madrid seem to us, we who are used to the dazzling and enchanting luxury of the Parisian cafés, veritable fifth-rate suburban places; the way in which they are decorated recalls very happily the booths at fairs in which the bearded women and the living sirens are exhibited; but this lack of luxury is very much redeemed by the excellence and the variety of the refreshments which are served there. It must be admitted that Paris, so superior in everything, is behind in this respect: the lemonade-maker's art is still in its infancy. The most celebrated cafés are the *Bolsa*, at the corner of the Calle Carretas; the *Nuevo*, where the *exaltados* gather, the . . . (I forget the name), the usual meeting-place of those people who belong to moderate opinion, and who are called *cangrejos*, that is to say, crayfish; [that of] the *Levante*, very near the Puerta del Sol, which is not to say that the others are no good; but those ones are the most frequented. Let us not forget the *Príncipe* Café, the normal meeting-place of artists and men of letters*.

If you wish we will go into the café *Bolsa*, decorated with little mirrors cut underneath in grooves so as to form patterns, as you see in certain German glasses: here is the menu of *bebidas heladas*, of *sorbets* and of *quesitos*. The *bebida helada* (iced drink) is contained in glasses which are divided into *grande* or *chico* (large or small), and offers a very large variety; there is the *bebida de naranja* (orange), the *limón* (lemon), the *fresa* (strawberry), the *guindas* (cherry), which are as superior to these frightful little carafes of redcurrant juice and citric acid which they are not ashamed to serve you in the most splendid cafés in Paris, as the fine wine of Xerès is to the authentic wine of Brie; it is a kind of liquid ice, half consisting of strawberries or cherries, a sherry purée of the most exquisite taste. The *bebida de almendra blanca* (white almonds) is a delicious drink, unknown in France where you swallow, as a pretext for a syrup, I know not what abominable medicinal mixtures; they also give you iced milk, half filled with strawberries or cherries, which, while your body boils in the torrid zone, gives enjoyment to your gullet with all the snows and frosts of

* All these cafés vanished in the 1920s.

Greenland. During the daytime, when the ices have not yet been prepared, you have the *agraz*, a kind of drink made from green grapes and contained in bottles with incredibly long necks; the lightly acidulated taste of the *agraz* is one of the most agreeable; you can in addition drink a bottle of *cerveza de Santa Bárbara con limón*; but this demands some preparation: they first of all bring you a dish and a long spoon, like that with which you stir punch, then a waiter draws near carrying the bottle tied up with steel wire, which he uncorks with infinite precaution; the cork comes out, and the beer is poured into the basin into which beforehand has been emptied a little carafe of lemonade, then everything is stirred with the spoon, you fill your glass and you swallow it. If this mixture does not please you, you have only to go to the *horchaterías de chufas*, usually owned by Valencians. The chufa is a little berry, a kind of almond which grows well in the surroundings of Valencia, of which is made an exquisite drink, especially when it is mixed with snow: this preparation is extremely refreshing.

To finish with the cafés, we must explain that the *sorbets* differ from those of France in that they have more consistency; that the *quesitos* are hard little ices, moulded in the shape of a cheese; these are of all sorts, apricot, pineapple, orange, as in Paris; but they also make some with butter (*manteca*) and with unlaid eggs, taken from the disembowelled hen, a speciality of Spain, as I have only ever heard of this singular refreshment in Madrid. They also serve *espumas* of chocolate, of coffee, and others; these are a kind of whipped ice cream of extreme lightness, which you sprinkle with a kind of finely grated cinnamon, the whole accompanied by *barquillos*, wafers rolled into long cornets with which you eat your *bebida*, like a straw, sucking gently at one end; a little refinement which enables you to savour the freshness of the beverage longer. Coffee is not drunk in cups, but in glasses; besides, it is very rarely done . . . You see many more women in the cafés of Madrid than in those of Paris, even though people smoke cigarettes and even havana cigars there . . . – But here is eleven o'clock striking; it is time for bed; hardly any promenaders are walking along the Calle de Alcalá. There is no one in the streets except the *serenos* with their lanterns at the end of their pikes, their grey cloaks, and their measured cry; you hear nothing except a choir of

crickets singing their dissyllabic complaint in their little cages
prettified with glass trinkets.   *Gautier, 108–111.*

[94] De Amicis at the Café Fornos (1870)

... and any one not wishing to omit anything would speak of
the superb cafés: the Imperial in the square of the Puerta del
Sol, the Fornos in the street Alcalá, which are two immense
halls in which, if the tables were removed, a squadron of
cavalry could exercise; and innumerable others, that one meets
at every step, in which a hundred couples could easily dance.

De Amicis, 141.

[95] Ramón y Cajal at the Café Suizo (c. 1900)

(This café was on the corner of the Calle Alcalá, on the site
of the Banco de Bilbao. For Ramón y Cajal, see No. 18.)

But in addition to the physical landscape, the man of the
laboratory needs the oral landscape, the agreeable *tertulia*
where, in the warmth of friendship and mutual confidence,
he can bring forth the varied and spontaneous flowers of his
genius.

In truth my first tentative explorations of *tertulias* in Madrid
were rather unfortunate. I found, in the Café de Levante*, a
regular gathering of old friends, mostly military doctors whom
I had already known during the Cuban campaign†. Among
these friendly [*simpáticos*] comrades there reigned total frank-
ness and sometimes their conversation was lively, sparkling
and instructive. But a bad fairy pursued us. Almost every day,
fatally, irremediably the commentaries became directed towards muttering against superiors or towards the salary scale
of the military medical corps: that accursed pay scale, destroyer
of all noble inspiration, and all generous ambition, hindrance
to justice, asylum of the idlers and one of the worst calamities
from which we suffered in Spain!

---

* In the Puerta del Sol.
† That is, 1895–1898.

The evil lacked remedy. Those well-intentioned comrades, certainly not free from talent even if petrified by the useless life of cantoonments, barracks and clubs, only need the *gaceta* [the official gazette] and the bulletin of the medical corps.

With difficulty I abandoned the daily discussion with comrades who re-lived, in my memory, moments of war and youthful transatlantic adventures, and I sought another *tertulia* at which to stimulate my mind and utilize the idle fallow-land of my brain.

I think it was San Martín who first presented me to the *peña** of the Café Suizo, a gathering of ancient and splendid ancestry, since in it there figured politicians, literary men and even outstanding financiers. Even though from the political and literary point of view, the *peña* in question had declined, it still enjoyed at that time a justified renown. From there there emerged, as is notorious, senators, university lecturers, professors, rectors, legal advisers to great companies, even ministers . . . The discussions of the *peña* were so famous and so much commented upon that often, and with a serious risk of indiscretion, there were formed at the next tables parasite *tertulias* of listeners, who for the modest price of a cup of coffee acquired the right to know our more or less extravagant flights of fancy and to chatter about them without risk.

Among the companions the doctors dominated naturally, at the head of which there was Don Alejandro. Lawyers, proprietors, university professors and, in the end, persons of every type and condition were also present. Everyone was admitted on the condition of being presented by a formal member and of keeping three rules: 1, to talk with due respect for persons; 2, to talk about things which one did not understand or understood little (one had to avoid pedantic and academic bores); 3, to forget on leaving the café all the follies and incoherences provoked by the stimulation of the café or the horrors of the post-lunch digestion. Because it is important to note that our *tertulia* occurred in the first hours of the afternoon and rarely lasted more than one hour. By this good fortune, on

* A *peña* was, or is, virtually synonymous with a *tertulia* but historically a *tertulia* might have been in a private house and a *peña* is a group of friends who meet more formally in a public place.

rising from the session one found one's brain warmed up but lively enough to carry on the day's work. It is good to digress a little every day. But it is dangerous to prolong the distraction of the mind at the expense of the concentration on one's work.

With sadness I recall the changes that time and death brought to our dear *peña* in the Suizo. Those *tertulias* are living bodies with youth, maturity and decay; and like every organization they nourish themselves, grow, assimilate and fall apart. New cells are incorporated while others, alas!, die or disappear. And the deaths now are innumerable! . . .

I owe much to the lively *tertulia* of the Suizo. Apart from unforgettable chats of the most entertaining kind, I learned many things from it and corrected myself of some defects. There we elevated our spirits a little, expressing and discussing with warmth the doctrines of modern and old philosophers alike, from Plato and Epicurus to Schopenhauer and Herbert Spencer; and we rendered veneration and enthusiasm towards evolutionism and its popes Darwin and Haeckel, and abominated the satanic pride of Nietzsche. In the literary terrain, our table proclaimed naturalism against romanticism, or the reverse, according to the speakers of the moment and the mood of the day. Pepe Botella and San Martín, the most musically minded among those present, quarrelled over Wagner when in Spain there were scarcely more *Wagneristas* than Peña y Goñi.

Ramón y Cajal, 142–43.

[96] Pre-war *tertulias* (c. 1930): Agustín de Foxá (Agustín de Foxá (1903–59) was a charming and brilliant writer and diplomatist, whose wit during the Civil War was a redeeming feature of the Nationalist headquarters in Salamanca.)

The apothecary Martínez went every evening to the *tertulia* of the Café Varela, on the corner of the Plaza de Santo Domingo. This corner was the North American coast of the city, against which the liveliness of the native students and seamstresses of the Calle de San Bernardo was lapping.

Mirrors, with a blue steam from smoke and gilded frames complicated by leaves, mouldings and beading. Red sofas, chairs, carafes, and papers near the counter. Sometimes the black cat of the nearby lottery curled up lazily, greedy for milk.

At the tables on the right the brothers Machado* had their *tertulia*, with the painter Ricardo Baroja†, with his one eye, and the bad one adorned with a black crystal; the actor Ricardo Calvo and the Duque de Afil, Spanish diplomatist and author of sonorous hendecasyllabic sonnets:

– *Oh tú, de los Habsburgos hijo ilustre.*
– O thou, illustrious child of the Habsburgs.

Don Cayetano Martínez – envious of the *tertulia* of the *literati* – orated in a narrow world of humble engineers, modest lawyers, doctors without patients and sub-editors of *El Liberal*. He had his favourite phrase: 'Because I, in truth, am a Deist; even if I do not believe in any positive religion.'

Those simpletons who admired him were dazzled by his back-room or shop-counter Voltairism.

Lieutenant Moreno was a theosophist. He went every Friday to the Calle de la Madera where they studied the reincarnations of Krishnamurti and read the prospects of the 'Order of the Star'. 'Now,' he said, 'we are paying for the karma of Peru.'

Engineer Robledano asked ingenuously: 'What is this?'

'It signifies that we have to purge the blood which that barbarian Pizarro spilled.'

The chemist Giral‡ intervened warily: 'This is absurd. I am an evolutionist.'

The doctor, Sánchez Amador, loosed, greatly daring, his favourite phrase: 'And I. I have never found a soul when operating.'

Don Marcelino, the pedagogue, became conciliatory with his lore of Masonic lodges: 'One must recognize all the same that all this has a Creator. A grand architect, if you like.'

They diverted towards politics.

Nostalgic for pulque and iguana meat, the Mexican Guzmán

---

* Antonio Machado (1875–1939) and Manuel Machado (1874–1947), two great poets.
† Ricardo Baroja (1871–1953), brother of the novelist Pío.
‡ Presumably José Giral (1879–1962), professor of Biological Chemistry in Madrid, minister and briefly prime minister during the Civil War. Died in Mexico.

was talking of Madero and his conspiracies in Vera Cruz. He was still intoxicated by marijuana and sang, beating time with a little spoon which he tinkled against the coffee cup:

> 'If Adelita goes off with another,
> I'll follow her, by land and sea;
> If by sea, in a battleship;
> If by land, in an armoured train.

'And *Olé!* by the eagle and the snake.'

Don Cayetano lifted his glass full of *anís* del Mono, as if water sugared with tears, into which he dipped his fingers. Guzmán raised his brandy glass:

'To the future Spanish Republic!'
All drank the toast. Giral rose to go.
'Good evening, gentlemen!'
He had a rendezvous with Don Manuel*.
'Shall I see you tonight?'
Guzmán assented: 'I will be in the editorial offices of *El Sol* until dawn. There are rumours of a crisis.'

Agustín de Foxá, 32–35.

[97] Ritz Hotel: Salvador Dalí's visit
(This fine building was put up in the neighbourhood of the Prado in 1911–1912. Dalí had a drink there about 1926.)

Instead of going to the barber's when I reached the Ritz, I headed for the bar and asked for 'a cocktail.'

'What kind will you have?' asked the bartender.

'Make it a good one!' I said, not knowing there were several kinds.

It tasted horrible to me, but at the end of five minutes it began to feel good inside my spirit. I definitely dropped the idea of the barber for the afternoon and asked for another cocktail. I then became aware of this astonishing fact: in four months this was the first day I had missed classes, and the most stupefying part of it was that this did not give me the slightest feeling of

* Presumably Azaña.

guilt. On the contrary, I had a vague impression that this period was ended, and that I would never return. Something very different was going to come into my life.

In my second cocktail I found a white hair. This moved me to tears, in the euphemistic intoxication produced by the first two cocktails I had drunk in my life. This apparition of a white hair at the bottom of my glass appeared to me to be a good omen. I felt ideas and ideas being born and vanishing, succeeding one another within my head with an unusual speed – as if, by virtue of the drink, my life had suddenly begun to run faster. I said to myself, 'This is my first white hair!' And again I sipped that fiery liquid which I had to swallow with my eyes shut, because of its violence. This perhaps was the 'elixir of long life,' the elixir of old age, the elixir of the anti-Faust.

I was sitting in a dark corner from which I could easily observe everything, without being observed – which I was able to verify, as I had just said 'elixir of the anti-Faust' aloud and no one had noticed it. Besides, there were only two persons in the bar in addition to myself – the bartender, who had white hair but seemed very young, and an extremely emaciated gentleman, who also had white hair, and who seemed very old, for when he lifted his glass to his lips he trembled so much that he had to take great precautions not to spill everything on the floor. I found this gesture, betraying a long habit, altogether admirable and of supreme elegance; I would so much have liked to be able to tremble like that! And my eyes fastened themselves once more on the bottom of my glass, hypnotized by the gleam of that silver hair. 'Naturally I'm going to look at you close,' I seemed to say to it with my glance, 'for never yet in my life have I had the occasion, the leisure, to take a white hair between my fingers, to be able to examine it with my avid and inquisitorial eyes, capable of squeezing out the secret and tearing out the soul of all things.'

I was about to plunge my fingers into the cocktail with the intention of pulling out the hair when the bartender came over to my table to place two small dishes on it, the one containing olives stuffed with anchovies, the other *pommes soufflées*.

'Another?' he asked with a glance, seeing that my glass was less than half full.

'No thanks!'

With a ceremonious gesture he then wiped up a few drops that I had spilled on the table and went back to his post behind the bar. Then I plunged my forefinger and my thumb into my glass. But as my nails were cut very, very short it was impossible for me to catch it. In spite of this I could feel its relief; it seemed hard and as if glued to the bottom of the glass. While I was immersed in this operation an elegant woman had come in, dressed in an extremely light costume with a heavy fur hanging around her neck. She spoke familiarly, lazily to the bartender. Full of respectful solicitude, the latter was preparing for her something that required a great din of cracking ice. I immediately understood the subject of their conversation, for an imperceptible glance cast by the bartender toward the spot where I was sitting was followed after a short interval by a long scrutinizing gaze from the lady. Before fixing her eyes on me with an insistent curiosity she let her eyes wander lazily around the entire room, resting them on me for a mere moment, meaning in this clumsy way to make me believe it was by pure chance that her gaze settled on me. With his eyes glued to the metal counter, the bartender waited for his companion to have time to examine me at her leisure, and then, with rapid words and an ironic though kindly smile, he told her something about me which had exactly the effect of making the woman's face turn in my direction a second time. This time she did it with the same slowness, but without taking any precautions. At this moment, exasperated as much by this scrutinizing gaze as by my clumsiness in not being able to get out the white hair, I pressed my finger hard against the glass and slowly pulled it up, slipping it along the crystal with all my might. This I could do without being seen, for a column concealed half of my table from the lady and the bartender just at the spot where my hand and my glass happened to be.

I did not succeed in detaching the white hair, but suddenly a burning pain awakened in my finger. I looked, and saw a long cut that was beginning to bleed copiously. Out of my wits, I put my finger back into the glass so as not to spatter blood all over my table. I instantly recognized my error. There was no hair at the bottom of my glass. It was simply a very fine crack that shone through the liquid of my accursed cocktail. I had cut myself by mistake in sliding the flesh of my finger hard along this crack, with the impulsive pressure which the lady's second glance had increased in intensity. My cut was at least three centimetres long and it bled uniformly and without interruption. My cocktail became almost instantly colored a bright red and began to rise in the glass.

I was sure I knew what the bartender had said to the lady. He had told her that I was most likely a provincial who had dropped in here by chance, and that not knowing what kind of cocktail to order I had naïvely asked him to 'make it a good one.' In spite of the distance I could have sworn that I had seen exactly these syllables emerge from between the bartender's lips. At the moment when he finished telling his anecdote my blood had begun to color my drink, making it rise, and my hemorrhage continued. Then I decided to tie a handkerchief round my finger. The blood immediately went through it. I put my second and last handkerchief over it, making it tighter. This time the spot of blood which appeared grew much more slowly, and seemed to stop spreading.

I put my hand in my pocket and was about to leave, when a Dalinian idea assailed me. I went up to the bar and paid with a twenty-five peseta bill. The bartender hastened to give me my change – my drink was not more than three pesetas. 'That's all right,' I said with a gesture of great naturalness, leaving him the whole balance as a tip. I have never seen a face so authentically stupefied. Yet I was already familiar with this expression; it was the same that I had so often observed with delight on the faces of my schoolmates when as a boy I had exchanged the famous ten *céntimo* pieces for fives. This time I understood that it worked 'exactly' the same way for grown-ups and I at once realized the supremacy of the power of money. It was as if by leaving on the bar the modest sum of my disproportionate tip I had 'broken the bank' of the Hotel Ritz.

But the effect I had produced did not yet satisfy me, and all this was but the preamble to that Dalinian idea which I announced to you a while ago. The two cocktails I had just drunk had dissipated every vestige of my timidity, all the more so as I felt after my tip that the roles were reversed and that I had become the author of intimidation. An assurance and perfect poise now presided over the slightest of my gestures, and I must say that everything I did from this moment until I reached the doorstep was marked by a stupefying ease. I could read this constantly on the face of the bartender as in an open book.

'And now I should like to buy one of those cherries you have there,' I said pointing to a silver dish full of the candied fruit.

He respectfully put the dish before me. 'Help yourself, Señor, take all you want.'

I took one and placed it on the bar.

'How much is it?'

'Why, nothing, Señor. It's worth nothing.'

I pulled out another twenty-five peseta bill and gave it to him.

Scandalized, he refused to take it.

'Then I give you back your cherry!'

I put it back into the silver dish. He reached the dish over to me, beseeching me to put an end to this joking. But my face became so severe and contracted, so offended, so stony, that the bartender, completely bewildered, said in a voice touched with emotion,

'If the Señor absolutely insists on making me this further present . . .'

'I insist,' I answered in a tone which admitted of no argument.

He took my twenty-five pesetas, but then I saw a rapid gleam of fear flash across his face. Perhaps I was a madman? He cast a quick glance at the lady seated beside me at the bar whom I could feel staring at me hypnotically. I had not looked at her for a single second, as though I had been completely unaware of her presence. But now it was to be her turn. I turned toward her and said,

'Señora, I beg you to make me a present of one of the cherries on your hat!'

'Why, gladly,' she said with agile coquettishness, and bent her head a little in my direction. I took hold of one of the cherries and began to pull it. But I saw immediately that this was not the way to do it, and remembered my long experience with such things. My aunt was a hat-maker, and artificial cherries had no secrets for me. So instead of pulling, I bent the stem back and forth until the very slender wire that served as its stem broke with a snap, and I had my cherry. I performed this operation with a prodigious dexterity and with a single hand, having kept my other, wounded, hand buried in the pocket of my coat.

When I had obtained my new artificial cherry I bit it, and a small tear revealed the white cotton of its stuffing. Having done this, I placed it beside the real cherry, and fastened the two together by their stems, winding the wire stalk of the false one around the tail of the real one. Then, to complete my operation, I picked off with a cocktail straw a little of the whipped cream that covered the lady's drink and applied it to the real cherry, so that now the real and the false both had a white spot, the one of cream and the other of cotton.

My two spectators followed the precise course of all these operations breathlessly, as if their lives had hung on each of my minute manipulations.

'And now,' I said, solemnly raising my finger, 'you will see the most important thing of all.'

Turning round, I went over to the table I had just occupied and, taking the cocktail glass filled with my blood, and holding my hand around it, carried it cautiously and daintily put it down on the metal top of the bar; after which, quickly removing my hand from it and picking up the two cherries by their joined stems I plunged them into the glass.

'Observe this cocktail carefully,' I said to the bartender. 'This is one you don't know!'

Then I turned on my heels and calmly left the Ritz Hotel.

I thought over what I had just done, and I felt as greatly moved as Jesus must have felt when he invented Holy Communion. How would the bartender's brain solve the phenomenon of the apparition, in a glass which he had observed with his own eyes to be half empty a moment before, of the red liquid which now filled it to the brim? Would he understand that it was blood? Would he taste it? What would they say to each other, the lady and the bartender, after my departure?

From these absorbing meditations I passed abruptly and without transition to a mood of joyous exaltation. The sky over Madrid was a shattering blue and the brick houses were pale rose, like a sigh filled with glorious promises. I was phenomenal. I was phenomenal. The distance which separated the Ritz Hotel from my street-car stop was rather long and I was hungry as a wolf. I began to run through the streets as fast as my legs would carry me. It astonished me that the people I passed were not more surprised at my running. They barely turned their heads in my direction and continued about their business in the most natural way in the world. Peeved by this indifference, I embellished my run with more and more exalted leaps. I had always been very adept at high-jumping, and I tried to make each of my leaps more sensational than the last. If my running, unusual and violent though it was, had not succeeded in attracting much attention, the height of my leaps surprised all passers-by, imparting an expression of fearful astonishment to their faces which delighted me. I further complicated my run with a marvelous cry. 'Blood is sweeter than honey,' I repeated to myself over and over again. But the word 'honey' I shouted at the top of my lungs, and I pushed my leap as high and hard as I could. 'Blood is sweeter than HONEY.' And I leaped. In one of these mad leaps I landed right beside a fellow-student of the School of Fine Arts, who had never known me otherwise than in my studious, taciturn and ascetic aspect. Seeing him so surprised I decided to astonish him even further. Making as if to whisper an explanation of my incomprehensible leaps, I brought my lips close to his ear. 'Honey!' I shouted with all my might. Then I ran toward my street-car which was approaching and jumped aboard, leaving my co-religionist in study glued to the sidewalk and looking after me till I lost sight of him. The next day this student told everyone, 'Dalí is crazy as a goat!'

Dalí, 179–183.

Palaces

[98] Palacio de Alba: St Teresa rebukes the King
(1569)
(This was the palace in old Madrid long since abandoned
but still roughly identifiable in the Calle del Duque de Alba.
St Teresa de Ávila (1515–1582) stayed there in the 1560s).

. . . Remember, Sire, that Saul was anointed and yet he was
rejected . . .

Madrid, early in March, 1569.
*(Fragment of a letter to Philip II, containing a warning received
by the Saint during prayer.)*

While passing through Madrid on her way to make a foundation at Toledo, St Teresa gave the King's sister a letter for him
containing advice received by her from God concerning Philip's
most secret thoughts. Nothing remains of it but the fragment
given above. Much impressed by it, Philip exclaimed: 'Why can
I not see this woman? where is she?' Search was made, but the
Saint had left the city. Later on, Isabel of St Dominic said that

after holy Communion the thought of a certain person [the King] always presented itself to her and she believed she heard our Lord say: 'My daughter, I wish him to be saved.' St Teresa replied: 'The same thing happens to me. Pray for him, for God wishes it. That person has passed through great trouble and has more to come.' This was Philip II, who after a long and painful illness died a Christian death. St Teresa often wrote to him and used to call him jokingly: 'My friend the King'. He took her and her Reform under his special protection and obtained the separation of provinces for it from the Pope.

St Teresa, 'Letters', 50, 5.

[99] Palacio de Buenavista: the Duquesa de Alba's ball (1790)
(Cayetana (1762–1804), the thirteenth Duquesa, inherited the title from her father. This account is by a biographer of the 1920s.)

Their house had its usual entrance in the Calle Real del Barquillo and, in the part of the property behind the garden, there was under construction, under Villanueva's direction*, a large pavilion of two storeys, whose ballroom, in the central section of the first floor, was not a temporary building in any way . . . it communicated, at the level of the first floor, with the rooms of the Duque and Duquesa . . . [At the celebrations for the coming to the throne of the new King Charles IV] in various places, balls were held which, if the *Diario de Madrid* does not lie, were interminable, capable of exhausting dancers of iron since some, such as that in the Palace of the Osunas, lasted from eight at night to ten in the morning. The most brilliant, it was said, was the Albas' because of the larger space they had in which to spread out. The entrance in the Calle de Alcalá, through three gates and a gallery of six aisles, led to the ballroom by a double staircase. This ballroom, decorated in white with blue and white sofas, edged with gold, with curtains to match, had at each end platforms for the musicians. On the

* Juan de Villanueva (1731–1811) was the leading architect in Madrid at the end of the eighteenth century. He was also responsible for the Museum of the Prado.

ground floor there were rooms for gambling; an alcove for the King and Queen if they wanted to rest, with a boudoir, and tables, the first with twelve places laid for the royal family, very well served and decorated with bunches of flowers. At half-past eight the King and the Queen* arrived, the Queen and the Infanta María Josefa† coming in sedan chairs as far as the house itself, staying there about an hour. The fiesta, which was very lively, lasted till nine in the morning the following day.

Joaquín Ezquerra del Bayo, 'La Duquesa de Alba y Goya', Madrid 1928 163, 166.

[100] Palacio de Buenavista: the death of the thirteenth Duquesa de Alba (1804) – the one tribute
(The death of the thirteenth Duquesa de Alba was widely, if erroneously, as it now seems, thought to have been by poison. No one paid tribute to her generosity and capacity for friendship – except Francisco Sánchez Barbero (1764–1819), later imprisoned for liberal ideas by King Ferdinand VII.)

La Duquesa murió. La luz brillante	The Duchess is no more. The brilliant light
del astro de Alba entre ofuscadas nieblas	of the Star of Alba is concealed
se esconde; su semblante	By obscure clouds. Her face no more
las gracias halagüeñas abandonan,	With beauty is adorned
y en torno la coronan	And a yellow glare and the bleak shadows of death
sin fin amarillez, sin fin tiemblas.	Crown her instead.
. . .	. . .
¿qué será, de vosotros, oh leales	What will become of you, oh loyal

---

* King Charles IV (1748–1819) and Queen María Luisa (1751–1819).
† The Infanta María Josefa (1744–1801), sister of Charles IV, whose middle-aged features can be seen at the back in Goya's portrait of the Royal Family (1800).

vasallos? ¿Vuestra vida	servants? Who will make sure of
quién asegurará? ¿Quién vuestros hijos	Your life and lodging? Who will protect
defenderá? ¿La paz y regocijos	Your children? Peace and happiness,
de quién esperaréis? Ella viviendo	Who will give hope to them? When she was alive
la abundancia corría	Plenty flowed
para adormir vuestras dolientes penas,	To soothe your grievous pains and
para colmar de próspera alegría	To heap prosperous happiness
vuestra canosa edad. Ella viviendo	On your hoary age. When she was alive
aherrojada en cadenas	She shackled in chains
en sus estados la opresión bramaba,	The frightful oppression on her properties.
el huérfano afligido	The afflicted orphan
su madre la llamaba	Called her mother.
su amparo el desválido,	The helpless called her shield,
su gloria el español; y cual si fuera	The Spaniard his glory; and, as if
su diosa tutelar, la agricultura	She was its tutelary goddess,
sus dones imploraba . . .	Agriculture begged gifts from her . . .

Francisco Sánchez Barbero, 'Memorial Literario' No. LXV,
Dec. 5, 1804, qu. in Ezquerra del Bayo, 256–37.

[101] Palacio Liria (Berwick): Joseph Townsend
(1786)
(This palace, built by Ventura Rodríguez in 1770, is now
(having been rebuilt after the Civil War of 1936–39) the Madrid
palace of the Duques of Alba. It was made for the Duque de
Berwick (see No. 118, footnote ‡‡) whose grandson inherited
the Dukedom of Alba through the female line in 1804.

Joseph Townsend (1739–1816), a geologist and clergyman,
was a keen observer of Spain.)

For commodiousness and elegance, no house in Madrid is equal to the duke of Berwick's*. Built on a hill, with the principal front towards the city, it occupies, like other Spanish houses, the four sides of a square, yet is perfectly modern, both in style and furniture. You enter a spacious hall, then, ascending a wide staircase, you find a suite of magnificent apartments, communicating all round, and upon the same level with the garden to the south and to the east. From this circumstance, all the ground floor is kept exceedingly cool for a summer's residence, and the principal apartments are warm and comfortable in winter. Such an habitation would be ill-suited for the accommodation of numerous domestics, with their widows and their children, descending by tradition from his ancestors; and therefore the duke, very wisely, is satisfied with giving them small pensions, and leaves them to provide a lodging for themselves.

He was so obliging as to let me see his accomptant's offices, in which he has introduced a system of economy little known in Spain. They consist, as usual, of four departments, but then in these he has only one accomptant general, with three clerks; one principal secretary, with three under him; one treasurer, and one keeper of archives, with an assistant. On all his estates he has similar establishments, but upon a smaller scale . . .

Most families, especially the great, have their tertulia, or evening society for cards and conversation, after which, they, who are upon a footing of intimacy, stay and partake of a little supper. At these evening meetings you see the same faces from day to day. The society I chiefly frequented was at the duchess of Berwick's†; but I went often to the dutchess de la Vauguion's‡, sometimes to the countess del Carpio, and too seldom I visited count Campomanes§. Now and then, with a view to get an insight into the nature of society, I wandered away to other families, but not meeting anyone, with whom I had been previously acquainted, besides the lady of the family,

---

* This was the 4th Duke, Carlos Fernando Fitzjames Stuart (1752–1790).
† The Duchess was Catalina Augusta de Stolberg, daughter of Gustav Adolf, Prince of Stolberg.
‡ The Duchesse de la Vauguion was the wife of the French ambassador.
§ Pedro, Conde Campomanes (1723–1802), Asturian statesman.

I was soon weary, and could seldom prevail upon myself to prolong my stay.

Without any disparagement to the rest, I may venture to say, that the society at the dutchess of Berwick's was the most pleasing. It was frequented by the foreign ministers and, not only were the dutchess and her sister, the princess of Stolberg, most engaging in their manners, but the ease and freedom, which every one enjoyed, made the time pass delightfully. The dutchess herself, and three of her friends, occupied a whist table, some separated themselves for conversation, and the princess commonly, for a part of the evening, amused herself with drawing, under the inspection and tuition of the Prussian minister, who, for taste and execution, is one of the first masters in that line. Others were engaged at the piano forte. For my part, I commonly took up my pencil, and profited by the lessons given to the princess. At eleven o'clock we sat down to an elegant supper, and about one in the morning I retired, having nearly two miles to walk. The duke generally came home to supper, but he seldom sat long before he retired to his bed. *Joseph Townsend, 138–41, (1786).*

[102] Palacio del Infantado: Lady Holland's visit
(Elizabeth Vassall (1770–1845), who married the third Lord Holland, wrote a most interesting journal of her and her family's stay in Spain 1802–1803 and 1807–1808.)

On Wednesday morning [20 Dec. 1803], I went to the Duke of Infantado's*; he showed me his books, manuscripts, and pictures. His own apartment is very comfortable; his books and papers scattered about betrayed that his collection was more for use than ostentation. Ld. Hd. observed that if forcibly recalled to his mind the poor Duke's own apartment at Woburn, for here there is also a medley of the useful and ornamental models of machinery for manufacturers by the side of an inestimable *Rubens*, electrical apparatus, minerals, fossils, chemical instruments, fine porcelain, armory, and a thou-

* Pedro de Toledo, 14th Duke of Infantado (1773–1841), statesman and general.

sand curious, useful, and costly objects huddled together. In addition to every modern publication, he has some rare and precious manuscripts. A *Romance of the Rose* splendidly illuminated, *Les quatre dames d'amour*: most all the romances of chivalry enumerated as composing Don Quixote's library. A Mexican record, in hieroglyphics, of the early manner of communicating with them by signs or symbols. A beautiful portrait by *Vandyke*. Quantities of sketches by *Rubens*, several fine portraits on horseback by *Velázquez*, especially one of Christina on the brink of a river. Prince Emanuel de Salm, brother of the Duchess of Infantado, and uncle of the Duke, knowing my intimacy with the D. of Devonshire, came on purpose to meet me and enquire about them. He is a sensible, agreeable, well-informed old man, much connected in the early part of the Revolution with the Fayettists, having long been the lover of the Princess of Bouillon, who was one of 'the four inseparables', with Mde. d'Hesnin, Psse. de Poix, Dsse. de Biron.　　　　　　　　　　　　　　*Ilchester, 129–30.*

[103] Palacio de Medinaceli (1803)

(This palace on the corner of the Carrera de San Jerónimo and the Prado was built for the Duque de Lerma, favourite of Philip III, and soon passed by marriage to the Medinaceli. In the early twentieth century it was sold, 'for a song', to the founder of the Palace Hotel. The Medinacelis so criticized by Lady Holland (from whose candid journal this extract comes) showed themselves patriots in the war against Napoleon.)

Wednesday, 25th – The Nuncio obtained permission for us to see the Palace of Medinaceli; accordingly we went, and found him* and the Dss. of M. C. sitting waiting our arrival in the armory. She, her son, and daughter-in-law accompanied us everywhere with the utmost civility and attention – to the offices, kitchens, infirmary, school for servants' children belonging to the family, archives, secretaries' offices, stables for horses, ditto for mules, vaulted passages of communication from difft. parts of the house, others underground to get out to

* Luis María Fernández de Córdoba, 12th Duque de Medinaceli (1749–1806) married (1764) Joaquina María de Benavides, Duquesa de Santisteban in her own right.

the Prado, *dépôt* for *garde meuble*. Sumptuous apartments above. The mansion is immense; it covers several acres of ground, stands in three parishes, and communicates by covered galleries with three churches. 3,000 persons [including 500 servants with their wives and children] lodge under the roof. They alone preserve the custom of pages, *los caballeros*, dressed in yellow with black stockings. Many have the crosses of military orders, and are promoted to high posts in difft. professions. They are very devout . . .

There are tailors and shoemakers and many other mechanics living in the house, and employed only for the family. Every article of furniture almost is furnished from the estates of the family, and worked by his people; the marble from his quarries, the wood from his forests, the silk hangings from his estates and looms, the cloth and linen from his wool and flax. The mirrors only are from the Royal manufacture of San Ildefonso. They alone keep up a sort of sovereign state, formerly more common among the Grandees than at present. The D. and Dss. are served at table by *gentlemen* on their bended knees. They are both narrow-minded and illiterate, and associate with none of their equals, being constantly surrounded by monks and priests. The Medinaceli estates are the greatest in Spain. Among many great Houses sunk in Medinaceli, is Cardona, in Cataluña. As Cerdas they claim to be the rightful heirs of Castile, and on the day when the Kings are proclaimed the old custom is still retained of erecting a gallows opposite to the Medinaceli palace, and in taking the oath of fealty they present a protest against this act being construed into a renunciation of their claims.   *Ilchester, 135–36, 197–98.*

[104] Palacio de Medinaceli: fighting around the palace in 1808 (the account of Savary)
(Anne Jean Marie Savary, Duc de Rovigo (1774–1833), was a general and also a confidant of Napoleon.)

The progress of the Emperor had been so rapid that not one of the grand people of the court of Spain who had abandoned King Joseph to stay amongst the rebels, after having sworn loyalty to him, had had time to make plans to flee. Nearly all of those who had come to Bayonne would be found in Madrid.

Anxiety started to take hold of them; they saw no way they
could resist from within, and thought themselves lost if they
could not come to disarm the vengeance of an angry conquer-
or. They dreamed therefore of using their influence to make
him open the gates of a capital, of which one could not be made
master without rivers of blood and piles of ruins.

They all had spirits of moderation, and came, little by little,
to abandon the idea of useless resistance, to listen to the
propositions most in keeping with the interests of everyone,
most especially this last part being commanded by necessity.

Despite this, one could not get anything, and each time that
one got near to a wall or a gate one would be shot at. The
Emperor was determined to make three or four openings in the
wall where there was enough distance between it and the first
houses of the town to assemble the troops.

He selected, from the others, the outer side of the garden of
the Retiro, of which the brick wall with battlements was
demolished by cannon-fire . . .

The troops were then caused to enter there in good order.
This single movement freed the Alcalá gate, and carried the
troops right up to the edge of the Prado.

The three big roads which lead off the town at this promenade
were defended by cuttings behind which there was a good
parapet. In the first moments, there was a pretty lively row of
musket fire from the corner houses which are at the entrances to
those streets, particularly the Medinaceli palace, but it was
returned so promptly that it put a stop to it, and as they had
had the carelessness to tear the main entrance open, our soldiers
went in there, and killed all those they found with arms in their
hands; at the same time the house was pillaged, in such a manner
that any thoughts of others doing the same was quickly removed.

General Labruyère*, who was leading the 9th Light Infantry
regiment, was killed by a gun shot from one of those windows
of the Medinaceli palace.

This position opened the eyes of the members of the Junta,
who did not wish to expose Madrid to the inevitable sack if
once the troops spread out into the houses.

'Mémoires du duc de Rovigo' (Général Savary), 16–17.

* Général André Labruyère (1768–1808).

Royal Palace – Alcázar

[105] A visit of French ambassadors to the court of Juan II in Madrid in the fifteenth century: chronicle of the day as quoted by Mesonero Romanos

There came there the ambassadors of King Charles of France*, the archbishop of Toulouse who was called Louis de Molin; and a seneschal from Toulouse called Moses Jean de Moncays. And as the King† heard of their coming he ordered the Constable and all the other counts and gentlemen and prelates in his court to come out and welcome them. They went out of the town about a league and escorted them to the palace when it was almost night. They found the King in the Alcázar, accompanied by very noble people, with six torch-bearers each carrying four torches and the King ordered twenty of his younger courtiers with two torches to meet the ambassadors at the gate. The King was on his high dais, seated on his throne

* Charles VII, King of France 1422–61.
† John (Juan) II, King of Castille 1406–54.

adorned below by a rich canopy of crimson brocade, the whole covered by rich tapestries, and he had at his feet a very large tame lion with a brocade collar, a thing quite new for the ambassadors, who greatly marvelled at it, and the King stood up to receive them and made them a very happy reception and the archbishop began to shiver with fear of the lion. The King said to him that he had done well to have come and thus he embraced him and the Seneschal wished to kiss the King's hand and begged to do so; but the King did not wish it and gave him an entrance with a very gracious face and commanded the ambassadors to draw near and thus they sat themselves in two seats of Silk which the King had ordered to be placed there, the one on one side, the other on the other, divided from the King by six feet. The King asked for news of his brother the King of France and of other great lords of the realm, and having heard the news which they gave him the King commanded that a meal be brought, which was offered in the room of this great prince . . . They asked the King to name a day to explain the purpose of their visit. The King offered them the next Wednesday.

Mesonero Romanos, 8–9.

[106] The Comuneros Revolt (Sandoval, 1520)
(This was an important Castillian challenge to Charles V.)

The absurdities which were done in Madrid, which, as I said, had risen, were not less than in the other communities of Castille. There was in the Alcázar an honourable and faithful gentleman called Francisco de Vargas. The Comuneros did all they could to get rid of him or capture it . . . The town many times asked for it and threatened the *alcalde* that if he did not give up the Alcázar they would hang as many of those who were inside as they could. The *alcalde* [Hernán Gómez de Herrera] being so pressed and with so few men, left secretly one night for Alcalá six short leagues from Madrid to try and raise some men there to help him. He found forty men and in order to put them in such a way without them being seen he ordered them to ride in a procession, two by two in each group . . . [But this did not succeed and the *alcalde* fled again to Alcalá]. The Comune then fell with great fury on the Alcázar, and besieged it, though in no manner that they could get close to it, since those inside defended it very well and fired balls of fire at them, and used crossbows and stones.

The Alcázar being in this difficulty, Diego de Vera arrived near Madrid with people from Los Gelves. They were able to enter the Alcázar and provide it with supplies with which to punish the Comuneros of Madrid harshly. But he came tired from the journey and cross not to have received payments, nor his people for a long time . . .

The captain of the people of the town was a man called Negrete. He decided to mine the Alcázar in four places. Those inside realized that they were being mined and threw down on the besiegers many shots and told each and every one of them that they would throw down things in vast quantities and kill them, and so they left off mining by day and did so by night with protections and blankets, and they put before them the children and relations of those who were within . . . The wife of the *alcalde* who was within gave herself over with ingenuity to aid and even to animate the defenders so that they did not miss her husband, in such a way that she was the heart of the defence.

Those of the city sent to require her to give up; if she did not, they promised that no one would enter or go out unless they were dead or a prisoner.

She replied that they were whistling in the dark to think that just because the *alcalde* was absent she and the others would do any black thing or any disservice to the King; that all inside were decided to go on defending the fortress until death rather than commit such treason; and that where she was, her husband the *alcalde* would not be missed.

When the *Comunidad* heard this they became infuriated and said loudly: 'They will die and they will all die.'

Everyone then was armed and put on a war footing. They blocked all the gates of the Alcázar and placed before them big pieces of artillery. Those inside made further great efforts to defend themselves and fired all they could, on a large and effective scale, but they had few people to command them. Both sides began to use their artillery. Those inside the Alcázar destroyed the nearby houses, for inside there were two very skilful artillery men, even though they did not wish to do all the evil that they could.

Some monks tried to make peace between the two sides but when that had been half achieved, a knight left the Alcázar saying in thunderous tones, 'Oh wicked traitors, Jews of Madrid! What have you done? What an arrangement to make in respect of such damage to the King of your town? What are you going to do with such cowards?' And he went on and on saying such things in such a way that the town became agitated again, and burned with fury, some favouring him, others wishing to kill him. And between the two there was fighting and a bloody exchange, with knives and lances which disabled many.

The Knight was soon captured by the populace, and they wished to kill him. They kept him prisoner until they knew what had moved him to inspire such an upheaval which prevented the achievement of what had been planned . . . [soon] the artillery commander from outside killed the artillery commander inside and there was nobody inside who knew how to use the artillery.

Water and food became scarce and in the end they had to give up . . . The Comunidad entered the Alcázar with much enthusiasm.

[*Their triumph was short-lived. The rebellion collapsed in Castille and most of their leaders were executed.*]

Fray Prudencio de Sandoval, '*Historia
del emperador Carlos V*', I, 242–43.

[107] King François I visited by Emperor Charles V (1525)

(The King of France, captured at the battle of Pavia, was imprisoned in Spain 1525–1526.)

When the Emperor entered the room where the King was, he took off his hat and embraced him on the bed where he lay; and the King gathered himself in the bed and embraced the Emperor saying, 'Monsieur, you see I am your slave.' And the Emperor replied, 'No, you are my good brother and free friend.' And the King replied, 'No I am your slave.' And the Emperor replied: 'No, you are my free friend and good brother.'

And after this many other words were exchanged. The

substance of these was the Emperor had to tell the King that all he had to do was look after his health, that he desired that very much, and that certainly his affairs would go well. And with this the Emperor went out and passed to another room in the same Alcázar. And the King remained consoled, and felt notably better.

In Fray Prudencio de Sandoval, 'Historia del Emperador Carlos V,' I, 109–10.

[108] King François I tries to escape dressed as a black slave (1525)

Madame de Alanson*, seeing how little her requests and tactics profited her and how what was offered her turned out to be nothing, begged permission to return and see her brother on her way. She was given it and went to the Alcázar of Madrid to visit him, where she was several days inquiring how she could cautiously remove him from prison, since neither demands nor offers were enough.

The stratagem was that a black slave who put firewood in the room where the King slept would sleep in the King's bed, while the King would dress in the clothes of the negro, and black his face. And thus he would be able to leave the house when night fell, at an hour when nobody could see that the face had been falsely blackened.

At this time there was in the King's service there in Madrid a French gentleman who was called Monsieur de Larochepot and a waiter called Clemente Chapion. The two of them quarrelled one day and Monsieur Larochepot gave the waiter a blow, as a result of which he was very bruised and self-pitying.

The waiter, seeing that there was something strange going on and because the injury came from a man more powerful than he, did not give up his desire for vengeance and went from Madrid to Toledo where the Emperor was and revealed to him the entanglement which the King of France had woven to get

---

* Margaret Duchesse d'Alençon (1492–1549), the 'Marguerite des marguerites', was sister of François I and the centre of a brilliant salon.

out from prison. And that he was determined to do it a few days after his sister had left.

The Emperor marvelled that the King of France would want to use this scheme and humiliate himself in such an ugly fashion in order to fly . . . and the guards were warned.

[*The King of France found imprisonment in the Alcázar intolerable. He signed the Treaty of Madrid, giving away Burgundy. But as soon as he got back to France, he went back on his word.*]

Fray Prudencio de Sandoval, 'Historia de la vida y hechos del Emperador Carlos V', in 'Biblioteca de Autores Españoles', Tomo LXXXI (Madrid 1955), III.

[109] Arrest of Don Carlos (1568)

(This account is by Sir William Stirling Maxwell (1818–1878), a rich baronet – his grandfather had built up a fortune in Jamaica – who devoted his life to the study of Spanish painting and to a biography of Don John. Don Carlos, made into a figure of myth by Schiller's play and Verdi's opera based on it, was in truth an invalid.)

On the 17th January the King was again in his capital. Accompanied by Don John of Austria*, he immediately went to the Queen's† apartments; and they had not been there long when Don Carlos‡ entered to pay his respects to him. For a considerable time before Christmas the father and son had hardly spoken to each other when they met; but on this occasion the one was very respectful in his demeanour, and that of the other betrayed neither anger nor displeasure. When Don Carlos retired, he took Don John with him to his apartments, and there they remained closeted for two hours. Of

---

* Don John of Austria (1545–78), illegitimate son of the Emperor Charles V by Barbara Blomberg of Regensberg. A brave soldier and skilful diplomatist of whom King Philip II was jealous.

† Queen Elizabeth of Valois (1546–1568), third wife of Philip II, daughter of King Henry II of France, and Catherine de Medici. Briefly betrothed to Don Carlos.

‡ Don Carlos (1545–1568), son of Philip II of Spain and his first wife María of Portugal. Delicate, wilful, probably insane.

what passed at this interview there are several accounts. One, perhaps the more probable one, is that Carlos repeated his former efforts to induce Don John to join him, informing him that he had ordered fresh horses to be ready for his departure; that he begged him to bring at midnight the order necessary for his embarkation, and a paper declaring himself prepared to serve him at whatever time or in whatever manner his service might be desired; and that Don John, to gain time, promised these papers by the next day at one in the afternoon, and on that condition was suffered to retire. Another version is that Carlos, unable to prevail with his uncle, attacked him with sword or pistol, and that Don John defended himself until the servants, hearing a great noise, opened the doors and enabled him to withdraw. A third account makes it appear that Carlos, having given up all hope of enlisting Don John on his side, inveigled him to his room in order to punish his treachery; that he had placed a loaded gun ready, but that one of his people had withdrawn the charge; and that, finding himself thus baffled, he had attacked him with another weapon, and with intent to take his life.

Next day, the 18th of January, being Sunday, Don Carlos accompanied the King to mass. At one in the afternoon he received a note from Don John of Austria, excusing himself from keeping the appointment made the day before, being unwell, and proposing to wait on Don Carlos on the Wednesday following. The Prince himself then went to bed in order to avoid obeying any summons from the King, who, in fact, sent for him some time afterwards, and was informed that he was too unwell to rise. Some days before, the King had ordered prayers to be said in the churches of Madrid for divine counsel and guidance in an affair of importance; and on this Sunday it was noticed that frequent messages passed between the King and his minister, Espinosa. After the arrest of Don Carlos these prayers and messages were connected by the courtiers with that event; but up to the moment of its accomplishment, its approach does not seem to have been suspected.

At eleven o'clock on Sunday night the King summoned the Prince of Eboli*, and Count of Feria†, the prior Don Antonio

---

* Ruy Gómez de Silva, Prince of Eboli (1516–73). Philip II's chief adviser in the early part of his reign.
† The Conde de Feria had been Spanish ambassador in London.

de Toledo, and Luis Quixada, and addressed to them some
words, such, they afterwards said, 'as never man spoke before.'
At midnight, accompanied by two chamberlains, a lieutenant,
and a guard of twelve men, they proceeded to the apartments of
the Prince. The King wore armour under his dressing-gown
and a helmet on his head, and the Count of Feria walked before
him carrying a light. Don Carlos had lately caused to be made
an elaborate apparatus for securing his bedroom door, with
pulleys by which he could shoot or withdraw the bolts at
pleasure as he lay in bed. By the King's order the Frenchman
who had constructed this piece of machinery had now put it
out of order. The party therefore entered the room without
hindrance, the King keeping himself in the background until
some of the others had seized the sword, dagger, and pistol
which the Prince always placed by his bedside. Awakened by
the noise, Carlos called out: 'Who is there?' 'The Council of
State,' was the reply. He immediately jumped out of bed as if to
seize his arms. Observing the King, who now stepped forward,
he cried: 'Does your Majesty wish to kill me?' Philip assured
him that no harm was intended, and that they were come solely
for his good, and he advised him to return to bed. He then gave
orders for the nailing up of the windows, so that they could not
be opened, and for the removal of everything in the room that
could be used as a weapon of offence; and he himself proceeded
to make a careful search for the Prince's papers. These were
found in a small box, which was at once carried off to the
King's apartment. Amongst them was a list, in the handwriting
of Carlos, of his enemies and his friends. The first was headed
by the names of the King, the Prince of Eboli, and the Duke of
Alba*; the second, by those of the Queen, Don John of Austria,
'my most dear and beloved uncle,' and Luis Quixada.

On finding himself a prisoner the unhappy Prince fell into a
fit of passionate despair. He threw himself at his father's feet,
and entreated that he might be put to death rather than shut up.
'If you do not kill me I will kill myself,' he cried, and thereupon
tried to throw himself into the fire, but was held back by force
by the prior, Don Antonio. 'To kill yourself would be the act of

* Fernando Álvarez de Toledo (1508–1582), Duque de Alba, celebrated
for his campaign in the Netherlands, the reputed leader of the conservatives at Court.

a madman,' said the King. 'I am not mad,' replied Carlos, 'but driven desperate by your Majesty's manner of treating me.' He then burst into tears, reproaching his father in a voice broken with sobs for his tyranny and harshness. 'Henceforth,' said Philip, 'I am going to treat you not as a father, but as a King.'

Stirling Maxwell, 69–73.

[110] The death of Queen Elizabeth of Valois
(Queen Elizabeth, third wife of Philip II, was ill. Her mother wrote to her son-in-law suggesting the reason. He read this letter in the Palace in late September 1568.)

Monsieur mon Fils

Having been informed that the queen your wife is very indisposed, I write to state that I believe her indisposition proceeds from supping too heavily, and from not taking sufficient exercise; the which cannot fail to do great harm both to herself, and to her child. I entreat, therefore, that your majesty will give commands that she may not continue to act in this fashion, nor take more than two meals a day. If she cannot exist without eating between her dinner and her supper, I pray your majesty to order that she may take bread only, as in her youth she was never accustomed to eat meat excepting at her dinner, or her said supper. I have no doubt that this excess has done her harm; also I fear your majesty has been too anxious to please and satisfy her, to admonish the queen that such a practice is likely to produce serious illness. For this reason I have not hesitated to trouble you with this letter, and to implore you to forbid very strictly that the queen continues to pursue such a course. Praying the Almighty to grant your majesty your desires, I remain.

Votre bonne mère, et soeur, Catherine.
From Paris this 16th day of September, 1568.

[Elizabeth died in October, but not from over-eating – and not from poison as alleged by Antonio Pérez.]

MS. *Archivos de Simancas, 1394, A.B. 22, No. 161,*
Carta de la reyna Doña Catalina de Medici
al Rey Don Felipe II – Unpublished.

[111] A Nuncio's visit: Camillo Borghese (1593)
(For Borghese, see No. 22.)

The King [Philip II] since he turned seventy years old does not dine in public any more. But one can see the most serene prince [that is, the future Philip III] dining with much frequency, and at his table there is no majesty at all. He only eats at a small table, on which are placed four or six courses and his service is no better than the grandees have at their banquets and his meat is cut without the slightest elegance and his plate placed in front of him.

At this public audience [of the King] which did not serve for more than a complimentary occasion we were all present and on this occasion we did see the King, which would have been otherwise difficult . . . He is of small stature with a jovial look and large mouth, his hair white, which last fact gives gravitas. He was dressed wholly in black with a cap called a *gorra*, with cloak and sword.

When we entered, his majesty was seated in a chair of black velvet and as soon as *monseñor* was in the room he rose, leaning on a stool but covered in velvet, equally black, under a baldaquin. The room was not very big but it was hung with the most beautiful cloths, if without gold. Present at this audience there were at hand three or four grandees, on the right hand the Conde de Chinchón*, Don Juan de Idiáquez†, Don Cristóbal de Mora‡, with three or four pages, mostly sons of princes. His Majesty drew his cap down to his eyebrows and made *monseñor* so cover himself also, making a pleased expression.

After the audience which lasted a very short time we went to see the most serene Prince§ and Infanta¶ who saw *monseñor* at the same time in the room of the Infanta. She was dressed in black, of embroidered velvet; aged twenty-eight, of a look more beautiful than ugly, not very tall in stature although her high

---

* Diego Fernández de Cabrera, Conde de Chinchón, minister to the King.
† Juan de Idiáquez, secretary to the King (d. 1614).
‡ Cristóbal de Mora (1538–1613), a Portuguese in the service of King Philip II.
§ i.e. Philip, later King of Spain as Philip III.
¶ The Infanta Isabel, who later married her cousin the Archduke Albert of Austria.

heels helped her; a large gross mouth in the usual Austrian style, olive skin and on her head she wore a white feather. The prince was dressed in white in breeches, cloak and cap in the same style as his father but with big white plumes. In height he is not very tall, being now sixteen years old. He has a large mouth and will be a very pretty prince. These serene highnesses were standing beneath a baldaquin which only held him and the Infanta in spite of the fact that *monseñor* tried to approach them. Their chamber was decorated by Flemish tapestries like that of the King and there were many ladies and matrons waiting on the Infanta and six or eight gentlemen and some other pages. After saying goodbye to their Highnesses he went to see the most serene Cardinal of Austria* and when the audience with him was over he returned home in a coach accompanied by the same troop of prelates and gentlemen.

The royal palace, in which there did not live anyone other than His Majesty, the Prince, the Infanta and the Cardinal, does not seem too big for such a King. There are two big *patios* with a series of magnificent columns which almost reach the roof of the palace; and leaving the stairway there are beautiful galleries; but the rooms are small and one only sees rooms opening out of each other since the whole palace is full of galleries. It is full of many beautiful pictures and at the end of it there are beautiful stables. To guard the palace there are a good number of halberdiers dressed in black with breeches, who serve to guard the King, the Prince, the Infanta and the Cardinal.

The following day Monseñor went in a carriage to see the Empress† who lived in another palace, and is a most saintly old lady dressed as a nun with her cloak over her head with a face very like the King's. In her room there were many lords and ladies and at her gate a guard of halberdiers.

Camillo Borghese, in García Mercadal,
'Viajes', I, 1478, 1471–72.

---

* The Cardinal de Austria was another Albert v. Habsburg.
† Isabel of Portugal, the widow of Charles V.

[112] The Prince of Wales's visit (1623)

(Charles, Prince of Wales, and George, then Marquis of Buckingham, came to Spain in 1623 to pursue the Infanta (see No. 7). They reached Madrid on 26 March and stayed with the English Ambassador in the Calle de Alcalá for six difficult months. This joint letter is a personal one.)

Dear dad* and gossip†,

That your majesty may be the more particularly informed of all, we will observe our former order to begin still where we left, which was, we think, at the king's private visit in the night. The next day your baby desired to kiss his hands privately in the palace, which was granted, and thus performed. First, the king would not suffer him to come to his chamber, but met him at the stair-foot; then entered into the coach, and walked into his park. The greatest matter that passed between them, at that time, was compliments, and particular questions of our journey; then, by force, he would needs carry him half way home, in which doing, they were both almost overthrown in brick-pits. Two days after, we met with his majesty again in his park, with his two brothers; they spent their time in seeing his men kill partridges flying, and conies running with a gun. Yesterday, being Sunday, your baby went to a monastery called St Jerónimo's, to dinner, which stands a little out of the town‡. After dinner all the councillors came in order, to welcome your baby; then came the king himself, with all his nobility, and made their entry with as great triumph as could be, where he forced your baby to ride on his right hand, which he observes always. This entry was made just as when the Kings of Castille come first to the crown: all prisoners set at liberty, and no office or matters of grace falls, but is put in your baby's hands to dispose.

Wilson thus relates this circumstance: – 'About ten of the clock that night, the King of Spain came in a close coach to visit the prince, who having intimation of his coming, such secret hints among princes being suitable invitements, he met him in

* James I, King of England.
† A slang word for godfather which Buckingham used to the King out of affection.
‡ The Convento de San Jerónimo, in the Prado.

the way, and there they spent some time in those sweet yet formal caresses and embraces that are incident to the interviews of the great princes, though their hearts and tongues do seldom accord. Gondemar in consort was not without his strain of compliment, for he told the prince upon a visit next day, that he had strange news to tell him; which was, that an Englishman was sworn privy-councillor to the King of Spain, meaning himself, who he said was an Englishman in heart, and had lately received that honour.'   *Halliwell, 182–83 (1623).*

[113] Letter of the Conde Duque de Olivares to Rubens (1628)

(Peter Paul Rubens (1577–1640) spent nine months in Madrid in 1628, partly with a diplomatic role, partly on a painting commission. He had been before in 1603.)

Even though you have not told me yourself of the loss which you have experienced by the death of your companion [i.e. Isabelle Brant] showing thus your habitual discretion I have learned of it and I sympathize with you in your solitude, you who loved and esteemed her so much. I count greatly on your prudence and it seems to me that, in such cases, one does well to keep up one's courage and conform to the divine purpose than to seek motives of consolation. I have more need than anyone in the world when I coldly examine the causes of the sadness I feel myself having seen my nephew Cardinal Guzmán die at twenty-two years old, and a few days after, my only daughter, on whom I had founded the hope of continuing my family and whom I loved less because she was my daughter than because she was remarkable for her virtue, intelligence and character, marks worthy of an esteem higher than most. God carried her off in consequence of a bad labour and so I have lost everything and remain without being able to fear or hope for anything on earth. But it has pleased God to give me reliefs and consolations proportionate to my grief and I am glad that your natural affection acts with such tenderness that I can show from my side such as I can in these grievous moments. I speak to you as to a discreet man so that you can see that in the middle of my cares and heavy work, I esteem in you the qualities and favours which God has accorded you and the satisfaction that I have of the affection that you bear me. An excellent witness which you provide is the portrait which you have arranged to be printed [a portrait which Pontius would engrave]. It shows at the same time that affection finds appropriate ideas, that it knows how to represent real appearances and that it makes us conceive hopes which go beyond our merits.

As for the emblems [i.e. around the picture], I tell you that being now disembarrassed of temporal and personal cares, I am more than ever obliged to give an account of the public affairs which have been confided to me. May God give me the light and the force necessary for my task and then I will think I can esteem the portrait as it deserves and the things which it promises are not entirely lies.

God keep you as you deserve.

Madrid 8 August 1626

signed DON GASPAR DE GUZMÁN

Qu. in Brown and Elliott, 'A Palace for a King'.

[114] Rubens reports on his stay (1628)

. . . Here I keep to painting, as I do everywhere, and already I have done the equestrian portrait of His Majesty, to his great pleasure and satisfaction. He really takes an extreme delight in painting, and in my opinion this prince is endowed with excellent qualities. I know him already by personal contact, for since I have rooms in the palace, he comes to see me almost every day. I have also done the heads of all the royal family, accurately and with great convenience, in their presence, for the service of the Most Serene Infanta, my patroness*. She had given me permission, on my return, to make a tour of Italy, . . .

The King alone arouses my sympathy. He is endowed by nature with all the gifts of body and spirit, for in my daily intercourse with him I have learned to know him thoroughly. And he would surely be capable of governing under any

* This was the Infanta María, who had been courted by Charles Prince of Wales and would soon become Queen of Hungary and Empress.

conditions, were it not that he mistrusts himself and defers too much to others. But now he has to pay for his own credulity and others' folly, and feel the hatred that is not meant for him. Thus have the gods willed it.

Rubens, letter CCCCVII (1626), 'Letters', 454–55.

[115] Antoine, Maréchal-duc de Gramont (1604–1677), comes to negotiate a marriage (1659)

(This negotiation led to the most important marriage in European history: that of the Infanta María Teresa with Louis XIV, leading to the arrival of the Bourbons in Spain.)

And since it had to seem as if it had been a matter of post-horses, the marshal, having judged that as he had been sent by a young gallant and loving monarch, there was no other way of entering Madrid except as the most speedy messenger to show to the Infanta the impatience and passion of his master (which greatly pleased the Spanish who had not yet forgotten the idea of the ancient gallantry of Abencerrajes), he rode the entire way from the gate of the city to the palace at the gallop . . . The Marshal entered by the gate of the Prado [i.e. the Alcalá] which he traversed from one end to the other and then went to the Calle Mayor. There were there a great number of carriages which were, however, so arranged that they did not interrupt the passage and such a quantity of people that the streets, which are very broad, and the balconies as far as the fourth floor, could not contain them . . . it is impossible to conceive and express the joy and enthusiasm of the people. One only heard on all sides, 'Long live the Maréchal de Gramont who comes from the same blood as ourselves, who brings peace and who is here to conclude of the wedding of our most Serene Infanta* with the Most Catholic King, so good, so beautiful and so young. God bless them!'† . . . The Marshal de Gramont always had his hat off to reply to the civilities of the ladies and gentlemen. At last, he arrived at the palace and went on

---

* The Infanta María Teresa (1638–1683), later Queen of France.
† The Gramonts were supposed to have come originally from Spain.

horseback into the waiting room at the foot of the great staircase where he met the Admiral of Castille . . .

The Marshal could not go up the staircase because of the great crowd which gathered there. Those who had seen him before wished to see him again . . . As for me*, who was then extremely young, good-looking and well turned out, I was carried off like a saintly body by the *tapadas*, who are the 'femmes de joie' of Madrid, and who took me by force, after having taken all my ribbons, and were about to violate me publicly: that would have certainly occurred had it not been for the help of the Admiral of Castille and one or two other grandees, who saw the risk that I ran and extracted me, with some roughness, from the arms of these frenzied jades. The Marshal, meantime, had reached the rooms of the King . . . after having made three traditional bows he read as follows:

'Sire:

The King my master sends me to Your Majesty to bear witness to the extreme joy which he feels in seeing that God has blessed the holy intentions that Your Majesties have always had in wishing to end a long war, giving rest not only to the great number of peoples which are ruled by them but to all Christianity, which has for so long desired such a great and necessary work. And because the King, my master, desires nothing more than a good and lasting union among Your Majesties, he believed that nothing could better establish such a thing than to demand, as I do in his name to Your Highness, the most serene Infanta Dona María Teresa, eldest daughter of Your Majesty, in marriage.'   *Gramont, 312–314.*

[116] A royal wet-nurse's self-justification (seventeenth century)

(The wet-nurse of Felipe Próspero's son and so, till he died, heir of King Philip IV, replies to the King's accusation that she is responsible for the child's illnesses. (The Prince soon died.))

* This was Antoine, Comte de Louvigny (1638(?)–1720), second son of Gramont and eventually his heir.

Sire, I have three children, the loveliest in the Court, nurtured at my breasts, flourishing on my milk and care; when they cried, I rocked them; I cured their rashes and pimples with my saliva; they slept on my breast and I gave them love; I ate, at my usual time, seasoned food. *Here* they give me everything without spices, seasoning or salt; I spend the nights awake and if I must rest I am forced to retire to an attic: they lift my skirts to see if I have the curse; the fuss and noise is great; my milk, with so many annoyances, cannot be so good. That is how things are and it seems there is no remedy; as far as I am concerned I do what I ought and all I want is to serve Your Majesty.

.Paz y Meliá, A, 'Avisos de D. Jerónimo de Barrionuevo 1654–1658', 4 vols, Madrid 1892, quoted John Nada, 46.

[117] Verse addressed to María Luisa, Queen of Spain, encouraging her to give birth

(King Charles II was impotent, so it was not surprising that his French Queen could not bear a child. She died in mysterious circumstances. She was daughter of 'Monsieur', Duc d'Orléans, and Charles II of England's favourite sister, Henrietta Maria.)

Parid, bella flor de lis,	Procreate, beautiful *fleur de lis,*
Que en aflicción tan extraña	Thou that has such a strange malady
Si parís, parís a España,	If thou beget a child, it is Spain;
Si no parís, a París.	If dost not, go back to Paris.

to which was added:

si no parís, paraíso.	If you don't beget, Paradise.

Source: unknown

[118] Saint-Simon's visit to King Philip V (1721)

(Saint-Simon, ambassador of France, was acquainted with King Philip V (1683–1746) from the time when he had been at Versailles as Duc d'Anjou. The plans for a marriage between the Infanta María Ana and King Louis XV were unsuccessful.)

We arrived at the palace as the King was on the point of returning from mass, and we waited for him in the little salon which is between the salon of the Grandees and that of the Mirrors, into which only those who have been commanded enter. Shortly after, the King entered by the Salon of the Grandees. Grimaldo* alerted him as he entered the little salon: he straight away came towards me, preceded and followed by several courtiers, who were nevertheless not at all like the crowds with us. I made him a deep bow; he indicated to me his pleasure at my arrival, asked for news of the King, of the Duc d'Orléans†, of my journey and news of my eldest son, whom he knew to have remained ill at Burgos, and then entered alone the cabinet of Mirrors. Immediately I was surrounded by the entire court, with their compliments and their tokens of joy at the marriage and at the union of the two crowns. Grimaldo and the Duque de Liria‡ named the noblemen to me, practically all of whom spoke French, with innumerable civilities to which I endeavoured to respond with my own.

Five or ten minutes after the King had returned, he sent for me. I entered into the Salon of Mirrors alone, which is very large, and less wide than long. The King, and the Queen on his left, were nearly at the end of the salon, standing, and very close to each other. I approached with three deep bows, and I noticed at once, as always, that the King never wears a hat except at public audiences, and when he goes to and comes from the mass in chapel, a habit which I will explain in due course. The audience lasted half an hour (as it is always they who take leave), to witness to their joy, their desires, their impatience, with an infinite outpouring, especially concerning the Duc d'Orléans, and concerning the wish to make Mademoiselle de Montpensier§ happy, concerning a portrait of her and another of the King which they showed me. At the end of

* José Gutiérrez Grimaldo (1660–1733), principal minister in Spain after the fall of Cardinal Alberoni.
† Philippe Duc d'Orléans (1674–1723), Regent of France 1715–1723.
‡ James Fitzjames, Earl of Tynemouth by James II's creation, Duque de Liria in Spain (1696–1738), succeeded his father as 2nd Duke of Berwick.
§ Louise-Elisabeth d'Orléans (1709–42), daughter of the Regent Orléans, called Mademoiselle de Montpensier, married to Luis Prince of Asturias, and briefly Queen of Spain 1724–25.

the conversation during which the Queen spoke much more than the King, whose joy nevertheless sparkled with delight, they did me the honour to tell me they wished me to see the children, and commanded me to follow them. In their train, I crossed this room alone and the Queen's cabinet, an interior gallery where there were two ladies in waiting and two or three noblemen in charge, who had apparently been forewarned, as I have elsewhere explained, and went with this little procession the whole length of the gallery, at the end of which was the apartment of the children. I have never seen such pretty children, nor better made, than Don Ferdinand and Don Carlos, nor a more beautiful baby than Don Felipe*. The King and Queen† took great pleasure in letting me see them, and in making them walk and turn about in front of me very becomingly. Then they went to the Infanta's room, where I was at pains to express as many compliments as I was able. Indeed, she was charming, with a little rational air and not at all bashful. The Queen told me that the Infanta was beginning to learn French quite well; and the King, that she would very soon forget Spain. 'Oh!' cried the Queen, 'not only Spain but the King and myself, so as to attach herself only to the King her husband,' upon which I endeavoured not to remain dumb. I went away from there in their Catholic Majesties' train, which I followed across this little gallery and their apartments. They bade me farewell immediately with many tokens of kindness, and, returning to the salon with all the company, I was once again surrounded with many compliments.

A little later, the King summoned me back to see the Prince of Asturias‡, who was with Their Majesties in this same Salon of Mirrors. I found him tall and truly worthy of an artist's brush; fair and with beautiful hair, white-skinned with some colour, a long face, and agreeable, beautiful eyes but too close to the nose: I found him very graceful and polite. He asked me insistently for news of the King, then of the Duc d'Orléans and then of Mlle Montpensier, and the time of her arrival.

---

* These princes were the subsequent Spanish monarchs Ferdinand VI and Charles III, and Philip, Duke of Parma, founder of the family of Bourbon-Parma.
† Elizabeth Farnese (1692–1766), daughter of Odoardo of Parma, second queen to Philip V.
‡ Luis, Prince of Asturias (1707–1725), King of Spain 1724–1725.

Their Catholic Majesties gave me much evidence of their satisfaction at my diligence, told me that they had delayed their journey so as to give me time to prepare myself for my audiences, that a single one would suffice to ask for the Infanta's hand, and to grant it; that the articles could be signed on the eve of that audience, and in the afternoon of the same day of this audience the contract be signed. Finally he asked me when everything would be ready; I told them that it would be whatever day they pleased, since all that I was preparing was only for me to pay my court to them. I thought to succeed the better with less time so as not to delay their departure, than to postpone it in order to stall all that for which I was still working. It seemed to me that this reply pleased them greatly but they wished keenly to fix the day, upon which I finally suggested the following Tuesday. The joy at this promptitude appeared in their faces, and they were deeply grateful to me. Thereupon, the King drew back a little, spoke to the Queen in a low voice, and she to him, and fixed their departure for the following Thursday, the 27th of the month. Straightway they invited me not only to follow them, but ordered me to do so closely, because the inconvenience would permit only the most needed officers to accompany them on the way. That was the end of the entire audience . . .

The Queen, whom I saw a quarter of an hour later, just as I have recounted above, frightened me by her lined face, scarred and disfigured by smallpox; the Spanish costume for ladies of that time entirely differs from the ancient one, and, invented by the Princess des Ursins, is as flattering to young ladies with good figures as it is unbecoming for others, whose age and figure allow all their defects to be apparent. The Queen was shapely, at that time, but with bust and shoulders well set up, fairly plump and very white, as were her arms and hands. She had an elegant, fine and well-proportioned figure, extremely slender, standing a little taller than average; she had a slight Italian accent; spoke French very well, using well chosen words unhesitatingly, her voice and pronunciation being extremely agreeable. A charming, ceaseless, natural grace, which was not at all contrived, emanated from her conversation and her bearing, and varied as they did. She joined an air of goodness, kindness, also of politeness, with propriety and proportion and, often with an attractive familiarity, to a grand and majestic manner which never left her. From this mixture, it seemed natural that when one had the honour of seeing her in any privacy, though always in the presence of the King as I have said elsewhere, one was immediately at ease with her without ever forgetting who she was, and one became very quickly used to her face . . . We had to return to the palace for the ball which the King had had prepared in the Grandees' Salon, and which lasted until after two in the morning.

This Salon, which is also enormous and superb with its bronzes, marbles, gilding and pictures, was magnificently lit; at the far end opposite the door there were, as there had been at the signing ceremony, six armchairs facing, in which the King and Queen, etc, sat down in the same order. Close beside the King's armchair on his right, no distance away and much less than two feet to the rear of it, there was a sprung seat, heavy with crimson velvet with gold fringes and gilt woodwork, for the King's senior major domo, who seated himself exactly at the same moment as the King placed himself in his armchair. To the left hand of the armchair of the last Infante there was placed, in a similar position, a stool of black velvet, with no gold, having black tassels at the corners, for the Queen's chief lady-in-waiting who was dressed in somewhat modified widow's weeds since the Queen could not endure all this great nunnish paraphernalia, which is the wear for widows whoever they may be, in which I saw the Duchess of Linares* at Bayonne. For the same reason, the stool was black when it would otherwise have been of crimson velvet with gold. This lady could have had a sprung seat similar to the one on the right, but from force of habit she preferred the stool, which is as distinguished. Behind the armchairs there were red velvet stools with gold fringes and gilt wood, for the captain of the King's guard, the high butler, the Queen's high steward, the Infanta's governess, and the Duke of Popoli†, the Prince of Asturias' tutor. In a false doorway, right behind the armchairs on the side of the High Steward, but not directly at his back, were two sprung seats of red velvet with gold fringes and gilt work to

---

* Lucrecia Ladrón y Silva, Duquesa de Linares (1655–1729).
† Rostaing Cantelmi, Duque de Popoli (1651–1723), Neapolitan major domo of the King of Spain.

which Gaspard Girón led us, Maulevrier and myself, with no screen placed in front of us which was a singular favour, and no one at all in front of us, so that we could clearly see all this beautiful spectacle as well as the dances.

A little lower down than the High Steward, ranged against the wall, some way apart towards the far end, there were stools like ours mingled with other stools for ladies of red satin, likewise gilded, for the wives of the Grandees of Spain and those of their eldest sons, who sat down where they liked, but the wives of the grandees on the velvet ones and the wives of the eldest sons' on the satin or damask ones. These stools were placed about almost a half or thereabouts of the length of the long side of this salon; the rest was occupied by ladies of quality, wives or daughters, seated on the floor on the vast carpet which covered the entire salon, several of them standing, which they were free to do, and right by the last seats, several young ladies-in-waiting of the Queen, placed there to dance. Opposite this long row of ladies on the other side were all the men of the Court, grandees and others, all standing, their backs to the windows which were some distance from them, which distance was filled with lesser spectators, just as was the space opposite them, between the wall and the ladies. At the far end of the men's side, almost in a T-shape, were the King's four stewards to give orders to everybody. Opposite the armchairs, at the far end, stood the dancers, the grandees and others, the officers who had come to Spain with me, and spectators of quality; behind them there was a barrier across the salon, behind which were the crowds of onlookers.

In a room off the side of the entrance were all sorts of refreshments, pastries, wines, in great profusion but well arranged, to which, during the confusion of the quadrilles, repaired those who wished to eat and who took some to the ladies. The finery blazed sumptuously: it must be admitted that the general appearance of our most beautiful dressed-up balls in no way approaches it.

What appeared most strange to me were three bishops, wearing rochets and capes, near the high end of the men's side during the ball; they were the Duque de Abrantes, the Bishop of Cuenca*, and two bishops *in partibus*, suffragans in

---

* Juan Emanuel de la Cruz, Bishop of Cuenca, Duque de Abrantes (d. 1733).

Madrid of the Archbishop of Toledo; and the ball-dress of the chief lady-in-waiting, who held a large exposed rosary, and who was chatting and gossiping about the ball and the dancers, all the while mumbling paternosters, which she regularly let fall, throughout the entire time. What I also found very annoying was that not a single man sat down there . . .

The Queen . . . opened the ball with the King; this prince's dancing, which he loved, was a great subject of surprise to me; while dancing he was another man altogether, his back and his knees upright, with precision, full of grace. As to the Queen, who afterwards partnered the Prince of the Asturias, both of whom had extremely good figures, I have seen no one of any sort, neither man nor women, dance better in France, nor approach anywhere near them, least of all as well; the two other Infantas also danced very prettily for their age.

In Spain, men and women wear all sorts of colours at all ages, and dance when they wish, even up to over sixty years of age, without the least ridicule, or without it even seeming extraordinary, and I saw many examples of that among both men and women: the youngest Infante took the Princesse de Robecq*, who was not far off fifty, and they seemed to go well together.

As soon as she had danced with the Infante, because being a foreigner she was not subject to the Spanish rules for widows, she crossed the whole length of the salon, gave a beautiful curtsey to their Catholic Majesties, laughing and with a deep curtsey came to dislodge me from my retreat in order to get me to dance. I answered her that she was mocking me; arguments and flattery followed, and at last she went to the Queen who called me to her and who told me that she and the King wished me to dance. I took the liberty of suggesting that they wanted but to amuse themselves; that this could not be a serious command; I pleaded my age, occupation, the number of years since I had danced, in a word everything that I could. All was useless, the King became involved, both of them begged me, endeavoured to persuade me that I danced very well, finally commanding me in a manner which could not be disobeyed; so I managed as best I could.

---

* Isabelle de Croÿ-Solre, Princesse de Robecq (1672–1739), *dame du palais* to the Queen of Spain.

The Queen arranged to make all our French witnesses dance, except the Abbé of Saint-Simon*, who was not dressed for it, and towards the end of the ball, two or three of the most distinguished officers of the King's troops who had come with me . . .

The ball over, the Marqués de Villagarcía†, one of the stewards and one of the most honest and gracious men I have ever met, who was subsequently Viceroy of Peru, would not hear of letting me go until I had rested in the refreshment area, where he made me swallow a glass of excellent pure wine, as I was perspiring profusely as a result of the exercise while wearing a thick costume. The King and Queen of Spain and the Prince of Asturias seemed to enjoy it very much.

Saint-Simon Vol. 38, 337–42, 345–46; Vol. 39, 4–5, 6–9.

---

* Claude de Rouvroy, Abbé de Saint-Simon (1695–1760), later Bishop of Metz, cousin to the ambassador.
† Antonio José de Guzmán, Marqués de Villagarcía, aide to the Prince of Asturias, later Viceroy of Peru.

Royal Palace – 'New' Palace

[119] Beckford's visit (1787)
(William Beckford (1759–1844) visited Portugal and Spain after the death of his wife in 1786.)

The new palace front did not gain grace in Mr Beckford's eyes. The interior court he described as of pure classical architecture. The doors and window recesses gleaming with the richest polished marbles. The walls thick and fortress-like, while in the casements double panes of the strongest glass excluded the keen blasts which range almost uninterruptedly over the plains of Castille; thus sustaining an admirable temperature throughout all the royal apartments, the grandeur of which can scarcely be exceeded. As the King and Prince of Asturias, with their principal attendants, were absent hunting at the Escorial, and the Chevalier Roxas had joined a party of the body guard in another apartment, Mr Beckford was left to ramble in solitude over the palace, surrounded with the works of the great Spanish, Italian, and Flemish painters. Not a door was closed, and he penetrated through the chamber of the throne into the old king's sleeping apartment, remarkable for its extreme neatness. He found there a book of pious orations adapted to the exclusive use of majesty, and ornamented with engravings. An enamelled picture of the infant Saviour, and of St Anthony, by Mengs, was placed by the richly ornamented but uncurtained bed. In all the rooms were cages with gilded wire, each containing an exotic bird, some in full song, and with their notes chimed musical clocks sounding like the tones of harmonic glasses.

. . . He now met one of the officials, who asked where he was going so fast, having before been sent to seek him. It appeared that the Infanta and Don Gabriel wanted to have an interview with him, in order to inquire about Portugal. The messenger presumed that this wish was expressed from the letters of which Mr Beckford had been the bearer from the Marqués de Marialva, and more particularly from the Archbishop.

'You must kiss their hands this very evening. I am to be your conductor,' said his friend Noronha.

'What! in this unceremonious dress?'

'Yes, I have heard you are not a pattern of correctness in these matters.'

Mr Beckford was at that moment in no train of mind or body for a courtly introduction. His head was full of the pictures he had been looking at, and the exotic birds, and he had rather be presented to a cockatoo than to the greatest monarch in Christendom. There was no choice, and he proceeded to that part of the palace occupied by Don Gabriel* and his Portuguese bride. The doors of sundry antichambers flew open before him, and passing through rooms peopled with biped animals the most uninteresting in the world, and some mere children, such as pages and lords and ladies in waiting, he entered a lofty chamber, hung with white satin and formed into compartments by rich embroidery, at the further extremity of which stood the Infante Don Gabriel, leaning against a table covered with velvet, upon which lay a case of golden antique medals, which he was contemplating. The Infanta was seated near him. She rose at once to hold out a beautiful hand, which

---

* The Infante Gabriel (1752–1788) married Ana María de Braganza (1768–1788).

was kissed with unfeigned fervour. Her countenance was prepossessing, and she had the same florid complexion and handsome features which distinguished her brother, the Prince of Brazil.

The Princess said, 'You have lately seen my dear mother, and walked, perhaps, in the garden of which I was so fond. Did you notice the fine flowers that grew there, particularly the blue carnation? We have no such flowers in Madrid. This climate is not so pleasant as that of Portugal, nor are our views so pleasant. I miss the Tagus and your ships continually sailing up. When you write to your friend Marialva and the Archbishop, tell them I possess, what no other prospect upon earth can equal, the smiles of my adored husband.'

The Infante then approached with a manner so frank and kindly, that it exhibited no trace of senseless Austrian hauteur or Spanish stiffness, but partook more of the gentlemanly carriage of the Bourbons. The Infante then discoursed about books and the English universities, somewhat at the expense of the Portuguese academicians. He asked if English books were printed now as handsomely as in the days of the Stuarts, and said he was in possession of some that had belonged to Lord Oxford. The Infante had made a translation of Sallust, which Mr Beckford complimented. The Infante declared that he found the work laborious, and lost many a day's exercise in the parks and forests in doing it; but such as it was, he had performed his task without any assistance, 'though,' said he, 'you have, perhaps, heard to the contrary.'

Noronha, Mr Beckford's friend, who had introduced him, then began complimenting the Infante in the court mode, and the latter looked, as princes do under such circumstances, always more kind and gracious than before. The Infanta again reverted to her home on the banks of the Tagus, and was so affected as to awaken all her visitor's sympathies, and, while making his farewell bow, saw her eyes suffused in tears, while she kept gracefully waving her hand to bid him a happy good night.   *Beckford, 28–32 (1787).*

[120] Lady Holland's visit (1803)

4th [Aug. 1803] – Morning at the palace; the Court quitted it the preceding day. Apartments magnificent, infinitely more splendid than any palace I ever saw; the pictures are very fine, and so numerous that it would require many visits to do justice to them. The large saloon, in which are placed the equestrian pictures by *Velázquez* and *Titian*, is very striking, Charles V equipped in armour with his lance in arrest is admirable, and the figure so very *chevaleresque*. King's private library large, and contains a number of excellent books in different small rooms, also much theological *lore*. One book-case full of MS. relating chiefly to the secret history of Spain during the reign of the House of Austria. The present Governt. is as jealous of the circulation of political opinions and papers against the Court of Philip II and downwards, as against the present . . .

[What follows was written a year later.]

25th [July 1804] – To dinner Conde Fernan Núñez*, his brother del Rios, Marqués Peñafiel, 'Périco' Girón†, Marqués de Santa Cruz‡, B. Frere§. Much conversation about ye etiquette and ceremonial of the Sp. Court. King and Q., and even the little *Infantes*, served with drink by the gentlemen-in-waiting on their knees. Old custom retained of tasting what the King is to drink and eat. When the cup is carried through the apartments or corridors of the palace, every one by whom it passes must take off his hat. At the Escorial once lately an obstinate fellow refused, upon which the bearer of the cup threw it down, with the exclamation of '*Copa profanada*'; the man was imprisoned for the insult. Duty of the gentlemen-in-waiting excessively hard. There are 12, Fernan Núñez and brother are of the number. Scratch King's back at night when he is in bed. Gives water, & c., *par extraordinaire*, but not since

* Carlos Gutiérrez de los Ríos, 7th Conde de Fernan Núñez.
† Pedro Girón (1786–1851), son of the Duke of Osuna, later Marqués de Jabalquinto and a successful general.
‡ José Gabriel de Silva y Bazán, 16th Marqués de Santa Cruz.
§ Bartholomew Frere (1778–1851), secretary of legation in the British Embassy, brother of the minister.

English improvements have been introduced. *Sumiller de cuerpo* (Marqués de Ariza) put on K.'s shirt. Forms observed when K. is sick, even continued after his death. '*¿ No quiere comer el Rey?*' till he is interred, when the *Sumiller* breaks his wand or staff of office, and exclaims with surprise '*¡Está muerto el Rey!*'

Ilchester, 82, 156 (1803, 1804).

[121] Napoleon before the portrait of Philip II
(José María Queipo de Llano, Conde de Toreno (1786–1843), was an active politician as well as a historian.)

Napoleon stayed in Chamartín and only once very early in the morning did he go into Madrid and go to the Palace. Even though the royal dwelling appeared sumptuous to him, he asked for nothing with a more vehement interest than the portrait of Philip II. He stood before one of the most notable of them* for some minutes and it seemed as if a strong instinct took him to consider carefully the appearance of a monarch who, if in many ways was unlike him, resembled him in a remarkable way in respect of his love for a hard and unlimited domination both over his own people and over foreigners.

Toreno, 309.

[122] Quin's visit (1821)
(M.J. Quin visited Spain in 1821 and wrote a vivid account of the constitutional interregnum caused by the Revolution of 1820.)

One day I happened to be in the square before the palace, when I observed a number of state carriages going towards the principal entrance. I was told that the King† and the whole of the Royal Family were just about to take their usual promenade, and I had the curiosity to see how they appeared. The principal entrance is a gateway, which, during the daytime,

---

* This portrait by Titian is probably the one sent to Mary Tudor in England for her to see what Philip looked like. It is now in the Prado.
† Ferdinand VII (1784–1833).

is a common thoroughfare, as it leads to the interior square of
the palace, in which all the offices of state are situated. On the
right hand is the grand staircase: it was lined with battle-axe
guards; a party of the carabineers before noticed, and four or
five grenadiers, occupied the lower steps, and stood on each
side of the King's carriage, which was in waiting. The infantry
guards were drawn up in the square before the palace, and a
body of horse guards, to the number of five or six and twenty,
was waiting also in the square to escort [i.e. to guard] the royal
carriages. In the passage there were two or three military men
in undress, and seven or eight old women, who were waiting to
present memorials to the King; though they could scarcely have
been ignorant that the time for asking favours from the King of
Spain was passed. After waiting some time, the King and
Queen* descended the staircase, attended by several officers
of state, in full dress: dark blue coats, turned up with crimson,
laced with gold, in the usual military fashion, white small-
clothes, and white silk stockings. Such was also the dress of the
King, in addition to which he wore a blue riband over his left
shoulder, and a star on his breast. The Queen, a slight, genteel
figure, with a small round countenance, feminine and timid,
and not more, I should think, than eighteen or nineteen years
old, appeared in a pink satin hat, very plain, and a blue silk
mantle, edged with ermine, which covered the remainder of her
dress. Her face has a mild beauty in it, which strongly interests
a spectator. It looked on this occasion pale, and oppressed with
inward suffering. The face of the King is remarkable for the
vacancy – I fear I must say, the deformity of its expression. The
chin and lower lip protrude considerably beyond the line of the
upper features, and seem scarcely to belong to them. The upper
lip is enveloped in mustachios; and yet, with these features
almost of the dumb animal tribe, there is a mixture of intelligence, loftiness, and feebleness in his eye, which indicates a
very peculiar character. Two of the officers of state placed
themselves at each side of the carriage door, offering their
shoulders to the assistance of her Majesty, while getting in. I
observed that she merely took the hand of the King, and got in,

* María Josefa of Saxony (1805–1829). She, the third wife of Ferdinand,
had no children.

not without some effort, without availing herself of the assistance proffered by the officers of state. She smiled not; she scarcely looked around her, and addressed not a syllable to any body. The King, who is a good portly figure, before he followed the Queen, looked around like a man who wished to give an impression that he was a free agent, but who betrayed his real state of duress by a certain awkwardness which he could not control. He was as reserved and silent as the Queen. There is only one step, which is firmly fixed outside, beneath the door of the carriage, and this is so high that both their Majesties were obliged to ascend to it by means of a footstool. The footstool was then strapped behind, where it hung dangling as the carriage drove off. Before he left the palace, his Majesty put out his hand from the window, and received the several petitions which were presented to him. I was rather surprised that this custom was permitted to remain, as it might easily have been made the vehicle of private communications to the King, which the whole system of the household was framed to intercept . . .

[Two months later:]

. . . It was observed, however, that about seven o'clock in the evening, a collection of between four and five hundred persons, formed of groups which had come from different quarters of the capital, went down in a body to the palace. They were followed, or soon after joined, by perhaps as many more, who were curious to witness their proceedings. The whole found admittance into the square before the palace, immediately under the windows of the King's drawing-room. Attempts were made to penetrate into the palace, but this the guard on duty prevented, and the gates of the building were shut. The drums beat to arms; the militia infantry, and cavalry, were called out; they formed in an uninterrupted line in front of the palace, and they kept the crowd at a distance of ten or twelve paces from it.

From different parts of this crowd I heard a confused sound of voices; some discussed aloud the question of the removal of the ministry, reprobating it in acrimonious terms; and others directing their eyes towards the windows of the drawing-room cried out, *Presencia, Presencia* – the presence – that is calling to the King to come out to the balcony. This cry they accompanied with others, such as '¡*Viva el ministerio!*' and '¡*Regencia!*' 'The ministry for ever!' 'A Regency!' – thus intimating to the King, if he heard them, that he must re-appoint the ex-ministry, or submit to be deposed by a Regency. These cries were repeated every moment by distinct, though unvarying voices, from different parts of the crowd; and sometimes a particular group would shout them in chorus, accompanying them with execrations and expressions of a seditious character. One man, a militiaman, not on duty, stood before the balcony, and pointing towards the window, as if the King were there, he expressed himself to the following effect:–

'Tyrant, it is now nine years since you were restored to your throne by the valour and generosity of the Spanish people. Where is your gratitude? How have you evinced a sense of the foolish love which we bore you? You destroyed our Constitution as soon as you came amongst us; and now that it has been happily re-established, you have attempted, tiger that you are! to destroy it a second time. Citizens! is this man fit to be our King?' 'Down with the tyrant.' 'Depose him from the throne.' 'Deprive him of his crown!' 'Kill him.' 'Imprison him in a fortress.' These were literally some of the answers which he received from a few individuals in the crowd. I observed that the person who made this speech went afterwards among other groups, and endeavoured to excite them in the same manner. I observed also that by far the greater part of the crowd were mere spectators who took no part in the proceedings.

At nine o'clock – still no ministry was appointed. The number in the Palace square was on the decline. A militia officer was going about among the crowd inculcating, with as much energy as he could command, this maxim, 'that he who removed the ministry would rob Spain also of her liberty.' There were four or five militia-men unemployed in duty, though their uniforms appeared under their cloaks; who I plainly saw were making it their business to go about from group to group, uttering violent harangues, and calling the king *un tonto*, – an idiot, who was unfit to reign. It was industriously circulated that when the ministers asked the King to consent to his removal from Madrid, he abused them not only in violent but ungentlemanlike terms; and that he had even descended to make use of a low and ribaldrous dialect, which is among the privileges only of the most abandoned characters. This I suppose was a report in answer to one which had prevailed in the morning, and which imputed the uncourteous terms to the ministers.

Between nine and ten o'clock the Ayuntamiento, or municipality, sent a deputation to the King, with a remonstrance stating that agitation prevailed in the capital, and calling on his Majesty in strong terms to restore the ministry. The cries of the agitators in the crowd – for by this name I must distinguish them from the inactive spectators – acquired by this time fresh vigour, and they loudly threatened the King, that unless he reinstated the ministry, they must have a Regency. ¡Regencia! ¡Regencia! was resounded from different parts of the crowd by isolated voices. I observed a few persons of mean, and I must add of ferocious aspects, who carried poniards and swords under their cloaks. The council of state was sitting.

By the time the palace clock struck eleven, the crowd was considerably diminished, and was now lessening rapidly. At length it became generally known amongst those who remained, that the King had agreed to restore the ministry, and they dispersed with shouts of triumph . . .

. . . It was said that in order to work up the King's mind to this measure, strong representations were made to him upon the agitated state of the capital; and among other things it was insinuated that the people of the lower *Barrios*, or wards, of the capital, that is to say, the very lowest order of the inhabitants – were all arming and preparing to march on the palace, and massacre the King and royal family. This, it is said, disheartened the King very much, as he was under the impression that these classes were all in his favour.

The insinuation as to the arming of these classes was without the slightest foundation, as I was confidently assured by a gentleman who made it his business to inquire into the state of these *Barrios*, that, to use his expressions, 'not so much as a mouse was stirring there.' He had traversed several parts of the capital during the evening, and he stated that they presented no signs whatever of agitation. I staid at the palace until a quarter past eleven. In coming to my residence I had to traverse Madrid from one end to the other, and I can safely say, that in all that distance I observed, beyond the precincts of the palace, no crowd of people, heard no cries, encountered nothing whatever which could justify the statement that peace was disturbed. The streets were perfectly quiet . . .

The day after this scene occurred, I walked down to the royal palace accompanied by a friend, and, after passing through it, we proceeded towards the palace of the Cortes, where the permanent deputation was then sitting. We were attracted to that quarter by some shouts which we heard, and on proceeding to the entrance we found it surrounded by an assembly of persons about four hundred in number. A few were military men; the rest of the very lowest classes. A young woman was elevated on a block of stone that was placed near the entrance of the palace of the Cortes, and she harangued this mob incessantly. Her stature was short, her face rather strongly, though regularly, formed, and she was dressed in a plain cotton body, a basquine, or black silk petticoat, a red cloth shawl, and a black silk mantilla, or veil. She was possessed of an amazingly powerful voice, and she exerted it in all its force in urging the mob to demand of the permanent deputation that it should appoint a Regency forthwith. The mob frequently cried out 'a Regency,' in obedience to her dictates, – 'We want no king.' 'We want no moderates.' 'We want a Regency, and nothing else.' Whenever the cries relaxed, the young woman renewed her exertions and bade them to cry out for a Regency, and to stay there all night, until they succeeded. She frequently repeated this exhortation, and excited herself into such a rage against the King, that she foamed at the mouth. One of the guards on duty endeavoured to reason with her, but she attacked him so violently, calling him a moderate, and a servile, that he was glad to escape from her. She held her pocket handkerchief in her right hand, waving it now and then when she saw her dictates obeyed; and strange to say, the mob listened to her as if she were a sibyl. Whenever she desired them to cry out, they did so; when she uttered the word 'Regencia,' they echoed her voice.

During this scene, Galiano*, a leading deputy of the

---

* Antonio Alcalá Galiano (1789–1865), Liberal statesman.

Masonic party, came out from the interior of the palace, and as soon as he presented himself a number of persons collected around him and addressed some words to him, which, on account of the noise, I could not distinctly hear. The word *Regencia*, however, was clearly audible, and Galiano, from his manner, according to my impressions, seemed anxious to forward any wishes they expressed upon the subject.

Even in this assemblage, I must observe, the number of persons who took an active share in the business was limited to between twenty and thirty, and these too, with very few exceptions, men and women who probably knew not the meaning of the demand which they made. This continued for some time, when at last a man came out from the interior of the palace of the Cortes*, and having stated that he had a communication to make, the female commander immediately desired that he should be heard. She ordered silence and attention, in the most peremptory manner, and the man delivered himself in the following terms: 'I am,' said he, 'of a deputation from the Ayuntamiento, who have come here to represent to the permanent deputation the necessity of assembling the extraordinary Cortes again without delay. The deputation have said in answer to us, that the ordinary Cortes are to meet on the 1st of March; that even if they had resolved upon it, they could not summon the extraordinary Cortes before the 25th of this month, and that it would make a difference of only a few days to wait for the ordinary Cortes.'

'We want a regency,' uttered some voices in the crowd led on by the woman; 'we want a regency, and that quickly; we must have the Cortes immediately, we will not wait until the 25th.'

'What do you wish me to do then?' asked the man; 'is it your desire that I should go back to the Ayuntamiento, and tell them, that you demand that the Extraordinary Cortes should be again assembled?' 'Yes,' exclaimed the voices, 'that is what we wish.' 'Very well, then,' he replied, 'let us go to the Ayuntamiento.' . . .

. . . By these and other means, the government succeeded in collecting a sum sufficient for the expenses of the journey; and it was finally arranged that the King and royal family should

* The 'Cortes' constitute the parliament of Spain.

leave Madrid at eight o'clock on the morning of the 20th, and
travel by short stages to Seville. Although this arrangement was
generally known, the concourse of spectators on that morning,
in the square of the palace, was far from being numerous. But
there was a considerable crowd at the gate of Toledo, which
leads directly to the Andalusian road, and through which it was
generally understood the cavalcade would pass. This belief was
confirmed by the guards, who attended at the gate from an
early hour. Amongst the crowd there were, of course, persons
of a thousand different sentiments, but all seemed dejected.
They were mostly of the class of artists, tradesmen, shopkeepers, lodging-house keepers, and of those citizens who were
likely to suffer severely in their different individual interests by
the removal of the government. Several, also, of the families of
those of the local militia, who volunteered to go with the King
to Seville, were present to take a final farewell of their husbands, fathers, and other relatives, as they passed through the
gate to join the escort which was stationed at some distance on
the road.

In front of the palace, which looks toward the country,
there is a private road appropriated solely to the use of the
royal family, which opens, at a short distance from the
palace, on the public way. At a quarter before eight the
King and Queen were removed from the palace in sedan
chairs through the private road to the gate, which opened to
the high road, where their carriage was waiting. The rest of
the royal family followed in the same direction, their carriages being also in waiting. A slight escort was stationed at
the gate; the main body, consisting of about 4,000 men,
infantry and cavalry, was stationed on the road leading to
Andalusia. They then drove rapidly round to the Andalusian
road, attended by the great officers of state, and thus avoided
passing through the gate of Toledo, where the crowd waited
until nine o'clock, when they were informed that the King
had left Madrid an hour before, and they dispersed quietly,
though evidently disappointed.

Quin, 122–25; 231–27; 256–75 (Dec. 1821 – Mar. 1822).

[123] Inglis and Don Carlos (1830)

I was witness, another time, to a strange scene of rivalry between the King [Ferdinand VII] and Don Carlos. When the king's carriage drove up to the gate of the court, Don Carlos* and his wife† and family were seated in the area, and his carriage was in waiting: upon this occasion, the king arrived in state; a party of dragoons attended him, and his coachmen were in court dresses. The carriage of Don Carlos was in strange contrast with that of the king; it was drawn by six mules, harnessed with ropes; in place of postilions in court dresses, his servants were in the dress of Spanish peasants in their holiday clothes, – one on the coach-box, – the other employed as a runner by the head of the mules. Don Carlos affects all this appearance of simplicity and Spanish usage, to please the people; and for the same reason, his wife generally appears in a mantilla. The moment the king's carriage appeared, Don Carlos left the court with his wife, and continued to walk in the most crowded part of the garden while the king and queen‡ remained, dividing the attention which their majesties would otherwise have received, and indeed engrossing the larger share of it. I could not avoid remarking the greater popularity of Don Carlos among the lower orders: while they only took off their hats as the king passed, they bowed almost to the ground at the presence of the Infante. The appearance of the queen, however, always produced a favourable impression, especially when contrasted with that of her aspiring rival. One cannot look at the spouse of Don Carlos, without perceiving that she covets a crown; while in the countenance of the queen, we read indifference to it.

Upon frequent other occasions while in Madrid, I had proofs of the anxiety of Don Carlos to recommend himself to the people. The most marked of these, was upon the evening when the queen gave birth to a princess§: not an hour after this was

---

* Don Carlos (1788–1855) subsequently founder of the 'Carlist' cause and recognized by his followers as King Charles V.
† María Francisca de Braganza (1789–1834).
‡ This was Isabella II (1830–1904), Queen of Spain 1833–1868.
§ This was the King's fourth wife, Maria Cristina (1806–1878), his first cousin, daughter of the King of Naples.

known, the Infante drove through the streets and along the
Prado, in an open carriage, along with his three sons who . . .
were that day cut out of their inheritance.   *Inglis, 128–9.*

[124] George Borrow and Mendizábal (1836)

Early one morning I repaired to the palace, in a wing of which
was the office of the prime minister. It was bitterly cold, and the
Guadarrama, of which there is a noble view from the palace
plain, was covered with snow. For at least three hours I remained
shivering with cold in an anteroom, with several other aspirants
for an interview with the man of power. At last his private
secretary made his appearance, and after putting various questions to the others, addressed himself to me, asking who I was
and what I wanted. I told him that I was an Englishman, and the
bearer of a letter from the British Minister. 'If you have no
objection, I will myself deliver it to his Excellency,' said he;
whereupon I handed it to him, and he withdrew. Several individuals were admitted before me; at last, however, my own
turn came, and I was ushered into the presence of Mendizábal*.

He stood behind a table covered with papers, on which his
eyes were intently fixed. He took not the slightest notice when I
entered, and I had leisure enough to survey him. He was a huge
athletic man, somewhat taller than myself, who measure six
feet two without my shoes. His complexion was florid, his
features fine and regular, his nose quite aquiline, and his teeth
splendidly white; though scarcely fifty years of age, his hair was
remarkably grey. He was dressed in a rich morning gown, with
a gold chain round his neck, and morocco slippers on his feet.

His secretary, a fine intellectual-looking man, who, as I was
subsequently informed, had acquired a name both in English
and Spanish literature, stood at one end of the table with
papers in his hands.

After I had been standing about a quarter of an hour,
Mendizábal suddenly lifted up a pair of sharp eyes, and fixed
them upon me with a peculiarly scrutinizing glance.

---

* Juan Alvarez Mendizábal (1790–1853), a liberal financier and prime
minister.

'I have seen a glance very similar to that amongst the Beni Israel,' thought I to myself . . .

My interview with him lasted nearly an hour. Some singular discourse passed between us. I found him, as I had been informed, a bitter enemy to the Bible Society, of which he spoke in terms of hatred and contempt; and by no means a friend to the Christian religion, which I could easily account for. I was not discouraged, however, and pressed upon him the matter which brought me thither, and was eventually so far successful as to obtain a promise, that at the expiration of a few months, when he hoped the country would be in a more tranquil state, I should be allowed to print the Scriptures.

As I was going away he said, 'Yours is not the first application I have had; ever since I have held the reins of government I have been pestered in this manner by English, calling themselves Evangelical Christians, who have of late come flocking over into Spain. Only last week a hunch-backed fellow found his way into my cabinet whilst I was engaged in important business, and told me that Christ was coming. . . . And now you have made your appearance, and almost persuaded me to embroil myself yet more with the priesthood, as if they did not abhor me enough already. What a strange infatuation is this which drives you over lands and waters with Bibles in your hands! My good sir, it is not Bibles we want, but rather guns and gunpowder to put the rebels down with, and, above all, money, that we may pay the troops. Whenever you come with these three things you shall have a hearty welcome; if not, we really can dispense with your visits, however great the honour.'

Myself. – There will be no end to the troubles of this afflicted country until the Gospels have free circulation.

Mendizábal. – I expected that answer, for I have not lived thirteen years in England without forming some acquaintance with the phraseology of you good folks. Now, now, pray go; you see how engaged I am. Come again whenever you please, but let it not be within the next three months.

Borrow, 165–68 (1836).

[125] Odd uses of the Royal Palace
(Pérez Galdós (c. 1868) gave a vivid picture in his novel *La de Bringas*.)

Don Francisco's workshop was in the great embrasure of one of the windows looking out on the Campo del Moro. For the Bringas family lived in the Palace; in one of those apartments on the second floor which shelter the employees of the Royal Household . . . I have forgotten to say that at about this time, that is in February '68, Bringas was appointed a First Officer of the Privy Purse with a salary of thirty thousand reals, living quarters, medical attention, drugs, water, firewood and other perquisites which seem to be inherent in the vicinity of royalty. This appointment had realized the aspirations of his whole life, and he would not have exchanged his position – so exalted, so secure, so respectable! – for the throne of the Primate of Spain. The only thing that ever disturbed his perfect satisfaction were the rumours that were going round in that accursed year of '68, about the possibility of popular disturbances and the fear that the 'so-called revolution' might break out with violence. Although the suggestion that the Monarchy could come to an end sounded as absurd to our good man as the idea that the planets might cease to revolve, nevertheless, when he happened to be present in some café or *tertulia* where he heard prognostications of rebellion, or announcements that The Moment had arrived, or lugubrious comments on the unpopularity of the Government or of the Queen, he shivered and felt his heart contract.

To reach his home on the second floor, Don Francisco had to climb no less than a hundred and twenty-four steps up the Ladies' Staircase from the patio. This Second Floor along with the Third make up a veritable city supported on the splendid ceilings of the Royal dwelling. There the aristocracy, middle classes and people mix peacefully together. It is a sort of royal republic, which the Monarchs wear as a crown; and linked together in its immense circuit it has diverse examples of every class of person.

The first time I ever went there I was accompanying Don Manuel Pez on a visit to Bringas in his new abode, and we began by losing ourselves completely in that labyrinth, where

neither of us had ever been before. We had climbed the Ladies'
Staircase to the Second Floor and been met there by a porter
wearing a three-cornered hat, who asked us our destination.
When we told him, he pointed in the direction we should go
and said:

'Turn left, then right, then go up a small staircase, then go
down again . . . Number 67.'

Pérez Galdós, 'La de Bringas', 24–25 (c. 1868).

[126] News of the revolution of 1868: Pérez Galdós recalls the mood

When the news of the battle of Alcolea* reached Madrid, the
poor man almost had an apoplectic fit. And that was the day
that Madrid declared itself for the revolutionaries too. Paquito
brought the bad news. He had been passing through the Puerta
del Sol and had found it packed with people. A general was
haranguing the crowd, while another was tearing off his
epaulettes. And afterwards the people dispersed and went
running down the streets, showing every sign of rejoicing
rather than of panic. Groups were marching up and down
shouting *Long Live the Revolution – the Navy – the Army*, and
saying that Isabella II was no longer Queen. Men went by
carrying banners with various revolutionary inscriptions on
them, while others were busy taking down the Royal Crowns
from the shop fronts . . .

. . . 'There is nothing more to be done,' Bringas said, drawing strength from the very intensity of his despair. 'It is time to
prepare ourselves. God's will be done. Resignation. The
crowds will soon invade the Palace to loot it, and they will
spare no one. Let us show ourselves worthy, accept our
martyrdom . . .'

He choked on something in his throat. They were all silent,
listening to the sounds that came in from the passages and from
the great courtyard below. There was great alarm in the Palace-
city. All the inhabitants kept coming to their doors to get news

* This battle signified the defeat of the royal army by Generals Prim
(1814–1870) and Serrano (1810–85).

or to communicate their own impressions. And some of them even went downstairs, anxious to learn if anything was happening outside. But the silence reigned in the courtyard, and though the doors were open, not a living creature entered. Then when they were least expecting it, Doña Cándida suddenly appeared in a terrible state, saying between stifled groans:

'It's coming . . . it's coming . . .'

'What is coming, Señora, for heaven's sake, what is it?'

'The sack of the Palace . . . Oh, my dear Don Francisco, I've seen the crowds coming down the Calle de Lepanto. Oh, what horrible people, what criminal faces, what rough beards and filthy hands! We will all have our throats cut.'

'But what has become of the Palace Guard . . . the halberdiers?'

'They must have risen too. They are all the same. God help us!'

There was a moment of panic, but it was of short duration, for when the Bringas went out into the passage they found some of their neighbours walking up and down as calmly as if nothing were going on.

'But what is happening?'

'Nothing. A few boys made a disturbance in the doorway, and the Town Council have sent a guard.'

Pérez Galdós, 'La de Bringas' 230–31 (1868).

[127] The Infanta Eulalia is pleased (1876)
(The Infanta Eulalia (1864–1958) was daughter of Isabella II. She was at this time a little girl; later she married Antonio Duke of Galliera (1866–1930), son of the Duc de Montpensier.)

We arrived in high spirits at the royal palace, and I was glad to find it not only gorgeous, but most comfortable. It had been built by Charles III. – as everything in Madrid seems to have been built – but my brother* had had it modernized with those conveniences of heating and plumbing which our antique

* That is, the new (young) King Alfonso XII (1857–1885).

splendour had hitherto done without in Spain. He had allotted a whole wing for us three Infantas (my sister Pilar*, my sister Paz†, and I), and we each had our own maids and servants from Seville, so that we made quite a household. He had installed in another wing my sister the Infanta Isabel‡, whom I hardly knew, because she had not been with us in France during the Revolution. She was to take our mother's place towards us. She had been married at sixteen to a Prince of Naples; she had lived all her life among the forms and traditions of Royalty, and she was genuinely devoted to their maintenance. I should have been afraid for my new liberty if I had not foreseen that her direction over us would be tempered by my brother's indulgence. I knew that he had as much impatience as myself for what we called, jocularly, between ourselves, the *'singeries'* (monkey tricks) of Royalty. And so I began, with great expectations, what proved to be the happiest period of my life.

I was able to rise early, because my brother was always up at half-past seven, to ride in the Casa de Campo for an hour, and I rode horseback with him – to my great joy. Then, at nine, we girls had our lessons while he met his Ministers. Early rising is not a Spanish habit. My mother, when she was Queen, had met her Ministers after the theatre, at midnight, and worked with them more in the night-time than during the day. And my brother's Ministers had protested against his nine o'clock Cabinet meetings; but he had won them to it with the smiling and tactful determination that always secured him his own way.

At midday we lunched with him, the whole household together, a score at table, with ladies and gentlemen-in-waiting, officers, and aides-de-camp; but, on account of the presence of the latter, conversation was always formal. It was different on the afternoon drives. Then we were alone, for he drove himself, and I sat beside him; there were just the two servants on the rear seat, and no one to overhear us. Best of all were the visits I

* The Infanta Pilar (1861–1879).
† The Infanta Paz (1862–1946) married Ludwig of Bavaria (1859–1949).
‡ The widowed Infanta Isabel (1851–1931) had married the Conte de Girgenti (1846–1871).

paid him in his apartments, where it was not considered necessary that I should be followed by a lady-in-waiting, since I was under the protection of the King. The guards only took me across the public gallery in the centre of the palace – a soldier on each side of me and an officer in front, because in this gallery some attempts had been made to kill my mother when she was Queen – and the ushers, who led me down the halls, left me when I entered my brother's antechamber. He had collected a large library for his own use, and he made me free of it on condition that I should not tell anyone. At last I had books! And more than I could read.

Infanta Eulalia, 43–46 (1875).

[128] Alfonso XIII: Harold Nicolson (1911)

(Alfonso XIII (1886–1941) was King from his posthumous birth till 1931. Sir Harold Nicolson (1886–1968) was a secretary in the British Embassy for a few months in Madrid in 1911.)

Raised high upon a dais, each step to which was flanked by a golden lion pawing a golden globe, [the King and Queen] would assume an impression of being unaware that there were people around them. They would gaze with vacant eyes upon the clouds that drifted, white upon blue, beyond the great windows, down from Guadarrama towards the south. The grandees of Spain were grouped behind them: the diplomatists, embassy by embassy, were aligned with their backs to the windows: along the avenue thus left in front of the throne, the Ministers, the Officers of State and finally the members of the Cortes filed in slow procession, bowing to their sovereigns as they passed. These salutations were not returned. The eyes of Alfonso and Victoria Eugénie continued to gaze with languid inattention at the floating clouds.

'Diary', quoted by Lees Milne, Nicolson, I, 45.

Palacio del Buen Retiro

[129] Olivares describes the palace in a letter to
Juan Chumacero (c. 1635)
(The Conde-Duque was the driving force behind the idea of
the new palace of the Retiro.)

I confess that I am very happy to see you touch on this question
of the Retiro . . . because, as something which seems to affect
me closely, I am always pleased to see the charges and so be
able to draw up the defence; and although I do not claim to
excuse myself in any way, in order to avoid offending against
the truth, I will say a few words. I can assure you that what was
begun in the Buen Retiro, and for which I am responsible, cost
closer to ten thousand than to ten million ducats. Once this was
done, it was decided to continue, and in the process I lost
everything I had there, and everything I had tried to construct,
consisting of four rooms for passing Holy Week and those few
days when His Majesty can get away to the countryside, far
from the madding crowd.

Here a number of different charges arise . . . I think it can be established in the first place that there is not a king or potentate in all Europe who has not built himself a house, and a good house at that; and while I have seen judges condemned for building themselves houses, I have never heard of kings meeting such a fate. Let us now consider our own kings . . .

His Majesty's father built the palaces and gardens in Valladolid, those of Lerma, and the houses of the dukes of Lerma* and Uceda† here in Madrid. Look at the expense of all this to the royal treasury, and if the Retiro cost the patrimony a tenth of this sum, I am prepared to accept the criticisms . . . Now let's look at his grandfather [Philip II], the first of all kings in wisdom . . . Not one *maravedí* did he spend which was not drawn from the royal patrimony, but merely the acquisition of pasturelands cost four times more than the Buen Retiro. His great grandfather [Charles V], than whom the world has seen no greater nor more embattled monarch, built the Pardo, Aranjuez, Balsaín, Segovia‡, and innumerable other residences which I shall not even mention – and all this at such splendour and expense that every one of these houses cost infinitely more than the Retiro. And observe that there is probably not a single king who does not have a second residence in his capital. Here I should add that this is a positive necessity, because if there should be smallpox in the palace, all the royal family would be exposed, or else would have to take refuge in some nearby house till the epidemic ends . . . On top of this there is a host of other reasons which I shall not bother to rehearse, because if all kings have a second residence there is no need to say any more.

Let us turn now to Ferdinand the Catholic, that king of kings . . . He built an infinite number of great houses. From all of which it follows that all monarchs have two palaces in their court and capital, and that Spain's greatest kings, so far from restricting themselves to one, have built several, all of them impressive in respect both of adornment and architecture. The king, our master (whom God preserve) has built one, which is

* The Palacio de Lerma soon became by inheritance the Palacio de Medinaceli (now destroyed); see No. 103.
† The Palacio de Uceda is still visible on the corner of the Calle de Bailén and the Calle del Sacramento.
‡ These were all royal country-houses.

comfortable and in good taste, and he has built it with a great deal of piety, and not a trace of ostentation.

The furnishing, as regards pictures and tapestries, is of consideration, but not excessive; and if I say that the Retiro did not involve one-twentieth of the costs of what Philip III built at the expense of the royal patrimony, I should have to say that it did not amount to a five hundredth of the sum spent by other kings. In fact, *señor* Don Juan, I must speak plainly. The Buen Retiro, in terms of the royal patrimony, excise dues, sales tax, royal returns and dues, benevolences and other contributions and grants, has not cost His Majesty five hundred ducats, the only exception being that the Count of Monterrey* sent three or four hangings and a bed, which were paid for out of the royal treasury and patrimony.

> *Olivares to Chumacero, Oct. 22, 1632 qu.*
> *Brown and Elliott, 'A Palace for a King', 233.*

[130] French impressions in 1659 (Bertaut)
(This was during the mission of the Marquis de Gramont; see No. 115.)

During this time there was some disquiet over the fever which the surviving prince had suffered for some days because of the teeth which they took out, which were called eye teeth. During these events I went to see the Buen Retiro. The Marqués de Salinas, son of the Marqués de Velada, took us there, that is the Chevalier de Charny and myself.

It is a house which the Conde Duque had built without a second storey and as some say without a design. The whole scheme is low-built and at the beginning it was known as '*El Gallinero*', the chicken run, because of some strange chickens which were put in a little house and garden which was on the other side of the Prado, where one walks, in which there are many fountains; but since the Retiro is higher than the Promenade, it was necessary to spend an enormous sum to make the water flow there, especially a great tank and canal which

---

* Gaspar de Acebedo y Zúñiga, 5th Conde de Monterrey, Viceroy of Mexico 1595–1603.

there is in the park which runs all round the Convento de San Jerónimo and which extends as far as Our Lady of Atocha. That is a miraculous picture of Our Lady, whose church is very rich, as all the churches of Madrid are, and where there is a great quantity of silver and lamps but it is at the same time very dark. There, just as in the church of the Jeronomites, there is a great balcony where the King and Queen go to hear mass without being seen.

In this park, which is more than a league in length, there are great avenues with very thick trees. You can see well that much money has been spent to make these avenues straight. There are also there many isolated hermitages which would be pretty houses for private persons. There is even a theatre and a place to show comedies which is open and very well designed. There are also there two blocks of buildings and another two of lodgings which are shaped as galleries. They are full of pictures. The Conde Duque arranged to put there the statue of Philip II on horseback, which is rare because the horse is only standing on two rear legs*. At the end it is believed that the Retiro cost a million more than the Escorial.

Don Juan of Austria lives in the floor of the concierge†. Of all the bastards of the King of Spain, of which there were a great many, he is the only one who has been recognized. He is the son of an actress whom the King loved passionately. They say that in spite of being very vigorous, he delayed a long time before he grew up. Desirous of being a full adult he talked to his surgeon who visited him and found a thin covering which was the cause of the obstacle and after that was cut he could satisfy his desires.   *Bertaut (1659), 567.*

[131] The French ambassadress visits the Retiro in 1679 (Marquise de Villars)

Madrid 15 December 1679
I went yesterday to the Retiro where the King and Queen‡ now are. I entered by the room of the chief lady-in-waiting who

* This was Pietro Tacca's famous sculpture of Philip I, brought to Spain in 1640.
† Don Juan (1629–1679) illegitimate son of Philip IV by the actress María Calderón; a popular prince who became Prime Minister in effect in 1677.
‡ That is Charles II and Marie Louise (María Luisa).

came out to receive me with every type of attention. She conducted me by narrow passages to a gallery where I believed I would only find the Queen. But I saw to my great surprise that I was meeting the entire royal family. The King was seated on a great armchair and the Queen on cushions. The lady-in-waiting indicated by a wave of the hand the number of bows that I had to make and that I should begin to do so to the King. She made me go up to the Catholic King's chair and he did not know what I wanted to do. I did not think that I had to do more than make a profound bow. Without vanity he did not return it to me, though it did not seem that he was disgusted to see me. When I said this to Monsieur de Villars* he said that, without doubt, the lady-in-waiting would have liked me to have kissed His Majesty's hand. So I thought, but I did not feel inclined to do it. He added that he had proposed to the Princesse d'Harcourt† to kiss his hand and by the consultation which he had with that Princess had found that he had not got to do it.

Here I was then in the middle of these three majesties: the Queen Mother‡ saying to me, as she had done the previous evening, many friendly things and the young Queen being very pleased apparently to see me. She did what she could to do what she had to. The King had a Flemish dwarf there who understood and spoke very good French. He greatly helped the conversation. They made one of the young ladies-in-waiting with one of the guards of the Infante go with me and see this person. The King asked me to say what I thought and the dwarf replied that he did not think that he had been invented to fill a human body. I agreed. They made me take a cushion. I sat only for one instant in order to obey. And then I took advantage of a slight diversion to put myself on my feet again because I saw many maids of honour who were not seated and I thought I would please them by standing, even though the Queens frequently asked me to sit. The young Queen took a light meal served on their knees by their ladies who had admirable names and did not set out to be less than of all the great houses

* Villars had been in Spain as ambassador in 1668–69, as well as in 1671–73, before this mission.
† Marie-Françoise, Princesse d'Harcourt (d. 1715), married to Alphonse, Prince d'Harcourt.
‡ The Queen Mother was Mariana of Austria.

of Aragon, Castille and Portugal. The Queen Mother took chocolate. The King took nothing.

The young Queen, as you can imagine, was dressed in Spanish style with those beautiful fabrics which she had brought from France: very well combed, her hair crossed in front and then allowed to fall on to her shoulders. She has an admirable complexion, lovely eyes, and a very agreeable mouth when she laughs. What a wonderful thing it is to be able to laugh in Spain! But it is right that I make you a full portrait of the Queen.

The gallery is fairly large, tapestried in bright red damask, gathered in roll upon roll of broad fringes of gold. Stretching from one end to the other there is the most beautiful carpet that I have ever seen; tables, desks, and braziers, on the tables, candelabras; and from time to time you can see the maids of honour, very well dressed, coming in to change the two silver candelabras when it is necessary . . . Rather far away from the Queens there were some girls seated on the ground and various ladies of an advanced age in their widows' weeds leaning against the wall. The King and Queen left after three-quarters of an hour, the King going first. The young Queen took her mother-in-law by the hand, passing first through the door of the gallery but then coming back quickly to see me. The lady-in-waiting did not come back and it seemed that she was being allowed every type of liberty in order to talk to me. There only remained an old lady, a long way off. She told me that if that old lady had not been there she would have kissed me. Even though it was not yet four when I arrived there, it was seven-thirty when I left. And it was I who wished to leave.

I assure you, madame, that I would like the King, the Queen Mother and the chief lady-in-waiting to hear everything that the Queen told me, and what I said to her . . . the young Queen, in her new beautiful dress, and her numberless diamonds, was enchanting.

Imagine for once that black and white are no more different than the life of Spain and that of France. It seems to me that this young Princess does very well. She wanted me to do her the honour of seeing her daily. I assured her that I would be delighted. But I begged her to allow me not to do so until the day when we could see clearly that the King and the Queen

Mother wanted it as much as she. The chief lady-in-waiting
came to escort me to the door. There I met some of the French
maids of the Queen, whom I told that they ought to learn
Spanish and avoid . . . saying a word to the Queen in French. I
knew that there were many who were furious when they talked
too often in it. I said in Spanish to the chief lady-in-waiting
what I had said to those French girls and she thanked me very
much . . . Had you been here today you would have had the
pleasure of seeing across a gateway the prettiest and most
eloquent Nuncio in the world. He speaks an entirely natural
Spanish. I received him ceremoniously, but in great comfort,
sitting on cushions and he on an armchair. He talked a lot
about Charles V to me. I felt a little ashamed to be so ill
informed. But I did not let him see it.

Marquise de Villars in García Mercadal, 'Viajes' II, 850.

[132] Lady Holland's visit (1804)

17th June, [1804] *Sunday*. – Mr Anglboult and Mr Willing to
dinner. The former mentioned that a *cédula* had lately been
issued ordering all the cotton machines in Spanish America to
be burned or destroyed; also prohibiting all persons to come to
Spain from her colonies – without a permission from the Court
of Madrid. Great improvements lately made in the China
manufactory at the Buen Retiro by the use of a magnesian
earth containing a mixture of the carbonate of magnesia*.
Spanish Govt. loses considerably by its cloth manufactory at
Guadalajara. Confirms the common remark that the number
of directors and inspectors with large salaries who are placed
over the RI. manufactory are more than sufft. to absorb all the
profits of the manufactory, tho' supported by every sort of
monopoly and exclusive privilege, both in the purchase of the
raw material and sale of the manufactured produce. Royal
fabrics are often established in order to create a place for some
creature or dependent of the Minister, and a decayed member
of the *consejo* is not unfrequently recompensed for bad services

---

* This factory had been founded in the gardens of the Retiro by Charles
III, bringing workmen from Naples on his accession.

by the place of Inspector of some manufacture of the very name
or existence of which he was ignorant till he received his patent.

Ilchester, 147 (1804).

[133] Napoleon to Maréchal Berthier (1808)

(Louis Berthier, 1753–1815, was Marshal of France and
chief of staff to Napoleon, and he became Prince de
Wagram in 1809.)

My Cousin, the commandant of the Retiro must never leave the
enclave of the Retiro. I was three hours in this palace today
without finding a soul. M. Turenne being ill, I must be presented
with a superior officer with the intelligence to command the
Porcelaine, with orders not to leave its environments. It is
necessary to withdraw from the Retiro all ranks who are found
there and shut the beautiful rooms . . . Give firm orders that no
Spaniard, neither man nor woman, enters the Retiro. As for the
Porcelaine, give orders to the engineer to construct a stockade
which no Spaniard will enter; in the Retiro, the palace-keepers
only will be able to enter; to this effect, they will be given a card.
The engineers who are at the Retiro or near the *Porcelaine*, must
place themselves according to rule under the surveillance of the
C.O. of the square, and the officers and soldiers must also do the
duty as customary. They must adopt military airs. In general you
must make known to the C.O. of the Retiro, that he takes enough
measures to keep this position, which should be considered as a
citadel; at eight o'clock in the evening all the doors must be shut.
Give the order that from tomorrow all the furniture coming from
the houses of individuals condemned as traitors will be transferred to the Retiro; in this way the officers who arrive with single
men will be accommodated, and in a comfortable situation.

NAPOLEON

Napoléon 'Correspondances Inédite', 576.

[134] Henry Inglis sees Ferdinand VII (1831)

My evening walk in Madrid was more frequently to the *Retiro*
than to the Prado; this is a vast and ill-laid out garden and

shrubbery, three or four miles in circumference, situated upon an elevation behind the Prado, the entrance to which is by the court of the old palace, which was destroyed during the war. The Retiro possesses no particular attraction, excepting its fresh air, and freedom from dust. There are some elevations in this garden, from which an extensive prospect is enjoyed; but it embraces little that is interesting, excepting the city, and the skies – an object of no small interest to one accustomed to the dense atmosphere and cloudy heavens of a northern latitude. During the several months that I remained in Madrid, I scarcely ever saw a cloud; and I frequently walked to the Retiro for the sole purpose of looking at the glorious sky, and the gorgeous sun-set: such skies are glorious, even when they canopy a desert. From the Retiro, the eye ranges over nothing but a desert, bounded on one side by the Sierra Guadarrama, on the other by the Toledo mountains; and Madrid, standing alone in the midst of this treeless and lifeless plain, seemed, when the setting sun flamed upon its domes and spires, to have been placed there by enchantment . . .

. . . A few days before leaving Madrid, while walking in the Retiro about six in the evening, in one of the most private walks, I observed a lusty gentleman, in blue coat and drab trowsers, with one companion, about twenty paces in advance; and, as my pace was rather quicker than their's, I caught a side look of the lusty gentleman's face: it was the king*, accompanied by a new valet, who had just succeeded Meris, who died a week or two before, of apoplexy. I had frequently seen the king without guards; but never before at so great a distance from attendants, or in so retired a place; and that I might be quite certain that this was indeed the redoubtable Ferdinand, I followed, in place of passing. He walked the whole length of the Retiro, parts of which are more than a mile from any guard or gate; the garden is open to every body; some of the walks are extremely secluded; so that he was, the whole of the time, entirely in the power of any individual who might have harboured a design against him; and all this struck me the more forcibly since, upon that very day, it had been announced for the first time, in the *Gaceta de Madrid*, that the refugees had

* i.e. Ferdinand VII.

passed the frontier; and in the same paper the ordinance had appeared, for closing the universities. The king walked like a man who had nothing to fear; and never once looked behind him, though his companion occasionally did. Before making the circuit of the Retiro, he reached the frequented walks, which were then crowded, and where he was of course recognized and received as usual.   *Inglis, 96–98; 118–9.*

[135] Baroja recalls *la belle époque* c. 1897
(Pío Baroja's novel *Las Noches del Buen Retiro* gives a romantic picture of late nineteenth-century Spain.)

For many people of the poorer Madrilenian bourgeoisie, the gardens of the Buen Retiro offered the charm of being able to meet there people of the aristocracy whom in winter it was impossible to see or mix with because of their more lavish life.

During the summer one could run all the scales of society from high to low and the greater and more petty bourgeoisie drew close to the old and modern aristocracy, to the people with grand titles and to the plutocracy with more substantive values.

Representatives of one or the other fraternized on the dance-floor of the gardens to the music of 'La Gran Vía,' or 'La Verbena de la Paloma' or of the symphony known as 'Poeta y Aldeano'.

The aristocracy believed itself triumphant then and let itself be seen. The modest bourgeoisie and even that with some pretensions, the employees and the students, knew at least by sight the ladies of the highest society as much as they did the *divas* at the opera, the comedians, the *toreros* and the famous politicians.

When the grand ladies returned in their carriage in the evenings of autumn or winter by the Carrera de San Jerónimo or afternoons the Castellana, the young men said to each other:

'There goes Lady So and So. Here comes the famous "Missi".'

In the gardens of the Buen Retiro the occasions when one could see these high-born ladies were more frequent and they seemed closer.

It was not only the elegant high society which one could meet in that garden but also the world of the courtesans: La Blanca, La Puri, La Tropical or La Nadadora, a big woman, blonde and painted, and others who rubbed shoulders with the public. There were also odd-looking ladies who had a certain fame, of whom strange things were told. One of these was Lola la Valkiria, who was said to have challenged a rival in love with a French sword in the Casa de Campo and who that night had appeared in a box of the Teatro Real with her arm bandaged. Another was a woman who was nicknamed 'The Venus of the Necropolis' either because she made rendezvous in the cemeteries or because she considered herself sepulchral.

Among the men there was great variety. The most regular in the gardens were: one who was known as Radames because of his lively look and malign expression; another young man who was said to be the second most beautiful *objet d'art* of Madrid; a painter of doves who wore long hair; a very pretentious officer in the Hussars who, according to rumour, had performed heroic deeds in Melilla; and an aristocrat whose chief preoccupation was to be the double of the Prince of Wales who soon would reign as Edward VII.

It is worth saying that foreigners simply did not see the point of the Gardens of the Retiro. Frenchmen found very little licence to talk to women and Germans asked, surprised:

'But where can one get something to drink?'

The spectacle was exclusively *madrileño*, a little courtly, a little provincial, elegant but at the same time slightly shabby . . .

Baroja, 'Las Noches', 202–03.

The Ateneo

[136] Pérez Galdós
(Pérez Galdós's picture of the Ateneo comes from his
volume 'Prim' (1906) in the *Episodios Nacionales*.)

The Ateneo (Atheneum) was then like an intellectual temple,
established, for want of a better site, in one of the most prosaic
of bourgeois houses, a temple where nave, pulpit and side
chapels had been built by knocking down partition walls, and
doing away with alcoves and cabinets to form large spaces
where the multitude could congregate. It was a poor church,
once a house of *nouveaux riches*, where years before such
people had lived on fortunes made from business and had never
known anything of philosophy, literature or history. And with
the edifice being so shoddy, and so miserable in respect of
architectural style, it had an atmosphere of thoughtful seriousness propitious for study, while its unadorned ceilings gave a
sobriety suitable for the porticos of academies. People of all
ages went there, with different ideas, though the liberals and
democrats were dominant, and the moderates who had refined

their culture by visits abroad. There went too the '*neos*', not the sulky and intolerant, for the disputes there were always courteous, and a spirit of fraternity soothed the aggressive flight of opposing ideas. The divergencies of judgement there fluctuated with the spirit of an affectionate mother, and a general esteem.

One entered by the Calle de la Montera an ample gateway which, if it had not been clean and white, would have been equal to the *posadas* in the Cava Baja*. On the right hand the in-no-way-monumental stairway led in two flights to the first floor: there a screen of oilskin nailed to the wood gave access to the temple. Having passed the corridor where there were the porters and the concierge, one reached a long and broad *cul-de-sac* of a passage, fairly obscure in the day but lit at night by gas stoves. Springy sofas which the weight of innumerable bodies had softened invited one to rest on either side, or at the far end of the passage.

In the library, there were writing pads on which to read and write, shelvings of the sort which middle-class families have-built in order to keep books which are never read; there, one read, certainly; but the books had a certain look of not wishing to be read, preferring their comfortable rearguard position behind the glass . . . the reading-room or reading-rooms constituted a great irregular space composed of two distinct galleries communicating with each other by arcades of masonry with good light from the interior patio; a common kind of enclosure which would have as well served for a workroom of seamstresses as for a printer's, or perhaps a Protestant church. Large tables offered to members all the press of Madrid, much of the provincial press, the best foreign newspapers, some scientific reviews, partly illustrated, partly not, from all countries. It was an immensely varied intellectual dining-room in which each person found the dish most to his taste. In that white precinct, light, blessed with no more adornment than some map or a table of statistics, a silence of peace and reflection lived like a permanent guest, and in the refuge of it the readers crowded together, each one looking

* The Calle de la Cava Baja is a long narrow street which runs along the line of a ditch outside the old Arab walls. Tradition has it that most of the Arabs of Madrid fled this way after the Christian Conquest. For several centuries there have been rough inns there. Some remain.

after his own interests, never worrying about the others. Nobody interrupted with vain whisperings that tranquillity reminiscent of the activity of silkworms working through mulberry leaves. One heard no more than the turning of the pages of the newspapers, which were put into wooden holders for the greater ease of the reader.

There one saw strange types of gluttons for reading. One gentleman would seize *The Times* and not let it go for three hours. Another had the mania of taking six or eight of the best-known newspapers, sitting on them and then drawing them out one by one from under his buttocks and leaving them on the table when he had read them. Others still pecked here and there, standing up. Most ate sitting down, without taking their eyes off their plates, like gastronomes. Through this vast place there passed all the literary and political celebrities of the century, not excluding a great many of the military men. People remember Martínez de la Rosa* reading *Le Journal des Débats*; and Antonio Alcalá Galiano† recharging himself from the entertaining caricatures of *Punch*, and explaining the meaning of them, scarcely intelligible to those who had not talked English in England itself. The good man was already old, with a lined large face, buried in a grey gaberdine, and entered slowly and sat at the periodicals' table. He leafed through some, stopping here and there, seeking the best sweets in the tray of new pieces of knowledge. The circle of admirers which sometimes formed around him heard his hoarse voice, which even in private conversation sounded like oratory, being pointed in the most perfect grammatical forms. In the seasoned irony of his voice, he had no master to equal him, and, at times, his inflexions would have intimidated the bulls of Miura‡.

Pérez Galdós, 'Prim', 39–54.

---

* Francisco Martínez de la Rosa (1787–1862) – statesman.
† Antonio Alcalá Galiano (1789–1865) – statesman.
‡ Eduardo Miura was a famous breeder of fighting-bulls from Sevilla.

Casa de Cisneros

[137] The torture of Antonio Pérez in 1590
(Marañón)

(The Casa de Cisneros, still standing, was reconstructed in the
twentieth century, having been built by a nephew of the great
Cardinal Cisneros in the 1540s.

This account of the torture of a famous ex-confidant of King
Philip II comes from the great biography by Gregorio Marañón. Pérez had been arrested in 1578 (see No. 41) but this test
only came in 1590.)

[Pérez] in a few days begged that they would relieve him since
he was 'crippled in his arms and legs' and he could not support
the chain and the irons. The reply was torture. Probably
Antonio Pérez never thought that the King and his assistant
would stoop to this terrible and humiliating extreme. That
same day he had sent via Gil de Mesa to Father Chaves* a copy

---

* Father Chaves, the King's confessor, adept at finding good legal or
theological reasons for his master's ill-doing.

of that priest's letter in which he ordered that 'on reaching a confession about the murder [of Escobedo], in no way was he to say the causes of it.' Pérez could not understand that the King's confessor, master of his conscience, could command one thing and the King would contradict it . . . It was 23 February 1590. Rodrigo Vázquez and Juan Gómez*, intimated to him once more that he had to reply to the royal warrant. In face of his new negative, they 'ordered him to be put to the torture; and said that if he were to die or suffer damage to some part of his body it would be his fault and responsibility.' Antonio protested as being a gentleman (*hidalgo*) and since it was known that he was 'lame and crippled from eleven years' long imprisonment'. They did not heed this and ordered that his irons, chains and clothes should be removed, less some light linen; and Diego Ruiz, the executioner, showed him the staircase and apparatus of torture. The sight of the fearful instruments did not persuade him to talk. Then they extended his arms in the form of a cross and gave him the six first turns on the rack. Juan Gómez was present at the torture while Rodrigo Vázquez waited in the next room. Antonio complained in a loud voice that they were crippling one of his arms but he still refused to say anything of what they wanted. Another two turns and the threat of going on decided him and he exclaimed: 'Señor Juan Gómez, for the plague of God, finish with me once and for all, leave me, as much you want of me I will speak: for the love of God, brother, have pity on me.' They thus gave him some clothes, the executioner left the room, and he made a declaration.   *Gregorio Marañón, Vol. I, 466–67.*

* Royal officials.

Casa de la Villa

[138] A ball for Wellington (1812)

The municipality gave last night [August 13, 1812] a very superb ball to Lord Wellington, to which all the officers of the Guard being invited, I attended. Nearly 600 persons were there and the display of beauty rivalled London but the affability of the Spanish ladies is not less conspicuous than their beauty and, at every town where we have been, they have shown such marks of attention without the formality of being introduced as has made a deep impression. Already the French language is abolished and, in compliment to the British, no lady, although they all speak it well, will acknowledge that she understands it!

Aitchison, 183

The Cortes Españolas

(This parliament building is on the site of the *convento* of Espíritu Santo, built 1594 and burned down in 1823, while the commander-in-chief of the French army, the Duc d'Angoulême, was at mass. The building was designed by Narciso Pascual y Colomer and built between 1843 and 1850.)

[139] De Amicis (1870)

I was more amused by the deputies of the Cortes than by either the cocks or bulls. I succeeded in procuring a small place in the tribune of the journalists, and I went there every day, and stayed there to the end with infinite enjoyment. The Spanish parliament has a more juvenile aspect than ours; not because the deputies are younger; but because they are neater and more carefully dressed than ours. There, one does not see the disordered hair, unkempt beards, and those colourless jackets which are seen on the benches of our Chamber: there the beards and hair are nicely arranged and shining, the shirts embroidered, coats black, trowsers light, gloves orange-colored, canes silver-headed, and flowers in the button-hole.

The Spanish parliament follows the fashion plates. The dressing and speaking are alike: both lively, gay, flowery, and sparkling. We lament that our deputies are more governed by the form than is fitting political orators; but the Spanish deputies cultivate it more studiously still, and, it is only fair to confess, with better grace. They not only speak with a marvellous facility, so much so that it is a rare occurrence to hear a deputy interrupt himself in the middle of a sentence to seek for a phrase; but there is no one who does not strive to speak correctly, and to give to his words a poetical lustre, a classical flavor, and a little of the imprint of the grand, oratorical style. The gravest ministers, the most timid deputies, the most rigorous financiers, even when they are speaking on subjects quite foreign to those allied to rhetoric, embellish their speeches with the fine forms of anthology, graceful anecdotes, famous verses, apostrophes to civilization, liberty, and the country; and proceed quite rapidly, as if they were reciting something committed to memory, with an intonation always measured and harmonious, and a variety of poses and gestures which leaves no place for ennui. The newspapers, in criticizing their speeches, praise the elevated style, the purity of the language, *los rasgos sublimes*, the sublime flashes, which one admires – if it concerns their friends, be it understood; or, they say, with scorn, that the style is sesquipedal, the language corrupt, the form, – in a word, that blessed form! uncultivated, ignoble, unworthy of the splendid traditions of the art of Spanish oratory. This worship of form, this great facility of speech, degenerates into bombastic vanity; and while it is certain that one must not seek for the models of true political eloquence in the parliament of Madrid, yet that, which is universally admitted is not the less true, viz.: that this parliament is, among those of Europe, the richest in fruitful oratory, in the ordinary sense of the word. One ought to hear a discussion on a subject of important political interest, which stirs the passions. It is a veritable conflict! They are no longer speeches, but inundations of words, calculated to drive stenographers mad and confuse the minds of the auditors in the tribunes! There are voices, gestures, impetuosity, and rhapsodies of inspiration, which make one think of the French Assembly in the turbulent days of the Revolution!

There you hear a Ríos Rosas*, a very violent orator, who dominates the tumult with a roar; a Martos†, an orator of the chosen form, who slays with ridicule; a Pí y Margall‡, a venerable old man, who terrifies one with gloomy prophecies; a Collantes§, an indefatigable speaker, who crushes the chamber under an avalanche of words; a Rodríguez, who, with marvellous flexion of reasoning and paraphrase, pursues, confuses, and stifles his adversaries, and among a hundred others, a Castelar¶, who vanquishes and fascinates both enemies and friends with a torrent of poetry and harmony. And this Castelar, noted throughout Europe, is really the most complete example of Spanish eloquence. He pushes the worship of form to the point of idolatry; his eloquence is music; his reasoning is the slave of his ear; he says or does not say a thing, or says it in one way better than in another, according to the turn of the sentence; he has harmony in his mind, follows it, obeys it, and sacrifices to it everything that can offend it; his period is a strophe; in fact, one must hear him in order to credit the fact that human speech, without poetical measure and song, can so closely approach the harmony of song and poetry. He is more of an artist than a politician; has not only an artist's intellect, but an artist's heart also; it is the heart of a child, which is incapable of hatred and enmity. In none of his speeches can one find abuse; in the Cortes he has never provoked a serious personal dispute; he never has recourse to satire, nor does he adopt irony; in his most violent philippics he never lets drop a dram of gall, and this is a proof of it, that though a republican, adversary of all the ministers, a warlike journalist and perpetual accuser of him who exercises any power, and of him who is not a fanatic for liberty, he has never made himself hated by any one. However, his speeches are enjoyed, not feared; his style is too beautiful to be terrible; his character too ingenuous to admit of his exercising a political influence; he does not know how to tilt, plot, and to

---

* A. de los Ríos Rosas (1812–73), Andalusian lawyer and politician.
† C. Martos, Democratic politician.
‡ Francisco Pí y Margall (1824–1901), Catalan democrat and federalist, president of the first republic of Spain 1873.
§ Antonio Collantes (1806–1870) politician from Santander.
¶ Emilio Castelar (1832–99), president of the first republic 1874.

make way for himself by bribes; he is only fitted to please and to shine; his eloquence, when it is grandest, is tender; his most beautiful speeches draw forth tears. To him the Chamber is a theatre. Like improvisators, in order to have a clear and serene inspiration, he is obliged to speak at a given hour, at a fixed point, and with a certain allowance of time before him. Therefore, on the day he is to speak, he takes certain measures with the president of the Chamber; the president arranges matters so that his turn comes when the tribunes are crowded and all the deputies are in their places; newspapers announce his speech the evening before, so that the ladies may procure tickets; for he requires a certain amount of expectation. Before speaking he is restless, and cannot keep quiet one instant; he enters the Chamber, leaves it, re-enters, goes out again, wanders through the corridors, goes into the library and turns over the leaves of a book, rushes into the café to take a glass of water, seems to be seized with fever, fancies that he will not know how to put the words together, that he will be laughed at or hissed; not a single lucid idea of his speech remains in his head; he has confused and forgotten everything.

'How is your pulse?' his friends ask, smilingly.

When the solemn moment arrives, he takes his place with bowed head, trembling and pallid as a man condemned to death, who is resigned to losing in a single day the glory acquired with so many years of fatigue. At that moment even his enemies feel pity for his condition. He rises, gives a glance around him, and says:

'Señores!'

He is saved; his courage returns, his mind grows clear, and his speech comes back to him like a forgotten air; the president, the Cortes, the tribunes, disappear; he sees nothing but his gestures, hears nothing but his own voice, and feels nought but the irresistible flame which burns within him and the mysterious force that sustains and upholds him. It is beautiful to hear him say these things.

'I no longer see the walls of the room,' he exclaims, 'I behold distant people and countries which I have never seen.'

He speaks by the hour, and not a deputy leaves the room, not a person moves in the tribunes, not a voice interrupts him, not a gesture disturbs him; not even when he breaks the regulations has the president sufficient courage to interrupt him; he displays at his ease the picture of his republic, clothed in white and crowned with roses, and the monarchists do not dare protest, because, so clothed, they, too, find it beautiful. Castelar is master of the Assembly; he thunders, lightens, sings, rages, and gleams like fireworks; makes his auditors smile, calls forth shouts of enthusiasm, ends amid a storm of applause, and goes away with his head in a whirl. Such is this famous Castelar, professor of history in the university, a very fruitful writer on politics, art, and religion; a publicist who makes fifty thousand francs a year in the American newspapers, an academician unanimously elected by the *Academia Española*, pointed out in the streets, fêted by the people, beloved by his enemies, and a charming, vain, generous, and handsome youth.

De Amicis, 210–14.

[140] General Pavía's *coup* (3 January 1874)

The moment then had arrived to '*montar al caballo*'. Pavía* established himself before the palace of the Cortes, and ordered his aides, Cubas and Villalonga, to talk to the President of the Chamber, in the name of the Captain General of the Region, and tell him to leave, in the peremptory time of five minutes. At the same time the colonel of the civil guard, Valencia, went to tell the forces of that body and other representatives of public order who were doing service in the Congress.

At the moment of being intimidated, Salmerón† as president of the Cortes – seven in the morning – was preparing to take the vote for the president of the executive power, an investiture which, by agreement with the different opposition parties, was going to fall on Eduardo Palanca‡, ex federal minister of gloomy personality, native of Málaga. Salmerón, trying to dominate the assembly by the noise of his voice, more solemn than ever because of the tumult, announced that the vote could not be taken, since the representatives of the nation were being

* General Manuel Pavía y Rodríguez (1827–95).
† Nicolás Salmerón (1838–1908), philosopher, president of the first republic.
‡ Eduardo Palanca (1834–1900), Republican lawyer and politician.

threatened by the forces of order, and that the Cortes would be henceforth in permanent session resisting the dissolution by violence. Castelar, still president of the Executive power, rejected the vote of confidence which, in this critical moment, someone wanted to propose on his behalf and claimed himself to be perpetually disqualified, not only for the Government but to be a political personality of any sort, yet showed himself prepared to resist in his seat. 'I will die and everyone will die,' he exclaimed, sinking no doubt in a sea of contradictory impressions. Benot replied: 'To die; no, to conquer.' Chao proposed that General Pavía should be taken to a Council of War . . . But the civil guard did not act. In anticipation that it might be necessary to make a better show of force, Pavía had ordered some cartridges without balls to be manufactured, for which a piece of artillery was established in the Calle de Floridablanca. But the civil guard had only to fire some shots in the air to precipitate the dispersal of the legislators. Salmerón tried an airy reply: 'Is it agreed by everyone that we must resist? That we cannot be murdered in our seats?' Various deputies replied: 'Yes, yes all of us,' while at the same time they sought hastily the doors of the salon and then those of the building . . . A deputy for Granada, Enrique Molinero, fell on jumping out of a downstairs window: the only casualty of the day.

El Diario de las Sesiones records the last moments of the *Cortes Constitutuyentes* of the Spanish Republic.

Various deputies: 'What a scandal!' Señor Castelar – 'What shame!' Various deputies: 'Soldiers, *viva* the Federal Republic. *Viva* the sovereign assembly!' Other deputies addressed the soldiers who fell back in the gallery, and then several shots were heard, the session coming to an end instantly. It was half-past seven in the morning.

Melchor Fernández Almagro, I, 209–210

La Residencia
de Estudiantes

(The Residencia ('*la Resi*') was a wonderful establishment which seemed a college in the English style for liberal students at the University of Madrid. The great film-maker Luis Buñuel was there in 1917 with, among others, Federico García Lorca and Salvador Dalí.)

[141] 1917–1925: Buñuel

I had not been in Madrid more than once with my father for a few days. When I returned with both parents in 1917 to look for a place where I could continue my studies I felt at the beginning paralysed by my provincialism. I observed discreetly how people dressed and carried themselves, in order to imitate them. Even now I recall my father in his straw hat giving me instructions in a loud voice in the Calle de Alcalá and pointing things out with a stick. I, with hands in pockets, looked around as if I were not with him.

We visited various madrilenian pensions of a classic type in which every day one eats *cocido a la madrileña* with *garbanzos* (chick peas), potatoes, bacon, sausage and sometimes a slice of meat or chicken. My mother did not want to hear even talk of leaving me there, not only because of the food but because one might find there a very definitely free way of behaving.

Finally thanks to the recommendation of a senator Don Bartolomé Esteban I was inscribed in the Residencia of Estudiantes where I would remain for seven years. My memories of that time are so rich and vivid that I can assure you without fear of going wrong that had I not passed through the Residencia my life would have been different.

The Residencia was a kind of university campus in the English style and it did not cost more than seven pesetas a day for a private room and four pesetas for a double one. My parents paid these fees, and in addition gave me twenty pesetas a week for my expenditures, a considerable sum which nevertheless was inadequate for me. Every time that I went to Saragossa for holidays I asked my mother to charge the administrator to pay the debts accumulated during the term. My father never knew.

The director of the Residencia was Don Alberto Jiménez, a citizen of Málaga, of great culture. In it one could prepare a degree of any sort and it had conference rooms, five laboratories, a library and various sporting fields. One could remain there all the time that one wished and could change one's faculty during the course.

When, before leaving Saragossa, my father asked me what I wanted to be, I, who only wished to leave Spain, replied that my chief desire was to become a composer and I wished to go to Paris to study the Schola Cantorum. A rotund 'No' from my father. What I needed was a serious profession and everyone knew that composers die of hunger.

Then I spoke of my interest in Natural Sciences and Entomology. 'Make yourself an agronomist,' he advised me. Thus I began to study to be an agricultural engineer. Unfortunately though I passed first in Biology, I failed Mathematics during three consecutive courses. Abstract thoughts have always defeated me. Certain mathematical truths have been self-evident but I was incapable of following and reproducing the meanders of a demonstration . . .

It was also in the Residencia that I acquired a passion for sport. Every morning in short trousers and with bare feet, even when the ground was covered in frost, I ran in a training field for the cavalry of the civil guard. I founded the athletic team of the college and took part in various university matches, and I even practised amateur boxing – though in all I only had two combats: one, I won because of the non-appearance of my opponent, the other I lost on points after five rounds for lack of combativity on my part. In truth – I did no more than think of how to protect my face.

Whatever exercise I could find appeared good. I even climbed the façade of the Residencia.

During my whole life – or nearly so – I have kept the fitness which I acquired then, especially in the abdomen. I even managed to make a kind of circus turn of it. I lay on the ground and my friends jumped on my stomach. Another of my specialities: to test wrists. Up till a very advanced age, I have disputed innumerable rounds of this sort on tables of bars and in restaurants.   *Buñuel, 54–57*

Museo del Prado

('The Prado' became a museum of pictures in 1819, having been built between 1785 and 1808 as a museum of natural history by Juan de Villanueva.)

[142] Richard Ford (1830)

(Richard Ford (1796–1858) was a barrister who never practised but drew, travelled and lived in Sevilla. His *Handbook for Travellers in Spain* (1840) for John Murray is remarkable.)

The worst part of this noble institution is a gang of restorers who are established below and carry on their processes which the Spanish writers justly term *horroroso* and *espantoso* with a zeal and indefatigable energy worthy of a better cause. Every picture in the gallery seems destined to undergo their discipline; and neither age nor school escape their merciless grasp. They appear to view the inestimable productions which are successively doomed to pass through their hands with the same indifference a school of anatomists have for the 'subjects' brought before them.   *Richard Ford, 'Handbook', 683*

[143] Manet (1865)

(Édouard Manet (1832–83) went to Madrid after the scandal associated with his *Olympia*, sent to the Salon in 1865.)

Oh, what a pity you are not here; what pleasure it would have given you to see Velázquez, who alone is worth the whole journey. The painters of every school who surround him in the Madrid Museum, and who are very well represented, all seem second-rate in comparison with him. He is the painter to beat all painters. He didn't astonish me, he enchanted me. The full-length portrait in the Louvre is not by him; only the authenticity of the Infanta can't be doubted. There is an enormous picture here, filled with small figures like those in *The Cavaliers*, in the Louvre, but the figures of the women in this one are perhaps better, and all of them are perfectly free from retouching. The background – the landscape – is by a pupil of Velázquez.

The most astonishing work in this splendid collection, and perhaps the most astonishing piece of painting that has ever been done, is the one entitled in the catalogue, *Portrait of a Celebrated Actor in the Time of Philip IV*. The background fades into nothing; the old boy, all in black, so alive, seems to be surrounded by air. And, ah, *The Spinners*; and the beautiful portrait of Alonso Cano; and *Las Meninas* – another extraordinary picture! *The philosophers* – what astonishing works! And all the dwarfs too! – one in particular, seated full face with his hands on his hips: a painting for the real connoisseur. And his magnificent portraits! – one would have to include the lot; they are masterpieces. The well-known portrait of Charles V by Titian, which certainly deserves to be appreciated and which anywhere else would undoubtedly have seemed to me good, here, in comparison, looks wooden.

And Goya! surely the most curious painter since the Master (whom he imitated too much and in the most servile way). But in spite of this he has great verve. There are two equestrian portraits by him in the museum, painted in the manner of Velázquez; but all the same, they are much inferior in quality. What I have seen of him up to now does not please me enormously.

Letter from Manet to Fantin-Latour, dated
Madrid, 1865; quoted in Moreau-Nealaton, Vol I.

[144] Meier-Graefe (c. 1906)

(Julius Meier-Graefe (1867–1933), a famous art critic in his day, went to Madrid to study Velázquez but fell in love with El Greco.)

MADRID – 15TH APRIL

We went to bed after the night journey and had only just gone to sleep when Mynheer knocked at the door. Ten o'clock. On to Velázquez! I murmured something. He could go alone. – John was going too. – Very well then, go together, I must sleep. Mynheer mumbled something. John laughed. I heard them go downstairs. I simply couldn't. The same silly feeling of hesitation. Down below me the newspaper vendors shouted in exactly the same tone as the Parisian *camelots*. In our well-lit sitting-room there was a photograph hanging on the wall which I had hardly noticed when we had arrived early in the morning. The equestrian portrait of Olivares by Velázquez. I had a copy in Berlin. It seemed as if the motion of the horse was transformed into the rhythm of my pulse; I could hardly stay still another second. At noon the other two came in without ado. I was just shaving. Mynheer quite excited. Can't be beaten! Very swell indeed! – John quiet and pale. He inquired from the porter where to buy canvas. Without anyone noticing it I crept out; I told Jeanne that I had to go to the telegraph office. I leaped into a cab. Prado! The fellow drove so slowly that I could have beaten him, and when I tapped on the window, in a rage, he stopped the cab and inquired politely after my wishes. At last! I mounted the stairs calmly, bought a catalogue and walked slowly through the rooms. Pictures – pictures. I saw practically nothing until I reached my goal. The El Grecos, which one must pass, looked like inebriated phantasies. Goya's *Mayas* dreadful rubbish. That was moreover about what I had expected, and anyhow it didn't matter. Nothing but the one, the great, the unique Velázquez! It seemed to me as if for years I had lived for no other purpose than to experience this moment.

From the very first moment in the Velázquez room I felt that something painful and ludicrous was happening. It wasn't even altogether unexpected. It happened with the deadly certainty with which the train enters the station. I went from picture to picture, at first very quickly, like counting bank-notes, then slowly and more slowly. What happened was really quite natural. What were these pictures to be like? What did it concern them what I thought of them? For years I had written touching letters to an unknown friend concerning the most important things, then finally I succumbed to the temptation of getting to know him personally, and one should not do those things. Moreover, perhaps nothing was to be blamed except the ghastly cold day in Salamanca, or the garlic last night, or something else. Perhaps I simply lacked a certain impulse. Courage! Once in it, the rest would come by itself. Look at the colours, nothing can be said against them; and above all the *allure!* The only trouble is that one has heard of this *allure* too often on the barrel organ. The others, the organ-grinders, Whistler and company, have made this *allure* banal. One must subtract all these things in one's mind. But I wasn't thinking of them in the least, in fact I was not thinking at all, I was just waiting. I looked and forced myself to look with all the tension of my visual powers. I tried again with every picture. If only there was one single one there! . . .

The collection of portraits in the Prado is like the ancestral gallery of humanity. One's joy in its beauty is mingled with respect for this gathering. It seems quite a matter of course that Charles V was painted by Titian, this cardinal by Raphael, this queen, the mother of three kings, by Rubens, the princess of Mor, those burghers by Dürer and by the *Master of the Virgin Mary*. The painters, so to speak, fit in with their sitters. And this suggestive power applies even to Goya, the plebeian among these painters.   *Meier-Graefe, 38–40, 100*

[145] Trotsky (1916)

(Leon Trotsky came to Spain in 1916 after being expelled from wartime France.)

From San Sebastián, where I was delighted by the sea and appalled by the prices, I went to Madrid, and found myself in a city in which I knew no one, not a single soul, and no one knew me. And since I did not speak Spanish, I could not have been lonelier even in the Sahara or in the Peter-Paul fortress. There remained only the language of art. The two years of war had made one forget that such a thing as art still existed. With the eagerness of a starved man, I viewed the priceless treasures of the Museum of Madrid and felt again the 'eternal' element in this art. The Rembrandts, the Riberas. The paintings of Bosch were works of genius in their naïve joy of life. The old caretaker gave me a lens so that I might see the tiny figures of the peasants, little donkeys and dogs in the pictures of Miel. Here there was no feeling of war; everything was securely in its place. The colours had their own life, uncontrolled.

This is what I wrote in my note-book in the museum: 'Between us and these old artists – without in the least obscuring them or lessening their importance – there grew up before the war a new art, more intimate, more individualistic, one with greater nuances, at once more subjective and more intense. The war, by its mass passions and suffering, will probably wash away this mood and this manner for a long time – but that can never mean a simple return to the old form, however beautiful – to the anatomic and botanic perfection, to the Rubens thighs (though thighs are likely to play a great rôle in the new post-war art, which will be so eager for life). It is difficult to prophesy, but out of the unprecedented experiences filling the lives of almost all civilized human beings, surely a new art must be born.'   *Trotsky 'My Life', 223–224*

Prison

[146] Brunel (1655)
(The Palacio de Santa Cruz remained the Cárcel de Corte, a
prison for noblemen till 1850. It was built by Cristóbal de
Aguilera and José de Villarreal between 1629 and 1643.
The palace afterwards became the Ministerio de Ultramar
(1850) and the Foreign Ministry (1900).)

There are no houses in this town that I find more beautiful than
the prison; but there are none where I would less like to live. It
is a massive building, long and wide, whose windows are well
woven with good iron bars, which look as if they had been put
there as much for ornamentation as for security; indeed, apart
from the fact that they are not in little squares and that they are
much bigger than those of nuns' grilles, they are gilded and
worked with art; so much so that it would not be strange if I
had been taken in and that I had mistaken this house, at the
beginning, for that of some Grandee of Spain.

Brunel, 141 (1655)

[147] Casanova (1767)

My carriage was at the door, and I was just taking leave of
Mengs* when an officer appeared on the scene, and asked the
painter if the Chevalier de Casanova was in his house.

'I am the Chevalier de Casanova,' said I.

'Then I hope you will follow me of your own free will to the
prison of Buen Retiro. I cannot use force here, for this house is
the king's, but I warn you that in less than an hour the
Chevalier Mengs will have orders to turn you out, and then
you will be dragged to prison, which would be unpleasant for
you. I therefore advise you to follow me quietly, and to give up
such weapons as you may possess.'

'The Chevalier Mengs will give you the weapons in question.
I have carried them with me for eleven years; they are meant to
protect me on the highways. I am ready to follow you, but first
allow me to write four notes; I shall not be half an hour.'

'I can neither allow you to wait nor to write, but you will be
at liberty to do so after you have reached the prison.'

'Very good; then I am ready to follow you, for I have no
choice. I shall remember Spanish justice!'

I embraced Mengs, had the weapons put into my carriage,
and got in with the officer, who seemed a perfect gentleman.

He took me to the Castle of Buen Retiro, formerly a royal
palace, and now a prison†. When my conductor had consigned
me to the officer of the watch I was handed over to a corporal,
who led me into a vast hall on the ground floor of the building.
The stench was dreadful, and the prisoners were about thirty,
ten of them being soldiers. There were ten or twelve large beds,
some benches, no tables, and no chairs.

I asked a guard to get me some pens, ink, and paper, and
gave him a duro for the purpose. He took the coin smilingly,
and went away, but he did not return. When I asked his
brethren what had become of him they laughed in my face.
But what surprised me the most was the sight of my page and
Marazzini, who told me in Italian that he had been there for

* Antonio Raphael Mengs (1728–1779), the Bohemia-born court painter in Madrid. He left twenty-two children.
† The Buen Retiro, in disuse after Charles III went to the Royal Palace,
was temporarily used as a prison.

three days, and that he had not written to me as he had a
presentiment that we should soon meet. He added that in a
fortnight's time we should be sent off under a heavy escort to
work in some fortress, though we might send our pleas to the
Government, and might possibly be let out after three or four
years' imprisonment.

'I hope,' he said, 'not to be condemned before I am heard.
The *alcalde* will come and interrogate you tomorrow, and your
answers will be taken down; that's all. You may then be sent to
hard labour in Africa.'

'Has your case been heard yet?'

'They were at me about it for three hours yesterday.' . . .

. . . I passed such a night as Dante might have imagined in
his Vision of Hell. All the beds were full, and even if there had
been a spare place I would not have occupied it. I asked in vain
for a mattress, but even if they had brought me one, it would
have been of no use, for the whole floor was inundated. There
were only two or three chamber utensils for all the prisoners,
and everyone discharged his occasions on the floor.

I spent the night on a narrow bench without a back, resting
my head on my hands.   *Casanova, 108, 114.*

[148] Trotsky (1916)

In my hotel, I read the Spanish papers with the aid of a
dictionary and waited for an answer to the letters I had sent
to Switzerland and Italy . . .

On November 9, the maid at the small pension in which
Gabier had placed me called me out into the corridor with a
frightened air. There I found two young men of unmistakable
appearance who invited me, in not very friendly fashion, to
follow them. What to? But, of course, to the Madrid prefecture
of police. Once there, they seated me in a corner.

'Am I under arrest, then?' I asked.

'*Sí, para una hora, dos horas* (for an hour or two).'

Without changing my position, I sat there in the prefecture
for seven hours. At nine o'clock in the evening, I was taken
upstairs. I found myself before a fairly well thronged Olympus.

'What is it that you have arrested me for, precisely?'

This simple question nonplussed the Olympians. They offered various hypotheses in turn. One of them referred to the passport difficulties that the Russian government raised for foreigners going to Russia.

'If you could only know the amount of money we spend in prosecuting our anarchists,' said another, appealing to my sympathy.

'But surely I cannot be held answerable at the same time for both the Russian police and the Spanish anarchists?'

'Of course, of course, that is only to give you an example.'

'What are your ideas?' the chief asked me at last, after deliberating for a while.

I stated my views in as popular language as I could.

'There, you see!' they said.

In the end, the chief informed me through the interpreter that I was invited to leave Spain at once and that, until I left, my freedom would be subject to 'certain limitations'. 'Your ideas are too advanced for Spain,' he told me candidly, still through the interpreter.

At midnight, a police agent took me to the prison in a cab.

[The police agent entrusted with this task presented himself in a state of inebriation, and a large crowd gathered around the police car while the agent tearfully told Trotsky of his great love for the people of Russia.] 'In all this,' recalled Trotsky, 'there was something extremely Russian.' [At the Model Prison he was instructed to remove his hat, but refused, sensibly replying, 'It is not a church' . . .]

There was the inevitable examination of my belongings in the centre of the prison 'star', at the intersection of five wings, each of them four stories high. The staircases were of iron, and were suspended. The peculiar prison night-silence, saturated with heavy vapours and nightmarishness. Pale electric lights in the corridors. Everything familiar, everything the same. The rumbling of the iron-bound door when it opened; a large room, semi-darkness, heavy prison odours, a miserable and repulsive bed. Then the rumbling of the door as it was locked. How many imprisonments did this make? I opened the small aperture in the window behind the grating. A draft of cool air blew in. Without undressing, with my clothes all buttoned up, I lay down on the bed and covered myself with my overcoat. Only then did I begin to realize the full incongruity of what had happened. In a prison – in Madrid! I had never dreamed of such a thing. Izvolsky* had done his job well. In Madrid! I lay on the bed in the Madrid 'model' prison and laughed with all my might, laughed until I fell asleep.

When I was taking my walk, the convicts explained to me that there were two kinds of cells in the prison – the free cells and those for which one paid. A cell of the first class cost one and a half pesetas a day; one of the second class, 75 céntimos. Every prisoner was entitled to occupy a paid cell, but he had no right to refuse a free one. My cell was a paid one, of the first class. I again laughed heartily. But after all, it was only logical. Why should there be equality in prison, in a society built entirely on inequality? I also learned that the occupants of paid cells walk out twice a day for an hour at a time, whereas the others have only a half-hour. Again, this was perfectly right. The lungs of a government thief who pays a franc and a half a day are entitled to a larger portion of air than the lungs of a striker who gets his breathing free of charge.

On the third day, I was called up for anthropometric measurements, and was told to paint my fingers with printer's ink and impress their marks on cards. I refused. Then 'force' was resorted to, but with a studied politeness. I looked out the window while the guard courteously painted my hand, finger after finger, and pressed it about ten times on various cards and sheets, first the right hand, then the left. Next, I was invited to sit down and take off my boots. I refused. The feet proved more difficult to manage, and the administration presently was walking about me in confusion. In the end, I was unexpectedly allowed to go and talk to Gabier and Anguiano†, who had come to see me. Anguiano had been released from prison – another one – the day before. They told me that all the agencies to bring about my release had been set in motion. In the corridor I met the prison chaplain, who expressed his Catholic sympathies with my pacifism and added consolingly: '*Paciencia, paciencia.*' There was nothing else possible for me, anyway.

* Alexander Izvolsky (1856–1919) was Russian foreign minister, 1906–1910, and then ambassador to Paris until 1917.
† Daniel Anguiano was a veteran socialist leader who helped to found the Communist Party in 1922.

On the morning of the twelfth, the police agent informed me that I was to leave for Cádiz that same evening, and asked if I wanted to pay for my railway ticket. But I had no desire to go to Cádiz, and I firmly refused to pay for the ticket. It was enough that one had to pay for accommodation in the 'model' prison.

And so, in the evening, we left Madrid for Cádiz. The travelling costs were dear, at the expense of the Spanish king.

Trotsky, 224–26.

LIFE, CUSTOMS AND MORALS IN MADRID

LIFE, CUSTOMS AND
MORALS IN MADRID

Men and Women – Manners

[149] Sir Richard Wynn's view of Spanish women (1623)

Towards evening I went to my Lord of Bristol's, to wait upon my Lady; and in my return through one street, I met at least five hundred coaches; most of them had all women in, going into the fields (as they usually do about that time of the day) to take the air. Of all these women, I dare take my oath, there was not one unpainted – so visibly, that you would think they rather wore vizards than their own faces. Whether they be handsome or no I cannot tell, unless they did unmask; yet a great number of them have excellent eyes and teeth; – the boldest women in the world, for as I passed along, numbers of them called and beckoned to me: whether their impudence or my habit was the cause of it, I cannot tell. I saw more good horses under saddles, foot-cloths, and in coaches, than ever I saw in all my life . . .

After some time's expectance, enters the Queen's ladies, by two and two, and set themselves down upon the carpets that lay spread upon the ground. There were some sixteen in number of them: handsome I cannot say any one of them was, but painted more (if it were possible) than the ordinary women; not one of them free from it, though some of them were not thirteen years old. Rich enough they were in clothes, although not over costly.   *D'Ewes II, 445–46, 447.*

[150] A French view of Spanish women in 1655 (Brunel)

As to the women . . . they often counterfeit the passions, and borrow the transports of a real love. The Count of Fiesque who, when he arrived in Madrid, made a strong set at the sex, recounts as a pretty tale, a trick, which one of these good ladies played on him: in the middle of the Court she grabbed him by the hair, bewailing his infidelity, and calling him traitor and scoundrel, because she had learnt that he had some new loves! Monsieur de Mogeron was also very surprised to find himself being attacked, one evening, by a woman who treated him in the same way, pulling his hair, and belabouring him with injuries and reproaches, because he had not gone to see her as he had promised her that he would do, at the promenade, where he had met her the day before. They act out many jests and extravagances of this sort . . .

They are ridiculous in the way they beautify themselves, and wear their best dresses underneath wretched ones, which means that if you should see them on some feast day when they deck themselves out, or when they walk making their skirts rustle underneath, you cannot judge one prettier than another. The linen they use is a light-coloured cloth, which is usually the most used in Spain: they are so fond of paint that not only do they cover their entire faces with it, but in addition they change the colour of the parts that do not show. They also wear chemises edged with lace in places seen only by their admirers; it is true that they are made of that shabby lace which they get from Lorraine and Provence, and which here orna-ments the linen of countryfolk; because they know nothing of Flanders lace, unless they pick up a few little pieces from foreigners, by snatching their ruffles or jabots.

Besides this prodigiously large number of abandoned women that exists in Madrid, you can count seven or eight brothels established by public authority in various areas to serve as prostitutes to all those who want to go and find one. They are called *cantoneras*, ladies of the crossroads, as one might say; they are paid some wages by the town, which means that this infamous employment is sought after, to such an extent that when one of these sluts is missing either through death or some evil spell, the position is solicited for of the magistrate. I do not know what their price is; but those who have told me about this villainous establishment have told me that each person who sees them is obliged to pay them twelve quartos, which is six of our sous.

The doctors have to visit them from time to time, to see if they are clear of those accursed evils which they earn in their marvellous trade. In addition they have an old lady near them who is obliged to let the magistrate or the doctor know when they discover that they are infested. People who have described to me the life which these miserable creatures lead, have told me that they are not seen at all once there is someone with them, where there is never any noise, because those who go in there leave their swords and daggers at the entrance to the room and those who then arrive, seeing them outside the door, retire without a word.

Sinning thus with impunity because of the public authority's consent, they hardly ever leave off this vice which they so openly profess. Nevertheless there is one day dedicated to exhorting them to repentance. It is a Friday in Lent, on which they are led by one or two *alguazils* to the church of Las Recogidas, which is for the repentant women of our areas. There they are placed at the foot of the preacher's pulpit, who does his best to touch their hearts; but rarely does he achieve his end. After having exhorted them in vain to amend for quite a long time, he comes down from the pulpit, and presents them with the crucifix, saying 'See the Lord, embrace him,' and if there is then some one who embraces it, she is taken and shut up in the convent of the Repented. But more often they only kiss the cross and shed tears without touching what is presented to them, and with this grimace go on to continue in their evil life, and the story of the Magdalen, the whole of which is told them, does not touch them enough to make them want to imitate her. *Brunel, 216–217.*

[151] Saint-Simon calls on a marquesa (1722)

The first person I called on when I arrived in Madrid was the Marquesa de Grimaldo*. No one had warned me of the manner in which ladies receive. I found her at the far end of the small room opposite the door, with a little gathering of men and women on either side of her. She rose as soon as she saw me enter, but without stirring a step, and bowed her head, when I approached, as nuns do, which is their form of curtsey. When I left, she did the same again, without advancing from a line, nor with any excuse for not doing more: it is the custom of the country. The men, however, come more or less far in front, and accompany one to the door depending on one's standing, since everything is laid down and definitive, and yet nevertheless it does not remove the obtrusiveness of compliments. One way or another, much more is made of prolonging the ceremony than is done here. Both parties know exactly how far it must go, that nothing must either shorten it or extend it, that everything that is said on both sides is utterly useless, that the one would be blamed and the other rightly offended were the whole not carried out in its entirety exactly as it should be. None of that prevents one stopping all the time, and these compliments take up half the visit; it is insupportable: people now speak here of ceremonious visits; but once familiarity is established, people exist together more or less as here. Women never go to visit men; but they do go to them when they are besought for an evening of music or a ball or some fireworks or something similar. And if there is a supper as well as refreshment, they sit down at table with everyone else.

Saint-Simon, Vol. 39, 356 (1722).

[152] Beaumarchais has his revenge on José de Clavijo for deceiving his sister (1764)

(Beaumarchais told the following story during his visit to Madrid, Clavijo – the villain of the tale – being present. See Goethe's curious novel, *Clavigo* (1771).)

---

* Marquesa de Grimaldo, wife of the prime minister.

A certain French merchant, with a family and only moderate means, had nevertheless many business connections in Spain. One of the richest of these, passing through Paris nine or ten years ago, made him this proposal: 'Let me have two of your daughters to take back to Madrid. I am an old man, without relatives; they can take charge of my business and will eventually succeed to the richest establishment in Spain.' The eldest daughter, already a married woman, and one of her sisters were put in his charge, the father undertaking to provide the new branch in Madrid with all the French merchandise that they might want.

Two years later, the old Spaniard died, leaving the Frenchwomen without any benefit, and in the awkward position of having to carry on a commercial enterprise. Good behaviour and wit preserved to them some friends, who hastened to increase their credit and their business. At about this same time, a young man from the Canary Islands got himself introduced into the house. [Here, says Beaumarchais, Clavijo's smile 'froze on his face'.] In spite of his lack of means, the ladies, finding in him a great enthusiasm for the study of the French language and of sciences, provided him with the means of making rapid progress in these . . . Finally he conceived the idea of giving the city of Madrid the novel pleasure of reading a periodical journal on the lines of the English *Spectator*, and then, spurred on by hope of success in making his name, he dared openly to propose marriage to the younger of the two Frenchwomen . . . Touched by the merit of the man who sought her, she refused several advantageous matches, and, preferring to wait until he who had loved her for four years had fulfilled the hopes of success which all his friends entertained for him, she encouraged him to publish his first philosophical journal, under the imposing title of *El Pensador*. ['Here', says Beaumarchais, 'I saw my man ready to faint.']

The work [pursued Beaumarchais icily] had a prodigious success; even the King gave public marks of goodwill to the author. He was promised the first honourable employment which should fall vacant. Then he drove away all other suitors by paying open court to the girl; the marriage only awaited the attainment of the promised appointment. At last, after six years of waiting on one side, and of cares and attentions on the other, the appointment materialized – and the man fled. [Clavijo was now breathing hard.]

The affair had caused too much stir for such an outcome to be viewed with indifference. The ladies had taken a house capable of holding two households; the banns had been published. The outrage incensed all their friends, who set about avenging the insult. The French Ambassador took the matter up. But when the man in question discovered that the French-women were employing more powerful support against him, fearing an influence which might overthrow him and destroy in one instant his rising fortune, he threw himself at the feet of his exasperated mistress. In his turn he enlisted the aid of all his friends to bring her back, and as the anger of a deceived woman is hardly ever more than disguised love, everything was set right. The preparations for the marriage were resumed, the banns were published again, and the wedding was fixed to take place in three days' time.

He came back, indeed, two days later; but instead of leading his victim to the altar, he sent word to the poor girl that he had changed his mind a second time and would not marry her. Her indignant friends rushed to him at once; the insolent wretch no longer beat about the bush, but defied them to do their worst, saying that if the Frenchwomen sought to worry him, they had better take care that he did not bring about their final ruin, in a country where they had no protection.

At this news, the young French girl fell into a state of convulsions which caused fears to be held for her life. In their despair, the elder one wrote to France of the public affront which had been put upon them; this account so moved the heart of their brother that, instantly demanding leave to come to Spain and elucidate such a complex affair, he leapt at one jump from Paris to Madrid. '*I am that brother*,' said Beau-marchais, 'who have left everything – country, duties, family, pleasures – to come to Spain to avenge an innocent and unhappy sister, to unmask a traitor and write his infamy in letters of blood upon his face – and *you are that traitor!*'

[Note – *This was Beaumarchais' version. It was not widely accepted. The 'innocent girl' was thirty-three. Beaumarchais stayed a year in Madrid but was unsuccessful in numerous speculations. He returned richer than he himself realized; for he was carrying in his head the outlines of those sharply cut and original characters Figaro, Rosina, Count Almaviva, Bartholo and Basilio.]*

Beaumarchais, quoted in Cynthia Cox, 'The Real Figaro', 22–24

[153] Alfieri's month in Madrid (1769)
(Count Vittorio Alfieri (1749–1803), the Piedmontese dramatist, had left England in haste after a scandal, and travelled in Spain and Portugal 1769–1771.)

I passed then to Madrid and such was the pleasure which I had in this gypsy life that I soon gave up Madrid as tedious, and I only stayed there a month. I talked to nobody, I knew nobody, except for a clock-maker, a young Spaniard, who had just returned from Holland where he had learned his trade. This young man was full of natural intelligence and, having seen something of the world, spoke frankly to me, very sorrowfully of the many barbarities which embittered his country. And here I will describe briefly a senseless brutality which occurred to me in relation to my servant Elia, when I was in the company of this young Spaniard. One night when the clockmaker had dined with me, and when we were still chatting round the table, after having finished dining, Elia entered in order, as was his custom, to treat my hair, before we all went to bed and, in combing my hair, pulled my hair. I, without saying a word, leapt up more rapidly than a shaft of light and gave him from behind a most brutal blow on his right temple with a candle stick which I had grabbed. The blood shot out as if from a fountain, reaching the face and the body of the young Spaniard who was sitting in front of me on the other side of the ample table where we were dining. This young man believed, with reason, that I had suddenly gone off my head, not having seen what had happened nor being able to believe that a hair pulled out could have occasioned my momentary furore. He, however, leapt towards Elia, intending to shelter him. But then the lively and offended and horribly wounded Elia flung himself on me in order to hit me and quite rightly, too. But now I, very rapidly, escaped from his arms and rushed forward with my sword which was in the next door room on a table and I had time to unsheath it. Elia, livid with rage, turned against me and I placed the sword at his chest. And the Spaniard then overcame first Elia, then me, and the whole household was awakened and the servants came running in, with which concluded this tragic-comical and scandalous quarrel.

Tempers being somewhat pacified, we passed to explanations. I said that, having felt my hair pulled, I was beside myself. Elia said that he had not noticed it, and the Spaniard cleared everything up by saying that if I was not mad, neither was I in my right mind. Thus ended that terrible quarrel as a result of which I remained sorrowful and ashamed. I said to Elia that he would have done very well to have killed me. And he was man enough to have done it, being a hand bigger in height than I (who am very tall) and of a valour and strength in no way inferior to his height. The wound on the temple was not deep but it bled much and if I had given it a little higher up I should have found myself the killer of a man whom I greatly loved, however much he had pulled my hair. I was appalled by this vile excess of anger, and, even though I saw that Elia was somewhat placated, but not entirely appeased by me, I did not wish to show nor feed any lack of confidence in him, and thus a couple of hours after the wound, having put all in order, I went to bed leaving the door to the room of Elia, next to me open on purpose, and without wishing to hear the Spaniard who advised me not to invite in this way a man offended and recently wounded to any vengeance. On the contrary, I told Elia who had already retired that he could kill me that night if he wanted to, since I deserved it. But he was a hero when dealing with me and he did not wish to take any vengeance other than to keep two handkerchiefs full of blood with which I had restrained at the beginning the blood flowing from the wound. This reciprocal mixture of ferocity and generosity on both our parts could not be easily understood by those who do not know our habits . . .

Vittorio Alfieri, in García Mercadal, 'Viajes' III, 641–42 (1769).

[154] Advice on love (Ramón de la Cruz, 1780)

In Ramón de la Cruz's *sainete, El No*, the following advice is given by an aunt to her young niece: 'Love is a wicked thing we must avoid. Love is a child to be feared more than a giant ten yards tall . . . and when a girl, absent-minded, leaves the side of her mother or aunt, love approaches stealthily, seizes her, and carries her away . . . to a cave where he cuts her into bits and eats her up . . . As he sometimes takes the gallant form of a man, one must always be armed against men and flee from them and their conversation . . .'   *Qu. Kany, 454, (1780).*

[155] Calling on a lady (Townsend, 1786)

When you pay a visit to a lady, (for, wherever there is a lady in the family, the visit is to her) you neither knock at the door, nor ask any questions of the porter, but go straight forwards to the room where she usually receives her company, and there you seldom fail to find her, morning, noon, and night; in winter, sitting near the brazier, surrounded by her friends, unless when she is gone out to mass. The friends are mostly gentlemen, because ladies seldom visit in a familiar way; and, of the gentlemen thus assembled, one is commonly the *Cortejo**; I say commonly, because it is not universally the case. During the whole of my residence in Spain, I never heard of jealousy in a husband, nor could I ever learn, for certain, that such a thing existed; yet, in the conduct of many ladies, whether it proceeds from the remains of delicacy, from a sense of propriety, or from fear, you may evidently see caution, circumspection, and reserve, when their husbands are in sight. Some have address enough to keep the *cortejo* in concealment; and this, in Spain, is attended with no great difficulty, because, when the ladies go to mass, they are so disguised, as not to be easily distinguished. Their dress upon that occasion is peculiar to the country. They all put on the *basquiña*, or black silk petticoat, and the *mantilla*, which serves the double purpose of a cloak and veil,

---

* *Cortejo* means escort, or *cavaliere serviente*, not necessarily lover; see No. 159.

so as completely, if required, to hide the face. Thus disguised, they are at perfect liberty to go where they please. But should they be attended by a servant, he is to be gained, and therefore he becomes little or no restraint. Besides this, every part of the house is so accessible by day, and the husband is so completely nobody at home, so seldom visible, or, if visible, so perfectly a stranger to those who visit in his family, that the lover may easily escape unnoticed. This, however, will not always satisfy the Spanish ladies, who, being quick of sensibility, and remarkable for strong attachment, are miserable, when their *cortejo* is out of sight. He must be present every moment in the day, whether in private or public, in health or sickness, and must be every where invited to attend them. There have been recent examples of women, even of high fashion, who have shut themselves up for months, during the absence of their *cortejos*: and this, not merely from disgust, but to avoid giving them offence. If the lady is at home, he is at her side; when she walks out, she leans upon his arm; when she takes her seat at an assembly, an empty chair is always left for him; and if she joins in the country dances, it is commonly with him. As every lady dances two minuets at a ball, the first is with her *cortejo*, the second with a stranger; with the former, if she has any vivacity, she makes it visible, and if she can move with grace, it then appears; but with the latter she evidently shews, not indifference, but disgust; and seems to look upon her partner with disdain.

As soon as any lady marries, she is teased by numerous competitors for this distinguished favour, till she is fixed in her choice; when the unsuccessful candidates either retire, or submit to become, in future, what may be called *cortejos* of the brazier, without any pretensions beyond that of sitting round the embers to warm themselves in winter.

It is reckoned disgraceful to be fickle; yet innumerable instances are seen of ladies who often change their lovers. In this there is a natural progress; for it cannot be imagined, that women of superior understandings, early in life distinguished for delicacy of sentiment, for prudence, and for the elevation of their minds, should hastily arrive at the extreme, where passion triumphs, and where all regard to decency is lost. As for others, they soon finish the career. It is, however, humiliating to see some who appear to have been designed by nature to command the reverence of mankind, at last degraded, and sunk so low in the opinion of the world, as to be never mentioned but with contempt. These have changed so often, and have been so unfaithful to every engagement, that, universally despised, they end with having no *cortejo*.

I have observed, that jealousy is seldom, if ever, to be discovered in a husband; but this cannot be said in favour of the new connection, because both parties are tormented by suspicion. This, it must be confessed, is natural; for, as both are conscious that there is no other bond between them, but the precarious tie of mutual affection, each must tremble at the approach of any one, who might interrupt their union. Hence they are constantly engaged in watching each other's looks, and for want of confidence, renounce, in a great measure, the charms of social intercourse. Even in public, they seem to think themselves alone, abstracted and absorbed, attentive only to each other. He must not take notice of any other lady; and if any gentleman would converse with her; in a few minutes she appears confused and filled with fear, that she may have given offence. In all probability she has; and should she be the first dutchess in the kingdom, and he only a non commissioned officer in the army, she may be treated with personal indignity; and we have heard of one who was dragged by the hair about the room. But if, instead of giving, she should happen to have taken the offence, even the more delicate will fly like a tigress at his eyes, and beat him in the face till he is black and blue. It sometimes happens, that a lady becomes weary of her first choice, her fancy has fixed upon some new object, and she wishes to change; but the former, whose vanity is flattered by the connection, is not willing to dissolve it. In lower life, this moment gives occasion to many of those assassinations, which abound in Spain; but, in the higher classes, among whom the dagger is proscribed, the first possessor, if a man of spirit, maintains possession, and the lady dares not discard him, lest an equal combat should prove fatal to the man of her affections. In this contest the husband is out of sight, and tells for nothing.

In a Catholic country, with such depravity of morals, it may be naturally inquired, what becomes of conscience, and where is discipline? It is well known, that all are under obligation to confess, at least once a year, before they receive the eucharist. Every one is at liberty to choose his confessor and priest; but before he leaves the altar, he takes a certificate that he has been there, and this he delivers to the curate of his own parish, under pain of excommunication, should he fail to do so. When, therefore, a married woman appears, year after year, before her confessor, to acknowledge that she has been, and still continues to be, living in adultery, how can he grant her absolution, or how can he be moderate in the penance he enjoins. Without penance, and unless the priest is satisfied that there is contrition, with full purpose of amendment, there can be no absolution; without absolution, no participation of the eucharist; and, in the neglect of this, excommunication follows. Yet, from the universal prevalence of this offence, we may be certain, that there must be some way of evading the rigour of the law. Nothing is more easy. As for the penance, it is imposed by those, who can have compassion on the frailties of mankind, and is therefore scarcely worthy to be mentioned. In many instances, it is ridiculous. Were any confessor severe, he would have few at his confessional. The absolution is commonly a more serious business; because the penitent must not only testify contrition, but must give some token of amendment, by abstaining, at least for a season, from the commission of the crime, which is the subject-matter of confession. The first absolution may be easily obtained; but when the offender comes, year after year, with the same confession, if he will obtain absolution, he must change his confessor; and this practice is not only disgraceful, but sometimes ineffectual. Here, then, it is needful to adopt some new expedient. Two naturally present themselves: for, either some priest, destitute of principle, may be found, who for certain considerations, will furnish billets; or else, which is a prevailing practice at Madrid, the common prostitutes, confessing and receiving the holy sacrament in many churches, and collecting a multitude of billets, either sell, or give them to their friends. I have certificates before me. As these carry neither name nor signature, they are easily transferred. They are simply thus: *Comulgó en la Iglesia parroquial de San Martín de Madrid. Año de mil setecientos ochenta y seis.* Joseph Townsend II, *142–49 (1786)*

[156] Instructions to a *cortejo* by a lady (as in Cadalso's play *La Óptica del Cortejo*)
(José Cadalso (1741–1782), a romantic satirist, famous for his *tertulias* in the café San Sebastián, was killed at the siege of Gibraltar when serving as a colonel.)

In the first place you are to speak with no lady except me, even when I am not present. You are to take chocolate with me in the morning and perhaps to fasten my bodice, and in the afternoon you are to take me walking. In the evening I like to play a game of ombre or *malilla* (manille), and you will be my partner. If perchance you wish to attend some party or pay a visit, you must first obtain my consent. You must provide me with the most exquisite flowers of the season, for I am fond of their perfume. You must inform me of the very latest fashions, so that I may dress accordingly. For this purpose you are to employ a discriminating agent who will know just what is being worn, and who leaves no stone unturned to apprise me directly some new fan or coif arrives from abroad, so I may be among the first to use it . . . It is necessary that on my saint's day, as well as on yours, I wear a new *bata* with all the indispensable paraphernalia . . . And although I am not one of those ordinary women who arrange with their *cortejos* for a monthly allowance of pin money . . . yet I cannot dispense with a daily box at the theatre, and I need as well a seat in the *cazuela* (gallery for women) for occasions when I wish to attend veiled in order to engage in free conversation with friends, or when some relative has died and I am not to appear in public . . . It goes without saying that I need a steady hairdresser, a coach ready for my service at all times, and a special shop where you can procure ribbons, laces, and other finery which may be necessary for my adornment . . . And remember that should I unfortunately be taken ill, no one but you may be at my side to give me medicines. And then, as at other times, you must have a capable and trustworthy servant attend to your business, because you cannot leave my presence.

Qu. Cadalso, 'La Óptica del Cortejo',
(Barcelona 1796), 21–22, qu. Kany, 211

Dress

[157] A Nuncio's thoughts (Camillo Borghese, 1594)

The native dress of these men is long breeches, jacket, hat and short cloak with a collar, or alternatively cloak and cap (*gorra*). It would be a grave error in etiquette to wear the cap and the short cloak at the same time. This dress would certainly be beautiful if the breeches had not been cut so wide, which give them a disproportionate effect; and some, though few, wore hose in the *sevillana* fashion, which they describe as Greek, with which they mean neither cape nor cap, but short cloak and hat.

The women are generally dressed in black, as the men are also and around their face wear a veil as nuns do, carrying their shawl (*manto*) on their heads which they wear over their faces in such a way that one scarcely sees them. Had it not been for the royal ordinance which the King had given on this, they would be covered up entirely as they used to do a few years ago. And when they do not wear this veil around their face they put on collars, with enormous neckcloths; all the women using as a rule the rouges whereby they alter their naturally brown complexions and they put on so much that they really seem painted. They are naturally small but they wear heels, called *chapines*, so high as to make them seem tall. So much so that one can say that in Spain every woman has the same coloured face and they are all of the same height.

When the main ladies of the Court go in a carriage either they do so in a covered seat in the Genovese fashion; or they do so on a horse or a donkey led by a man. They are by nature impudent, presumptuous and importunate and even in the street talk to men whom they do not know, yet take it heresy to be introduced to them. They admit every type of man to their conversations. But what is even greater impudence is that even when they are talking of something less than honest they are not scandalized . . . One day four of us, walking along the edge of the river, saw a woman in the water who had on nothing more than a linen vest and a petticoat, under which she was showing one leg, and exposed openly a breast. And on our arrival another woman who was out of the water began to talk to us while the other continued in the water; and the shirt falling off, she said, without the slightest shame, '*Señores*, you have seen the pot which has got such a lot of meat in it.' In a short time she dressed herself in our presence.

Gentlemen, who never go on horses and only rarely in a carriage, usually have behind them a throng of pages and two bodyguards who are called lackeys, being forbidden to have more by royal ordinance and the grandees have four, thereby differentiating themselves from the others.

Horses wear cloths of cotton from October to March, and the rest of the year have a saddle of velvet, that being arranged by royal ordinance. And their pastime is to go up and down the Calle Mayor from twenty-one hours till nightfall. And, ladies, the day of fiesta, go to the Prado of San Jerónimo which stands out as among the most celebrated things in Madrid, and their chief recreation is for about eight or ten of them to shut themselves up in a place to dine, being all night a mixture of men and women. And they say that a few years ago they would, one after another, make a speech, and that the ladies would call on the gentlemen to speak, and develop the taste of speaking and of joking over the table. The men as well as the women are very coarse, since they publicly do their necessities in the streets without the least respect for others, since they eat with little breeding, and live miserably, and he who wants to please a lady, gives her something to eat which, scarcely having been received, she as a rule eats with great greed, and one sees people walking about in the street eating blades of grass as if they were goats.

Camillo Borghese, in García Mercadal, 'Viajes' I, 1473 (1594).

[158] Sir Richard Wynn's judgements (1623)

All the women's ruffs are of a deep wachet. They wear high chopeenes, and hoops about their skirts. These women are so cloistered up (and they need not) that they see not men at all, but at these times in public, where they dare not speak to any. The better sort of women are much carried up and down in chairs of velvet by two footmen. In all places in the world, there be not so many that walk in the streets, converse, and eat in spectacles, as in this town: you cannot meet ten, but you shall find one of them with a pair of glass eyes.   D'Ewes, II, 448.

[159] Brunel (1655)

The women, abandoned as they are, but nevertheless wishing to seem less so, immediately beg the stranger to remove any outstanding or bright clothes, for fear of their being too much noticed when they visit them.

These clothes are a robe with long shirts, very tight-fitting from the neck to the hips: they wear a belt of Moroccan leather on the waist, or a little lower than the navel; their breeches are so very tight that in order to pull them on they have buttons up the sides which they do up in the morning and undo at night. Their shoes are shaped to the foot, and so as to be dainty, the soles are very narrow; a small foot and a large calf are so much admired, that the gallants tie up their feet with ribbons so as to make them appear small and are martyrs to the suffering, at the same time as, with false calves, they attempt to be absolutely in fashion. The silk stockings they use are loosely knitted and look like netting; they wear them very tight and underneath them white stockings which show through.

They no longer wear hats with large brims. They now wear fairly small ones which they line with black taffeta. It is a great ornament and a mark of extraordinary magnificence to have a quantity of broad black lace as a hat band, which no doubt costs just as much as a beautiful bunch of feathers, since it comes from Flanders or from France. Their linen is not sumptuous, and you hardly ever see lace; most people wear *la golilla*, a smock with broad sleeves, two or three of which are enough for a year.

The reason they always begin to dress from the top down and to button up below is not because they do everything the opposite to other nations but because of the air, which is so penetratingly cold here that, unless you take good care . . . you run the risk of becoming ill, which is why they cover up . . . so thoroughly. And people have been seen who, because they neglected to do this, met with great disasters, and lost the use of their limbs, as much as if they had slept through the night with open windows.

Bayette and black petersham are the dress materials they use in winter; in summer they wear clothes of taffeta, but they always keep the cloak and the *roupille* of bayette*.

Brunel, 174–75.

[160] The ban on the long cape – the royal ordinance (1767)

It not being enough to banish from the Court the evil-favoured and dangerous disguise or abuse of muffling oneself with a long cloak, hat in *chambergo* style or slouching cap pulled over the eyes, cap or hairnet [as provided in] the Royal Orders and public announcements of 1716, 1719, 1723, 1729, 1737 and 1740 prohibiting these things and especially the Royal Order . . . renewed in the year 1745, I [i.e. King Charles III] order that nobody, of whatever condition, quality and state he may be, can use in any place, site or suburb of this Court and these

---

* *Bayette* was a woollen material, *roupille* a robe.

Royal Palaces nor in their *paseos* or fields outside their walls, the aforementioned dress of long cloak and round hat for a disguise; that I will and order that all public servants and all of any class by which one understands all who live by their incomes and on their properties or from the salaries of their offices or who have honorary positions or their domestics and servants who do not wear the livery of those for whom they work, wear the short cloak (which at least shall have a distance of a quarter's length between it and the ground) or riding coat or capingot or wig or their own hair and three-cornered hat in a way that in no fashion does it enable disguisement or hide the face.

'Novísima recopilación de la leyes de España . . .', Libro III,
Título XIX, Ley XIII (1767), quoted in Díaz Plaja, III.

[161] Inglis and the fashions (1831)

The stranger who walks for the first time through the streets of Madrid, is struck with the sombreness of the prospect that is presented to him: this, he speedily discovers, arises from the costume of the women. It is the varied and many-coloured attire of the female sex, that gives to the streets of other great cities their air of gaiety and liveliness. No pink, and green, and yellow, and blue silk bonnets nod along the streets of Madrid; for the women wear no bonnets, – no ribbons of more than all the hues of the rainbow, chequer the pavement; for the women of Madrid do not understand the use of ribbons. Only conceive the sombreness of a population without a bonnet or a ribbon, and all, or nearly all, in black! yet such is the population of Madrid. Every woman in Spain wears a *mantilla*, which varies in quality and expense, with the station of the wearer: and, for the benefit of those who, though they may have heard of a *mantilla*, have an imperfect idea of what it is, I shall describe it. A *mantilla*, is a scarf thrown over the head and shoulders; behind, and at the sides, it descends nearly to the waist; and falling in front over a very high comb, is gathered, and fastened, generally by something ornamental, just above the forehead, at the lower part of the hair. Of old, there was a veil attached to the fore-part of the *mantilla*, which was used or thrown back, according to the fancy of the wearer; but veils are now rarely seen in Spain, excepting at mass. Of the rank and means of a Spanish woman, something may be gathered from the *mantilla*, though this cannot be considered any certain criterion, since Spanish women will make extraordinary sacrifices for the sake of dress. Yet there are three distinct grades of the *mantilla*: the lady in the upper ranks of life, and most of those in the middle ranks, wear the lace *mantilla*; some of blond – some of English net, worked in Spain; and these vary in price, from 4*l* or 5*l* to 20*l*. The bourgeoises generally wear the *mantilla*, part lace and part silk; the lace in front, and the silk behind, with lace trimmings; and the lower orders wear a *mantilla* wholly of silk, or of silk trimmed with a velvet. Spain is the only country in Europe in which a national dress extends to the upper ranks; but even in Spain this distinction begins to give way. In the streets, no one yet ventures to appear without the *mantilla*; but French hats are frequently seen in carriages and in the theatre; and the black silk gown, once as indispensable as the *mantilla*, sometimes gives place to silks of many colours; and even a French or English printed muslin, may occasionally be seen on the Prado.

But although the sombre dress of the women, and the consequent absence of bright colours, seemed at first to give a gloomy cast to the exterior of the population of Madrid, a little closer observance of it disclosed a variety and picturesqueness not to be found in any other of the European countries. The dress of the women, although sombre, bears in the eye of a stranger a character of both novelty and grace. The round turned-up hat and crimson sash of the peasant; the short green jacket and bare legs and sandals of the innumerable water-carriers, who call *agua fresca*; the sprinkling of the military costume; and above all, the grotesque dresses of the multitudes of friars of different orders, gave to the scene a character of originality exclusively its own. No feature in the scene before me appeared more novel than the universality of the fan; a Spanish woman would be quite as likely to go out of doors without her shoes, as without her fan. I saw not one female in the streets without this indispensable appendage. The portly dame, and her stately daughter; the latter six paces in advance, as is the universal custom throughout Spain, walked fanning themselves; the child of six years old, held mamma with one hand, and fanned herself with the other; the woman sitting at her stall selling figs, sat fanning herself; and the servant coming from the market, carried her basket with one arm, and fanned herself with the other. To me, who had never before seen a fan but in the hands of a lady, this seemed ridiculous enough.   *Inglis 66–70, (1836)*

[162] The Marquis de Custine's view (1831)

All the women wear the same costume in the street; foreigners find fault with this uniformity; I am charmed by it. It allows for nuances, though so delicate as to be nearly imperceptible, and which only make them the more precious in the eyes of those who can discern them. The *mantilla*, which every woman wears on her head to go out in, is not the same garment for all; some make a veil of it, others a single ornament. It is a mantlet of black taffeta, embroidered with lace or velvet according to the rank and fortune of the wearer, or else a veil made entirely of lace; it hangs down from a tortoiseshell comb. The rest of the costume is not at all original; European fashions have spoilt Spain; but the bearing, the feet, the eyes, all recall the special charms of the Spanish ladies. They are pretty rather than beautiful, flirtatious rather than affectionate, brilliant rather than charming, or at least their charm is of the sort which dazzles rather than attracts; it is what is described here by an untranslatable phrase: *La sal española* (Spanish salt!).

Men's clothes are more varied than the women's. The gentlemen are more or less dressed as everywhere else, unless it be that they hide our dresscoat under their cloak, the obligatory complement of all Spanish dress.

A crowd of costumes from the neighbouring provinces can be seen in the streets of Madrid; each differing from the other in their shape or colour. I have seen peasants wearing a full jacket, the colour of Spanish tobacco, as a coat, a red woollen belt and a large pair of trousers similar to the jacket. Everyone wears a little round sugar-loaf hat, with a little turned up brim like a gutter. This brim is turned down when it rains. The Spanish hat is susceptible to ornament; people add piping, velvet, ribbons.

They all look alike, but each is different. In this country men give as much attention to their appearance as women do. They have remained as in the Middle Ages, when so much importance was attached to beautiful clothes. I have been assured that this passion for brilliant dress is even more general in Andalusia than in Madrid.

. . . Here is a costume very often seen: it has a jacket and breeches of black sheepskin, with gold lashings and buckles. This very fine, very soft and very warm fur resembles astrakhan. People wearing it have a proud look, and one of obliging self-confidence, which raises them above the common crowd: they usually hold in their hand a long stick of bare wood, nearly as tall as themselves, ending in a fork, on which they nonchalantly lean. These are the street swells: here they are called *majos*. Even the grandest noblemen are not always too proud to copy them. Others dress in short trousers, with embroidered leather garters which they leave semi-undone at the calf, and which are not without elegance. Others again, and these are the most distinguished, are adorned with jackets of velvet decorated with patches of various colours and edged with little silken pompoms and golden lashings. Sometimes they wear a double waistcoat, the under one is fitted tight, a little like a corset: that is of scarlet stuff; a second waistcoat, usually of brown cloth, covers the first; short trousers of the same material are joined to elegant gaiters; and a full jacket, likewise brown, is thrown over the left shoulder like a dolman. It completes the costume and replaces the cloak. The collar and sleeves of this jacket are slashed with several pieces of cut-up coloured materials, a little like some bits of Harlequin's costume, or, rather, like the sleeves of the Montmorency livery. The costume of this sort of country *majo* is of a particularly light elegance.

The less a people is civilized, the more it attaches importance to its adornment. The richest clothes are worn by semi-barbarians. The costume of the Spanish peasants confirms this. They are withdrawn from civilization but I infintely prefer their style of dressing to ours. We entertain a very false idea of their habits when we imagine that they are poorly nourished or poorly dressed: the poverty of the country is hardly noticeable except in the interiors of houses in the middle of the fields; but the few people who live in these seemingly sterile plains are less wretched than the greater part of those who inhabit the most flourishing States. Spain can only be revolutionized by communicating a moral malaise to her; the physical malaise is rarer there than in the rich populated countries of Europe. The dress of the simple Castillian peasant indicates more wealth than that of the richest men with us . . .

The Madrid theatres are rather sad: but what gives them originality is the national costume of the women. Unfortunately a few Parisian hats have slid in among the *mantillas*; this innovation is a victory for feminine vanity over national pride: the women think to gain by the change; they are mistaken. I regret the time when a foreigner could not walk about Madrid without dressing in Spanish costume. That time is not very distant; it is hardly twenty five years since the *madrileños* have allowed French dress on their streets. In each Madrid theatre there is a place whither my eyes are always carried: it is an amphitheatre which the men do not enter: a sort of feminine pit. This reserved area is not occupied by grand ladies but by women of the middle class; at least these still keep their costume. Would you believe me? The law condemns any man who penetrates this sanctuary to four years in the galleys. Such severity recalls the Arab customs, and it has its comic side . . . since these same virtues of the theatre, so correctly guarded by the public police, are very badly defended outside the auditorium, when they become private duties.

Custine, 150–53, 256–7 (1831).

[163] De Amicis (1869)

An hour passed there is sufficient to enable one to know by sight the people of Madrid in its various aspects. The common people dress as in our large cities; the gentlemen, if they take off the cloak which they wear in winter, copy the Paris models; and are all, from the duke to the clerk, from the beardless youth to the tottering old man, neat, adorned, pomaded, and gloved, as if they had just issued from the dressing-room. They resemble the Neapolitans in this regard, with their fine heads of hair, well-kept beards, and small hands and feet. It is rare to see a low hat; all wear high ones, and there are canes, chains, trinkets, pins, and ribbons in their buttonholes by the thousand. The ladies, with the exception of certain fête days, are also dressed like the French; the women of the middle class still wear the mantilla, but the old satin shoes, the *peineta*, and bright colors, – the national costume, in a word, has disappeared. They are still, however, the same little women so besung for their great eyes, small hands, and tiny feet, with their very black hair, but skin rather white than dark, so well formed, erect, lithe, and vivacious.   *De Amicis, 120 (1869)*.

[164] Pérez Galdós (c. 1870)

Ah, what a place Madrid is, all show! A gentleman I know says that it's as if the Carnival went on all the year round, with the poor dressing up as rich people. For here, except for half a dozen families, everyone is poor. Façade, nothing but façade. These people have no idea of comfort in their houses. They live in the streets; and so that they can dress well and go to the theatre, some families eat nothing but potato omelettes all the year round. I know wives of small officials who are unemployed half the year, and they dress so that it's a pleasure to meet them. They look like duchesses, and their children look like princes and princesses. How do they do it? I simply can't imagine. A gentleman friend of mine says that Madrid is full of these mysteries. Some people, as I say, don't eat, so that they can dress instead; but others manage it in other ways – Oh, I have heard stories, I've seen a lot of the world. Women like that are out for what they can get – they buy their clothes in any way they can. And then they talk about other women – as if they weren't worse themselves!

Pérez Galdós, from 'La de Bringas', 217 (c. 1870).

[165] The cape in the twentieth century: Nina Epton
(Nina Epton, half-Spanish, lived in Madrid as a child.)

'Need I emphasize,' continued Don Pedro, 'the importance of the cape in courtship? The young people of today do not know what real romance is because they do not wear a cape. An essential ingredient of love is mystery, and a cape is the essence of mystery. Lovers practised what was known as the *embozo*: this was the act of wrapping oneself around the lower face and neck with a wing of the cape, thus. If this was effected in a halting or lifeless manner, it signified that the attachment was overpowering. Three foldings made as if in a bad humour signified that the difficulties were appalling. To raise the cape thus – and then let it fall back – was to solicit an assignment. To throw open the cape and adjust the hat by the brim with the thumb and forefinger was to beg for favour. If the hat was left slanting and half-adjusted, thus – it threatened fury, as the payment for disdain; but if the suitor wished to affect disdain he would throw over his cape carelessly from right to left, put one arm akimbo, smile, yawn, light a cigarette. The cape,' said Don Pedro with mounting enthusiasm, 'was of universal service. It could be used as a sack, a bucket, a fan, a dummy, a lure, a life-preserver, everything in almost every crisis of a man's life from birth to death, battle, murder, shipwreck, fire . . .'

'Don Pedro, Don Pedro,' I interrupted laughingly, 'now you are going too far even for an Andalusian. How could a cape be of any use in a fire? On the contrary, it must be a hindrance.'

Recovering some of his youthful agility in defence of his beloved cape, Don Pedro leaped on to a chair and gave a demonstration. 'Look,' he exclaimed, swirling his cape round at arm's length and inclining it slightly. 'Here I am standing upon a balcony. There is a fire in the house behind me. When my cape has attained a certain speed of gyration and lies exactly in the right position for the cast, I release it – thus – and it falls like a parachute. I leap with both feet into the middle of the swirling garment as it touches the ground.'

'And you seriously want to make me believe that it would have broken your fall?'

Don Pedro folded his cape with a caressing gesture and ignored my comment. 'With a cape and a horse,' he concluded, 'an Andalusian could face and conquer the world.'

Epton, 110 (c. 1950).

Various Customs

[166] Advice to writers (1787): Anonymous satire

After you have selected your title, think of your prologue. Make it long and it will consequently be boring. Add a foreword to the readers. Be sure to have it printed in type much larger than the ordinary. Do not forget the dedicatory epistle which you will address to a person of high rank, whether he has given you permission to do so or not. Generally, this dedicatory letter closes thus: 'I am, sir, your Highness' most humble, devoted, and obedient servant.' If you know how to manage it, this sentence alone will suffice to fill a whole page, without its seeming that you have done it intentionally.

Divide your book into chapters, and, preceding the text of your work, put a table of contents. Here you can gain more space. You will also gain space by putting in large capitals BOOK 11, and at a great distance below it CHAPTER X, etc. All this will contribute not only to increase the bulk of your work, but also to beautify it.

Be especially careful to arrange your material with such dexterity that at the end of each chapter you will have two or three lines to spare, which will be placed upon the following page. To fill the rest of the page have recourse to a flower-pot supported by cherubs, or some pretty little animal, or a parrot perched upon a branch . . .

And thus having made the number of volumes greater than was necessary, announce them most vigorously. In order to arouse the reader's curiosity, mention the number of presses employed in printing your book. And if, as sometimes happens, your book has the misfortune of a slow sale, be shameless – add to the title page: 2d, 3d, 4th, 5th, 6th, edition, although half of the first may still be unsold . . . But whither is my enthusiasm leading me? I am revealing professional secrets. I must go no farther.

Correo de los Ciegos de Madrid, Jan. 5, 1787, qu. Kany 353–54.

[167] Ancestors (Blanco White, c. 1820)
(José Blanco White (1775–1841), Anglo-Spanish author, wrote several illuminatory works.)

. . . to make sure of their nobility, one of the fellows of the college* was to repair to the birthplace of the elected member's parents, as well as to that of his two grandfathers and grand-mothers, in order to examine upon oath from fifteen to thirty witnesses at each place, who had to swear that the ancestor in question had never been a menial servant, a shopkeeper, a petty tradesman, or a mechanic; that neither he himself, nor any of his relatives, had ever been punished by the Inquisition, and that he was not descended from Jews, Moors, Africans, Indians, or Guanches (aborigines of the Canary Islands).

Blanco White, 105.

[168] Cemeteries (Baroja, c. 1900)

Beltrán told truculent stories of what went on in the cemeteries of his old quarter. According to him all the tombs of rich persons buried there had been violated and searched. There was the tradition that the first body which was taken to the

---

* i.e. of a *colegio mayor*, or residence for students in Madrid.

cemetery of the North was that of a mistress of Pepe Botellas* and that the day following they robbed the coffin with the body and buried it in the garden of a house. In some tombs they had found bodies which without doubt had been buried alive since one could see how they scratched the top of the coffin with their nails.

The stories of Beltrán were enough to make anyone's hair stand on end. The man had a taste for the macabre. He explained those who were buried alive as having been victims during times of epidemic.   *Baroja, 'Las Noches', 80–81.*

[169] The cost of portraits by Velázquez: Fulvio Teste (1639)

(Diego de Velázquez (1599–1660) was court painter in Madrid from 1623 until his death. This letter from Fulvio Teste (1593–1646) to Francesco I d'Este, Duke of Modena (1610–1658) describes a painting now still in Modena.)

Velázquez is making the portrait of your highness, which will be marvellous. However, like other men of talent, he has the defect of never finishing and of not telling the truth. I have given him 150 pieces of eight on account, and Marchese Virgilio (Malvezzi) has arranged a price of one hundred doubloons. It is expensive but he does good work. And I can assure you that I hold his portraits in no less esteem than those of any other famous painter, either ancient or modern.
          Fulvio Teste, March 12, 1639, qu. Brown and Elliott, 144.

[170] Dances: *bolero, fandango* (Townsend, 1786)

At a ball, to which I was invited by the Duchess [de la Vauguyon], I had the happiness to see Madame Mellow dance a *bolero*†. Her

---

* Joseph Bonaparte.
† A three-beats-in-a-measure dance, danced by several couples as a rule, performed to the accompaniment of castanets or singing. The movement of arms is an important part of the dance. It was apparently not of popular origin, having been invented by Sebastián Cerezo about 1780, perhaps, but deriving from an old dance.

motions were so graceful, that whilst she was dancing she appeared to be the most beautiful woman in the room; but she had no sooner retired to her seat than the delusion vanished.

This dance bears some resemblance to the *fandango**, at least in sprightliness and elegance; but then it is more correct than that favourite, yet most lascivious pantomine. The *fandango* itself is banished from genteel assemblies, and justly so. As danced by the vulgar, it is most disgusting: as refined in higher life, covered with a most elegant yet transparent veil, it ceases to disgust; and, from that very circumstance, excites those passions in the youthful breast, which wisdom finds it difficult to curb. This dance must certainly come to them by tradition from the Moors. The music of it has such a powerful effect on young and old, that all are prepared for motion the instant the instruments are heard; and, from what I have seen, I could almost persuade myself to receive the extravagant idea of a friend who, in the warmth of his imagination, supposed that were it suddenly introduced into a church or into a court of judicature, priests and people, judges and criminals, the gravest and the gay, would forget all distinctions, and begin to dance.

Joseph Townsend, 281 (1787).

[171] Dinners: with Floridablanca (Townsend, 1786)

José Moñino, Conde de Floridablanca (1728–1808) was an enlightened minister of Charles III, and was responsible with Aranda for that monarch's reputation as a reformer. He lived in the Calle Nueva, now Bailén.)

Soon after my return to Aranjuez, I had the honour to dine with the prime minister, Count Florida Blanca. The company consisted of the foreign ministers, who are invited every Saturday, and his under secretaries. This assemblage may appear incongruous, but

---

* The *fandango* is said to have been devised early in the eighteenth century by muleteers during their halts on the way from Andalusia to Madrid. It became popular in good society in the 1780s and was partly responsible for the return of the guitar to the drawing-room. It is a dance in triple time and a fast tempo.

it is not so; because these gentlemen, having been well educated, and trained up in the various civil departments of the state, and from thence dispatched into foreign countries as secretaries of the embassy, where they learn the language, and acquire knowledge, they have higher claims than those, who have similar employment in the other courts of Europe. When they return to Spain, considered as servants of the public, they are received into various offices, and have each his several department, one France and England, another the Italian courts, where they assist in expediting business. To them a foreign minister can explain at leisure, with clearness and with freedom, in his own language, all that he wishes to have distinctly stated to the prime minister. From this office they are commonly promoted to some honourable and lucrative employment, as the reward of their long services.

I was struck with the elegance of the dinner, in which there was great variety, yet every thing was excellent; and had I been intending to form judgement of the count, merely from the arrangement of his table, I should have pronounced him a man of sense. It is an old, and perhaps a well-founded observation, that no man is fit to govern an empire who cannot give a dinner to his friends. The manners of the count are easy and polite, such as evidently mark the school in which he has been trained, distinguished not by familiarity but by the most pleasing attentions . . .

Like the French, the Spaniards drink their wine at dinner; but as soon as they have finished their dessert, and taken coffee, they retire to their couch.   *Joseph Townsend, 328–9; II, 138.*

[172] Funerals: according to E. Clarke, a fellow of St John's College, Cambridge (1760)

The funeral rites of the rich in SPAIN are splendid, as well as decent; they are solemnly interred with their best suit clothes, with hat, cloak and sword.

> *Nam vivis quis amor gladii, quae cura togave*
> *Mansit, & haec eadem remanet tellure repostis.*

And I am firmly persuaded, that the old knights, condes, and grandees of this kingdom were antiently buried, just as we see their *sculptured figures* upon their tombs; armed *cap-á-pee*, and at all points; just as if they had been harnessed out for battle with their beaver, coat, cuirass, the target, lance sword, spurs, and jackboots. And this shews the great propriety of that famous joke of old SCARRON, who, when he was receiving extreme unction, told the anointer, 'Pray, sir, take care to grease my boots well, for I am going a very long journey.' . . .

The late Queen of SPAIN, consort of the present King Charles III died September 27th, 1760, aged 35, after she had reigned only one year and fourteen days. She was a daughter of the present King of POLAND, and had suffered greatly for the distresses of her father, who has been driven from his electorate by the King of PRUSSIA: She had lived twenty years with his present Majesty. She was in a bad state of health when he came first into Spain, catched the meazles at SARAGOZA, then a cold: and afterwards was taken ill with a fever and flux at ST ILDEFONSO, in September, and upon its increase returned to MADRID; when both those disorders still kept harassing and weakening her, till they at last ended in a delirium and mortification. Every art of physic was used to save her, and every *Spanish Saint* invoked, but all in vain. They brought the *image* of ST ISIDRO to her, and some were fetched even from TOLEDO and ALCALÁ DE HENARES: But neither the interposition of saints or subjects could avail any thing; tho' all the churches of MADRID were crowded with people, offering up prayers for her recovery, fate was inexorable, and death relentless. The *nuncio* came and gave her the last papal benediction, and by that means conveyed to her the first notice of her approaching dissolution; she received the shock with some surprise, but with much piety, resignation, and resolution. Upon her observing to the nuncio the insignificance and emptiness of all human grandeur; and that it was now of no advantage to her, that she ever was a Queen – He replied, 'Your Majesty has certainly had much greater opportunities of doing good, and which have not been neglected.' She lingered a day or two after this, till the delirium came on, attended with convulsions, and at length expired on the twenty-seventh of September, about three o'clock in the afternoon.

CEREMONIES OF A ROYAL FUNERAL

On the twenty-eighth, she was laid in state in the *casón*, or great-hall of the BUEN RETIRO: she lay upon a spond covered with gold tissue, under a canopy of state: She was dressed in a plain cap, tied with a broad white sattin ribband, and with a small black egret over her forehead: On each side the spond were fixed large *girandoles*, of *Mexican* silver, about four feet high, with large tapers burning, and round the room were several altars with gold and silver candlesticks. On the right hand side of the spond, at the feet, knelt the dutchess of MEDINA SIDONIA, behind her another lady of distinction, and then an exempt, and on each side stood two *pursuivants* bearing the crown and sceptre. The ladies were relieved every hour by others, such as the dutchess of BURNOMBILE, the dutchess of ARCOS, &c. but the pursuivants were obliged to remain the whole twenty-four hours – Thus lay the Queen all that day and night; on the twenty-ninth, she was carried to the ESCORIAL in this manner: About seven o'clock in the evening the procession began from the gate of the BUEN RETIRO in this order: First came forty *Carmelite*-monks on horse-back, each with a torch in one hand, and the bridle in the other; then as many *Cordeliers*, and last of all the *Dominicans*, all with torches in their hands: Then a body of the guards on horse-back, without tapers, headed by the duke of VERAGÜEZ, or duke of BERWICK*. These were followed by the sacrist in his cope, bearing a gold crucifix, at the head of the curates. Then the state-coach with the Queen's body, followed by two *carosses de respect*; then the duke of ALVA; behind him the inquisitor-general, with some other people of distinction, such as the duke of ARCOS, & c. then followed another body of the guards, and last of all a suite of coaches. These were obliged to travel in this manner all the night, with their torches burning, which must be a vast expence; it being eight leagues to the ESCORIAL, and they proposed burying her Majesty about eight o'clock the next morning. The monks are paid for this journey, and they commonly share the tissue pall between them.

Clarke, 116–118

---

* This was the 3rd Duque de Berwick, of King James II of England's creation.

[173] Gambling: Beaumarchais (1764)

A long time ago, the Count de Buturlin, son of the grand-marshal of Russia and the ambassador in question, received me at his house with that partiality that indicated that he and the very pretty ambassadress were in love with me. In the evenings, there was either gaming or music and supper, of which I seemed to be the life and soul. The company was augmented by all the ambassadors who, before this one, had lived with little contact with the outside world. Before the return of the Count to this town, they gave charming suppers, charming, so they said, because I was there. One evening I won 500 livres off the Count and 1,500 off the Countess at whist, although for petty stakes, at 10 écus a stake; after that time we played no more at brelan, and they suggested faro to me, which I had not the slightest wish to play. I had not been paid my 2,000 livres; I said nothing. Everybody knew it; it seemed that I acted as ambassador, and the Count was particularly broke . . . At last one evening, annoyed by the Count winning a hundred louis and not speaking of what he owed me, I said out loud: 'If the Count will lend me gold, I will be a fool and be the banker at faro;' he had no answer, and passed me the 100 louis he had just won off me, and I held the bank: in one hour my poor bank vanished. The Duke of San-Blas won 50 louis off me, the English Ambassador 15, the Russian 20, etc. So there I was a little as if I had won nothing. I rose laughing and said: 'My dear Count, we are quits.' 'Yes,' he said: 'but you will no longer say that you won't play faro, and we expect that you will not in the future give us the slip.' 'Capital! For punting a few louis but not for being banker for 100 louis.' 'That,' said he, 'costs you hardly anything.' 'That is all that could be said to me,' I replied, 'if I had to deal with a bad debtor.'

Thereupon the Countess disrupted the conversation. Madame de la C . . .* rose, and told me to take her arm. I left. Two days of sulking; nevertheless I went as usual to the Russian house and, so as not to give the impression of being desperate

---

* La Marquise de la Croix, the chief affection of Beaumarchais during his stay in Madrid. When he left for Paris, it is said that he left her to the recently widowed King Charles III.

for money, each evening I lost a punt of 10 or 12 louis, or I won a few. One evening when I had won 20 louis on a bank of 200, I rose and, before leaving, I put all my winnings on 2 cards which both won. All succeeded; I broke the bank which was held by the Marqués de Carrasola. The Knight of Guzmán quadrupled the stake 100 times saying: 'Sirs, don't go, I wager that M. de Beaumarchais will break this new bank also.' I felt myself obliged, having gained 200 louis, to reply to this provocation; I played, everyone else stopped because there was no one else playing for such high stakes. Having put 50 louis on one side and wanting to pay back the rest so as not to have to play any more, I put 10 louis on each card; when the card won, I doubled. In short, in 2 hours I had the 100 quadrupled. I rose, and went to bed with 500 louis, of which the next day I lost 150. Madame de la C . . . told me I had played very nobly to have paid back such a sum of my winning, and that I could keep the rest . . .

[After some days of dispute with the Russian Ambassador] Each person said what he knew of his role, then followed much music, a grand dinner. Good humour reigned. Everyone on all sides was on his honour never to speak to me again of gaming, and that we would amuse ourselves with livelier pleasures, which do not have such consequences. The Countess, very pleased at this, had sent me by a page a note containing four lines in my praise in bad verse, which she had written that very day. Here they are:

> O thou whom nature has given as your portion
> The talent to charm with the wisdom of a sage,
> If Orpheus, like thou, had had such glittering sounds,
> Pluto would have made him happy without conditions.

'A plague on it! These are not mutual honours,' I replied. Our intimacy is as good as ever: the ball, the concert, no more gaming, and I have still got 14,500 livres. Since then, I have written some French words for a new Spanish seguidilla. There are 200 copies of it; it is being snatched up; it is jaunty in the style of *Est-il endormi*! . . .   *Loménie, 145.*

[174] Gambling: Beckford (1788)

Though cold and tired, recollecting an engagement to a concert and ball, at the house of Señor Pacheco, that very night, he [Beckford] determined to go, and put on his dancing dress for the purpose. There he found Achmet Vassif, the Turkish ambassador, and others, but felt little delighted with Turkish music, and actually volunteered to make one in a dance after the Spanish manner, which the French present severely criticised. There he became acquainted with a card-playing old Countess of Benavente* who lured fashionable people into play, in which Mr Beckford joined for fashion's sake, but soon from fatigue begged leave to retire. Nothing could be more expressive of her play-going art on his taking leave, – the croak of a vulture scenting its prey from afar – '*Caballero inglés, mañana a la misma hora!*'   *Beckford, 27.*

[175] Grandees of Spain: 1878 (Infanta Paz)
(The Infanta Paz married a Bavarian prince and published diaries later, after her survival in Germany of two world wars.)

I may as well make some remarks about the ceremony of bestowing the Grandeza†. Last Thursday [she was writing 9 March 1878] I saw it. As is well known, Grandees have the right to keep on their hats in the King's presence if they wish. It is from this ceremony that they acquire that right; and it is therefore called 'covering' and they are called 'covered Grandees'. Besides this they can take part in the Capillas Públicas and other Court functions without invitation, and can see the King without first asking for an audience. The King can make a Grandee of whom he will, but it is usually the sons of Grandees, or the husband of a lady who is a Grandee in her own right, who are accorded the honour.

As at the bestowal of the Golden Fleece a Grandee godfather is necessary. He leads his grown-up godchild to the King. This

---

* The Condesa de Benavente, mother of the Duquesa de Osuna.
† Or naming Grandees, of whom there were then only about ninety.

time, as often happens, there were a good many to be covered. They each came in turn with his godfather to the King, who says: '*Cubríos, y hablad.*'* Then each in turn reads aloud, with his hat on, a long speech – mostly about the nobility, age and heroism of his family and ancestors (to show how worthy he is of the honour about to be bestowed). Then taking off his hat he kisses the king's hand and embraces his colleagues . . .

For the Grandee Ladies – or shall I call them Lady Grandees? – the word has no English feminine – the formula is quite different. There is no hat, but instead they are invited to sit down on a cushion! So the ceremony is called *Tomar la Almohada*†. It probably dates back to the time of the Moors when the Spanish ladies, perhaps following Oriental fashion, sat, as a special honour, on cushions on the floor instead of mats. It was a much more brilliant scene than the Covering of the Male Grandees because it took place at night and the ladies were in full Court dress with jewels. Round the room on the floor were placed rows of cushions for the ladies who were already Grandees. For the Queen‡ alone there was chair, and for her Mistress of the Robes a stool. One by one each of the aspirants for the cushion comes in, accompanied by her godmother, and one by one, after making three low curtsies to the Queen, is told by Her Majesty to sit down, which she does (as best she can) on a cushion placed immediately at the feet of the Queen and there remains until Her Majesty after a short conversation tells her to rise, which she does (again as best she can) and goes to take her rightful place – as a full-blown Grandee Lady of the Cushion – beside her sisters of that rank. The whole ceremony might be called an exercise in gymnastics, and was terribly trying particularly for the stouter ladies – as I counted that they had to sit down and stand up thirty-six times and curtsy each time – and all this with long trains! . . .

María de la Paz, 'Memoirs' (1878) 66–67.

* 'Put on your hat and speak.'
† Taking the cushion.
‡ The Queen was the delightful Mercedes (1860–1878), daughter of the Montpensiers. She died soon after this, aged eighteen.

[176] Masters and servants: as seen in Ramón de la Cruz's *sainetes* (eighteenth century)

'What time is it?'

'I don't know, because the clock in the square and mine in London have stopped.'

'Why do you reply like that to your master? Heavens, what a woman! I for one am fed up with you.'

'Well, sir, take a little rhubarb. That always helps people who are filled up.'

'If your tongue could only stop wagging!'

'And yours too.'

'I'll wager that this is your last day here!'

'And I'll wager that I'll win out: if you are thinking of dismissing me at six, I'll leave at four.'

'I never saw such a depraved servant!'

'Why don't you have one made to order in China?'

'El Trueque de las criadas', qu. Kany, 253–54.

The hairdresser:

Madame is seated: 'Towels!'

The servant: 'There aren't any.'

'You lie. I bet I'll find them.'

'I bet you won't!'

'Well, where are they then?'

'Disappointed because you never send them to the river [to be washed], they went down by themselves. But they'll soon be back, if they're honorable.'

'Don't talk so much, and bring me your master's towel.'

'Here it is. Don't tell me it's torn.'

'Which corner shall I use so as not to begrime myself more than I am already? They're all alike, I guess. Let's begin!'

'Please let me know when you've finished scratching, madame.'

'I don't know why on earth my head itches so, *señor maestro*. Can it be some humor?'

'To judge from the tangled thicket you have, it is probably due to an abundance of livestock which can't find an outlet, and there are more cattle than there is pasture-ground.'

'I hope you don't believe that. I have never in all my life picked a louse from my head.'

'That's why there are so many of them now.'

'Come, come, dress my hair and don't talk so much! Bring the ornaments and other paraphernalia, my girl.'

'Here they are.'

'*Señor maestro*, be sure to put on everything today.'

'What wretched pins!'

'Well, there are no others. Ouch, ouch!'

'Never mind!'

'Since when have you become so obnoxious? Be sure to powder the hair well!'

'And pray, where is the pomatum so that the powder will hold?'

'Heavens, what a bore and nuisance you are today!'

Now her hair is combed, and here begins the most arduous task.

'Put on a huge *tururú* in the latest style and very high, with only a few used ribbons, a few rags, an old plume, a crumpled sprig of flowers, and a few rooster feathers, and try to make it all look becoming and effective.'

And what does she do? Sighing deeply, she gives me two *pesetas* at the most, and then ruins my reputation by appearing in drawing rooms and at the theatre. Let the devil comb her hair, for I shan't!   *'La Fonda del Escorial', qu. Kany, 198–99.*

[177] Nobility: the Duke of Wellington (1836)

(Wellington was somewhat condescending to foreigners.)

The reason why the Queen had a spite against the Duchess* was, *qu'elle lui avait soufflé un amant*, I believe. The fact is – I am sorry to say it of my colleagues – that the grandees are just like my servants or your servants. They are very good-natured, good-humoured people, but they have no idea beyond the Court. It is really most extraordinary how exactly they have both the good and the bad qualities of menials.

Stanhope's 'Notes of Conversation with the Duke of Wellington'.

---

* The 13th Duquesa de Alba.

[178] *Tertulias:* Gautier's view (1840)

(The word '*tertulia*' means a regular gathering of the same people in the same place: either in a private house as in the eighteenth century, or in a café, as later.)

I saw a few evening gatherings or *tertulias*, they are not very remarkable; people dance to the piano as in France, but in an even more modern and deplorable manner, if that is possible. I cannot understand why people who dance so little do not frankly resolve not to dance at all, it would be much simpler and just as amusing; fear of being reproached with the *bolero*, the *fandango* or the *cachuha*, makes the woman utterly rigid. Their costume is very simple, in comparison with that of the men, and always made to look like fashion plates. I remarked the same thing at the Villahermosa palace*, at the benefit performance for the Foundlings, *Niños de la Cuna*, where the queen mother, the little queen and all that Madrid has to offer in the way of *beau et grand monde* were present. Women who were double duchesses and four times *marquesas* wore dresses that a Parisian modiste, going to spend the evening with a dressmaker, would have scorned; they no longer know how to dress in the Spanish style, but they do not yet know how to dress like French people, and, if they were not so pretty, they would run the risk of looking ridiculous. Only once, at a ball, I saw a woman in an outer petticoat of pink satin, adorned with five or six rows of black blond-lace, like that of Fanny Elssler† in the *Diable boiteux*; but she had been to Paris where she had been made to give up the Spanish costume.

The *tertulias* cannot cost those who give them very much. The refreshments shine by their absence; no tea, no wine, no punch; only on a table in the first room a dozen glasses of perfectly clear water are laid out, with a plate of *azucarillos*; but you are generally considered to be an indiscreet man and *sur sa bouche*, as Madame Desjardins said of Henri Mannier, if you are so effeminate as to sugar your water. This happens in

* This palace still survives, opposite the Palace Hotel, and has come to house the Museum del Prado's less distinguished pictures of the eighteenth century.
† Fanny Elssler (b. 1818), a famous dancer from Vienna specially celebrated for the *cachuha*. Retired to Hamburg c. 1845.

the richest houses: it is not because of greed, but such is the custom; besides, the hermit-like sobriety of the Spaniards goes perfectly with this régime.

Gautier, 'Voyage en Espagne,' (1840), 119–120.

[179] A thank-you letter of Goya's
(This letter was written about 1800 to Goya's great friend from old days in Saragossa, Martín Zapater.)

Most powerful generous and splendid Sr Don Martín Zapater . . . who would have grasped the thought that a knave and cannibal like you could have surprised our spirits with such gallantry, disposed as we were to celebrate and applaud our good fortune? No one; and thus we've rejoiced almost to the point of excess. What toasts! What repetition of bottles! What coffee and more good coffee! Indeed the glasses in the banqueting room were scarcely replenished before one could hear the joyful acclaim of 'Long live Zapater! What an excellent man! What a good friend! Long may he live and go on drawing winning lottery tickets still more to come!' And just after our party ended with so much festivity, what a surprise greeted us at that moment! For an attendant brought us back a hackney cab with a message from our host saying that he'd arranged a balcony for us to overlook the city where we could continue to enjoy ourselves but also relax from the rigours of the feast. We who are your most grateful and attendant servants kiss your hand. Like servants, ladies, not like rural ill-bred fools.

There follow two columns of illegible signatures, slogans, drunken greetings and allusions to bars and the pleasure of the feast – cakes the size of coach wheels and eel pies, with some sketches.

In 'Cartas a Martín Zapater', edited by
Mercedes Agueda and Xavier de Salas.

[180] Tobacco and chocolate: Saint-Simon (1722)

One day when I saw the Queen [Elizabeth of Farnese] taking tobacco several times, I said that it was a rather extraordinary thing to see a King of Spain who took neither tobacco nor chocolate. The King replied to me that it was true that he did not take tobacco: whereupon the Queen made excuses for taking it, and said that she had done all she could, because of the King [Philip V] to stop taking it but that she had not been able to carry the design through, in consequence of which she was extremely annoyed. The King added that, as for chocolate, he sometimes took it during the morning with the Queen but only during days of fast. 'How, sire,' I said with animation, 'chocolate on days of fast?' 'But after all,' the King said gravely, 'chocolate does not break it.' 'But, sire,' I said to him, 'it is all the same, to take something and that something is extremely good, which sustains one and which even nourishes.' 'And I assure you,' said the King, with emotion, blushing a little, 'that it does not break the fast, because the Jesuits take it every fast day, which is as a rule without bread though they dip bread into the chocolate all other days.' *Saint-Simon, 40, 336, 1722.*

[181] Walking: Inglis (1830)

. . . throughout all Spain, nobody walks for pleasure; at all events no woman: and this fact is I think sufficient to account for the superiority of the Spanish women in the art of walking, without making it necessary for us to suppose any deficiency in elegance of limb or symmetry of form among the women of other countries. An Englishwoman walks for health; she puts on her bonnet, and a pair of strong shoes, and a shawl, and walks into the country; and the nature of the climate creates a necessity for walking fast; there is no one to look at her, and she thinks of nothing so little as her manner of walking: but a Spanish woman never walks for health or exercise; she never goes out but to go to the Paseo, and never without having paid the most scrupulous attention to her toilette. On the Paseo, she studies every step, because the object of going there is to be seen and admired, and the nature of the climate, obliges her to walk slow.   *Inglis, 95.*

The Church

[182] Santo Domingo
(St Dominic's letter (1220) to the *convento* which he established during his visit to Madrid (which lasted a little under a year). Santo Domingo was founded in 1217, before the saint's visit, near the square of Santo Domingo. It was destroyed precipitately in 1869.)

Friar Dominic. Master of the Preachers, to the dear prioress and to the whole convent of the nuns of Madrid, health and daily progress.

We greatly rejoice and give thanks to God that He has granted you the favour of such a holy life and has liberated you from the sordidness of this world. Wage war by your fasts, daughters, against our ancient enemy, for only he who has honourably fought will be crowned.

Up to the present you had not a suitable place for carrying out your religious life; now you can no longer plead this excuse for, by the grace of God, you possess buildings sufficiently well adapted for the maintenance of regular life. I therefore wish you for the future to keep silence in all the places where speaking is normally forbidden – refectory, dormitory and oratory; as to all other places observe your rule. Let no one cross the threshold to go out, let no one come in, unless it is the bishop or some prelate to preach to you or to make a visitation. Spare neither disciplines nor vigils. Obey your prioress. Do not chatter among yourselves and do not lose your time in gossip.

Not being able to help you in economic matters, we do not want to burden you by empowering any of the brethren to receive women into or impose them on the community. Only the prioress has this power, with the council of her convent.

Moreover we prescribe to our most dear brother*, who has gone to very great trouble to enable you to embrace this most holy estate, to dispose and ordain all things as it shall seem useful to him so that you may conduct yourselves in a most holy and religious fashion. Finally, we give him power to visit and correct you, even to depose the prioress in case of necessity, with the consent of the majority of the nuns, and we grant him permission to dispense you in certain points, if it seem good to him.

Fare you well in Christ.   *Vicaire*, 145.

[183] San Francisco: the Inquisition discusses the Moorish problem (1525)

(San Francisco was established as a *convento* outside the walls in 1217. The *convento* was destroyed in 1760 but a new church built in 1761–1770.)

After the Emperor came to Spain and finished with the riots in the Kingdom of Valencia, those who had been made Christians by force, wished of their own good will to return to be Moors and in their mosques made the *zala* and the *guadoque*, circumcised their sons and had many wives, kept Ramadan and finally did all the things which the Koran required, and the worst of it was that the nobles who were their lords not only put up with them but defended them.

* This was in fact St Dominic's own brother, Manes.

The reason why the nobles consented with great inappropriateness was because the Moors said that if they were compelled to be Christians they would not have to pay the old tributes as Moors, and the noblemen wanted their incomes more than they did the souls of their vassals.

At that time the Inquisitor General was Don Alonso Manrique, Archbishop of Sevilla. The inquisitors of Valencia told him of the offence which had been made to Our Lord in that realm. The Court was then in Madrid. A Junta was formed in the monastery of San Francisco in which, within twenty-two days, the Consejo Real de Castilla and of Aragón and of the Inquisition and of the Orders and of the Indies would try and dispute as to whether those Moors had been baptized by force . . . All were agreed that, since the Moors of Valencia had not made any resistance when they baptized them, without wishing it, the faith that they had been made to take, whether they liked it or not, had to be kept by them.

This Junta was made in the month of March of this year and on the 23rd of that month the Emperor came in person to find them, and the Inquisitor General went there referring to the case and the resolution which he had taken and approved it and confirmed it as a Catholic Prince should . . . at Valencia, the common people received the news well; but the Knights very ill. It could have been fifteen or sixteen thousand Moors which had been baptized and afterwards apostasized; most of whom fled and went up to the Sierra de Bernia.

[*This story had a tragic end:* 4,000 German soldiers under imperial orders eventually killed 5,000 Moors.]

> *Fray Prudencio de Sandoval, 'Historia*
> *del Emperador Carlos V,' II, 121–22.*

[184] San Francisco: the Royal Confessors (Sobieski, c. 1613)

(Jacob Sobieski, a Polish traveller, was father of the Polish king John Sobieski.)

The confessors of the Kings of Spain enjoy the most high authority, and they are named bishops, archbishops and cardinals. The order privileged for this office is that of St Dominic.

No one can be confessor of the King if he does not belong to this religious order. The Duque de Lerma* ordered one of these confessors to be drowned for communicating privately with the King, not only in the confessional but also in political matters. He had much authority with the King and as a result the Duque de Lerma developed hatred for him because the King was (as they say) *unum velle, unum nolle*.

The Queens of Spain were obliged to have their confessors from the order of San Francisco which gave them less importance than the Dominicans.

Sobieski, in García Mercadal 'Viajes', II, 334.

[185] Encarnación Benita, *Convento* (San Plácido): Philip IV's passion for a nun (c. 1625)

(This nunnery, still surviving, in the Calle San Roque, was built in 1623–1624. It was the only one of the Benedictine nuns.)

Having inherited the Crown young, Philip IV had as favourite the Conde de Olivares†, third son of the house of Medina Sidonia, who had as a great friend Don Jerónimo de Villanueva‡, prothonotary of Aragon and aide of the bedchamber, and all three were young. And the prothonotary was patron of the nunnery of the Blessed Incarnation, next to his house. Being one day the three of them in conversation, he [Villanueva] said casually that there was in his convent a nun who was an exceptionally beautiful girl. The curiosity of the King and the ardour of the prothonotary led to the King wishing to see her. He went disguised to the place where Don Jerónimo, being patron, was able to arrange by his authority that the King could see the girl.

The King fell in love, the Conde with his power arranged matters, and, in the end, the royal visits [to the nunnery] were nightly and prolonged. One could not hide this gallantry in

---

* Francisco de Sandoval (1552–1625), Duque de Lerma, first minister to Philip III 1598–1618.

† For Olivares, see No. 129.

‡ Jerónimo de Villanueva, minister of Philip IV and associate of the Conde-Duque de Olivares.

such a way that it was not condemned in the nunnery but the King, carried away by the fire of his appetites, trampled under foot the inconveniences.

The presents and offerings of the Conde, the dexterity of the prothonotary, the proximity of the houses, made it possible to break the traditional ban on the sisters leaving the precincts by use of a cellar in the patron's house, which gave on to a passage to a vault in the nunnery, which had in the past been used to keep coal.

The nun, half resolute, half shy, did not dare embark on any sacrilege without telling the abbess, who communicated secretly with the Conde and with Don Jerónimo, and tried with all prudence to dissuade them from the adventure. The two courtiers, determined to humour the King, responded to her with determination, which she bravely replied to by arranging that, the night when the plan had been fixed, there was laid out in her cell a platform on whose cushions the girl laid down and by her side a bare cross with judges painted on it. There entered into the passage Don Jerónimo first, leaving the King and the Conde in his house, and at the sight of this spectacle returned confused and then suspended the execution.

[In the text there is then a paragraph making it clear that despite this 'suspension', the gallantry began and then 'criminal relations' ensued over a long period] . . .

This could not be held secret. The prelates of the church learned everything. But they were confused, vacillating between religion and power. In the end the news reached the Holy Office [that is, the Inquisition]. At that time Don Antonio de Sotomayor* was inquisitor-general, being a Dominican monk, archbishop of Damascus, Confessor of the King. He had repeated audiences with the King, advising him of the many errors which he had committed. Philip IV gave his word to abstain from further communication with the beautiful nun and said that he had done all these things by mistake. Then the Conde-Duque came to discuss the correction of what had transpired.

The Holy Office took up a plaint against Don Jerónimo, who in secret declarations had been incriminated, and they

* Antonio de Sotomayor (1548–1648), Inquisitor General 1631–42.

proceeded to arrest him . . . [On 30 August 1644 he was taken to the Inquisition's prison in Toledo; this was, however, after Olivares had fallen from power]   *Mesonero Romanos, 376–7.*

[186] *Convento* of Capuchin friars (Calle de las Infantas): the persecution of the 'New Christians' (1635)

(This account is by Isaac (Fernando) Cardoso (1604–83), present at that time in Madrid.)

There came from Portugal to the Court some Portuguese Jews with their wives and little children, who were sent to school and, while conversing with the other children, the teacher gave them sweets and titbits and began to ask them if they were Jews, and whether at home their parents mistreated or whipped a Christ. At first they denied it, but, persuaded by the sweets which the others gave them, and by the teacher, who had little affection for this nation, and possessed more feigned than perfect piety, without realizing what they were saying they came to admit that which was imputed to them, and although these were minors of five or six years of age, when testimonies are null and void, for those influenced and prompted statements they took the parents who were ill in bed with tertiary fever occasioned by the heat of the summer and the hardships of the journey, and submitted them to torture, old, poor, and infirm, exhorting them to confess and thereby be dealt with mercifully. Unable to endure the pain, they confessed that of which they were accused. Six or seven persons were burned, the sentences first being read to them in a public meeting, at which it was declared that they flagellated a Christ, that they afterward burned it, and that between the lashes which they gave it, it said to them: 'Why do you mistreat me?' But the physician who treated them, and the surgeon who bled them, saw clearly that in their house they had no figure or image whatsoever, of wood, metal nor of paper.

The house was destroyed, and on its site was put as a memorial an infamous marker in the Calle de las Infantas*,

---

* This still surviving street lies two blocks north of the Calle de Alcalá. The *convento* has long since also vanished.

which referred to the fact of a Christ having been whipped and burned. But afterwards, since it seemed indecent, they took it away, and established on the site a Convent of Capuchin Friars. Such is the power of false testimonies and rigorous tortures that there are many who would prefer a single death, rather than to suffer interminable pains.

Isaac Cardoso, 'Las Excelencias de los
Hebreos' (Amsterdam, 1679), 405–06.

[187] The Atocha: Saint-Simon (1722)

Our Lady of Atocha, or the Atocha, as she is normally called in abbreviation, is a miraculous image of the Holy Virgin, in the rich chapel of an otherwise rather ordinary church belonging to a vast and superb Dominican convent outside Madrid, but less than a gunshot from the last houses, and adjoining the end of the park of the Buen Retiro Palace, which also encloses a large and beautiful Jeronomite monastery, whose church serves as a chapel to this palace, whence one can go everywhere under cover, even into the monastery*. The Atocha is so much the most important object of devotion in Madrid, and in all Castille . . . it is in front of this image that are offered up the vows, the prayers, the public thanks for needs, and the prosperity of the realm, and, in the instance of the King being dangerously ill, for his recovery. The King never embarks on a real journey, and this since time immemorial, without going ceremoniously to pray in front of this image, which is exactly as if he were to go and take leave of Our Lady of Atocha, and he goes and does exactly the same as soon as he returns. The riches in gold, precious stones, lace and sumptuous materials belonging to this image are prodigious. It is always one of the grandest and richest ladies who bears the title of her tire-woman, and it is a very sought-after honour, though expensive, since it costs her 40,000 livres and sometimes 50,000 livres each year to keep her in lace and stuffs, which soon return to the convent's

* Our Lady of Atocha was founded as a *convento* in 1523. Both church and *convento* were damaged in the Napoleonic wars, and a new church was built in the 1890s. In the forecourt there is now a pantheon dedicated to the memory of illustrious men and women.

profit. I will not stop to dwell on these devotions. The Duchess of Alba*, whom we knew in Paris when she was the Spanish ambassadress, held the post then. I do not know who succeeded her in this employment. She died a few days after my arrival in Madrid . . .

I never saw monks so stout, so big, so coarse and such rogues. Pride leapt from their eyes and from their whole faces. The presence of Their Majesties in no way enfeebled it, even when they were talking to them; I speak of the air, the manner, the tone, since they spoke only Spanish, which I did not understand. What surprised me to such an extent that I could not believe my eyes the first time, was the arrogance and effrontery, almost brutality, with which these master monks pushed their elbows into the ladies' faces, and equally into that of the gentlemen who, at this signal, all made a deep bow, humbly kissed their sleeves, then redoubled their bows, without the monks stirring in the least; they seldom after addressed them and then only a few words in a brazen manner, and without showing the slightest civility, to which, when that happened, these ladies replied in the most respectful manner in the world. I have sometimes seen some lord also kissing their sleeve, but as at the unrobing, with an air both hurried and ashamed . . . Although this rare ceremony was renewed each time the King went to the Atocha, it always took me by surprise and I could never get used to it.

Saint-Simon, Vol. 39, 350–52 (1722).

[188] The Church in the streets (E. Clarke, 1762)

The noise made by the intinerant bodies of psalm-singers in the streets, or the ROSARIOS, as they call them, is very disagreeable in the evening; the frequent processions, particularly those of the HOST, troublesome; at Easter especially, when the sight of those bloody disciplinants, the *flagelantes*, is extremely shocking†.

E. Clarke, 343 (1762).

---

* The Duquesa de Alba at this time was Isabel Ponce de León, widow of the 9th Duke who had been ambassador in Paris in 1703.
† Flagellation in the streets was abolished in 1778.

[189] The case of Olavide before the Inquisition (1786)

(Pablo de Olavide (1725–1802) was a Peruvian-born minister of Charles III. The account (1786) is by Jean François Bourgoing (1748–1811), later a French minister.)

[Olavide] knew, by another way, that since the previous year, the vindictive monk had accused him, to the minister, of lacking respect for religion, and of possessing forbidden books; and that he had recently denounced him to the Inquisition.

These discoveries did not as yet disturb his sense of security. He sought apologists near the throne. He went to find the Grand Inquisitor to protest the purity of his belief, offered to retract utterances with which he could be reproached. For more than a year while he had been at Madrid, he lived in the most exemplary way; but nothing could ward off the storm which threatened his head.

On 14 November 1776, a grandee of Spain in the role of *alguacil mayor* of the Inquisition, accompanied by ministers of justice, came to arrest him and took him to the prisons of the Holy Office, whilst, at La Carolina*, where his wife had remained, which was his usual home, his goods, his books and his papers were seized. From this moment, he was lost to his wife, his parents and his friends. For two years they had no idea in which part of the globe he was living, or if he was still alive, and they had all given up all hope of seeing him again . . .

The trial of Olavide was continued in the greatest secrecy. His fate was finally decided after two years and seven days of rigorous detention which had separated him from the whole world.

On 21 November 1778, an assembly was held in the interior of the palace of the Inquisition†, to which were invited forty persons from different orders, among whom were to be found several Grandees of Spain, officers, priests and monks.

The guilty party appeared there wearing yellow carrying in

* La Carolina was a new city on the way to the south, so called because it was founded by Charles III.
† The headquarters of the Inquisition were at No. 4. Calle Isabel la Católica. There is no sign of this building now.

his hand a great candle and attended by two ministers of the Holy Office. All the details of the proceedings were read out to him. The most interesting piece was the circumstantial account of his whole life which he himself had made. He confessed that on his voyage abroad, he had consorted with free-thinkers, namely Voltaire and Rousseau; that he had returned to Spain imbued with biases against the clergy, and persuaded that its privileges and the views of the Roman church were opposed to the prosperity of states; that, since he had found himself at the head of the colonies in the Sierra Morena, he had explained boldly and without reflecting, the obstacles which held up their progress on the infallibility of the Pope and on the tribunals of the Inquisition.

There followed the testimony of seventy-eight witnesses, who accused him of having often used the free-thinkers' language: and having cast ridicule on the fathers of the church, etc. The accused confessed several of these indictments, denying some, insisting moreover that the remarks which were imputed to him had all sprung from the purest objectives: that some of them had been for the purpose of getting the colonists confided to his care to work, since they only lazily understood the outward practices of the religion as a masque: that bringing to their attention the drawbacks of celibacy, he had in mind to encourage the growth of population which was so necessary to the prosperity of his country.

These means of exonerating himself had seemed neither respectful nor conclusive. He was accused above all of the crime of resorting to all sorts of methods to evade the justice of the Holy Office, of intercepting their letters, of getting the witnesses who were put up to oppose him to retract; and these statements of grants of appeal were proved by the writings of his own hand.

In brief, the tribunal judged him guilty in fact and law of all the faults imputed to him, and pronounced the sentence which declared him formally heretical. He interrupted the reading to deny this qualification. It was the last effort of his steadfastness. He fell fainting on to the bench on which he was sitting. When he had recovered, the reading of the sentence continued. It carried the confiscation of all his goods, declared him unfit for any responsibility, exiled him twenty leagues from Madrid, from the royal palaces, from Sevilla, from the theatre of his eclipsed authority, from Lima, and from his country house; it condemned him to eight years' incarceration in a monastery where he would have to read pious works as directed, and to go to confession once every month. He then made his solemn recantation, and was absolved of the censures he had brought upon himself, with all the pomp and ceremony prescribed by law . . .

Hardly had M. Olavide been shut up in a convent in La Mancha than he complained that his health was deteriorating and he obtained permission to go and take the waters that were nearby; soon after to go and seek others in Catalonia, which he hoped would be better for him. There, near the frontier, he easily eluded the vigilance of his guards, as he had doubtless hoped; and saying, or thinking he was saying, a last farewell to his native land, he went into France, where his reputation had preceded him, and where he was welcomed as a martyr to intolerance.   *Bourgoing, 378–85.*

[190] *Autos de fe* in the eighteenth century

On 9 May 1784, at half-past eight in the morning, there emerged from the Holy Office in Madrid a man and two women in penitents' garb. The man and one of the women wore a *sambenito de media aspa* (a penitential garment with a half-cross; that is, one with only one band of color across the front and the back); each carried a green candle, had a halter about the neck, and a conical mitre (*coroza*) with an inscription explaining what crime had been committed. The Tribunal was preceded by cavalry and a company of grenadiers of the Murcian regiment. There followed, in two rows, the Inquisition officers and between them marched the culprits. Then came the censors (*calificadores*), and in their midst an ecclesiastic and a secular minister carrying a box covered with crimson velvet and containing the sentences. The procession was closed by the court inquisitor Don José de Quevedo y Quintano, the secretary (*secretario del secreto*) and *alguacil mayor*, the Excelentísimo Sr Marqués de Cogolludo, and the two supernumerary secretaries, the Excelentísimos Sres Conde de Altamira* and Duque de Frías†. The procession was flanked on either side by a row of halberdiers, and behind it marched the rest of the royal troop beating drums, as did the grenadiers in the vanguard. Behind them came the *alguacil mayor's* retinue of carriages and coaches. In this order they reached the church of Santo Domingo el Real, which was being guarded by the company of grenadiers belonging to the African regiment . . . The clergy emerged from the church to receive the Tribunal, and the procession then entered. The criminals were led to some benches on a platform constructed on the epistle [or right] side, near the middle of the church; and at their back were stationed the *alcalde* (jailer), the lieutenant, the nuncio, and the surgeon, as guards. Ministers and officials occupied the center of the church . . . In front of the inquisitor was an image of Christ crucified, the ritual, and the stole and candle for the absolution of the criminals. When he gave the signal with a handbell, the introit of the mass began . . . after which . . . the secretary read from the pulpit the various charges, which consisted of obscene acts, superstitions, idolatry, diabolic pacts, and other abominable crimes, for which the man and one of the women were sentenced to abjuration *de vehementi* (abjuration of vehement suspicion of heresy). Both were to be taken through the public streets, the man to receive two hundred lashes, one woman the punishment of *vergüenza* (that is, to be stripped to the waist and paraded through the streets while the town crier proclaimed the sentence, but to receive no lashes). Then they were to be taken to the penitential prison for five years and finally exiled for ever at a distance of forty leagues from the court and royal residences . . . The other woman was sentenced to abjuration *de levi* (abjuration of light suspicion of heresy), she was to be banished from Madrid and the royal residences for a period of four years . . . Then the criminals were conducted to the chancel, where, kneeling before the inquisitor's table and in the presence of the senior secretary, they abjured. When they were absolved and the half-cross (*media aspa*) was removed, the green candles they carried were lighted. They then kneeled at the main altar, heard mass,

---

* Vicente Osorio de Moscoso, Conde de Altamira (d. 1816).
† Diego Fernández de Velasco, 11th Duque de Frías (d. 1811).

and gave their candles to the priest, kissing his hand, after which they were taken back in the same order as they had entered the church. At ten o'clock the following morning the man, who was to suffer two hundred lashes, and the woman, who was sentenced to public *vergüenza*, were led from the Tribunal, accompanied by mounted inquisitorial officers and secular ministers in two rows, the procession being preceded by a troop of cavalry and closed by the *alguacil mayor* with his carriages and coaches. On each day crowds of people had assembled. *'Memorial Literario'*, *May 1784, qu. Kany, 457–58.*

[191] The case against celibacy of the clergy (Townsend, 1786)
(Townsend was a clergyman, who himself married twice.)

The principal *cortejos* in the great cities are the canons of the cathedrals; but where the military reside, they take their choice, and leave the refuse for the church. In the country villages, the monks bear rule; at least within their limits, and even in the cities, they set up their pretensions. As for the parochial clergy, one thing is certain, that many of them have families, and all are involved in the common censure. Even in the Asturias, my friend, the good bishop auxiliary of Oviedo, a man of high principle, yet of great humanity, severe only to himself, but compassionate to others, made it a rule, that none of his curates should have children in their families. This sacrifice, at least, he insisted they should make to decency. Beyond this he did not think it right to be too rigid in his enquiries. In short, during my residence in Spain, I never found one person inclined to vindicate the curates from the common charge; but, at the same time, all, with united voices, bore testimony to the superior virtue of the bishops. Indeed, these venerable men, from all that I could hear, and from what I saw in the near approach, to which they graciously admitted me, for purity, for piety, for zeal, can never be sufficiently admired; but too few of the clergy, either secular or regular, till they begin to look towards the mitre, seem to think it necessary, that they should imitate these bright examples, or aspire after such high perfections.

This universal depravity of morals, if I am not much mistaken, may be traced up to the celibacy of the clergy . . . this mistaken principle, that *conjugal affection is inconsistent with the due discharge of the ministerial functions*. In conversing freely with the clergy on this subject, I never met any one, besides the archbishop of Toledo, who attempted to vindicate this principle; and wherever I was, I had no difficulty in declaring war against it, because they do not consider it as an article of faith.

The purpose of the law is however frustrated; for nature is like a rapid river, which, checked in its progress, scorns restraint, and, when diverted from its proper course, either overflows the country, or forms new channels for itself. What then is gained? The parochial clergy, and these are the only clergy who should be suffered in a state, have their connections and their children, but not as they ought, in the most honourable way. They are disgraced in the eyes of the people, who are taught by their example to live in the violation of the laws; and their children, for want of a proper education, are fitted only for the vilest employments in the community . . .

Should the Spanish government resolve to set the clergy free, more ample provision must be made for their maintenance, because at present it is scarcely sufficient for their own support; and this might be easily accomplished out of the vast revenues of the bishops, or the suppression of some useless convents.

Joseph Townsend, 150–53.

[192] Colegio de San Isidro: 'Cathedral Church' (1809)

(Joseph Bonaparte enters the Collegiate Church. This splendid church, built by the Jesuits between 1622 and 1661 on the site of an earlier Jesuit church, became the parish church of San Isidro after the Jesuits were expelled in 1769. It was elevated to be a cathedral in 1885 (provisionally) on the creation of the new diocese of Madrid-Alcalá. Joseph Bonaparte reigned as king in Spain off and on between 1808 and 1813.)

The Court being thus re-established, the King prepared to make his entry into Madrid. This took place on 22 January

1809, but the procession was altogether a military one. The King and his suite were on horseback. I was present, and had an opportunity of observing all that took place. The streets through which the procession passed were not deserted, occasional shouts were raised, and if there were neither warmth nor enthusiasm, there was no positive antipathy visible on the part of the spectators. In general there was an expression of curiosity, in some few cases one of resignation, in others there was hope, but no signs of dislike or contempt were exhibited. The King dismounted at the Collegiate Church of San Isidro and made a simple and manly speech. One phrase only was remarkable. 'The unity of our holy religion,' it ran, 'the independence of the Monarchy, the integrity of its territory, and the liberty of its citizens, are conditions of the oath I took on receiving the crown, which shall not lose in dignity while I wear it.'

He endeavoured by these words to refute the rumours that had been circulated concerning the intentions of his brother, and bound himself in some sort to the nation by engagements which it was out of his power to fulfil. This indication of independence was of course very displeasing at Paris.

After the religious ceremony the King proceeded to the Palace, where he found a large concourse of persons awaiting him in his apartments. The next and following days he went out, showed himself in the town, and inspected the public institutions, especially the hospitals. He was tolerably well received. There were decided symptoms of a favourable change in the feelings of the inhabitants and in the aspect of the town. Aversion was diminishing, hope and confidence seemed about to revive, and it must be said that this change was due to the King personally. His natural disposition was of the greatest service to him under the then circumstances; his amiability, his popularity, and above all the preference he evinced in all things for Spaniards over Frenchmen, were pleasing to the nation.   *Miot de Mélito, 313–315.*

[193] A Spanish catechism (1808)
(This was a catechism typical of the Napoleonic Wars.)

Chapter I

Tell me my son, what are you?

I am Spanish, by the grace of God.

And what does it mean to be Spanish?

A good man.

What obligations has someone who is Spanish?

Three: to be a Christian, and defend Country and King.

Who is our King?

Ferdinand VII.

With what degree of ardour should he be loved?

With the most lively ardour, as his virtues and misfortunes merit.

Who is the enemy of our happiness?

The Emperor of the French.

Who is this man?

An evil man, an ambitious man, prince of all evils, end of all good and composed of and deposit of all vices.

What characteristics does he have?

Two: one diabolic, one human.

How many emperors are there?

One true one in three deceiving personages.

Which are?

Napoleon, Murat, Godoy.

Chapter II

Who are the French?

Old Christians and modern heretics.

Who has conducted them to such state of slavery?

False philosophy and the corruption of old customs.

When will we finish with its atrocious despotism?

Already it is within sight of its end.

Whence comes this hope?

From the effort which is being made by our beloved country.

What is 'Country'?

The union of many governed people under one King according to our laws.

What punishment is reserved for a Spanish person who defaults on his just duties?

Infamy, material death reserved for the traitor and civil death for his descendants.

Chapter III
Is it a sin to kill a Frenchman?
No, father: one does a worthy work, thereby liberating the country from these violent oppressors.

Chapter IV
What should we do in battle?
Increase the glory of the nation, defend our brothers and save the country.
Who must take up arms?
Everyone who can: those designed by the government less those needed for public positions.

Chapter V
What should be the politics of the Spanish people?
The maxims of Jesus Christ.
Who are our enemies?
Those of Machiavelli.
In what consist these things?
Egoism.   *In Díaz Plaja, 'Documentos III', 73.*

[194] A nun takes her vows in the Descalzas Reales (Inglis, 1830)

(This *convento* was founded by Juana de Austria, daughter of Charles V, mother of the fatal Sebastián, King of Portugal. She was regent of Spain in the 1550s. She established her *convento* in 1560, in a converted palace, and the present church was finished in 1564. Numerous princesses were thereafter *descalzas* (barefoot). The architect of the original conversion was Antonio Sillero; of the church, Juan Bautista de Toledo.)

At the hour appointed, the abbess entered the room on the other side of the grating, accompanied by all the nuns, and by several ladies, friends and relatives of the novice. She entered a moment after; and immediately knelt down, with her face towards the grating, so that I had a near and distinct view of her. She was attired in the novice's robe of pure white, and wore a crown of flowers upon her head. Her countenance was gentle, sweet, and interesting; – there was an expression of seriousness, but not of sadness, in her face; and a skin, fairer than usually falls to the lot of Spanish women, was sensibly coloured with a fine carnation, – the glow of youth, and health, and happiness, yet lingering on her cheek; and connecting her with the world of light, and life, and freedom, about to close upon her for ever.

The administrator now entered by the chapel, and placed himself in a chair close to where I was stationed, and at the side of an opening in the grating of about a foot square. The novice then rose, and walking forward to the grating, presented him with a paper, which he read aloud: this was the act of renunciation of all property, then and for ever; and during this ceremony the novice retired and knelt as before, holding in her hand a long lighted taper, with which the abbess presented her. The preparatory service then commenced by reading and chanting; and this, although monotonous, was pleasing and impressive, according well with the solemnity of the scene that had introduced it; and in this service the novice joined, with a clear sweet voice, in which nothing of emotion could be distinguished. When this was concluded, the novice again rose, and advanced to the grating, and pronounced slowly and distinctly the three vows that separate her from the world, – chastity, poverty, and obedience. Her voice never faltered; nor could I perceive the slightest change of countenance; the colour only, seemed to be gradually forsaking her. The lady abbess, who stood close by her side, wept all the while. Ah! if each tear could have told why it flowed, what a history might have been unfolded. Indignation was the feeling produced in my mind. I wished for the cannon of the Constitutionalists, to throw down these most odious of prisons; and even to the priest, who stood by me in his crimson and gilded surplice, I could not restrain myself from saying, half audibly, 'Qué infamia!'

When the vows that could never be recalled had been pronounced by this misguided child, she stepped back, and threw herself prostrate upon the ground, – this is the act confirmatory of her vows, – symbolical of death, and signifying that she is dead to the world. The service was then resumed, – a bell continued slowly to toll; and the priest read; while the nuns who stood around their new-made sister, responded – 'dead to the world – separated from kindred – bride of heaven!' and the nun who lies prostrate is supposed, at the same time, to repeat to God in secret, the vows she has already pronounced aloud. When this was concluded, a slow organ peal, and a solemn swell of voices rose, and died away; and the abbess then raised the nun from the ground, and embraced her; and all the other nuns and her relations also embraced her. I saw no tear upon any cheek, excepting upon the cheek of the abbess, whose face was so full of benignity, that it half reconciled me to the fate of the young initiated who had vowed obedience to her. When she had embraced every one, she again knelt for a few moments, and then approached the grating along with the abbess; and the priest handed to the abbess through the opening, the vestments of a nun. Then came the last act of the drama: – the crown was lifted from her head; the black vestment was put on, and the girdle and the rosary; and the black hood was drawn over her head; – she was now a nun, and she again embraced the abbess and all the sisters. Still I could not discover a single tear, excepting on the cheek of the abbess, who continued to weep almost without ceasing to the very end: the countenance of the young nun remained unmoved. The crown was again replaced upon her head, to be worn all that day; the sacrament was administered, and one last embrace by friends and relations terminated the scene.   *Inglis, 160–3 (1831).*

[195] The Marquis de Custine's judgements (1831)

The Spanish clergy are not at all united; the priests detest the monks. The latter have a mysterious influence, which is much more widespread than that of the secular clergy. To influence a half-African, extremely passionate people, and one in consequence swayed by the imagination, even truth itself has to be presented in extraordinary shapes! . . . Nothing is as romantic as convent life in Spain, nor, I have been told, as barbaric as the teaching given to children in these religious sanctuaries . . .

It is instructive to study the Spanish character; you learn that religion goes even as far as love in the matter of indulgence, and that the truly philosophical Christian's pardon is almost equal to the mercy of God. Here religion tolerates so much weakness that it seems almost as if faith will be injurious to morals: faith pardons all, since it conceives that everything is involuntary. Since I have been in Spain, my faith has grown, and my indulgence of human weakness has increased in the same proportion . . .   *Custine, Vol. I, 173, 222.*

Between man and his Redeemer, between the creature and the Creator, between the nation and God, this people's faith has established a familiarity which even the most sublime philosophy could not achieve unless as an exception by favour of some élite intelligence; philosophy and Protestantism which derive from it are the aristocracy of wisdom; with Catholicism, faith is no longer the privilege of genius, it becomes genuinely popular, without losing any of its sublimity. *Ibid, Vol. I, 244.*

. . . The King has converted the convent of the Inquisition into a barracks: thus this tribunal has been abolished, but only since 1820. In previous times, when the victims were led in front of their hangmen disguised as judges, the wheels of the carts in which the accused were transported by night were covered in cloth, and the mules' hoofs were enclosed in padded slippers. The dungeons were named Valencia, Sevilla, Vitoria, Barcelona, so that they could, without explicitly lying, reply to the parents who came to ask after the fate of a prisoner: he is in Sevilla, or Saragossa, etc.

I have thought it worth while to mention this Jesuitical respect on the part of the people of the Inquisition for scruples of conscience. On the road to evil there is always some point at which the consciences of men who seem to us the most abominable stop before that of people whom we think to be honest. For example, I myself thought up till now that I was morally better than the people of the Inquisition, although it has been proved to me by the above-related facts that the hangmen of the Holy Office fear lying more than I do, which does not prevent me from blaming their equivocation; but this self-same hypocrisy is a homage rendered to sincerity. I speak only after the account I was given this morning; if it is false, so much the worse for the person who has deceived me, I cannot answer for the truth of facts at which I was not myself a witness; but while conceding the need to describe to you at second hand the scenes I could not myself witness to, I warn you to be on your guard.

If the tribunal of the Holy Office had remained faithful to the spirit of its founders, and if it had restricted itself to maintaining discipline among the ecclesiastics, one would respect it when it concerns the punishment of a crime which only a few months ago was committed by the monks of Saint Basil's convent*. Their abbot, a conscientious man of rare piety, wanted to reform them; he undertook this perilous task: but one day eight of the most unruly monks in the community went into his cell and cut his throat.

A little after this event, the convent barber noticed wounds on the heads, the necks and hands of some of the monks: he told the police; at last, upon some other indications which confirmed the suspicions, strict searches were made, and the proofs of the murder were discovered. Seven monks are in prison, convicted of having taken part in it. They cannot be executed! The monks have the privilege of assassination!!

Nevertheless, another person, for whose veracity I cannot answer, came to tell me that one monk had been publicly executed some years ago, for having been found guilty of having stabbed his unfaithful mistress. This monk belonged to an order instituted for preparing the dying for a good death; and he swore that he had not neglected to fulfil his holy ministry by the victim. If these facts are true, if these really are the customs and the guiding lights of the regular clergy, what can one reply to the revolutionaries?

Ibid, Vol. I, 185–87.

---

* This *convento* in the Calle Desengaño was disestablished in 1838.

Processions and Fiestas

[196] Carnival (Quin, 1821)

Little would any person who had seen the streets of Madrid
during the Carnival [Sunday 9 to Tuesday 11 February]
imagine that at this period Spain was harassed by internal
factions, threatened with a foreign invasion, and reduced almost to the verge of national bankruptcy. The jubilee of this
festive season is displayed chiefly in the number, diversity, and
gaiety of the masques, which animate the principal streets.
About noon they begin to make their appearance, traversing
the streets in groups, and between four o'clock and half-past
five, they all meet in the Prado, which is crowded with visitors,
and they perform such antics as are suitable to the characters
which they represent. On the first day there was a slight
sprinkling of these masques on the Prado. The most amusing
fellow amongst them was a shoemaker, who carried a rule of
an immense size; with this machine in his hand he claimed the
privilege of approaching the handsomest ladies in the Prado, in
order to measure their feet. They complied with the operation,

particularly those who had delicately shaped feet to display, with the utmost good nature. A number of women, who were collected in the middle of the street of Alcalá, raised an incessant shout of laughter, mingled with attempts at singing, while they tossed a stuffed figure of Sancho in a blanket. The representation of this faithful follower of Don Quixote, when whirled aloft in the air, excited irrepressible mirth, and the shout was doubled when, by the awkwardness of the women in tossing the figure, it fell upon some of the bystanders. No man was permitted to assist them in this operation, as time out of mind it belongs exclusively to the other sex. It is impossible to give an idea of the enjoyment which poor Sancho created. It was a scene of downright fun, shout after shout, talk, laughter, song, such as the weeping philosopher himself could not resist, had he witnessed it.

At night there was a masquerade at the Teatro del Príncipe*, and so great was the demand for admission, that at half-past ten, when the doors were opened, not a ticket was to be had, except from the retailers – persons who buy up a number of tickets in the morning at the common price, one dollar each, and at night sell them for two, and sometimes even three dollars. It was calculated that at least eighteen hundred persons were present, and of these, perhaps, not more than fifty were without masks. There is this difference between a Spanish and an English masquerade, that, at the latter, scarcely any person is seen dressed in character, who does not at the same time attempt some exhibition in which that character is developed. A hermit assumes the language of the cell, a doctor offers his prescriptions, and a poet pesters every body with his rhymes. But at a Spanish masquerade the character reaches no farther than the dress, and, under different disguises, all meet for one purpose, that of spending the whole night till morning dawns in dancing. Indeed, it can scarcely be said that, in the generality of the dresses, any character is intended to be represented. The object seems to be to effect the most complete concealment by the comic aspect of the masks, and by dresses which have little relation to their features. The voice too is disguised, and there is kept up a constant din of feigned tones and squeaking saluta-

* See No. 215.

tions. The dances follow each other in the order of country-dances, rigodoons, and waltzes; and as this is an amusement to which the Spaniards are passionately attached, one may imagine the spirit with which it was maintained till a late hour of the following morning. Several persons of distinction were present, who, under cover of their masks, mingled without fear of discovery in the joyous scene, and frequently danced, for aught they knew, in the same circle with their wives and husbands, though perhaps not exactly intending such a rencontre.

It is impossible to avoid the urbanity and decency which presided over the amusements of the night. Not the slightest incident occurred to disturb the harmony of the meeting, crowded as it was. An excellent band occupied the orchestra, and the different successions of the dances were arranged by two or three officers, whose dictates were instantly obeyed, as law, by every part of the company. There were guards of soldiers in attendance; but, from the great order which prevailed, their presence seemed almost unnecessary. In the coffee-room refreshments were served at a moderate price.

The number of masks on the Prado on the second day (Monday) was very considerable. In the evening several ladies and gentlemen attended Lady A'Court's *tertulia* in fancy dresses*. The young Marqués de Santa Cruz appeared very elegantly dressed as a Moorish prince†. The naturally dark Spanish countenance becomes this dress exceedingly. His mother, the marchioness, who is yet in the prime of life, and who, before her marriage, was considered the most beautiful woman in Spain, was arrayed in a vest and turban of silver tissue, which set off her person to great advantage‡. The young Marquesa of Alcañices presented herself in the ancient dress of Andalusia, which, without being costly, is extremely beautiful. Her two younger sisters appeared also in provincial dresses, which became them remarkable well, particularly that of the youngest, who was dressed as a Mallorquine, or native of Majorca. The Duquesa of Frías was attired as Cleopatra, with

---

* Lady A'Court was María, daughter of Lord Radnor, and married to Sir William A'Court (1779–1860), later Lord Heytesbury, the British Minister.
† This was Francisco, 11th Marqués de Santa Cruz.
‡ Joaquina, daughter of the Duquesa de Osuna.

a long flowing white veil, her bosom starred with diamonds
. . . The company began to pour in at ten o'clock. Soon after
that hour the rooms were crowded, and dancing commenced. It
was an extremely interesting sight to view the various Spanish
provincial dresses, set off by so many fine forms, mingling
together on this gay occasion. The Spaniards seemed to enjoy it
much, and to the foreigners who were present it was productive
of equal delight. The company did not separate till a late hour
the following morning.

On the third and last day of the Carnival (Shrove Tuesday),
'all the world and his wife', to use a Spanish saying, were out.
There were at least a thousand persons of both sexes, young
and old, masqued, who traversed the Prado in groups; a task
which they would have found difficult enough, on account of
the vast crowd which attended, if every disposition had not
been shown to accommodate them. One of the first groups
which appeared was headed by a watchman, who held before
him an old iron lantern. Some of this group were dressed in a
very fantastic manner. Another group was headed by a musician, who played on a broken old guitar with one string. In
another quarter were seen Don Quixote and his man Sancho.
One mask excited great amusement, who had a stuffed figure
so attached to him that he appeared to be riding upon a man's
back. In the conception of these and innumerable other masks,
a great deal of the spirit of broad comedy prevailed. But a
group of five masks, one of whom was seated on an ass, his face
turned towards the animal's tail, afforded the greatest amusement of all. By an inscription which appeared on his hat, it
appeared that he was intended to represent a 'Diplomatist of
Verona.' He held in his hand some sheets of blank paper, and
he observed a most important silence. On his right hand he was
attended by a mask, the representative of the Regency of Urgel;
and on his left the Russian and Prussian ambassadors. The
King of France was stationed at the ass's tail. They were
received with shouts of laughter wherever they appeared. An
old clothes man, with a bag on his shoulder, and hat of rush
matting, with a leaf a yard wide, presented also a droll
appearance. From the Prado he pursued his way into the
streets, stopped before the balconies where he saw any ladies,
viewed them for awhile through his immense tin eye-glass, and

then ran off to another part of the street. A mask with the face behind, giving the idea of a man walking backwards, shook all the sides of all the old women with laughter. Some grave masks appeared on horseback; others in calèches, giving curious ideas of contrasts; and, in fact, all Madrid seemed to have taken leave of their senses on this occasion. It was observable, however, that, in all this crowded scene, not the slightest disturbance occurred, no altercation of any sort, no picking of pockets (as would have happened in London if such a scene were exhibited there), and, above all, not the least approach to indecorum was to be discovered. . . .

At night the masquerade at the Teatro del Príncipe was crowded. The theatre was not cleared until eight o'clock on the morning of Ash Wednesday. This being the first day of Lent, the Prado presented a very different aspect from that of the last three days. A penitential stillness reigned in the streets, and the churches were crowded with those persons who, during the Carnival, were perhaps the gayest of the gay. The theatres were all ordered to be shut during the Lent, as no public amusements of any sort were permitted, except musical concerts, which were conducted upon a minor scale, at an assembly-room called the Cruz de Malta*. In the course of the Lent, however, this rule was a little relaxed for the first time, as operas were allowed to be performed twice a week.

[197] Holy Week: the Moroccan ambassador (1690)

Palm Sunday is the day when the Messiah entered Jerusalem, according to his Gospels . . . the Christians celebrate this day as a fiesta. They come together in a church, pray, and recite the history of what happened. They take out the cross and walk through the streets. Each one of those who take part carry in their hands a palm or a branch of olive or of some other tree, fresh and flexible, or something similar. Afterwards, they take back the cross and put it back in its place.

* The Cruz de Malta was a famous hotel in the Calle Caballero de Gracia.

I have seen, on Palm Sunday, the King* entering a chapel situated inside his palace and hearing there every impiety – may God preserve us from that! – which was ever said. After the ceremony, he went out with all the priests, the friars and the archbishop, whose role is that of Mufti, and the Nuncio, who is 'the Vicar of the Pope'. The friars were dressed in rich cloths encrusted with jewels. Each one of them had a palm in his hands. They carried before them a cross of silver on which there was an image covered by a silk cloth. They were preceded by a group of friars who sang admirably and carried instruments of music and similar things. The monks carried papers which they read, singing psalms. Behind there were their superiors, followed by the highest personages of the Court. The King came last, carrying with him a palm adorned with flowers. After having carried the cross round the Royal Palace, they returned it to its place in the church. The same ceremony is celebrated in every church. One meets on this day and the following day, all Christians carrying in their hands a palm or a branch of olive . . .

The next day they all meet also in the churches, and pray, and tell what happened to the Messiah with the children of Israel when they were excited against him and consulted together as to how to seize hold of him and kill him.

The fourth day is the fiesta of the breaking of the fast which is known as La Pascua. That day the King arranges a meal for the poor, inviting thirteen men among the poor and makes them enter the Palace and seats them on his chairs. The Archbishop, the Mufti, and the Nuncio, Vicar of the Pope, arrive and help the King who with his own hands presents the food to the above-mentioned poor, and occupies himself in offering plates, and changing them and returning them as a servant does for his master in such a way that the thirteen poor men are each offered thirty dishes of food, without meat, it being understood that during Lent the Christians do not eat . . . The King gives them fish only to eat but of every kind, and concludes the thirty dishes with every kind of fruit, fresh or dry, in such a way that everyone is very well fed. Water and wine are also distributed. When they have finished eating, the super-

* i.e. Charles II.

ior of the church arrives. He has in his hand a wooden basin. The Nuncio, Vicar of the Pope, brings water and the King washes the feet of the poor and dries them with specially prepared towels. When he has finished drying them, he kisses the feet of each of them and gives them clothes and some money. They then go away, taking what the King has given them, as well as the remains of the meal, and the plates on which it has been served. They sell all this in the streets where the multitude gathers, because of the belief that they have in the blessing which is united to these foods.

The Queen* and the mother of the King† do the same; each of them gives a meal to thirteen poor women and offers them a meal comparable to what the King has served the men.

This washing of the feet is, in its origin, according to what was written in the Gospel, a pious work and practice kept in imitation of what the Messiah did the day of Pascua.

While the King was giving the food to the poor on the day of Pascua, and while the poor were leaving the palace, all the Christians, the priests and the friars, the other dignitaries and the lower clergy, take all that they have in the way of crucifixes and images which adorn them and make them pass by all the streets and the city. They have an incalculable number of candles lit in full daylight . . . The people pass in this manner from one church to another showing in this way their grief and their piety. As they insist, the Crucified Christ was treated in this way. As a result they carry his image which represents him standing up in a garden and in an attitude of prayer; an angel has come down close to him, carrying in her hand the cup of death, towards which he extends his hand to grasp hold of it. They carry too another image accompanied by a group of guards. In this way, they assure us, they became infuriated against Christ. In continuation, the figure of the Messiah appears after having been beaten and bearing the marks of the torment on his shoulders. They also represent him carrying the Cross on his shoulder. Afterwards they carry the crucifixion, and sometimes they depict him taken down from the Cross. Among the Christians there are those who imitate the Crucified Christ. They have their faces covered with the

* i.e. Mariana of Neuberg.
† i.e. Mariana of Austria.

intention, as they believe, of hiding themselves and not being recognized. But one of their servants or friends walks behind them for fear that they will faint in consequence of the many lashes that they receive on their backs. One sees the blood run down to their feet. Others imitate the Crucifixion. With their hands and their heads tied to a column of steel, they pass in this way through the streets the day that the processions pass. They have their face covered so as not to be recognized.

The following day the Spaniards take again the image of the Crucified Christ, at the moment that He had just been nailed to the Cross, and carry it under the Christ; then covered with sheets in the tomb. They read at the same time psalms full of sadness. They take him back then to the church and hide him. They then walk round the church with torches and candles, cover the church with black cloth, close the doors of the church, whose bells are not rung while the procession is going on. Nor do the parishioners go on horseback or in their coach during the days that the procession lasts. During these days, the whole world, grandees and humble, go on foot. They say that Don Juan de Austria* brother of the King . . . is the one who insists that one should go only on foot during the days of the procession.

The following day, the third day of La Pascua, they open the churches at mid-day, burn torches, and candles, take away the black cloths, and replace them with others of bright colours, and ring the bells. They give themselves over to happiness and print little papers on which there are tiny figures supposed to be those of angels. Among the figures letters are written in chaldaic letters, forming the word 'Alleluya' which means 'Rejoice! Rejoice!'† The moment that the bells are let go, they allow these little pamphlets loose too in the middle of the crowds which seize hold of them and distribute them, shouting cries of happiness and pleasure. They show how the Messiah went up to heaven, after having been crucified, so people thought, shrouded and then raised from the tomb to heaven:

* Don Juan 'of Austria' (1629–79). But 'scandal accused' his mother, the actress María Calderón, 'which must have rendered the paternity of Don John very dubious'. All the same, King Philip IV recognized him.

† This was the origin of the political Alleluya, so popular in Spain between 1750 and 1939.

'But they did not slay him, neither crucified him; only a likeness of that was shown to them. Those who are at variance concerning him surely are in doubt regarding him . . . and they slew him not of certainty – no indeed; God raised him up to Him . . .' (Koran, Sura IV, Verse 159).

These men who have deviated from the truth, persevering in their belief and in their evident error, have abandoned the right path and the great, brilliant, path of charity: 'decked out fair to them,' (Koran, Sura VI, Verse 13). They have deviated along an evil path. They have persisted in impiety. The Pope – may God defeat his abominable efforts – makes them deviate . . . From him and his acolytes the masses have picked up by contagion this incurable illness and this damage which only the sword can extirpate . . .

The Pope insists that all Christian peoples confess once during the Easter festival. All Catholics, men and women, go to church specially to make this confession . . . The great and the humble, the man and the woman, the boy and the little girl, confess all the sins that they have committed and take a firm decision to renew their repentance. They then receive tickets (*billetes*) in a number equal to the persons who have confessed . . . After the Easter days are over, a friar presents himself successively in each house and, having discovered the number of persons who live in it, collects these tickets one by one. When the friar finds someone who has lost his ticket, or if someone in a house has not confessed, it is a great abomination; and the person is held to have committed a great crime. He finds himself obliged to give a sum of money and to confess in order to be absolved.

> *Moroccan ambassador in Spain, 1690–91,*
> *qu. in García Mercadal, 'Viajes' II, 1265–70.*

[198] Holy Week: Custine's record (1831)

Today, throughout Madrid, there was the procession of the great good Lord. The ceremony was touching. People who were too ill to go to church to receive the Pascal Communion, waited for it at home; the holy sacrament is taken to them, with great pomp, and the whole town is affected, hangs tapestries from its balconies and adorns itself for this feast of the dying. Each parish has its own procession. The priest, with the monstrance, climbs into a magnificent carriage, belonging either to the Court or to some Grandee of Spain, who vie for the honour of consecrating their turn-outs and servants to the service of the good God and to the health of souls. A team of six mules, numerous lackeys in grand livery and carriages of the period of King Philip V obstruct the approaches to the churches, the façades of all the houses are hung with cloths, and the pavements are strewn with flowers. At the moment that the holy sacrament goes through the streets, the air is darkened by a cloud of little images of saints which are thrown from the upper floors of each house, and which troops of children fight over on the balconies on each storey, in the public road and right under the mules' hoofs, or under the golden wheels of the ancient and majestic carriage with its windows.

Custine to Victor Hugo, in Custine, 244 (1831)

[199] San Isidro: Sir Richard Wynn at the first celebration (15 May 1623)

The next day following, being Monday, was there a very great procession, in commemoration of a new Saint, canonized by the Pope the year before, and this was the first day that was ever kept for him. Desirous I was to know what this saint was, and how he came now to be thought of? On further inquiry, an English Jesuit; of whom I asked this question, told me, that, about four hundred years since, he lived in this town of Madrid. He was a ploughman by profession; his name, Isidro, and he was the proper saint of the place; for, when he lived, he never failed daily to go to a little chapel* hard by (where his body now lay) to mass, and when the bell rang, though he were at plough, yet did he leave his oxen in the field, and went to church, and while he was there, there came an angel and held the plough; that still, at his return, he found rather more work

---

* Actually, this was the church of San Andrés. San Isidro also found, miraculously, several springs, one of which was at the site of the hermitage of his name on the hills outside Madrid, where the fiesta was celebrated.

done than if he had been present himself; and now, being dead, he lay there incoffined in silver, and but the continual touching of that coffin wrought infinite number of miracles. This he told me with as much confidence as if it had been possible for him to have believed it. 'Then,' said I, 'how, after four hundred years, come he now to be thought on?' He told me, that the late King*, being wonderful sick, this coffin was brought and laid in bed with him, which instantly recovered him. So, in recompense of this cure, the King got him canonized by the Pope. This procession passed by the court gate. There were of friars at it between seven and eight hundred, of several orders, walking by two and two in rank, and between every several order was there a great cross carried, and intermixed amongst them in divers places, were morris-dancers, pageants, trumpeters, and a number of other light things, far unfit to be mixed with anything that had a show of religion. At the sight of these things most of the people as they passed by, fell on their knees.

This ceremony ended with the day . . .

D'Ewes, II, 450 (1623).

[200] San Isidro: Richard Ford in the nineteenth century
(Richard Ford was a passionate anti-Catholic.)

The grand pilgrimage . . . of this revered rustic . . . takes place on May 15 and is truly a national scene. Here may be studied most of the costumes, songs and dances of the provinces as the natives settled at Madrid congregate in parties with true local spirit, each preserving their own peculiarities. Booths are erected and eating houses in which the Gaita Gallega† resounds with the Guitarra Andaluza. Vast numbers of the saint's small pig-bells made of clay are sold, as they avert lightning when well rung; this fair is to the Madrilenian what Greenwich is on Easter Monday to the Cockney . . . By these and other melodramas, given gratis in a poor land, where amusements are rare, the church maintained its popularity:

---

* That is, Philip III.
† The Gallegan bagpipe.

labour was gladdened by a holiday which while it refreshed the body combined religious consolation for the soul: but Christianity was thereby dwarfed into a superstition and Paganism was virtually revived, for it might be the festival of Bacchus or of Venus: but the stock in trade of the old firm was soon taken by the early Popes and by these pilgrimages of piety and fun the infallible Vatican rendered acts of devotion sources of enjoyment ... and their flocks, wedded to festivals which suited themselves and their climate, will long prefer them to the dreary Sundays of our purer Protestantism, which has no machinery for canonizing whitebait.

Richard Ford, 'Handbook', 715.

[201] San Antonio de la Florida: the fiesta (13 June) in the mid-twentieth century (Nina Epton)
(The church of San Antonio de la Florida was built in 1797–98 by the Italian Francesco Fontana on the site of several previous hermitages or chapels. The dome is decorated by Goya. It was damaged in the Civil War.)

The fiesta is frequented by all classes of society, from sophisticated adolescents of the Serrano district to the gypsies of Altamira who come to tell fortunes and make a few pesetas. The staidest-looking, middle-aged Spaniard may, for all you know, be an inveterate fiesta-goer. I was surprised when a gentleman to whom I had been introduced by my Galician friend Ramón Piñeiro, a civil servant and bibliophile who looks like a Unamuno type, i.e. imbued with the tragic sense of life, offered to accompany me to San Antonio. 'It will bore you!' I objected. Ramón smiled.

'Don't you believe it. Enrique adores La Florida and he always makes his official visits to Madrid coincide with the date of the fiesta.'

'Nothing begins to happen until after midnight,' said Enrique, 'so we shall come to fetch you then.'

Strictly speaking – and unless you are very young and naive enough to wish to petition San Antonio for a sweetheart – nothing happens even after midnight except that half Madrid is to be found at La Florida, all the streets in the vicinity are blocked solid with honking traffic until the small hours of the morning and once you get there you spend most of the time dodging cars as you cross from the chapel to the fair stalls and back again or vainly endeavour to get the waiters in the overcrowded cafés to serve you.

The bridge over the Manzanares is black with people watching the couples dancing in the open-air cafés below. Students bring their instruments, there is a lot of noise, a lot of dust and *animación*. You are expected to dress in *manolo* style and here at least you will see *mantones de Manila*, flowers in the girls' hair and a faint echo of the gay scenes depicted on Goya's cupola across the road.

The mythical core, the *raison d'être* of the fiesta, is not to be found among the stalls and dancing couples; it is being enacted, very seriously, in the crowded chapel where an endless file of girls stream through the door with a lighted candle in one hand and a packet of pins in the other to ask the amiable saint to find them a *novio*.

Pins are the little magnets which, sanctified by holy water and accompanied by a fervent prayer to Saint Anthony, will not fail to bring a sweetheart. He may even be waiting outside the church door, for as the girls emerge they are confronted by a waiting throng of boys ready to make *piropos* [compliments] and invite the prettiest girls to dance.

First of all a candle is offered to the saint and stuck before his image. A priest stands in the centre of the brilliantly lit chapel and presents a relic to be kissed; at his side, a server rattles an offertory box. In the sacristy is a holy water font into which it is customary to throw the sweetheart-attracting pins. The font was already half full when we arrived. A plump girl at my side, who appeared to be in her late twenties and therefore in urgent need of a sweetheart, was performing the rite with the matter-of-fact conviction peculiar to women of the *pueblo*; she threw in her packet of pins and followed this by placing her hand in the holy water, palm downwards.

'What is that for?' I asked her. . . .

'If the pins stick to the palm of my hand, that means that I shall soon have a *novio*,' she replied simply. 'If they don't, I shall have to try again next year.' I watched, fascinated, while she breathed a prayer to Saint Anthony and waited a few seconds for the pins to stick to her hand. Several girls were waiting patiently behind her. The plump girl raised her hand – three pins were stuck to her palm. She blushed with pleasure, raised her skirt and attached the pins to the hem of her petticoat.

'And what is that for?' I persisted. . . .

'That,' said the plump girl, smiling broadly, 'is to make quite sure.' The gesture was obvious enough, I really did not need to ask.   *Epton, 64–65.*

[202] Corpus Christi: Gautier (1840)

We already knew Madrid, and we saw nothing new save the procession of Corpus Christi which has lost a lot of its ancient splendour because of the suppression of the convents and religious communities. Nevertheless the ceremony is not without solemnity. The path of the procession is powdered with fine sand, canvas stretched between one house and another makes the streets shady and cool; the balconies are bedecked and adorned with pretty women all dressed up; it is the most charming picture you can imagine. The perpetual play with fans, opening, closing, fluttering and beating the air like butterflies about to rest; the movements of women's elbows arranging themselves in their mantillas and correcting the shape of an unpleasing fold; the glances thrown at acquaintances from one crossing to another; the pretty movement of the head and the gracious gesture which accompanies the *agur* [greeting] with which the ladies reply to the gentlemen who salute them; the picturesque crowd intermingled with *Gallegos*, *Pasiegas*, Valencians, *Manolas* and water-sellers, all makes an animated and charmingly gay sight. The *Niños de la Cuna* (foundlings), dressed in their blue uniform, walk at the head of the procession. We saw, in this long procession of children, only a few with pretty faces, and Hymen himself, in all his conjugal carelessness, would be hard put to it to make uglier ones than those love-children. Then came the parish banners, the clergy, the silver reliquaries, and under a dais of black cloth, the Corpus Dei in a ray of diamonds of an insupportable brilliance . . .

One evening, as I was standing near the Hôtel de la Poste, at the corner of the Calle Carretas, I saw the crowd hastily moving aside and a pleiade of shimmering lights drew near the Calle Mayor: it was the holy sacrament which was on its way, in its carriage, to the bed of some moribund; since in Madrid God does not yet go on foot. This flight took place to avoid the necessity of kneeling.   *Gautier, 195 (1840)*

[203] Christmas: Quin (1822)

The Christmas festival is still observed in Madrid in the same manner that was practised a century ago. The evening of the vigil is scarcely dark when numbers of men, women, and boys are seen traversing the streets with torches, and many of them supplied with tambourines, which they strike loudly as they move along in a kind of Bacchanal procession. There is a tradition here, that the shepherds who visited Bethlehem on the day of the Nativity had instruments of this sort upon which they expressed the sentiment of joy that animated them, when they received the intelligence that a SAVIOUR was born. Hence for weeks before Christmas there is a fair in Madrid, where scarcely any thing but tambourines are sold, and every family, of the lower order at least, think it necessary to have one. If the younger branches do not issue into the streets with them, they use them in their houses: in some instances, aided by the guitar, they spend the whole night dancing to these tambourines, or to another instrument which they call a *zambomba**.

At twelve o'clock, the midnight mass is celebrated in all the churches. As soon as the clock strikes, the priests come forth vested from the sacristy, and repair to the altar, which is already lighted and prepared for the occasion. The organ peals forth a hymn of joy, and the mass is commenced. During the service several pieces of national music are performed, particularly that which is called the *Muñeira†*, which is a fine old

---

* The *zambomba* is a very noisy instrument. A skin of parchment, moistened, is tied on the mouth of an earthen vase; and to the centre of the parchment is fixed a reed, by the friction of which, when the parchment is dry, a sound like that of the tambourine, when rubbed by the finger, is produced. It can be heard still in Andalusia.

† Presumably the *Muñeira*, a popular dance of Galicia.

composition. But what is most remarkable in this ceremony is, that crowds of people, who perhaps had been traversing the streets the whole night, come into church with their tambourines and guitars, and accompany the organ.

Quin, 126–27 (1822).

[204] Beaumarchais' Christmas (1764)

The next night, in Madrid is the truest picture of a Roman Saturnalian feast; the amount consumed in sustenance, the uncontrolled licence reigning in the churches in the name of gladness, are incredible: there is one church belonging to the monks where they all dance in the choir with castanets; people make *paroli*, armed with cauldrons, whistles, balloons, clappers, and drums; cries, insults, singing, dangerous jumps, all are within the province of the feast; the uproar runs through the streets from church to church all night long, and gives itself over to all the excesses that can accompany such an orgy. In eight days, they have celebrated sung mass accompanied by this diabolical drone in a church right beside me, and all in honour of the birth of our Saviour, the best-behaved and quietest of men. *Beaumarchais, 'Correspondance' I, 128*

Bull-fights

[205] On the way to the bull-fight: Ford (1840s)
(Ford's *Handbook to Spain*, II, 674–75, has a lively
picture.)

The next afternoon all the world crowds to the Plaza de Toros.
You need not ask the way; just launch into the tide, which in
these Spanish affairs will assuredly carry you away. Nothing
can exceed the gaiety and sparkle of a Spanish public going,
eager and full-dressed, to the *fight*. They could not move faster
were they running away from a real one. All the streets or open
spaces near the outside of the arena present of themselves a
spectacle to the stranger, and genuine Spain is far better to be
seen and studied in the streets, than in the saloon. Now indeed
a traveller from Belgravia feels that he is out of town, in a new
world and no mistake; all around him is a perfect saturnalia, all
ranks are fused in one stream of living beings, one bloody
thought beats in every heart, one heart beats in ten thousand
bosoms; every other business is at an end, the lover leaves his
mistress unless she will go with him, – the doctor and lawyer

renounce patients, briefs, and fees; the city of sleepers is awakened, and all is life, noise, and movement, where tomorrow will be the stillness and silence of death; now the bending line of the *Calle de Alcalá*, which, on other days, is broad and dull as Portland Place, becomes the aorta of Madrid, and is scarcely wide enough for the increased circulation; now it is filled with a dense mass coloured as the rainbow, which winds along like a spotted snake to its prey. Oh the din and dust! The merry mob is everything and, like the Greek chorus, is always on the scene. How national and Spanish are the dresses of the lower classes – for their betters alone appear like Boulevard quizzes, or tigers cut out from our East End tailors' pattern-book of the last new fashion; what *Manolas*, what reds and yellows, what fringes and flounces, what swarms of picturesque vagabonds, cluster, or alas, clustered, around *calesas*, whose wild drivers run on foot, whipping, screaming, swearing; the type of these vehicles in form and colour was Neapolitan; they alas! are also soon destined to be sacrificed to civilization, to the 'bus and common-place cab, or vile fly.

The *plaza* is the focus of a fire, which blood alone can extinguish; what public meetings and dinners are to Britons, reviews and razzias to Gauls, mass or music to Italians, is this one and absorbing bull-fight to Spaniards of all ranks, sexes, ages, for their happiness is quite catching.

Ford, 'Gatherings', 296.

[206] Lady Holland's visit to the Madrid bull-ring (1803)

(Lady Holland vowed that she would never go to a bull-fight again after her first visit in Sevilla, but, in the event, she went often.)

Dined to-day [24 October 1803] at Freres' to enable the servants to see the bull feast, and to which I also went, it being probably the last I can ever see, as it closes the season of those *fiestas*. The *plaza* is of wood and compared to those of Valencia, Granada, Cádiz, Seville, &c., is very shabby. After fighting three bulls in the usual manner, the 4th was to be killed in a new way. A man on his knees was placed opposite the gate through which the animal was to enter; he held a thick pole, at the end of which a broad spear was affixed. The intention was that the animal should rush upon it and kill himself; this he did not do, however, he only threw the man over. The *bander-illeros** fought him with their *capas*** without the *picadores*†. For the last three bulls, the arena was divided by a high fence of wooden paling, which enabled them to regale the public with two *fiestas* or *corridas* at once; those animals were very furious, several horses were killed, and the *picadores* thrown. The only extra accident was the tossing of a poor fellow, whose eagerness carried him into the arena to see the bull come forth, who, instead of attacking the *picador*, attacked and threw him over his horns with the utmost violence. Such, however, is the indifference about a victim in so *great* a cause, that as yet I cannot ascertain how much he has been hurt. The only merit in my eyes of this representation is the eagerness of the people, who can neither contain their delight nor displeasure when the *matador* makes a bad stroke and the bull vomits blood; they cry '*Pícaro quiere hacer de caballero,*' alluding to the phrase that a high-born noble throws his noble blood in your face – '*il vous crache sa noblesse à la figure.*' An expert *matador* only inflicts one wound, but that is mortal. The *matadores* are the *toreros*†† admired by the ladies; the Dsses. of Osuna‡ and Alba‡‡ formerly were the rivals for Pedro Romero§. This evening when Rocca§§ fought, the Marquesa Santiago¶ withdrew to the back of her *balcone* [sic] not to see him in danger. The Santa Cruz¶¶ is suspected of beginning to follow her

* Those who place darts in the bull's side.
** Capes.
† Those who lance the bulls from horseback.
†† A *torero* is simply a man who fights bulls.
‡ See No. 226.
‡‡ See No. 99.
§ Pedro Romero (1754–1839), the most famous bull-fighter of his day, painted by Goya.
§§ Rocca, rival to Romero.
¶ The Marquesa de Santiago, though then middle-aged, had a wild reputation when younger.
¶¶ Joaquina, Marquesa de Santa Cruz (1784–1851). The prettiest woman in Madrid at that time. She was daughter of the Osunas.

mother in her tastes, as she goes in the *gradas*, where the
aficionados*, sit within reach of the *toreros*!!!

Ilchester, *107 (1803)*.

[207] Prosper Mérimée's description (1830)

(Mérimée was in Spain in 1830 and wrote his impressions
in *Mosaïque* (1833). They were very successful and
influential in Paris. His *Carmen*, based on a story which he
had heard on his journey in Andalusia, appeared in 1847.)

The evening before a bullfight is already a fiesta. The bulls are
only led into the ring stable (*encierro*) during the night to avoid
accidents; and, the evening before the day fixed for the combat
they are grazed in a pasture a little way from Madrid (*el
arroyo*). It provides an excuse to go and see the bulls, which
often come from very far. A large number of carriages, riders
and pedestrians go to the *arroyo*. Many young people wear the
elegant costume of the Andalusian *majo* on this occasion, and
display a magnificence and luxury which our ordinary clothes
do not allow. Moreover, this walk is not without danger: the
bulls are roaming free, their herdsmen cannot easily make them
obey them, it is up to the sightseer to avoid the horns' blows . . .
  The bull-ring at Madrid can hold about seven thousand
spectators, who go in and out with no confusion by a large
number of gates. You sit down on benches of wood or stone; a
few boxes contain chairs. His Catholic Majesty's is the only
one that is fairly elegantly decorated.
  The arena is surrounded by a strong palisade, about five and
a half feet in height. Two feet from the ground all around and
on both sides of the palisade, extends a wooden ledge, a sort of
causeway which helps the pursued toreador to jump the more
easily over the barrier, and is moreover protected by a double
rope fastened by strong stakes. It is a fairly recent precaution. A
bull had not only jumped the barrier, which happens often, but
had even flung himself on the tiers, where he had killed or
maimed dozens of sightseers. The tight rope is thought to
prevent the recurrence of a similar accident.

* Enthusiasts.

Four doors open on to the arena. One communicates with the bulls' stable (*toril*); another leads to the butcher (*matadero*), where the bulls are flayed and dissected. The two others are for the human actors in this tragedy . . .

The bull-ring looks very animated. The arena, well before the combat, is full of people, and the tiers and boxes provide a confused mass of heads. There are two kinds of seats: the ones in the shade are most expensive and the most comfortable, but the sunny side is always provided with intrepid amateurs. You see many fewer women than men and most of them are of the *manola* class (grisettes). However, in the boxes you can observe some elegant outfits, though few young women. The Spaniards have recently been perverted by French and English novels, and have removed their respect for their ancient costume. I do not think that ecclesiastics are forbidden to attend these spectacles: however I never saw but one in costume (at Sevilla). I have been told that several go there in disguise.

At a signal given by the president of the fight, an *alguacil mayor*, accompanied by two *alguaciles* in short cloaks, all three on horseback, and followed by a company of cavalry, evacuate the arena and the narrow corridor which separates it from the tiers. When they and their retinue have returned, a herald, escorted by a lawyer and more *alguaciles* on foot, comes to the centre of the ring to read out a ban which forbids anyone to throw anything into the arena, or to disturb the combatants with cries or signals, etc. Hardly has he appeared when, in spite of the respectable formula: 'In the house of the King, our lord, whom God preserve', whooping and whistling arises on all sides, and lasts the whole time of the reading of the rules, which in any case are never observed. In the ring, and only there, the people command the sovereign, and can say and do just as they please . . .

One of the mounted *alguaciles* receives a key in his hat, which is thrown to him by the president of the games. This key opens nothing; but nevertheless he takes it to the man responsible for opening the *toril*, and makes off straightaway at full gallop, accompanied by hoots from the multitude, who shout that the bull is already loose and behind him. This witticism is repeated at every fight.

Meanwhile the picadors have taken up their positions. Normally there are two mounted ones in the arena; two or three others stay outside, ready to replace them in case of accidents such as death, severe fracture, etc. A dozen *chulos* on foot are scattered about the place, for the purpose of mutual aid.

The bull, preferably expressly provoked while in his cage, rushes furiously out. Usually he reaches the middle of the plaza, in one dash, and there stops, astonished by the noise he hears and by the spectators all round him. On his neck he carries a little knot of ribbons attached by a little hook stuck in the flesh. The colour of these ribbons shows what herd (*vacada*) he is from; but a skilled amateur can tell at a single sight of the animal, what province and what race he is from.

The *chulos* draw the bull towards one of the picadors. If the beast is brave he attacks them unhesitatingly. The picador, his horse well gathered, places himself, his lance under his arm, exactly opposite the bull; he seizes the moment when he lowers his head, ready to charge with his horns, to give him a blow from his lance on the neck, and *not elsewhere*; he puts the whole force of his body behind the blow, and at the same time he makes his horse make off to the left, in such a way as to leave the bull to the right. If all these movements are properly exercised, if the picador is strong and his horse easy to handle, the bull, carried on by his own impetus, rushes by without touching him. Then the *chulos'* duty is to occupy the bull, so as to allow the picador time to make off; but often the animal recognizes only too well who has wounded him: he turns sharply, overtakes the horse, digs his horns into his stomach, and topples his rider. He is immediately aided by the *chulos*; some help him to get up, others turn the bull on to themselves by throwing their capes at his head, and escape him by reaching the barrier at a run, which they scale with amazing nimbleness. Spanish bulls run as fast as a horse; and, if the *chulo* were very far away from the barrier, he would escape with difficulty. Besides it is unusual for the riders, whose lives depend on the skill of the *chulos*, to venture into the middle of the arena; when they do so, it is seen as an extraordinarily daring feat.

Once back on his feet, the picador immediately remounts his horse, if he can also rise. It matters little if the poor beast is losing streams of blood, that his entrails trail along the ground and twine around his legs; as long as a horse can walk he is obliged to face the bull. If he remains defeated, the picador leaves the arena, and returns straightaway on a fresh mount.

I have said that the blow from the lance is only able to give the bull a slight wound, and its only effect is to irritate him. Meanwhile the shocks from the horse and the rider, the movement he puts into it, above all the reaction he feels in stopping suddenly on his haunches, tires him fairly quickly. Also the pain of the blows from the lance often discourages him, and then he does not dare to attack the horses again, or, to use the tauromachic jargon, he refuses to *go in*. However, if he is strong, he has already killed four or five horses. Then the picadors take a rest and the signal is given to implant the *banderillas*.

These are sticks of about two and a half feet, wrapped in cut paper, and ending in a sharp point, barbed so that it stays in the wound. The *chulos* hold one of these javelins in each hand. The best manner of using them is to advance quietly behind the bull, then to suddenly excite him by noisily knocking the *banderillas* one against the other. The bull turns round in astonishment, and unhesitatingly charges his enemy. At the moment he is practically touching him, and when he lowers his head to charge, the *chulo* pushes the two *banderillas* into him, both together, one on each side of his neck, something he can only do by holding himself for an instant close up to and directly in front of the bull and practically between his horns; then he stands aside, lets him pass him, and reaches the barrier to be in safety. One distraction, one hesitating or fearful movement, would be enough for him to be lost. Nevertheless, the connoisseurs consider the function of the *banderillero* the least dangerous of all. If by bad luck he falls while planting the *banderillas*, he must not try to get up; he stays immobile where he has fallen. The bull very rarely hits the ground, not at all from generosity but because he closes his eyes when he charges and passes over the man without seeing him. But sometimes he stops, smells him as if to be certain he is really dead; then drawing back a few paces, he lowers his head to lift him up on his horns; but then the *banderillero*'s comrades surround him and occupy him so well that he is forced to abandon the would-be corpse.

When the bull has been cowardly, that is to say when he has

not received four blows from the lance bravely, which is the required number, the spectators and sovereign judges condemn him by acclamation to a sort of torture which is at the same time a punishment and a means of reviving his anger. From all sides arises a cry of *¡fuego! ¡fuego!* (fire! fire!). So, instead of their usual arms, the *chulos* are handed *banderillas* of which the sleeves are surrounded with fireworks. The point is garnished with a piece of lighted tinder. As soon as it enters the skin, the tinder is thrown back on to the wicks of the fuses; they catch fire, and the flames, which are directed towards the bull, burn him to the quick and makes him jump and bound which amuses the public enormously. In fact it is an admirable spectacle to see this enormous animal frothing with rage, shaking the burning *banderillas* and becoming excited in the midst of the fire and smoke. Despite the poets, of all the animals which I have observed none has less expression in its eyes than the bull. One should say, changes expression the least; since his is almost invariably that of brutal and savage stupidity. Rarely does he express his pain in groans: the wounds irritate or frighten him; but never, if you will allow me the expression, does he have an air of reflecting on his fate; never does he weep like the deer. Thus he inspires no pity till he has displayed his courage.

When the bull is carrying on his neck three or four pairs of *banderillas*, it is time to finish him off. A roll of drums is heard; immediately one of the *chulos* designated in advance, who is the matador, leaves the group of his comrades. Richly dressed, covered in gold and silk, he holds a long sword and carries a scarlet cape, attached to a baton, so that it can be more easily handled. It is called the *muleta*. He advances under the president's box and with a deep bow asks permission to kill the bull. It is a formality that normally only takes place once during the whole fight. The president, of course, nods in the affirmative. Then the matador shouts 'viva', makes a pirouette, throws his hat on the ground and goes back to meet the bull.

There are rules in these corridas just as there are in duels; people who infringe them would be thought as infamous as someone who treacherously killed his opponent. For example, the matador may only strike the bull in the area where the neck joins the back, which the Spaniards call the *cross*. The blow must come downwards from above, as they say *en seconde*; never from below. It would be a thousand times better to die than to strike the bull from below, from the side or from behind. The sword used by the matador is long, strong, and has a cutting edge both sides; the hilt, which is very short, ends in a ball which you lean on with the palm of the hand. You have to be well accustomed to it and have a special skill to use this weapon properly.

To kill a bull well, you have to understand its character very well. Not only his glory but the very life of the matador depends on this knowledge. As you can imagine, there are as many different characters among bulls as among men; yet they can be divided into two clean-cut groups; the *light* and the *dark*. Here I am using the language of the ring. The light ones attack unhesitatingly; the dark ones, on the contrary, are cunning and try to get their man treacherously. These latter are extremely dangerous.

Before trying to strike a bull with a sword, the matador shows him the *muleta*, excites him, and watches closely to see if he rushes straight at it as soon as he sees it, or if he approaches quietly to gain space, and does not charge his adversary until the moment when he would be too near to avoid the shock. You often see a bull menacingly shake its head, paw the ground without wanting to advance, or even retreat a few paces, trying to draw the man to the centre of the arena, where he could not escape him. Others, instead of attacking in a straight line, draw near in an oblique way, gently and pretending to be tired; but as soon as they have judged their distance, they are off like an arrow . . .

After several passes, when the matador feels he has got to know his antagonist well, he makes ready to give him the final blow. Standing firm, he places himself directly in front of him, immobile, at a suitable distance. The right arm, armed with the sword, is doubled back at head height; the left, stretched forward, holds the muleta which, dragged a little on the ground, incites the bull to lower his head. It is in that moment that the matador gives him the mortal blow, with all the strength of his arm, aided by the weight of his body and by the bull's own impetus. The sword, three feet long, often goes right in up to the hilt, and if the thrust is well judged, the man has nothing to fear: the bull stops suddenly; his blood hardly flows; he raises his head; his legs tremble, and suddenly he falls in a heavy mass. At once deafening *vivas* ring out from all the tiers; handkerchiefs are waved; the *majos'* hats fly in the arena, and the conquering hero modestly blows kisses to all sides.

They say that, in the past, he never gave more than a stab wound; but everything degenerates, and now it is rare for a bull to fall at the first blow. However if he appears mortally wounded, the matador does not redouble his efforts; helped by the *chulos* he makes him turn in a circle while exciting him with the capes so as to daze him quickly. As soon as he falls, a *chulo* finishes him off with a dagger-blow well planted in the neck; the animal immediately expires.

It has been noticed that nearly all bulls have a place in the ring to which they always return. It is called the *querencia*. Usually it is the door by which they entered the arena.

You often see the bull, with the fatal sword stuck in him of which only the hilt is visible in his shoulder, walk across the arena with slow steps, scorning the *chulos* and the drapery which they pursue him with. He thinks only of dying comfortably. He seeks out his special place, kneels, lies down, extends his head and dies quietly, unless a stab of the dagger hastens his end.

If the bull refuses to attack, the matador runs towards him, and always at the moment that the animal lowers his head, pierces him with his sword (*estocada de volapié*); but, if he does not lower his head, or if he continues to run away, crueller means have to be used in order to kill him. A man armed with a long pole ending in a crescent shape (*media luna*), treacherously cuts his hamstrings from the rear and, as soon as he is beaten, he is finished off with the stroke of a dagger. It is the only episode in these combats universally disliked. It is a kind of assassination. Luckily it is rare to have to be reduced to that to kill a bull.

Fanfares announce his death. At once three mules in harness enter the ring at a smart trot; a knot of ropes is attached to the bull's horns, a hook is fastened and the mules drag him off at the gallop. In two minutes the dead bodies of the horses and of the bull have disappeared from the arena.

Each battle lasts about twenty minutes, and, normally, eight bulls are killed in an afternoon. If it has been a mediocre entertainment, the president of the corrida allows, by public demand, one or two extra combats.

You can see that the bull-fighter's trade is fairly dangerous. Two or three in the whole of Spain die in an average year. Few of them reach an advanced age. If they do not die in the ring, they are obliged to give it up early because of their wounds. The famous Pepe Illo* received twenty-six horn wounds in his life; the last killed him. The fairly high salary these people receive is not the only motivation which makes them embrace this dangerous sport. It is the glory and the applause which makes them brave death. It is so good to triumph in front of five or six thousand people! Moreover it is not unknown to see well-born amateurs sharing the dangers and the glory of the professional *toreros*. At Sevilla I have seen a marquis and a count filling the place of picadors in a public *corrida*.

It is true that the public hardly ever show themselves indulgent towards the *toreros*. The least sign of fear is punished by jeers and catcalls. The most atrocious insults rain down from all sides; sometimes, indeed, an *alguazil* by command of the people, and it is the most terrible sign of their indignation, approaches the toreador and instructs him, under pain of prison, to attack the bull as soon as possible.

Mérimée, 'Mosaïque', 269–86.

---

* Pepe-Illo, or Pepe-Hillo, nickname of José Delgado y Gálvez (1754–1801), a great bull-fighter from Seville, darling of the Madrid crowd, killed by the bull Barbudo in his favourite ring in Madrid, 1801.

Theatres

[208] A play in the Alcázar: Sir Richard Wynn
(1623)
(The first public theatres of Madrid began in the open in
corrales (yards) in the quarter near the Plaza Mayor in the
1560s. But there were also theatrical representations in the
royal palaces.)

Within two days after we saw a play acted before the King*
and Queen† in an indifferent fair room, where there was hung
up a cloth of state, and under it five chairs. There was a square
railed in, with a bench, which was all round about covered
with Turkey carpets, which to the stage side covered the
ground two yards from the forms. The company that came
to see the comedy were few besides the English, although there
were no difficulty in getting in; but the reason was, as I
conceived, because there are none admitted to sit – no, not

* Philip IV.
† Isabella of Bourbon.

the grandees, who may stand by covered between the forms and the walls. The players themselves consist of men and women: the men are indifferent actors, but the women are very good, and become themselves far better than any that ever I saw act those parts, and far handsomer than any women I saw. To say the truth, they are the only cause their plays are so much frequented.   *D'Ewes II, 447 (1623).*

[209] The two theatres of Madrid in the 1650s (Brunel, 1665)

Here we have two theatres* which are acted in every night. The comedians only take about one and half sols per person for themselves: you give as much again for the hospital, and later, to climb up to the seats, you give two sols which are for the town which owns the theatres: it costs seven French sols to sit down, so that, for the whole comedy it costs you about fifteen or sixteen sols. As to the construction and the subjects touched upon, I cannot tell anything for certain, since my knowledge of the language is not yet so far advanced that I can understand poetry which is always the most decorated manner of talking. The performance is practically worthless since, except for a few people who succeed, all the others have neither the manner nor the genius of real comedians. They do not play by torchlight, but in daylight which prevents their scenes from having any brilliance. The clothes of the men are neither rich nor suitable to the subject. A Greek or Roman scene is represented in Spanish costume. All those I have seen are composed in only three acts which are called *Jornadas*. They begin with some musical prologue, but the singing is so bad that their harmony sounds like the cries of little children. In the intervals, there is a little farce, a little ballet, or some special plot which is often the most entertaining of the whole thing. In any case people are so taken with this divertisement that there is hardly ever any

---

* These were the *corrales* de la Cruz and del Príncipe. Both began as open yards, later received covers and were rebuilt. The Teatro de la Cruz, newly designed by Pedro Ribera in 1737, was removed in 1860 to make way for the Calle Espoz y Mina; the Príncipe was on the site of the present Teatro Español, in the Plaza de Santa Ana.

room. The best places are always taken in advance, and it is a
sign of the excessive laziness of this country, since even in Paris,
where there is no theatre every day, you never see such
eagerness.   *Brunel, 142–143.*

[210] An *auto sacramental* (1762)

(An *auto* was a one-act play performed at Corpus Christi,
originally on the theme of the Eucharist but later
degenerating into farce.)

Not many years ago, in one of our theatres, the Pope and the
sacred college were ridiculed when, on hearing a *chacona* [an
old Spanish dance] played and sung, they one and all lost their
grave bearing and began to dance with great abandon . . . The
most tender and devout words produce laughter and jeering
when spoken by some actress whose conduct is well known by
the spectators to be diametrically opposed to what she is saying
. . . The same is true of the actors. To see, as I have seen, a man,
who, in the interlude, was dressed as a ragged ruffian smoking
a cigar, become, in the *auto*, one of the Holy Trinity, is just as
offensive to reason and nature as to see an actor who takes the
rôles of the Eternal Father in the *auto* called *Los alimentos del
hombre* transformed later, for the *sainete*, into a gate-keeper
stationed at one of the city entrances where goods are examined, making indecent remarks to a girl, who, in the *auto*, had
taken the part of an angel . . . In *Tres prodigios del mundo* we
had already seen an Elijah with an abundant beard, dressed in
rags and *wearing red slippers adorned with gold braid*, but to
see Christ with a powdered pigeon-winged wig (*ala de pichón*)
and a cravat, that indeed was reserved to crown the deformities
of the *autos*! . . . I believe the following incident happened at a
performance in the Corral del Príncipe: After a certain actor, in
the part of the devil, had recited a passage to the liking of the
people, one of the *mosqueteros* shouted, '¡*Viva el demonio!*'
Immediately a number of spectators, taking the remark literally, began to clamour '¡*A la Inquisición, a la Inquisición!*'
                    José de Clavijo, 'El Pensador', 1762, qu. Kany 318.

[211] The Spanish theatre seen by an Englishman (E. Clarke, 1762)

When I went first to the Spanish comedy, it was the season for acting the *Autos*, that is to say, plays in support of the Catholic faith; for *Auto de Fe* is in their language *an act of faith*. I found at my first entrance a good theatre, as to size and shape, but rather dirty, and ill-lighted; and, what made it worse was an equal mixture of day-light and candles. The *prompter's* head appeared thro' a little trap-door above the level of the stage, and I first took him for a ghost, or devil, just ready to ascend to these upper regions: But I was soon undeceived, when he began to read the play loud enough for the actors and the boxes too, who were near him. The *pit* was an odd sight, and made a motley, comical appearance; many standing in their night-caps and cloaks; officers and soldiers interspersed among the dirtiest mob, seemed rather strange. That which answered to our *two shilling gallery*, was filled with women only, all in the same uniform, a dark petticoat, and a white woollen veil. The side and front-boxes were occupied by people well dressed, and some of the first fashion.

When the play began, the actors appeared much better attired, that is, in richer clothes, than those in England; and these they change perpetually, in order to let you see the expensive variety of their wardrobe. After some scenes had passed, which were tedious and insipid, there came on an interlude of humour and drollery, designed, I suppose, for the entertainment of the pit. One of these comedians appeared tempting, with a bag of money, a lady who sung to him very prettily, and did not seem altogether averse to grant him some favours: in the meanwhile to my great surprise a man brought in three barber's blocks upon the stage: after these three said barber's blocks were placed upon the stage, the same man returned and dressed them first in *mens' clothes*, and undressed them again, and then dressed them once more in *women's clothes* . . .

However, I should not forget to tell you, that when these block ladies were properly attired, there came in three men, who had a fancy to tempt these three ladies likewise; but they were inflexibly coy, and I think it was not long before their gallants discovered the mistake. But to quit this interlude, and return to the play again: In process of time, and after some scenes had passed, which were long, tiresome, uninteresting, and full of sustain and bombast; the grand scene approached; an actor, dressed in a long purple robe, appeared in the character of JESUS CHRIST, or the *Nuestro Señor*, as they call him; immediately he was blind-folded, buffeted, spat upon, bound, scourged, crowned with thorns, and compelled to bear his cross, when he knelt down and cried, *¡Padre mío! ¡Padre mío!* 'My Father! my Father! why hast thou forsaken me?' After this he placed himself against the wall, with his hands extended, as if on the cross, and there imitated the expiring conclusion of this awful and solemn scene . . . Really, one every way suitable to the dignity and seriousness of the occasion: one of the actresses immediately unbound Christ, divested him of his crown and scarlet robes; and when he had put on his wig and coat again, he immediately joined the rest of the actors, and danced a *seguidilla*.

Spectatum admissi, risum teneatis, amici?

As to the *seguidilla*, or dance, it is little better upon the Spanish stage, than gently walking round one another; tho' when danced in its true spirit, in private houses, it much resembles the *English Hay*. After this one of the actresses, in a very long speech, explained the nature, end, and design of the *sacraments*; you must know also, that the Spaniards admit a great number of soliloquies, full of tiresome, and uninteresting declamation, into their plays. In the last scene, Christ appeared in a ship triumphant; and thus the play concluded. I forgot to tell you, that Christ, before his passion, preached to the four quarters of the world, in their proper dresses, upon the stage: *Europe* and *America* heard him gladly, and received the faith; but Asia and Africa remained incorrigible.

Some time after I had seen this *Auto* (for, to say the truth, my curiosity was a little abated with regard to the Spanish stage, from this specimen of it) I went to see a regular comedy; there were two English gentlemen in the box with me at the same time. We understood very little of the design of the first act; we saw a king, queen, an enchantress, and many other pretty, delightful sights: but the *interlude*, with which that act concluded, is, I think, not to be equalled either by ROME or GREECE; neither FARQUHAR, CIBBER, or any of our lowest farce-writers, have ever produced any thing comparable to it. The scene was intended for the inside of a Spanish *posada* (or *inn*) in the night; there were three feather-beds, and as many blankets brought upon the stage; the queen and her maids of honour personated the mistress of the *posada* and her maids; and accordingly fell to making the beds. After this, there came in six men to lie there, who paid three quarts a piece; one of them being a miser, had rolled up his money in twenty or thirty pieces of paper. Then they undressed before the ladies, by pulling off six or seven pairs of breeches, and as many coats and waistcoats, and got into bed two by two: When behold, the jest was, to see them all kick the clothes off one another, and then fight, as the spectator is to suppose, in the dark. The absurdity of this scene, and the incomprehensible ridiculous-ness of it, made us laugh immoderately. The sight of feather-beds, the men kicking and sprawling, the peals of applause, that echoed through the house, were truly inconceivable; tho', I believe, our neighbours in the next box thought we laughed at the wit and humour of the author. It was a scene that beggars all possible description, and I defy any theatre in EUROPE, but that of MADRID, to produce such another . . .

This, I hope, will serve at present for a short sketch of the *Spanish Stage*. Indeed, I had almost forgot to tell you, that TERESA, one of the actresses, was this winter imprisoned by the King's order, for being too free of her charms to some of the grandees*; it was said she would be condemned to the work-house for life. However that be, she remains in prison still, and, as far as I can learn, is like to remain so for some time longer.

E. Clarke, 102–107.

[212] Beaumarchais' description to the Duc de la Vallière† (24 December 1764)

The Spanish entertainments are two centuries at least behind ours, both for propriety and for acting; they can compare very

---

* The grandee was apparently the Duque de Osuna.
† Louis César La Baume Le Blanc, Duc de la Vallière (1708–1780), great-nephew of the famous Louise de la Vallière.

well with those of Hardy* and his contemporaries; the music, on the other hand, can be placed immediately after the beautiful Italian [music] and before ours. The warmth, the gaiety of the interludes, all with music with which they cut the boring acts of their insipid dramas, often compensate for the boredom one has endured listening to them. They are called *tonadillas* or *sainetes*. Dancing is absolutely unknown here; I speak of figure dances, since I cannot honour with this name the grotesque and often indecent movements of the Grenadine and Moorish dances which are the delight of the people. *Loménie, 154.*

[213] A masked ball in the Caños del Peral (Casanova, 1767)

(This theatre, approximately on the site of the modern opera house, was so called because there was once a font or conduit in a pear-grove there.)

The masked ball [in the Caños del Peral] quite captivated me. The first time I went to see what it was like and it only cost me a doubloon (about eleven francs), but ever after it cost me four doubloons, for the following reason:

An elderly gentleman, who sat next me at supper, guessed I was a foreigner by my difficulty in making myself understood by the waiter, and asked me where I had left my lady friend.

'I have not got one; I came by myself to enjoy this delightful and excellently-managed entertainment.'

'Yes, but you ought to come with a companion; then you could dance. At present you cannot do so, as every lady has her partner, who will not allow her to dance with anyone else.'

'Then I must be content not to dance, for, being a stranger, I do not know any lady whom I can ask to come with me.'

'As a stranger you would have much less difficulty in securing a partner than a citizen of Madrid. Under the new fashion, introduced by the Conde de Aranda†, the masked ball

---

* Alexandre Hardy (1560–1631), a French facile playwright in the style of Lope de Vega.
† Pedro Pablo Abarca de Bolea, Conde de Aranda (1719–1798), First Minister of Spain 1766–1773. He expelled the Jesuits, despised lawyers and sympathized with the Revolution in France.

has become the rage of all the women in the capital. You see there are about two hundred of them on the floor tonight; well, I think there are at least four thousand girls in Madrid who are sighing for someone to take them to the ball, for, as you may know, no woman is allowed to come by herself. You would only have to go to any respectable people, give your name and address, and ask to have the pleasure of taking their daughter to the ball. You would have to send her a domino, mask, and gloves; and you would take her and bring her back in your carriage.'

'And if the father and mother refused?'

'Then you would make your bow and go, leaving them to repent of their folly, for the girl would sigh, and weep, and moan, bewail parental tyranny, call Heaven to witness the innocency of going to a ball, and finally go into convulsions.'

This oration, which was uttered in the most persuasive style, made me quite gay, for I scented an intrigue from afar. I thanked the masked man (who spoke Italian very well) and promised to follow his advice and to let him know the results.

'I shall be delighted to hear of your success, and you will find me in the box, where I shall be glad if you will follow me now, to be introduced to the lady who is my constant companion.'

I was astonished at so much politeness, and told him my name and followed him. He took me into a box where there were two ladies and an elderly man. They were talking about the ball, so I put in a remark or two on the same topic, which seemed to meet with approval. One of the two ladies, who retained some traces of her former beauty, asked me, in excellent French, what circles I moved in.

'I have only been a short time in Madrid, and not having been presented at Court I really know no one.'

'Really! I quite pity you. Come and see me, you will be welcome. My name is Pichona, and anybody will tell you where I live.'

'I shall be delighted to pay my respects to you, madam.'

What I liked best about the spectacle was a wonderful and fantastic dance which was struck up at midnight. It was the famous *fandango*, of which I had often heard, but of which I had absolutely no idea. I had seen it danced on the stage in France and Italy, but the actors were careful not to use those voluptuous gestures which make it the most seductive in the world. It cannot be described. Each couple only dances three steps, but the gestures and the attitudes are the most lascivious imaginable. Everything is represented, from the desire to the final ecstasy; it is a very history of love. I could not conceive a woman refusing her partner anything after this dance, for it seemed made to stir up the senses. I was so excited at this Bacchanalian spectacle that I burst out into cries of delight. The masker who had taken me to his box told me that I should see the *fandango* danced by the Gitanas with good partners.

'But,' I remarked, 'does not the Inquisition object to this dance?'

Madame Pichona told me that it was absolutely forbidden, and would not be danced unless the Conde de Aranda had given permission. *Casanova, 78 (1767).*

[214] Lady Holland's visit to the Caños del Peral

[29 Nov, 1803] Went Wednesday, 23rd, for first *sortie* to see *Macbeth* in Spanish at Los Caños del Peral. It is whimsical that foreigners invariably object to Shakespeare's extravagances, and yet in their translations or imitations from him they out-Herod Herod and create absurdities and superfluous crimes to become sublime. For instance, in this tragedy, Lady Macbeth is represented with a son of six years old, who is introduced for no other purpose than that of enabling her to run upon the stage with bloody hands, fresh from murdering him in his bed. Mlle St Simon*, I took with me. Afterwards I went to the Comtesse D'Etty†, it was the first night of her opening her house, the company was treated with a game of blind man's buff. Mde Bourke††, by dint of extreme court, very fortunately for the society of foreigners, has brought many Spaniards into her society, and the Court wink at it at present, but how long this indulgence may be accorded unto them is doubtful. The next day the Duquesa de Osuna called upon me in the morning

---

* Daughter of the Duc de Saint-Simon, a grandson of the memorialist who was then in Spanish service.
† Wife of the Imperial Ambassador.
†† Wife of the Danish Ambassador.

to invite me to pass the evening at her house and to bring Charles*. It was a very splendid ball and supper; Charles was enchanted with her daughter, the Manuelita†, and her *futur* [*sic*], the young Duque de Berwick‡. I did not stay till 6 o'clock in the morning, otherwise I might have been her *fin de fiesta* Mass, which was said in the oratory of the Duquesa.

Ilchester, 119 (1803).

[215] Inglis at the Príncipe (1830)

The Teatro del Príncipe is miserably small for a metropolitan theatre: it will contain no more than 1500 persons; but it is light and pretty, painted in white and gold, and round the ceiling are the busts of the principal Spanish poets, dramatists and novelists, their names being inscribed under each. The six in front are no doubt intended to occupy the most honourable places: they are Calderón, Lope de Vega, Cervantes, Garcilaso, Ercilla, and Tirso. Calderón and Lope are placed in the front, where I think Cervantes ought to have been. The house was well filled; the ladies generally wore *mantillas*, but some were in full dress; and a few had ventured upon French hats. There is one peculiarity in the Spanish theatres, which seems at first sight, inconsistent with the state of society and manners. Excepting the private boxes, there is scarcely any place to which a lady and gentleman can go in company. In Madrid the only places of this description will not contain thirty persons; but, on the other hand, an ample provision is made for ladies. The greater part of the space occupied by the first tier of boxes in the English theatres, is thrown into one space, called the *cazuela*§; and here, ladies, and only ladies, have the right of entrée. The most respectable women go to the *cazuela*, and sit there unattended; nor is this arrangement unfavourable to intrigue. The entrée to the *cazuela* secures the entrée of the

---

* Charles Fox (1796–1873), Lady Holland's son by Lord Holland, born out of wedlock.
† María Manuelita, daughter of the Duque de Osuna, later, however, married the Duque de Abrantes.
‡ This Duque of Berwick also succeeded to the dukedom of Alba (1804).
§ Literally, stewpot.

whole house; and between the acts the *cazuela* is almost deserted, some having gone to visit persons in the boxes, but the greater number getting no farther than the lobby, where it is not unusual to meet a friend; and when the comedy ends, every lady finds an escort ready. It is a fact too, that if the *cazuela* be crowded during the first act, there is generally room enough during the second, and more than enough during the third. This needs no explanation.

I saw only one really beautiful countenance in the theatre; but there were some expressive faces, and inexpressibly fine eyes, almost worthy of a serenade. Here, the fan seemed a most indispensable companion; for besides its common uses, it exercised the powers of a critic, expressing approbation or dislike; and between the acts, it proved itself a powerful auxiliary to the language of the eyes . . .

The play being ended, the next part of the entertainment consisted in the Bolero. This is danced by two persons; the man, in the dress of an Andalusian peasant – for to Andalusia the dance properly belongs – with dark embroidered jacket, short white embroidered waistcoat, crimson sash, white tight small clothes, white stockings, and the hair in a black silk knot; his partner in a gaudy dress of red, embroidered with gold. These are nothing more than the usual holiday-dresses of the Andalusian peasantry. The dance itself, is a quick minuet; advancing, retiring, and turning; the feet all the time performing a step, and the hands occupied with the castanets. I had heard much of the indelicacy of the Bolero, but I could find nothing in it in the slightest degree indecorous.

Inglis, 104–06 (1831).

[216] De Amicis sees the Zarzuela (1869)

There is, too, a great rage for the *Zarzuela**, which is usually represented in the theatre to which it gives its name, and is a composition something between comedy and melodrama,

---

* A Zarzuela was originally a popular comedy with music. The hunting-seat so called, where the King now lives, was probably named from a Baile de Zarzuela of ancient origin. Very popular in the seventeenth century, the genre was revived in the nineteenth century.

between the opera and *Vaudeville*, with a pleasing alternation of prose and verse, of recitation and song, of the serious and comic; a composition exclusively Spanish in character and most entertaining. In other theatres they represent political comedies intermingled with song and prose in the style of Scalvini's review; satirical farces are the subjects of the day, – a species of *autos sacramentales*, with scenes from the passion of Jesus Christ, during Holy Week; and balls, silly dances, and pantomimes of every description. At the small theatres three or four representations are given during the evening, from one hour to another, and the spectators change at every representation. In the famous *Capellanes* theatre they dance every evening of the year a *can-can*, scandalous beyond the most obscene imagination, and there gather the fast young men and women, old libertines with wrinkled noses, armed with spectacles, eyeglasses, opera-glasses, and every kind of optical instrument which serve to bring nearer, as Aleardi would say, the forms advertised on the stage.   *De Amicis, 124 (1869)*.

[217] The Teatro Real at the height of the Regency (Baroja, c. 1897)

That night the Teatro [Real] ... played *Tannhäuser*. The luxurious decoration of the room, with warm red and gilded tones, shone with light. The great safety curtain was drawn down.

The public came to their places with more haste than usual. The stalls were almost full. At every instant the door of a box opened and there appeared standing there elegant women and men in full evening dress. The orchestra pit was being livened up by black-suited and white-shirted men and one could hear from time to time the notes of violin or cello being tested.

For the regular spectators the usual public was there, that which constituted society: the same ladies, the same uniforms, the same *fracs*, the same naked bosoms, the same faces.

In the boxes, white shoulders and bosoms, splendid dresses, jewels, muslin shawls. Diamonds shone, fans waved, bald pates shone like marble, opera glasses began to appear here and there. The half-Jewish, half-piscine countenances of Spanish aristocrats were to be seen in many elegant seats. The murmur of conversation was heard like a distant noise of storm.

In a very short space of time, the theatre became quite full.

At this moment there sounded the first measures of the Royal March*. The Queen† entered her box with her two daughters‡. It was not the royal box but an ordinary one. Most of the people in the lower part of the theatre stood up. There was some discreet applause and, then, silence in the gods! The Queen and her children smiled and waved, inclining their heads from right to left. The Queen was dressed in a violet dress, black coat with grey furs and pearls at her neck. Her two daughters, somewhat insignificant, wore simple little dresses, of schoolgirl-type, which appeared cheap, in pink. Their hair was combed back, with a very high bun (*moño*) and brilliant ribbons in the hair. One was blonde, and seemed like her mother. The other, a brunette, had a rather common face with dark complexion and sparkling eyes, black as jet, like a peasant.

In the box on the side there appeared the Infanta§, aunt of the child king, sister of his father, fat, heavy, herpetic, white hair, a Bourbon air and the rather cynical expression associated with that family. She was wearing a dress that was green like a parrot, and many diamonds, some of the size of large hazelnuts.

This good lady prepared to enjoy Wagner sleeping in the acts and chatting in the intervals.

At her side there was sitting an old lady, small, with an insinuating air and keen nose, with a dress the colour of a flea [*color de pulga*] and behind the chairs there remained standing up a stiff gentleman with white beard and aristocratic presence, and a tall, fair Infante, dressed as a cavalry officer, with a cross of one of the military orders on his uniform.

In the boxes *de gala* there shone the household staff of the palace, the courtiers with embroidered coats full of crosses and their ladies with red ribbons planted on their chests. One of

* The National Anthem was an eighteenth-century tune adapted as the Spanish Royal March in 1770. It has no words.
† Queen María Cristina, the Regent.
‡ The Infantas Mercedes and María Teresa.
§ Probably Isabel.

them was a lady with an important air, with a high diadem of precious stones, her nose hooked, solemn, eyes as if fallen on the outside ends, painted mouth and many jewels. The other was a *flamencota*, old and graceless but smiling, adequate to produce enthusiasm in the street among students and shop-assistants.

In one row of seats, there appeared a dark princess, Goya-esque in her appearance with black brilliant eyes, cheeks blushing, dressed in black silk, with very tight spangles, and big pearls.

The prince showed himself behind, tall, a man packed together in appearance, bald and with a great red beard. By the look of him he could have been a portrait of the Lombard school, but according to many people he had only the appear-ance of it.   *Baroja, 'Las Noches', 173–75.*

[218] Harold Acton sees 'La Cordobesita' in the 1920s
(Harold Acton (born 1904) wit, aesthete, man of letters, went to Madrid on a holiday from Oxford University.)

Night after night we went to a vaudeville theatre to see Dora, 'la Cordobesita', an incomparable dancer and *diseuse*. Her almond face was oiled instead of powdered, so that it shone with a moonlike lustre as she swayed her serpentine hips and stamped her heels to the castanets that whispered and hummed and shouted with every varying shade of emotion. More robust than the Parisian favourite Raquel Meller, she sang the same type of song ranging swiftly from smiling satire to murderous passion.

The visible sympathy of the audience was as exciting as the performance. They did not shout, for that would have stopped the magic but, when their enthusiasm overleaped itself, they gave forth a concerted sigh which had the effect of a roar: it was as if a lion could bellow *sotto voce*. This was also noticeable when Andrés Segovia played the guitar which he could convert into a harpsichord for Bach and Haydn and into a gitano voice for Albéniz* and Granados†. During the *seguidillas*, one feared

---

* Isaac Albéniz (1860–1909), Spanish composer and pianist, who cre-ated the modern Spanish school of music.
† Enrique Granados (1867–1916), pianist and romantic composer.

that the audience would have a mass apoplectic fit from their pent-up longing to cry out: *olé*. One was gripped and tossed in the air by their surges of applause. At most popular performances in Spain, I experienced this muffled thunderstorm.

'Memoirs of an Aesthete', London 1984, 143–144.

THE APPROACHES
TO MADRID

[219] Ramón y Cajal (c. 1900)

The surroundings of Madrid! It is not for me to show them now, vindicating once more both the much calumniated Manzanares, and the austere Castillian plain. It would call for someone with as biased a sense of colour as a caterpillar to be forever missing the damp and uniform green of the countries of the north, and to despise the penetrating poetry of the grey, the yellow, the dun-coloured and the blue. Nor is it correct that in the landscape of the Court of Madrid there is lacking the lively note of green. Far from being merely plains open to the winds or pieces of untilled land, the surroundings of Madrid – the Retiro, the Moncloa, the Casa de Campo, Amaniel, the Dehesa de la Villa, the Pardo, etc. – are the most leafy and picturesque parts of Spain. We live in the folds of a sierra, whose elegant profile embellishes our horizons and whose winds purify our atmosphere. And in the spring and autumn, the Castillian plain offers the picture of a lawn splashed with flowers. Nowhere else does the landscape offer such varied contrasts, according to seasons. Whatever may be the preoccupation of the spirit we always find there a solitary corner whose peaceful beauty soothes the shaking of grief and opens a new spring for thought. How many small discoveries are associated in my memory with that solitary path on the Moncloa, or with a riverside ash-tree next to the Manzanares, or some hill of Amaniel or the Dehesa de la Villa, splendid look-out places from which one can see so well the Guadarrama, visible among pine trees, in all their august majesty.

Ramón y Cajal, 142–43.

[220] The Manzanares: Tirso de Molina (c. 1610)

Título de venerable	Title of 'venerable'
merecéis, aunque pequeño	you deserve, even if you are small
pues no es bien viendos tan calvo	since you are not become so bald

que os perdamos el respeto.	that we must lose our respect for you.
Como Alcalá y Salamanca	Like Alcalá and Salamanca
tenéis, y no sois colegio,	you have, though you are not a college,
vacaciones en verano	holidays in summer
y curso sólo en invierno . . .	and your only course is in winter . . .
¿Qué es la causa, pues, mi río	So what is the cause, my river,
que tantos años sirviendo	that serving so many years
no os den siquiera un estado	you are not even given a settlement
que os pague en agua alimentos? . . .	which pays you alimony in water? . . .

Tirso de Molina, 'Romance del Maestro Tirso de Molina', qu. in Mesonero Romanos, 327.

[221] The Manzanares: the Marquise de Villars (1679)

I want to speak of a walk which I made yesterday, which is most fashionable when there is heat, and here there is much of it. It is along the much praised banks of the Manzanares. To be honest, the dust there is extremely trying. There are small trickles of water on one side and on the other – but not enough to water the frequent sandy stretches which rise under the feet of the horses – in such a way that this walk is not really supportable. It is not to tell you a bad joke but a really extraordinary truth . . . it is not possible to walk along the river because of the dust. But that is nothing. You might see the great and prodigious bridge that the King of Spain has made over this Manzanares [the Puente de Toledo]. It is not possible to mock the river. I thought that I could tell you this in five or six lines. But here you have much more.

Marquise de Villars, Letter to Mme de Coulanges (1679).

[222] The Manzanares: Charles Stanhope (1699)

TO THE EARL OF JERSEY*

Madrid, August 12, 1699.

His Catholic Majesty is well again, almost to a miracle; and, so far as I am able to judge by having seen him several nights lately in the river, has the very same looks I remember him in the time of his best health. Upon this unexpected recovery, the Queen and her party have resumed new courage and strength.

Paseo del Río. At that period it appears that the bed of the Manzanares, being dry in summer, was used as the fashionable promenade. Calderón says of the adjoining walk, La Florida, that it would be the most beautiful in the world if the river were not sometimes wanting the river!

Que para ser la florida	For this to be the flowered place,
Estación de todo el orbe	The most beautiful, rich and lovely spot
La más bella, hermosa y rica	In the whole world, only this river
Sólo al río falta el río.	Lacks the river.

But that, he adds, is an antiquated and long since exploded objection!

'*Mas ya es objeción antigua!*'

Alexander Stanhope, 184.

[223] The Manzanares: British officers bathe during the Peninsular War (1812)
(Bathing in this much maligned river continued till the twentieth century.)

The weather since we came to Madrid has been oppressively hot but every sort of refreshing drink is to be had iced and there are delightful baths on the river. These are formed by

* Edward Villiers, 1st Earl of Jersey (1656–1711), then Secretary of State for the Southern department.

digging in the river bed and built on every side with wood so it excludes all dirt, and the rain and the sun are kept out by mats laid over framework – the river is divided into regular streams, two for baths and the water constantly running and filtering itself through the sand is always clean – two streams on each side of the baths are for washing and here you may see all the washerwomen of Madrid at work, while they are protected from being wetted by wooden boxes which they sit in and from the heat of the air by canopies erected for the purpose.   *Aitchison, 189.*

[224] The Casa de Campo: two English impressions

a) The Prince of Wales, 1623

Not long since, the prince, understanding that the infanta was used to go some mornings to the *Casa de Campo*, a summer-house the king hath the other side of the river, to gather May-dew, he did rise betimes and went thither, taking your brother [Endymion Porter] with him; they were let into the house and into the garden, but the infanta was in the orchard, and there being a high partition wall between, and the door doubly bolted, the prince got on the top of the wall and sprung down a great height, and so made towards her: but she, spying him first of all the rest, gave a shriek and ran back. The old marquis that was then her guardian came towards the prince and fell on his knees, conjuring his highness to retire, in regard he hazarded his head if he admitted any into her company; so the door was opened, and he came out under that wall over which he had got in. I cannot say that the prince did ever talk with her privately, yet publicly often, my lord of Bristol being inter-preter; but the king always sat by to overhear all. Our cousin Archy* hath more privilege than any; for he often goes with his fool's coat where the infanta is with her *meninas* and ladies of honour, and keeps a blowing and blustering amongst them and blurts out what he lists.

Halliwell, qu. in 'The Letters of Kings of England', 215–16.

b) Lady Holland, 1803.

4th December, Madrid. [1803] – Went yesterday to see the Casa de Campo, a small hunting palace belonging to the King: it is not above half a mile from the town, on the opposite side of the Manzanares, across the bridge of Segovia. The house is small and insignificant; in the garden is a magnificent equestrian statue in bronze of Philip III, designed and begun by John de Bologna and finished on his death by Pedro Tacca, erected in 1616†. It is an admirable piece of workmanship, the defects are chiefly owing to the badness of the situation in which it is placed; the pedestal is too small and narrow, and the statue is so much larger in proportion than the house (close to which it is placed), that one might fancy a fly bite would impel him to leap over it, or like the good Alfonso in the *Castle of Otranto* the inhabitant of the castle had grown too big for it. In the garden there is also a beautiful white marble *jet d'eau*; the basin is richly sculptured and ornamented with the chains, & c., of the *Toison d'or* workmanship of the age of Charles V. There are some pictures mouldering on the chamber walls, chiefly bad portraits of the Austrian family. Some inexplicable allegories on human life by *Jérome Bosch*. The park is entered by a wall of two leagues in circumference; it contains an abundance of pheasants. Three large *estanques* abound in foreign ducks and geese. On an eminence is a small chapel built by the piety of Carlos III for the *gardes chasse*. The wood is very pretty, and the view of the palace in Madrid truly grand. On this side the town appears handsome, and does not betray the total nakedness and barrenness which disfigure its environs on every other side.

Ilchester, 120–21.

* 'Archy' was a celebrated court jester, and is mentioned by Ben Jonson as a 'sea monster' in allusion to this journey.

† This statue is now in the Plaza Mayor, since the 1840s. The Casa de Campo is now a splendid public park; the house and the immediate garden are dilapidated, though easily recognizable.

[225] The Pardo: Joseph Bonaparte's letter of resignation to his brother (1809)

(This palace in a large park to the north of Madrid has been used by many Spanish heads of state from Charles V to Franco. King Juan Carlos's house, La Zarzuela, is built in the park.)

Sire,

M de Urquijo* has communicated to me the legislative measures taken by Your Majesty.

I am covered with shame in front of my would-be subjects. I beg Your Majesty to accept my renunciation to all the rights which you gave me to the throne of Spain.

I will always prefer honour and integrity to power so dearly bought.

Despite events, I will always be your most affectionate brother, your most loving friend. I will become your subject

again and await your orders to go where it pleases Your Majesty that I should. *Balagny; 40.*

[226] The Alameda de Osuna: Lady Holland (1803)

Friday, 13th. [April 1803] – Went with Madame d'Osuna** to her country house, called the Alameda†; she conveyed us in an immense carriage, made to hold 12 persons. The party consisted of herself, M. de Peñafiel‡, 'Perico', P. Emanuel, M., M. de la Peña, Olmeda, an officer, and Manuelita§. The distance from Madrid is about a league and a quarter on the road to

---

* Minister of the Secretaryship of State of King Joseph.
** María Josefa Pimentel, 12th Condesa de Benavente (1752–1834), married Pedro Tellez Girón, 9th Duque de Osuna (1755–1807): 'The greatest lady of her time'.
† This charming park is now owned by the municipality of Madrid and open to the public.
‡ Francisco Girón, Marqués de Peñafiel, 10th Duque de Osuna (1785–1821), son of the Duquesa mentioned in 1.
§ 'Manuelita' was daughter of the Osunas.

Alcalá de Henares. It is a creation of her own, as she found 24 years ago the same sterility and nakedness which characterizes the environs of Madrid; it is now cheerful and woody. The garden is rather crowded with a profusion of difft. ornaments, some in the German sentimental taste, others in a tawdry, citizenlike style.

Gardens contrived for coolness, innumerable grottoes, temples, *chaumières*, hermitages, excavations, canal, ports, pleasure boats, islands, mounts, &c., &c *La Casa della vieja* [*sic*] is very pretty. The mansion is excellent and well fitted up. We had an agreeable day, altho' the weather was as unfavourable as rain and hail could render it. Returned by torch light at 9 . . .

Dsa de Osuna, heiress in her own right of the house of [Pimentel], Benavente, Quiñones, &c., &c., to the number of four or five *sombreros* alias *grandesses*, is the most distinguished woman in Madrid from her talents, worth, and taste. She has acquired a relish for French luxuries, without diminishing her national magnificence and hospitality. She is very lively, and her natural wit covers her total want of refinement and acquirement. Her figure is very light and airy. She was formerly the great rival of the celebrated Dss of Alba in profligacy and profusion. Her *cortejo*, Peña, has been attached for many years, and is now the only one established. She is rather imperious in her family. Her revenues are greater even than the D of Osuna's, who is a very tolerably sensible man and of considerable knowledge. *Ilchester, 143, 195.*

Bibliography

This list includes the books from which quotation is made, as well as one or two volumes of general value.

ABRANTÉS, *Mémoires de Madame la duchesse d'* . . ., Vols V and VIII, Paris, 1835

ACTON, HAROLD, *Memoirs of an Aesthete*, London, 1948

AGUEDA, MERCEDES (and XAVIER DE SALAS), *Cartas de Francisco Goya a Martín Zapater*, Madrid, 1982

AITCHISON, GENERAL SIR JOHN, *An ensign in the Peninsular War* (ed. by W.F.K. Thompson), London, 1981

ALEMÁN, MATEO, *The Rogue, or the Life of Guzmán de Alfarache* (tr. by James Mabbe 1623), New edition, New York, 1924

ALFONSO, *Memoria de Madrid, Selección y textos de Publio López Mondéjar*, Madrid, 1975

ÁLVAREZ DE COLMENAR, JUAN, *Les Délices de l'Espagne et Portugal*, 5 vols, Leyden, 1707

AMICIS, EDMONDO DE, *Spain and the Spaniards*, New York, 1885

AZAÑA, MANUEL, *Obras Completas*, ed. Juan Marichal, Vol IV, Mexico, 1968

BALAGNY, MAJOR, *Campagne de l'Empereur Napoléon en Espagne 1808–9*, 4 vols, Paris 1903

BAREA, ARTURO, *The Forging of a Rebel* (tr. by Ilse Barea), New York, 1946

BAROJA, PÍO, *Aurora Roja*, Madrid, 1910

—— *Desde la última vuelta del camino: Reportajes*, Madrid, 1948

—— *La Dama Errante*, Madrid, 1974

—— *Las Noches del Buen Retiro*, Madrid, 1940

BEAUMARCHAIS, PIERRE AUGUSTIN CARON DE, *Oeuvres Complètes*, Paris, 1805

BECKFORD, WILLIAM, *Memoirs*, 2 vols, London, 1859

BERTAUT, FRANÇOIS, *Journal du voyage d'Espagne*, Paris, 1669 (republished in *Revue Hispanique*, Vol 47, 1919)

BIGARRÉ, GÉNÉRAL, *Mémoires de . . .*, Paris, no date

BLANCO WHITE, JOSÉ, *Letters from Spain*, Madrid, 1822

BORGHESE see J. García Mercadal

BORROW, GEORGE, *The Bible in Spain* (with the notes and glossary of Ulick Ralph Burke), London, 1907

BOUFFLEUR, CHARLES, *Journal*, Manchester, 1812

BOURGOING, J.-FR DE, *Travels in Spain* (tr.) 3 vols, Paris, 1807

BROWN, JONATHAN (and ELLIOTT, J.H.) *A Palace for a King: the Buen Retiro & the Court of Philip IV*, New Haven & London, 1980

BRUNEL, ANTOINE DE, *Voyage en Espagne 1655*, in *Revue Hispanique*, Vol. 30, Paris, 1914

BUÑUEL, LUIS, *Mi último suspiro*, Barcelona, 1982

CARDOSO, ISAAC, *Las Excelencias de los Hebreos*, Amsterdam, 1674

CASANOVA DE SEINGAULT, JACQUES, *Memoirs of . . .*, Vol VI: *Spanish Passions* (complete tr. by Arthur Machen), London, 1960

CHAMPOLLION-FIGEAC, AIMÉ, *Collection de documents inédits sur l'Histoire de France, Prém. série: Histoire politique: Captivité du roi François*, Paris, 1847

CHUECA, FERNANDO, *Madrid: ciudad con vocación de capital*, Santiago de Compostela, 1974

CLARENDON, EARL OF, *The history of the Rebellion and Civil Wars in England*, Vol. 8, (ed. W.D. Macray), Oxford, 1888

CLARKE, E., *Letters Concerning the Spanish Nation*, London, 1763

CORTÉS CAVANILLAS, JULIÁN, *Alfonso XIII*, Madrid, 1956

COX, CYNTHIA, *The Real Figaro*, London, 1962

CRUZ, RAMÓN DE LA, *Sainetes*, 2 vols, Barcelona, 1882

CUSTINE, LE MARQUIS DE, *L'Espagne sous Ferdinand VII*, 4 vols, Brussels, 1838

DALÍ, SALVADOR, *My Secret Life* (tr. by Haakon Chevalier), New York, 1948

D'EWES, SIR SIMONDS, *Autobiography & Correspondence During the Reign of James I & Charles I* (ed. by J.O. Halliwell) 2 vols, London, 1845

DÍAZ PLAJA, FERNANDO, *La historia de España en sus documentos*, 4 vols, Madrid, 1954–58

DOBLADO, LEUCADIO see José Blanco White

DUMAS, ALEXANDRE, *Impressions de Voyage – De Paris à Cádiz*, 2 vols, Paris, 1861

ELLIOT, J.H., *The Count-Duke of Olivares: The Statesman in an Age of Decline*, New Haven, 1986

ELLIS, HAVELOCK, *The Soul of Spain*, London, 1908

EPTON, NINA, *Madrid*, London, 1964

EUGÉNIE, EMPRESS, *Lettres familiales de l'Impératrice*, Paris, 1935

EULALIA, H.R.H. THE INFANTA, *Court Life from Within*, London, 1915

EZQUERRA DEL BAYO, JOAQUÍN, *La Duquesa de Alba y Goya*, Madrid, 1928

FERNÁNDEZ ALMAGRO, MELCHOR, *Historia política de la España contemporánea*, 2 vols, Madrid, 1959

FERNÁNDEZ, ÁLVAREZ MANUEL, *Madrid en el siglo XVI*, Madrid, 1960

FERNÁNDEZ DE LOS RIOS, A, *Guía de Madrid*, Madrid, 1876

FORD, RICHARD, *Gatherings from Spain*, London, 1861

―――― *A Handbook for Travellers in Spain*, 2 vols (3rd edition), London, 1855

FOXÁ AGUSTÍN DE, *Madrid de Corte a Checa*, Madrid, 1976

FRANCOS RODRÍGUEZ, J., *El Año de la Derrota*, Madrid, 1930

GARCÍA MERCADAL, JOSÉ, *España vista por los extranjeros*, 2 vols, Madrid, 1919

―――― *Viajes de extranjeros por España y Portugal*, 3 vols, Madrid, 1952–62

GASSIER, PIERRE, 'Goya and the Hugo Family in Madrid, 1811–1812', in *Apollo*, Oct-Dec, 1981

GAUTIER, THÉOPHILE, *Voyage en Espagne*, Paris, 1845

GEOGRAFÍA MADRILEÑA (1634–1982), Museo Municipal, Madrid, 1982

GLOVER, MICHAEL, *Legacy of Glory*, London, 1972

GRAMONT, MARÉCHAL DE, *Mémoires du . . .*, in Michaud et Poujoulat, *Nouvelle collection des mémoires pour servir à l'Histoire de France*, Vol VII, Paris, 1851

GUERRA DE LA VEGA, RAMÓN, *Historia de la Arquitectura en el Madrid de los Austrias*, 1516–1700, Madrid, no date

―――― *Madrid* 1700–1800, Madrid, no date

―――― *Madrid* 1800–1919, Madrid, no date

―――― *Madrid* 1920–1980, Madrid, 1986

HALLIWELL, J.O., *Letters of the Kings of England*, 2 vols, London, 1846

HEMINGWAY, ERNEST, *Death in the Afternoon*, London, 1932

HOLLAND *see* Ilchester

HUGO, LÉOPOLD, *Mémoires du Général Léopold*, Paris, 1823

HUGO, VICTOR, *Oeuvres Complètes*, 48 vols, Paris, 1880–89

ILCHESTER, EARL OF, *Spanish Journals of Elizabeth, Lady Holland*, London, 1910

Illustrated London News, The, 24 October 1868

INGLIS, HENRY D., *Spain in 1830*, 2 vols, London, 1831

KANY, CHARLES, *Life and Manners in Madrid 1750–1800*, Berkeley, California, 1932

LEES MILNE, JAMES, *Harold Nicolson, A Biography, Vol I, 1886–1929*, London, 1980

LE SAGE, *Adventures of Gil Blas of Santillane*, London, 1716

LOMÉNIE, LOUIS DE, *Beaumarchais et son temps*, Paris, 1846

LORENZO, ANSELMO, *El proletariado militante*, Vol I, Mexico, no date

MADOZ, PASCUAL, *Diccionario geográfico estadístico: histórico de España y sus posesiones de Ultramar*, Madrid, 1847

MADRID EN EL SIGLO XVI, Consejo Superior de Investigaciones Cientificas, Instituto de Estudios Madrileños, Madrid, 1962. (*Note*: this includes 'El Madrid de Felipe II visto por Enrique Cock', 1586, and 'El establicimiento de la capital de España en Madrid'.

Madrid, Testimonios de su Historia, Museo Municipal, Madrid, 1979

MAHON, LORD (subsequently 5th Earl Stanhope) *War of the Succession in Spain*, London, 1836

MARAÑÓN, GREGORIO, *Antonio Pérez*; 2 vols, 2nd edition revised, Madrid, 1948

MARÍA DE LA PAZ, INFANTA (HRH Princess Ludwig of Bavaria), *Through Four Revolutions*, London, 1933

MAURA, MIGUEL, *Así Cayó Alfonso XIII*, privately printed, Mexico, 1962

MEIER-GRAEFE, JULIUS, *The Spanish Journey* (tr. by J. Holroyd-Reece), London, 1926

MÉRIMÉE, PROSPER, *Correspondance générale*, Vol II, Paris, 1942

——— *Mosaïque*, Paris, 1832

MESONERO ROMANOS, RAMÓN DE, *El antiguo Madrid*, Madrid, 1861

MIOT DE MÉLITO, ANDRÉ-FRANÇOIS, *Memoirs of . . .*, London, 1881

MOREAU-NEALATON, ÉTIENNE, *Manel raconté par lui-même*, Vol I, Paris, 1926

MOREL, FATIO A. (ed.), *Marquis de Villars; Mémoires de la Cour d' Espagne de 1679 à 1681*, Paris, 1893

MURAT, JOACHIM, *Correspondance de Joachim, Roi de Naples*, edited by A. Lumbroso, Turin, 1899

'NADA, JOHN' (John Langdon-Davies), *Carlos the Bewitched*, London, 1962

NAPOLÉON I, *Correspondance*, Vol XVIII, Paris, 1865

NAPOLÉON I, *Correspondance Inédite de . . .* (ed. by Léon Lecestre) 2 Vols, Paris, 1912

PÉREZ GALDÓS, BENITO, *Memorias*, Madrid, 1930

——— *el 19 de marzo y el dos de mayo*, Madrid, 1873

——— *La de Bringas* (tr. as 'The Spendthrifts' by Gamel Woolsey), London, 1953

——— *Tormento* (tr. by J.M. Cohen), London, 1952

——— *Prim*, Madrid, 1906

PONZ, ANTONIO, *Viaje de España*, Vol VI, Madrid, 1782

PRADT, M. DE, *Mémoires Historiques sur la Révolution d'Espagne*, Paris, 1809

PRITCHETT, V.S., *The Spanish Temper*, London, 1959

QUEVEDO, FRANCISCO DE, *El Buscón* (tr. as 'The Swindler' by Michael Alpert), Harmondsworth, 1969

QUIN, M.J., *Visit to Spain in 1822 & 1823*, London, 1824

RAMÓN Y CAJAL, SANTIAGO, *Historia de mi labor científica*, Madrid, 1981

RÉPIDE, PEDRO DE, *Las calles de Madrid*, Madrid, 1981

RINGROSE, DAVID R., *Madrid & the Spanish Economy 1560–1850*, Berkeley, California, 1983

ROCCA, A.J.M, DE, *Mémoires sur la guerre des Francais en Espagne*, London, 1814, 2nd ed., Paris, 1814

RODRÍGUEZ VILLA, ANTONIO, *Etiquetas de la Casa de Austria*, Madrid, 1913

ROVIGO, DUC DE (A.J.M.R. SAVARY), *Mémoires*, Paris, 1828

ROY, M.N., *Memoirs*, Bombay, 1964

RUBENS, P.P., *Correspondance de, et documents épistolaires* (ed. by Max Rooses), Anvers, 1900

—— *Letters* (tr. with new material by Ruth Saunders), Cambridge, Massachusetts, 1955

RUIZ PALOMEQUE, EULALIA, *Ordenación y transformaciones urbanes del casco antiguo durante el siglos XIX y XX*, Madrid, 1976

SAINT-SIMON, *Mémoires du Duc de . . .*, Vols 38, 39 and 40 (ed. by A. de Boislisle), Paris, 1926–1927

SANDOVAL, FRAY PRUDENCIO DE, *Historia del emperador Carlos V*, Vols I and III, Madrid, 1955

SAVARY *see* ROVIGO

SCHILLER, JOHANN CHRISTOPHER, *Historical Dramas*, 3 vols (tr. by R.D. Boylan), London, 1847

SECO SERRANO, CARLOS (ed.), *Cartas de sor María de Jesús de Agreda y Felipe IV*, Madrid, 1958

SENDER, RAMÓN, *Seven Red Sundays* (tr. by Sir Peter Chalmers Mitchell), London, 1936

STANHOPE, THE HON, ALEXANDER, *Extracts from the Correspondance of . . ., or Spain Under Charles the Second*, selected from the originals by Lord Mahon, London, 1844

STANHOPE, PHILIP (5TH EARL STANHOPE), *Notes of Conversations with the Duke of Wellington*, London, 1888. *See also* Mahon

STIRLING MAXWELL, SIR WILLIAM, *Don John of Austria*, Vol I, London, 1883

TERESA OF ÁVILA, ST, *Letters*, 2 vols, (tr. by the Benedictines of Stanbrook), London, 1919

TORMO, ELÍAS, *Las Iglesias de Madrid*, Madrid, 1979

TORENO, CONDE DE, *Historia del levantamiento, guerra y revolución de España*, Vol I, Paris, 1836

TOWNSEND, DOROTHEA, *Life & Letters of Endymion Porter*, London, 1897

TOWNSEND, JOSEPH, *Journey Through Spain in 1786–87*, London, 1792

TROTSKY, LEON, *My Life*, London, 1930

VAN AERSSEN, FRANÇOIS (real author ANTOINE DE BRUNEL, a French publisher), *Voyage en Espagne*, Paris, 1665

'VASILI, COMTE PAUL' (Madame Juliette Adam), *La Société de Madrid*, Paris, 1886

VICAIRE, M.H., O.P., *Saint Dominic and his Times*, (tr. by Kathleen Pond), London, 1964

VILLARS, MARQUISE DE, *Lettres de la Cour d'Espagne*, Paris, 1868

WELLINGTON, FIELD-MARSHAL, THE DUKE OF, *Selections from the Dispatches & General Orders of . . .*, (ed. by Lt. Col. Curwood), London, 1841

Index